Library of
Davidson College

FOR THE GOOD OF MANKIND

Pierre-Augustin Caron de Beaumarchais Political Correspondence
Relative to the American Revolution

Compiled, Edited, and Translated By
Antoinette Shewmake

UNIVERSITY
PRESS OF
AMERICA

Lanham • New York • London

Copyright © 1987 by

University Press of America,® Inc.

4720 Boston Way
Lanham, MD 20706

3 Henrietta Street
London WC2E 8LU England

All rights reserved

Printed in the United States of America

British Cataloging in Publication Information Available

Library of Congress Cataloging-in-Publication Data

Beaumarchais, Pierre Augustin Caron de, 1732-1799.
  For the good of mankind.

  Includes index.
  1. United States—Politics and government—
Revolution, 1775-1783. 2. Beaumarchais, Pierre
Augustin Caron de, 1732-1799—Correspondence.
3. Diplomats—France—Correspondence. 4. Dramatists,
French—18th century—Correspondence. I. Shewmake,
Antoinette. II. Title.
E211.B43   1987   973.3   87-10659
ISBN 0-8191-6447-X (alk. paper)

All University Press of America books are produced on acid-free
paper which exceeds the minimum standards set by the National
Historical Publication and Records Commission.

To Clio,

        Thalia,

                and Melpomene.

Tempora patet occulta veritas.

TABLE OF CONTENTS

Preface . . . . *vii*
Chronology . . . . *xi*
Illustrations . . . . *xvii*
Abbreviations . . . . *xix*

INTRODUCTION

I. *Historiography* 1
II. *The Decline of the French Monarchy* 5
III. *Beaumarchais and the Enlightenment* 10
IV. *Politics or Intrigue* 13

V. *Biographical Data*
     1. *The Caron family* 16
     2. *A business background* 18
     3. *The defendant* 18
     4. *London, school for politics* 21
     5. *Freemasonry* 26
     6. *Le Courrier de l'Europe* 29
     7. *The playwright* 31

VI. *Louis XVI and his ministers* 33

VII. *Beaumarchais, the king and the ministers* . . . 35

VIII. *Hortalez and Company* 38

IX. *A "Political Opuscule"* 44

X. *Epilogue* 52

CORRESPONDENCE

1775: A Vision of Glory and Peace 59

1776: Hard Work and Compromise 91

1777: Towards Saratoga 185

1778: The Alliance 277

1779: Open Protest 319
      Observations on the Justificative Memorial
         of the Court of London 349

1780-1798: The Aftermath 393

CHRONOLOGICAL TABLE OF CORRESPONDENCE 439
WORKS CITED 445
INDEX 447

PREFACE

The purpose of history is to safeguard the collective memory of nations and civilizations, for a knowledge of the past is as necessary to the mental health of nations as a good memory is to individuals. In order to be trustworthy, however, history should be free of undue contradictions, distortions, and obscurities, based on a disregard for truth, justice, and the integrity of the evidence. Truth alone is beauty to the historian, because truth alone is formative. The house of history should be cleansed of unsightly, expanding cobwebs, which hide the beautiful lineaments of reality. Such is the so-called "Deane-Lee controversy," which derives from the inaccurate record of the French alliance.

Students of history or of the literature of French Enlightenment will find here the materials for a beautiful and pathetic story, still untold after two hundred years, the story of a persecuted but indomitable man's efforts to engineer a plan which would insure the triumph of the American struggle for independence, sure as he was that "the cause of America was the cause of mankind." This man was at once a genial playwright who made his contemporaries laugh at themselves, a free lance statesman who succeeded in moving apathetic or fearful ministers, and an indefatigable man of action who got the needed artillery and artillerymen over the ocean and onto the battlefield of Saratoga. Having been actuated by sublime good will, he was repaid by slander during and after his life. American students today may read in their texts that "Deane and Beaumarchais defrauded Congress," and other gratuitous libellous statements. They are taught that the French Secretary of State, Vergennes, was "one of the greatest French statesmen," although as a Royalist minister he could not have wanted what he achieved, i. e. the violent uprooting of the monarchy by the French Revolution. Such incoherence never existed, except in the wrongful historical record.

The truth is that Beaumarchais was the driving force behind the Foreign policy attributed to Vergennes, from the secret aid, which he also single-mindedly and heroically implemented, to the 1778 treaties of alliance with America. I say, heroically, because he had to overcome the pusillanimity of the French ministers who, as England recriminated through her forceful ambassador, were ready to call it quits and tried to stop him. It stands to reason, at least for historians conversant with French history and literature, that the ministers' motivation differed from that of the future author of the *Marriage of Figaro*. A study of his politics should rest on the analysis of the Figaro trilogy of plays as well as on the heretofore overlooked evidence of his political writings. But as he was not the one seated behind the desk in the Foreign office and as he was not allowed to guide France through the conduct of the war, he failed to accomplish all that he had set to do. If he never was in a position of power in the government, if he was in fact always at their mercy, he had an effective fighting chance as an eloquent leader of public opinion, as a famous personality always in the public eye. By speaking out in a country deprived of freedom of expression, he always risked his life. His role in initiating and carrying out the policy of secret aid has never been fully disclosed. On this question, it has been alleged that documentary evidence is insufficient to establish the facts. The truth, however, is that, for two hundred years, **the extant essential primary sources have remained untapped.** The purpose of this book is to make them readily available to the public.

In preparing my first work, faced with the inconsistencies and contradictions contained in the authorities, I first sought an explanation in the conflicts of interests, private or public, American and European, which existed at the time and in which historians seemed to take sides even today. Finally, however, it became evident that the relative unavailability of the documentary evidence sufficed to explain the confusion. For Beaumarchais has been more successfully muzzled after his death than during his life. The piecemeal, inaccurate, partial and incomplete publication of the writings of a man who was prominent in so many fields of endeavor is a scandalous reality still today, almost two centuries after his death.

My discovery in 1965, in the microfilm edition of the *Papers of the Continental Congress*, of a significant piece of evidence (the 1783 letter to Congress, my Ariadne's thread), led to an inquiry to the Bibliothèque Nationale in Paris. This inquiry revealed that there existed only what appeared to be a draft of it. The Bibliothèque then attempted to collect the Beaumarchais manuscripts wherever they might be, and solicited the loan of documents from public and private collections in the United States and in Europe. In October 1966, the Beaumarchais exposition took place at the Galerie Mansard and a 160-page catalog was published.

That exposition in turn gave a new impetus to research, and the task of editing the general correspondence has been undertaken by Brian N. Morton: <u>Beaumarchais, Correspondance</u> (Paris: Nizet, 1969, vols. 1 and 2; 1972, vol. 3; and 1978, vol. 4). The collection unfortunately ceases with the year 1778. As I had, concurrently with Mr. Morton, collected the correspondence and collated the manuscripts, I have been able to review his work (<u>Revue d'Histoire Littéraire de la France</u>, 1978, 2:268-272), pointing out errors and omissions, and I can give from my own files a complete edition of the political correspondence. Many letters which I give in English translation have never been published in French. I refer to the Morton edition whenever possible, for the convenience of the reader.

The correspondence relative to the American Revolution, given here in English translation, has been selected, compiled and integrated in order to make, as much as possible, a complete and comprehensive whole. As a result, many problems of datation have been solved. Papers previously tentatively situated at different times by different historians, have found their proper chronological place.

I have done all of my graduate work on the subject of Beaumarchais' politics. In writing my Master's thesis ("The Role of Beaumarchais in the American Revolution," North Texas State University, 1967) I had fallen victim to an error contained in Charles Evans' American Bibliography, by which an official diplomatic paper (of 127 pages) published by the French government without author's name has been attributed to the playwright. This work bore the same title as a pamphlet which had been published by him (and suppressed by the government) a year before, <u>Observations on the Justificative Memorial of the Court of London</u> (1779). This bibliographical blunder has contributed to the complete coverup of that crucial piece of evidence. Further research gave birth to my doctoral dissertation, "Un Pamphlet clandestin de Beaumarchais, 1779, édition critique" (Madison, Wisconsin, 1971). This pamphlet, essential for a study of Beaumarchais' politics, is given here in its integrity for the first time.

The brightest son of French enlightenment, all his life Beaumarchais fought for the essential liberties which were sorely lacking in France in the last decades of the monarchy. He fought for justice, for freedom of the press and for equality, i.e. against the privileges based on birth, against class prejudice, as obscene as racial prejudice. The playwright immortalized this fight on the stage. "Where there is no freedom to criticize, there is no freedom to praise." Such understatement is still read in exergue in the daily Paris newspaper which bears the name of **Figaro**, Beaumarchais's spiritual offspring. "Unable to revile the spirit, they mistreat it for a revenge" (BMF 5:3). Figaro's words touch the heart and prevent pervasive slander from taking roots, even after two hundred years.

Answering Beaumarchais' detractors, refuting the inaccurate, insulting statements wantomly directed against him, would be an unrewarding task. "Go on with your nonsense if you must, but quit insulting people," Figaro tells his enemies (BMF 3:15, Mol 140). A careful verification of the documentation should suffice, if it will observe with due respect the hierarchy of sources, i.e. the priority of documentary evidence on secondary works and not fall in the common mistake of interpreting primary sources through secondary works written without their benefits. It is not my purpose here to write a new biography of the author, or even a comprehensive study of his politics. My objective is to present the evidence, and let it speak for itself. As a result, I have deliberately discarded the huge bibliography of works on the subject. It is difficult enough to put together a jigsaw puzzle in which pieces are missing, without taking extraneous material into the game. Obeying his often repeated but seldom answered prayer not to be judged without first being heard, I have let the author talk as much as possible, which he certainly does with a knowledge of circumstances, an accuracy, a conciseness and precision no one today could hope to match.

The basic theme illustrated in this study is the question of social justice by which a society should allow persons of merit and ability to live up to their potential, to get to the top and into positions of power where they can lead and serve, not primarily for their own sake but for society's sake. During the eighteenth century, the French monarchy was out of gear and the tragedy in France was that people of merit were not allowed to serve. The regime blindly kept on persecuting the men who could have save it. The "land of opportunity" is a phrase that carries that theme. It is the main underlying theme in Beaumarchais' theatre, as well as in certain famous nineteenth century literature such as the novels of Stendhal.

CHRONOLOGY

1732, 24 January: Birth in Paris of Pierre-Augustin Caron, son of Andre-Charles Caron, master watchmaker, and Louise Pichon. The only surviving son (out of four), he has five sisters. Of Calvinist stock, the bourgeois family is devout, closely knit, and acquainted with persecution.

1742-1745: In boarding school at Alfort (near Paris).
1745-1753: Caron, Jr. masters the watchmaking craft, and studies music.

1753-1754: He invents a new watch escapement, which permits greater accuracy and smaller sizes. He describes his invention in a paper addressed to the Academy of Science. An older watchmaker by the name of Lepaute claims credit for it. The Academy vindicates Caron. He creates a ring-watch for Louis XV and his current mistress, Madame de Pompadour, and similar objects for the king's family. Soon thereafter he gives music lesson to the king's daughters.

1756: He marries Marie-Catherine Aubertin.

1757: He adopts the name of Beaumarchais from a fief belonging to his wife.

1758: He meets Lenormant d'Etioles, Madame de Pompadour's discreet husband and financier, and subsequently Paris-Duverney. He starts writing sketches for the amusement of high society.

1761: He purchased the "ennobling" honorary title of "Secretary to the King," and two years later that of Lieutenant General of the King's Hunt, and until 1785 judged misdemeanors connected therewith.

April 1764-March 1765: Business trip to Spain. He submits a monograph on Spain to Choiseul.

1767, 29 January: Première of his first drama, Eugénie at the Comédie-Française (the royal theater).

1770: Premiere of Les Deux amis.
1 April: Paris-Duverney, eighty-seven years old, settles his accounts with Beaumarchais; dies in July. His heir, Count de LaBlache, challenges the settlement in court.

1771: Exile of the hereditary magistrature (Parlement)

and appointment of Maupeou magistrature.

1772: The Barber of Seville, as an opera, is rejected, then performed as a comedy.

1773: 11 February: Quarrel with Duke de Chaulnes about an actress. Chaulnes is jailed in Vincennes and Beaumarchais in Fort L'Evêque.
1 April: Maupeou judge Goezman is appointed in the LaBlache suit. The suit is quickly decided in favor of LaBlache. Beaumarchais' property is seized.
8 May: He is freed from the Fort L'Evêque jail. Goezman's wife had accepted presents for Beaumarchais (necessary to request an audience). Goezman sues for attempt to bribe.
September through December: Three judicial memoirs in the Goezman affair.

1774: 12 February: Fourth judicial memoir in the Goezman case which has taken political dimensions, as a challenge to the Maupeou Parlement.
27 February: Beaumarchais is "blamed," i.e. sentenced to "civil death."
April: He moves to England. Hoping to be rehabilitated by the king, he offers to suppress a libel printed in London against the king's mistress, DuBarry.
10 May: Death of Louis XV as a result of smallpox.
Fall: First Continental Congress in America.
October: Beaumarchais write a political paper entitled "Elementary Ideas on the Recall of the Parlements" submitted to Louis XVI who will follows the advice.

1775: Life in London, with frequent trips to France.
February: New performance of the Barber of Seville, revised to allude to recent events.
April: He starts urging Louis XVI to consider the political situation in England.
19 April: Lexington affair.
August: He meets with Chevalier d'Eon who asks for his help.
23 August: The colonies are declared in a state of rebellion.

1776, January: Publication of Common Sense in America.
February: Correspondence with Arthur Lee, Count de Lauraguais and the king.
March 5, Deane leaves Philadelphia, arrives in France May 4.
May 13: Controller General of Finances Turgot is

dismissed.
June 10: Subsidy of one million livres.
July: Silas Deane is directed to him in order to fulfill his mission to supply America.
August 18: news of the Declaration of Independence.
6 September: Restoration of Beaumarchais' civil rights.
October: <u>Courrier de l'Europe</u> starts circulating in France.
14 December: The Amphitrite, ready to leave since the month of August, finally departs from LeHavre; has to put in at Lorient on the 30th; sails again on January 31, 1777, and arrives in Portsmouth 85 days later.
December: Arrival of Benjamin Franklin in Paris.

1777: Intense secret shipping activities:
31 January: The Seine (alias Andromède) departs LeHavre for Martinique. Thence on 4 April heads towards America, captured the next day.
31 January: The Mercury leaves from Nantes.
26 May, the Thereze departs from Mindin for San Domingo.
5 June: The Mere Bobie departs from Dunkirk.
12 June, the Marie-Catherine departs from Dunkirk.
17 September: The Heureux (alias Flamand) leaves from Marseilles, stops over out of France to complete its load, and arrives at Portsmouth, New Hampshire in December. Commercial agent Thveneau de Francy on board.
4 December: news of Saratoga.
July: Memorial to Maurepas regarding the financial administration of the kingdom, defending the discount bank founded by a Swiss named Panchaud.

1778: 6 February: Signature of the Franco-American alliance in Paris.
4 March: Deane receives notice of his recall.
16 April: Francy obtains a contract from Congress, which will be not be ratified by the Commissioners. Beaumarchais continues shipping to America, to other parties than Congress.
April: <u>Courrier de l'Europe</u> will be reprinted in Boulogne.
21 July: Beaumarchais wins the LaBlache suit.
11 July: D'Estaing's fleet arrives in America, with Deane and Gerard on board.
14 September: Franklin sole plenipotentiary.

1779: Beaumarchais acquires in England the Baskerville type to be used for edition of Voltaire's works.
26 February: Memorial to the ministers in favor of

the Protestant merchants of Bordeaux.
Memorial on public finances and other matters.
13 March: Peace of Teschen between Joseph II, of Austria and Frederic II of Prussia.
July: Naval battle of Grenada, Admiral d'Estaing against Admiral Byron. The Proud Rodrigue participates in it.
November: Publication of the <u>Observations on the Justificative Memorial of the Court of London</u>.
December: Suppression of the pamphlet.

1780: Armed neutrality declared by Russia and northern countries.
18 December: Creation of the Company for the Edition of the works of Voltaire in Kehl, Germany.
27 July: Deane is back in France.
LaLuzerne, new French ambassador in the U.S.

1781: U.S. Articles of Confederation. Troop mutinies in Pennsylvania and New Jersey.
February: Necker's financial report to the king.
Beaumarchais organizes the Paris Water Company (Perrier).
29 September. Reading of the <u>Marriage of Figaro</u> at the <u>Comedie-Francaise</u>. The play is forbidden by the king.
October 17, Victory at Yorktown.
October: Beginning of the Kornman affair.
Resignation of Lord North.

1782: Business activities: invests one million in government bonds; lends 700,000 livres to Choiseul.
Readings of the <u>Marriage of Figaro</u> in private homes.
The play is prohibited by the Censoring Committee.
30 November: preliminary peace between U.S. and Great Britain.

1783-1790: Publication of the 70-volume works of Voltaire.

1783: 13 June: The scheduled performance of the <u>Marriage of Figaro</u> in Versailles, is forbidden by the king.
3 September: Treaty of Versailles, ending the war.
26 September: Private performance of the <u>Marriage of Figaro</u>. The play is still not approved by the Censorship Committee.
Calonne, new minister of Finance.

1784: 27 April. First of 67 triumphant performances of the <u>Marriage of Figaro</u>.

1785: Beaumarchais has a house built in London.
8-13 March: Beaumarchais is jailed in St. Lazarre for a letter published in the Journal de Paris, which has offended the king.
Thomas Jefferson, ambassador in Paris, until 1789.
8 May: Death of Choiseul. Beaumarchais, a creditor, is named as receiver of the estate.
18 August: The Marriage of Figaro is performed again with great success.
19 August: The Barber of Seville is performed at Trianon, in Versailles. The queen plays the principal female role.
November: The new Paris water company, providing water to the city on the London model, created by Beaumarchais and the Perier brothers, is attacked by the young and depraved demagogue, Count de Mirabeau. He replies by a witty satire, les Mirabelles.

1786: 8 March: He marries Therese de Willermaulaz, who has given him a daughter ten years before.
28 March| Tarare, an opera, music by Salieri, passes the censorship committee.
1 May: Premiere in Vienna of the Marriage of Figaro, opera by Mozart based on the play.

1787: January: In the U. S. Shays rebellion (re taxes and debts).
20 February: As a result of Beaumarchais' intervention in favor of Mrs. Kornman, imprisoned by request of her husband, a lawyer for Kornman, named Bergasse, sues him.
May-September: Constitutional Convention in Philadelphia.
Financial crisis in France: Calonne is dismissed.
Financial difficulties with the Perrier Company.
8 June: Premiere of Tarare, music by Salieri.
26 June: Purchase of a large lot near the Bastille, where he will build a mansion.

1788: Deane's stolen papers are sold to Thomas Jefferson, U.S. Ambassador in Paris.

1789: U. S. Constitution.
2 April: Bergasse and Kornman are condemned.
Convocation of the States General in Paris.
Spring: Beaumarchais is elected president of the district where he lives (Blancs Manteaux).
14 July: Fall of the Bastille.
August: He is elected to the Paris Commune.
22 September: death of Silas Deane.

1790: He drafts the Guilty Mother, or "The other
Tartuffe," which will be played two years later by
a minor troupe.
3 August: Tarare triumphs again.

1791: Hamilton organizes the bank of the U. S.
3 September: French Constitution and Declaration of
the Rights of Man.
Thomas Paine, in France, publishes The Rights of
Man.

1792: 4 March: Beginning of the affair of the Guns
from Holland, which Beaumarchais planned to
purchase for the French army.
20 April: France declares war on Austria.
4 June: Beaumarchais is accused of hoarding arms.
11 August: The populace invades his house, looking
for guns.
28-29 August: Imprisoned in the Abbaye with the
unfortunate destined to the guillotine; he is freed
by the Commune prosecutor, Pierre Manuel.
22 September: He leaves for Holland via England to
settle the gun affair, while in France his enemies
attack him at the National Convention. Reign of
Terror. He remains in England until 26 February
1793.

1793, 21 January: Execution of Louis XVI. England and
most of Europe declare war on France. U.S neutral.
20 March: Performance of the Marriage of Figaro in
Paris, with addition of Mozart music.
28 June: He leaves England for Holland and Germany
to settle the affair of the guns.
He drafts the self-defense, Mes Six Epoques.

1794, 14 March: He is listed among the emigres.
4 July: His family is arrested.
15 August: The Emigres law forces his wife to
divorce him.

1795: Exile in Hamburg. He suffers a first heart
attack. Appeal to the American people.

1796, 5 July: Return to Paris.

1797, 5 May: The Guilty Mother triumphs on the stage
of the Comedie-Francaise.

1798: Considerable amount of writing on various
subjects.
1799: Night of 17-18 May, death.

Illustrations

1. P.-A. Caron de Beaumarchais at the age of 23, by Jean-Marc Nattier. Page 1.

2. Beaumarchais in 1774, after his banishment, from an engraving by A. de Saint-Aubin. Page 59.

3. Charles Gravier, Count de Vergennes, by Charles Wilson Peale. Page 91.

ABBREVIATIONS

Ang. French National Archives. *Affaires de l'Angleterre et de l'Amérique*. Paris: Ministère des Affaires étrangères. Correspondance politique. Angleterre. Etats-Unis. France.

BN Dennery, Etienne, ed. *Beaumarchais (Catalog of the 1966 exposition)*. Paris: Bibliothèque nationale, 1966.

BBS Beaumarchais, *Le Barbier de Séville*.
BMC _____ *La Mère coupable*.
BMF Beaumarchais, *Le Mariage de Figaro*.

Dea Isham, Charles, ed. New York Historical Society Collec tions for the years 1886-1889: *Papers of Silas Deane*. 5 vols. New York: 1887-1891.

Don Doniol, Henri. *Histoire de la participation de la France à l'établissement des Etats-Unis d'Amérique*. 5 vols. Paris: Imprimerie nationale, 1886-1892.

Gai Gaillardet, Frederic. *Mémoires sur la chevalière d'Eon, suivis de douze lettres inédites de Beaumarchais*. Paris: Dentu, 1866.

Gibbon
Gibbon's Miscellaneous Works. J. Walker McSpadden, editor. New York: Fred DePau & Co., 1907.

Gudin 1809
Gudin de la Brenellerie, ed. *Oeuvres complètes de Beaumarchais*. 7 vols. Paris: LaPlace Sanchez & Cie.
Gudin 1888
Histoire de Beaumarchais, edited by Maurice Tourneux. Paris: Plon & Nourrit.

HR 220
U.S. House of Representatives, 20th Congress, First Session, Report no. 220, April 1828.

JCC *Journals of the Continental Congress*. Worthington C. Ford, ed. 34 vols. Washington, D.C.: GPO, 1904-1907.

Lau The Papers of Henry Laurens, Microfilm 6, South Carolina Historical Society.

Lin Lintilhac, Eugene. *Beaumarchais et ses oeuvres, d'après des documents inédits*. Paris: Hachette, 1887.

Lom   Loménie, Louis de. *Beaumarchais et son temps, d'après des documents inédits.* 2 vols. Paris: Michel Levy, 1858.

Marsan
      Marsan, Jules. *Beaumarchais et les affaires d'Amérique. Lettres inédites.* Paris: Champion, 1919.

Mol   Moland, Louis, ed. *Oeuvres de Beaumarchais.* Paris: Garnier, 1874.

Mor   Morton, Brian N., ed. *Beaumarchais: Correspondance.* 4 vols. Paris: Nizet. Vol. 1 (1745-72) and vol. 2 (1773-76), 1969; vol. 3 (1777), 1972 and vol. 4 (1778), 1978.

NA   U.S. National Archives. Papers of the Continental Congress. Microfilm 247, Roll 67, Item 54. Papers and Accounts of Silas Deane, Beaumarchais and Arthur Lee, 1776-1784. Washington, D.C.: 1952.

NCMH *New Cambridge Modern History,* Vol. 8. 1965.

RC   Beaumarchais, "Requête à la Commune de Paris."

RG 76 Records relating to French Spoliation Claims, 1791-1821.

S.F. B. F. Stevens Facsimiles of manuscripts in European Archives relating to America, 1773-1783. 25 vols. London, 1889-98.

VEM   Voltaire, *Essai sur les moeurs.*
VHPP   , *Histoire du Parlement de Paris.*
VL14   , *Siècle de Louis XIV.*
VL15   , *Siècle de Louis XV.*

Weaver, William A. *Diplomatic Correspondence of the United States, 1783-1789.* 7 vols. Washington: Blair, 1833.

Wha   Wharton, Francis, ed. *Revolutionary Diplomatic Correspondence of the United States.* 6 vols. Washington: GPO, 1889.

Pierre-Augustin Caron de Beaumarchais
at the age of 23
by Nattier

Pierre-Augustin Caron de Beaumarchais
in 1774.
from an engraving by A. de Saint-Aubin

INTRODUCTION

The following pages give the present state of publication of Beaumarchais' papers; the historical background of France in the Age of Enlightenment; biographical data for the author and for various personalities mentioned in the text; the novel story of the 1779 pamphlet; and a conclusion which includes data regarding the legal settlement of the Beaumarchais claim against the United States, the paltry ending of a great story. The index should be used to correlate text and introductory material.

For a lively introduction, written by the author himself, the reader is invited to turn to the eloquent, and heretofore unpublished letters of 1783 and 1795 in the last section of the correspondence.

I. Historiography.

A. The main biographies.

1. Paul Gudin de la Brenellerie, a friend of the author, who admired and shared his philosophic outlook if not his politics, was a historian in his own right and the first editor of the *Oeuvres complètes de Pierre-Augustin Caron de Beaumarchais* (Paris: Collin, 1809. 7 vols.), which included a selected number of letters. As an introduction to the complete works, he had nearly completed a biography, *Histoire de Beaumarchais* which he had to put aside in compliance with the wishes of the family. The "Beaumarchais story" remained unpublished until the end of the century, when it was edited by Maurice Tourneux (Paris: Plon, 1888). The reason for this sacrifice (and for the long inaccessibility of the documents) was the suit then pending between the Beaumarchais heirs and the government of the United States, which would not be settled until 1835.

2. Thus it was the French historian Louis de Loménie who in 1856 revealed, albeit in his own bowdlerizing way, the historical role of the famous French playwright. The documented, two-volume biography, *Beaumarchais et son temps*, 2 vols. (Paris: Michel Levy, 1858), which earned its author a seat in France's highest literary society, l'Académie française, can still be considered a masterpiece because of the insight it gives in the social and political situation in France during the decades immediately preceding the French revolution. Loménie also gave the text (always expur-

gated) of important and previously unknown documents. Writing under the reactionary Second Empire, Loménie admittedly (Preface, page x) bowed to the sensibilities of his contemporaries and cut out "liberties of language." He also (without admitting it) omitted or disguised in his narrative the liberties of action taken by the playwright and the evidence of his ardent democratic and revolutionary aspirations.

3. Since then dozens of biographies have appeared, the only one of which to bring out new documents is Eugène Lintilhac, *Beaumarchais et ses oeuvres* (Paris: Hachette, 1887). The rest of the biographies have failed to do so and are usually based on their authors' particular prejudice, or pet psychological theory. Although many of them are excellent reading, they need not be listed here because all of them are vitiated by the fact that the basic and paramount factor of the author's politics is entirely missing or inaccurate. They repeat striking but fabricated anecdotes. The biography which seems to ring true the most constantly is: Cynthia Cox, *The Real Figaro* (London, Longsman, 1962).

B. The Writings of Beaumarchais.

1. The "complete works."

There have been since the original Gudin edition several editions of the so-called complete works, which seldom added anything new. The most handy ones, because they are in one volume, are the Louis Moland edition (Paris: Garnier, 1874) and the Emile Fournier edition (Paris: LaPlace, Sanchez and Co., 1876). The plays have continually inspired new editions, contrary to the correspondence, the *Mémoires* (legal briefs) which are hard to find, and innumerable papers on a great variety of subjects, which have never been published. The correspondence has been the occasion in France, over the past two hundred years, for sundry short articles, all based on "documents inédits," but often revealing only poorly identified excerpts. Several compilations of specific correspondence have also appeared, in addition to what had already been included in the Moland and Fournier editions of the complete works.

2. The printed correspondence.

a. Limited editions include: Frederic Gaillardet, *Mémoires sur la Chevalière d'Eon* (Paris, Dentu, 1866), which includes in appendix twelve unpublished letters by Beaumarchais, and Jules Marsan, *Beaumarchais et les affaires d'Amérique, lettres inédites* (Paris, Edouard Champion, 1919), a compilation of the correspondence between Beaumarchais and his representative in America, Théveneau de Francy, mostly for the years 1780 to 1782, regarding the maritime business of Beaumarchais, which lies beyond the limits of our subject. The same remark goes for the most interesting works of Gustave Labat (*Actes de l'Académie de Bordeaux*, 1904) and Robert Lafont (*Beaumarchais, le Brillant Armateur*, Paris, 1928), both rich in writings by Beaumarchais, which have not been printed elsewhere. Other editions do not concern politics at all: Louis Thomas, *Lettres de jeunesse, 1745-1775* (Paris, Bocard, 1923), Maxime Formont, *Lettres à Madame de Godeville, 1777-1779* (Paris, Lemerre, 1928) and Gilbert Chinard, *Lettres inédites de Beaumarchais, de Madame Beaumarchais et de leur fille Eugénie, publiées d'après les originaux de la Clements Library* (Paris, Margraff, 1929). Inasmuch as they cover the years before 1779, they have been included in the Morton edition.

b. The political correspondence of Beaumarchais, inasmuch as it relates to America, especially for the crucial years between 1775 and 1778, the period which is focus here, has been partially printed in various collection of revolutionary correspondence in France as well as in the United States. The main ones are: Henri Doniol, *Histoire de la participation de la France à l'établissement des Etats-Unis d'Amérique*, 6 vols. (Paris, 1886-92), which printed some of the documents housed in the French National Archives. In the United States, some of the manuscripts to be found on this side of the Atlantic have found their way, in faulty translations, in various compilations: Jared Sparks, *Diplomatic correspondence of the American Revolution*, 6 vols. (Boston, 1829-1830), William A. Weaver, *Diplomatic Correspondence of the United States, 1783-1789*, 7 vols. (Washington, 1833) and Francis Wharton, *Revolutionary Diplomatic Correspondence of the United States*, 6 vols (Washington, 1889). Some documents included herein were first printed in the *Papers of Silas Deane*, edited by Charles Isham, 5 vols. (New York Historical Society Collections, 1887-1891).

c. The general edition now in progress, Brian N. Morton, *Beaumarchais: Correspondance* (Paris: Nizet, 1969, vols. 1 and 2; 1972, vol. 3; and 1978, vol. 4, in which Donald C. Spinelli is co-editor) covers the years up to 1778. This publication is a major step forward, although it is marred by the omission of several major political documents. The editing principles followed are also somewhat deficient: spelling and punctuation are inconsistent, whether the (unrevealed) source of the document is a printed one or not. Whenever a manuscript has been collated, the benefit of the doubt is not given the author, causing unnecessary obscurities; and most of all, sources are not given. It is a pity, however, that it is so slow in coming out. The editors appear to be in no hurry to finish the urgent enterprise they have preempted.

3. Manuscript sources of the correspondence.

a. In France, the most important private collection is, of course, that of the Beaumarchais family. Unfortunately these archives have not been made available in their entirety. Mr. Jacques de Beaumarchais wrote me in 1970 that he wanted to reserve the first use of unpublished manuscripts to his son, who had registered as a dissertation subject the politics of his ancestor. Mr. Morton apparently did not fare any better with him, and that explains why he has reprinted so many important documents in the form given by his predecessors. About the owners of private archives who refuse to open them to scholars we may say, using the words of Thomas Jefferson,[1] that they are "parricide to the memory" of their ancestor. Among the public collections, there are the French National Archives, Affaires étrangères, Correspondance politique, Angleterre, Etats-Unis (which can be consulted in the United States in the B. F. Stevens Facsimiles as well as in the Manuscript Department of the Library of Congress); the manuscripts housed at the Comédie-Française (some of which do concern diplomacy), Bibliotheque nationale and Bibliotheque de l'Arsenal.

b. In the United States, where many of the political records have come to rest because of the suit, the manuscripts are scattered in the National and States Historical Societies archives, among the papers of various protagonists of the American revolution or U.S. government officials later involved in the claim of the Beaumarchais heirs against the United States. Most of the manuscripts of the letters written by Beaumarchais to the Continental Congress still remain to be located. When such letters have been published in the United States, it was in the form of extracts and in transla-

---

[1] Jefferson applied these words in his *Autobiography* to Benjamin Franklin's heir who failed to include in his grandfather's works a paper concerning Franklin's negotiations with General Howe regarding a thwarted attempt at reconciliation, an essential piece in Jefferson's estimation. Boyd, ed. 1:164.

tion. The few incomplete English translations which are found in the various compilations of revolutionary correspondence are not always doing the job expected of a translation, that is, they do not always faithfully carry the meaning of the original French, to say nothing of the style or tone. Through those translations, even when the original in unavailable, a reader well-versed in French, often is able to tell what the original contained. Relying on this, I have occasionally corrected them. Microfilm and microprint editions are being made available and lend themselves to research, although they are not always catalogued or indexed. And as a result, they still conceal unpublished writings by the author.

II. **The decline of the French monarchy.**

By the end of the eighteenth century the French monarchy had reached an impasse, and it is not necessary to look very far to discover the main causes of that predicament. The descendants of Saint-Louis (1226-1270) and Henry IV, the Great (1553-1610), had lost all resemblance to their ancestors. The House of Bourbon was an international feudal family institution, no more French than Spanish or German, inbred as a result of the constant practice of marriages between relatives in the third or fourth degrees. The main inbred and permanent trait of the French Bourbons, starting with Louis XIV, was a monstrous narcissism, compounded by mediocre intelligence and incredible cruelty. The loyal people of France, looking for a father in their king, could only recall the last ten years of the reign of Henry IV two centuries earlier. Now the king was the State, the people were only "subjects" to be exploited. Political alliances were based on marriages and wars were fought for the aggrandizement of the dynasty. Louis XIV fathered six children from his cousin the queen (only one of which survived) and at least eleven natural children whom he recognized. He cherished above all his "legitimated" sons, gave them high rank and lucrative lands and married them to members of the royal family. The House of Bourbon (already composed of the collateral branches of Vendôme, Orléans and Condé), thus sprouted the "bastard branches" of Maine and Toulouse (titles given to the two sons born to the king and Madame de Montespan). Inbreeding probably caused the unusually high incidence of infant mortality in the royal family; poison (replacing the dagger used in the sixteenth century) probably caused the death of many a presumptive heir to the throne.[2]

Louis XIV reigned for more than half a century, surrounded by a huge family which was obviously the target of unseen enemies. Witness the Affair of the Poisons (1670-1684), in which several mistresses of the king were implicated. A new chemical enterprise, imported from Italy, manufactured "succession powder." It also furnished the wherewithal of abortion, as well as "love potions" and other insidious ways of influencing the lives of others. The Poison affair involved so many high-ranking people that Louis XIV had the "chambre ardente" investigation dismissed in 1684.

Louis XV differed from his great-grandfather in at least two respects: He did not care to add to his family and certainly did not wish to recognize his natural offsprings. There is evidence that abortion was resorted to, at least as far as the girls in his "Deer Park" harem (recruited by the police and bought for him) were concerned. Louis XV's favorites had a hand in the government. Louis XIV had not been influenced by his mistresses, except the last one, who became his morganatic wife, the pious Madame de Maintenon. With her assistance he persecuted the Huguenots and repealed the Edict of Nantes which had act enacted religious toleration a century earlier under Henri IV. Both, kings as they were by divine right, feared, not God, but the Church, that simulacrum of a church, Christian only by name, the barbaric and corrupt institution that Voltaire constantly exposed and for whose destruction he called for: "Smash the infamous!"

A carefully drawn genealogic tree of the house of Bourbon would show inverted branches resulting from marriages to first cousins or to nieces and the high in-

---

[2]This transpires from a reading of Voltaire's historical works, *Le Siècle de Louis XIV* and *Précis sur le Siècle de Louis XV*, published out of France, circulated clandestinely and several times suppressed. Author's name, date and place of publication cannot be given. Voltaire worked on them until his death in 1778. These are ironic works, written in a style devised to escape censorship, i. e. to avoid precise quotation. Voltaire's meaning will escape the reader unless he compares facts and ideas given in various places and weighs the tone of the writer: hyperbole is always ironic (for example, when Voltaire refers to his work on Louis XIV as "a monument raised to the glory of the Nation by the hands of Truth" in *Essai sur les moeurs*, 2:892), understatement serious.

cidence of death among the most promising heirs to the throne. Voltaire's "reasoned list of the children of Louis XIV" achieves the same unavowed purpose (VL14 2:160-4). Most suspicious were the deaths of the Grand Dauphin (Louis XIV's son) and his wife in 1711, and in 1712 the simultaneous deaths of the king's grandson Duc de Bourgogne, of his wife and first-born son, which left the future Louis XV an orphan at the age of two. The two-year old surviving heir (the future Louis XV) remained ill thereafter and Voltaire, who never wasted words, reported the rumor that the infant had been administered a counterpoison. Louis XIV had provided for power to pass to his legitimated son, Duke of Maine, in a testament which the judiciary declared null and void. Fifty years later, in 1765, Louis XV's son and presumptive heir to the throne and his wife died in close succession.

The title continually passing from father to son, more important than the individual (who often did not possess a distinctive name), blurred identities in the successive generations. Dates are required not only for the person but also for his tenure of the title in question to distinguish the various title holders. "There is as much confusion and uncertainty in all rights and titles in France," quipped Voltaire, "as there is order in the administration" (VL14 2:192).

The noblesse of France, unlike the British aristocracy, was a closed class. If the often repeated opposite contention were true, a large portion of French literature would be meaningless. The honorary offices (charges) sold by the king to commoners whom they purported to ennoble succeeded in enriching the royal Treasury but failed to remove the scornful prejudice attached to bourgeois birth. Both Voltaire and Beaumarchais played the game by the rules and tried to obtain admission to the ranks of the nobility; Voltaire was flogged by a nobleman's valets, Beaumarchais was called "mascaron mal plaqué" (a pun on the name Caron, "ill-plated mascaron") by one of his opponents (Chevalier d'Eon). The "silliest of the nobles felt superior" to the genial playwright (Mol 709c). In fact, herded around Versailles, the nobles had usually no other choice but to serve in the army or in the upper hierarchy of the Church (without necessarily having a religious vocation). The king traditionally led the nobles to battle, but when Louis XV proceeded to the front, it took more resources to keep him safe and comfortable than to fight the enemy. The nobles were wont to imitate the mores of the king.[3] The Prince of Talleyrand depicted in his memoirs the peculiar unhappiness of his youth. His family, having devoted him to the Church before he was born, avoided visiting him thereafter. When the child broke his ankle, no one noticed and he remained crippled for life. As a result of the emasculation of the noblesse, a feeling of superiority progressively built into the French middle class, busy, energetic, and having been nurtured in natural, loving families. But after Louis XIV, they were excluded from government positions, which (at the pleasure of the king) were the preserve of the nobles.

The more abject the social structure, the more successful the accomplishment of the intelligentsia in denouncing it, the more evident what Voltaire called "the progress of the human mind." Never was there among the people of any nation, together with the credulous good-nature of the lower class, a brighter intellectual elite. The pen, or rather the printing press, was a terrifying weapon against the monarchy, who used a gestapo as unprincipled as ever existed on the face of the earth. One of the rare sources for this seldom-revealed state of affairs is the work of the public prosecutor of the Paris Commune, Pierre Manuel, entitled (in translation) *The Paris Police Unveiled* and published in Paris "the year second of Liberty," i.e. 1791. Publicity, Manuel declared in exergue, is the safeguard of laws and mores, and he took it upon himself to publish material from the archives of the Bastille. Manuel revealed the various peculiar functions of the Police, which included the spying on the female population, aimed at recruiting candidates for the king's harem, the painstaking surveillance of printing presses and of the points of entrance of publications from abroad, and the constant tagging of the French refugees in London.

Thomas Jefferson witnessed "the monstrous abuses of power under which this people were ground to powder" and aptly listed them:

> The weight of their taxes and the inequality of their distribution [noblesse and clergy did not pay taxes]; the oppressions of the tithes, the taille [direct tax levied on commoners], the corvées [work gratuitously furnished by the peasants to the lords], the gabelles [tax on salt], the farms [tax collection agencies] and the barriers; the shackles on commerce by monopolies; on industry by guilds and corporations; on the

---

[3]Aristocratic mores are described in the *Liaisons dangereuses* of Louis Choderlos de Laclos (1741-1803).

freedom on conscience, of thought, and of speech; on the freedom of the press by the Censure; and of the person by Lettres de Cachet [arbitrary arrest orders]; the cruelty of the criminal code generally; the atrocities of the Rack; the venality of the judges and their partiality to the rich [illustrated in Beaumarchais' life and works]; the monopoly of military honors by the Noblesse; the enormous expenses of the Queen, the princes and the court; the prodigalities of pensions; and the riches, luxury, indolence and immorality of the clergy. Surely, under such a mass of misrule and oppression, a people might justly press for a thorough reformation, and might even dismount their rough-shod riders, and leave them to walk on their own legs" (Boyd 2:127).

Under the circumstances one can wonder why such a monarchy should have decided to go to the aid of the Protestant people who professed the principles of the Declaration of Independence. Revenge for the defeat of 1763? Yes, this was typical of the diplomacy of the age. But at such cost to itself? When an enlightened minister, Jacques Turgot, in the king's council had warned against it and prophesied that "a war with England should be shunned as the greatest of all misfortunes, as it would render impossible, perhaps forever, the reform absolutely necessary to the prosperity of the State and the solace of the people."

Historians have convincingly taxed as folly the British efforts to subdue America, but have seldom questioned the inevitability or sanity of the French intervention in the War of Independence. In fact, England suffered very little permanent damage as a result of her "folly," while the French monarchy reaped the harvest it had sown, its violent uprooting by the French Revolution.

Why have historians, on both sides of the Atlantic, heaped praise on the French Secretary of State, Vergennes they assumed to be responsible for that policy, while at the same time calling attention to its tragic effect and paradoxical nature? First, of course, because the Beaumarchais documents were missing. Secondly, because it was prestigious, and the more so as time went by. Aid to America, short of war, was indeed the wish of all enlightened Frenchmen who wanted democratic ideas to succeed. But for the monarchy itself, comprised of aristocrats who held on to ancient customs and values, to absurd privileges, it was an anomaly, a contradiction, a policy rooted in superficial or inferior motives. From the point of the view of the monarchy the policy does not stand to reason. From the point of view of the most eminent victim of the regime, however, it made sense. Its genesis can only be explained by the pervasive influence exerted by Caron de Beaumarchais upon the ministers. He was the Secretary of State's ghost writer, the real statesman behind him. Such is the missing link which solves the paradox and provides a solution to corollary controversies.

"Glory" was indeed promised Louis XVI by the banished playwright when he presented to the king his powerful analyses of the political conjuncture, and proposed a secret strategy by which France could assist the American insurgents without incurring the risk of bankruptcy or the risk of war. "An immense harvest of glory and peace" would be the result of an enlightened Foreign policy. The 1775 papers must be read as they are here gathered and properly dated here, for the first time. They need little introduction. Was he successful in influencing the king's ministers, and to what extent? The answer is novel and must be qualified.

III. **Beaumarchais and the Enlightenment.**

The two principal writers in eighteenth-century France were Voltaire and Rousseau. Voltaire was the great apostle of reason, common sense, intelligence, but not innovative in art. He was very much concerned with classical artistry, and spent much of his time writing tragedies and poetry. He fought, however, for social justice and tolerance from his little kingdom of Ferney, out of France. In the next generation, Rousseau came to counter Voltaire's dry intellectualism with an impassioned defense of the "eternal feminine," the equating of nature to goodness, or the idea that whatever is natural is good, and the defense of love, life and religion, the idea of Providence. Beaumarchais was conscious of being the fruit of those two influences. He admired both philosophers and looked wryly upon their open fight: "The Republic of Letters is one of wolves." He often reflected on both men's contributions and their comparative importance.

Beaumarchais devoutly carried on Voltaire's teachings. There are reminiscences or allusions to Voltaire in his writings, which I have brought to the reader's attention. They show what admiration he had for and how familiar he was with the man whose complete works and correspondence he would later carefully edit and lavishly publish at his own expense.

While Rousseau is blissfully outspoken, Voltaire's historical works, which have been called "a series of epigrams," (VHPP 268) are always couched in an ironic, clandestine style. As a result, they are difficult to read and often misinterpreted. It is sometimes assumed, for example, that the *Age of Louis XIV* is a panegyric of the "Sun King," when it is in fact a searing satire of the despot who persecuted one-sixth of his subjects on account of their religion, took children away from their parents and sent fathers to the galleys, for the illusory purpose of establishing unity of faith in the kingdom, and finally bled the country by forcing the Huguenots to emigrate, while he repealed the Edict of Nantes, by which a century earlier Henry IV had enacted religious toleration. When Voltaire praises Louis XIV, it is only to call attention to the shortcomings of his successors. Satire has seldom been so subtle and understated. Not being able to refer directly to France, Voltaire took a global point of view, discussing China, for example, when he meant to open his fellow countrymen's eyes on the absurdities of their own country.

The clandestine, often esoteric style in which those works are couched is a result of the conditions under which they were written and circulated among the public. The writers of eighteenth-century France could not publish without specific permission. The police hounded those who meddled with any subject related to politics. "It belongs only to freedom to know the truth and to speak it," noted Voltaire in his introduction to the Histoire du Parlement de Paris (VHPP, 260). The writers therefore had to find ways to make the reader think for himself and draw the obvious conclusions by himself, while communicating their intended message obliquely, without giving hold to censorship. Hence a clandestine style, the principles of which are diametrically opposed to those of classical rhetoric, and works which require careful reading and analysis and which are often misunderstood. Far from being unpleasant, however, their reading is often refreshing and amusing.[4]

The clandestine rhetoric used by Voltaire to baffle the censors, his way of publishing under an assumed name, or without author's name, and of disowning writings attributed to him, will appear timid compared to the practice of his disciple. The master himself expressed his awe before Beaumarchais' boldness, playing, as he put it, within the lion's claws. Although the thrust of the enlightenment had increased by the

---

[4]Sample for example this sentence: "The reign of Saint-Louis is a great era; almost all of the high barons of France being dead or ruined during his unfortunate crusade, he became absolute upon his return, albeit unhappy and impoverished." HPP 215.

time of Beaumarchais' maturity, the parallel between the two men is striking. Both were coached in business by the influential financier, Joseph Paris-Duverney (1684-1770) and secured a fortune under his leadership. Both of them were prosecuted for their writings and forced to find refuge in England. Voltaire in 1726, Beaumarchais in 1774. Both developed a great admiration for "English freedom" and acted on it. Both were successful playwrights, using the theater as a vehicle for political satire, both actively militating for freedom and social justice. Both played a political role, although not to the same extent. Under the "reign" of Madame de Pompadour Voltaire was appointed "historiographer to the king" (1745) and started a history of the reign of Louis XV, which he wrote in the office of the minister of war, Count d'Argenson, but soon became too disgusted with it to finish his work. He resided out of France from 1750 to the end of his life, while Beaumarchais lived in France and for more than six years, having penetrated the inner sanctum of power, was in a position to influence his country's foreign policy.

While Voltaire's relationship with Frederick the Great, whom he met in Belgium in 1740, eventually called him to Berlin (1750), where he sampled the pros and cons of enlightened despotism, Beaumarchais, under the influence of Rousseau, more optimistic about human nature, adopted as his own the democratic principles of Thomas Paine's Common Sense. Beaumarchais, heir to Montesquieu, Voltaire, and Rousseau, conceived a reign of justice, progress for mankind, a new era for Europe, and for that, he was willing to deploy an extraordinary talent for brinkmanship. The youthful playwright described his passion for politics in the following letter written in 1767 to the Duke of Noailles, a high-ranking aristocrat who admired his theater:

    I indulge in literature only in my spare time, Monsieur le Duc. As soon as I stop digging the soil and cultivate the garden[5] of my advancement, the whole clearing disappears under briars and I have to start from scratch again.

    Another folly of mine I have had to push aside, is the study of politics, a thorny and repulsive subject for anyone else, but as attractive as it is useless to me. I have loved it with a passion. Readings, writings, travels, observations, I did everything I could for it. The powers' respective rights, the pretensions of the princes which always upset the mass of

---

    [5]An obvious allusion to Voltaire, in the philosophical novel, *Candide*. "One must cultivate his own garden."

mankind, the interaction of governments on one another, those were interests meant for my soul. More than anyone else, perhaps, I have felt crossed by my need to take a large view of things, while I am the least of men. I have sometimes felt like protesting, in my unjust humor, against fate which did not place me in a position more appropriate to what I felt I was suited for. Especially when I considered that the mission given by kings and ministers to their agents certainly do not impress on them, like the ancient apostleship, a sort of grace which would make enlightened and sublime men out of the puniest brains (Mol 628).

At that time, he was 34 years old. His first play, Eugénie, had just been performed by the Comédie-Française (the house of Molière). He had been working with the financier Duverney for three years; had traveled for him on business to Spain. He was a successful businessman and a more successful playwright. He did not know that he would find time and opportunity, through indescribable tribulations, for the highest kind of both literature and politics.

In the last decades of the century, after the death of Voltaire and Rousseau, Beaumarchais was the most influential writer of the generation who carried the intellectual fight into action and finally to revolution, but his role was shrouded in secrecy, involved in State secrets which he was honor bound not to divulge, and still remains to be fully recognized.

IV. Politics or Intrigue?

The history of revolutions is bound to remain controversial, as long as the systems of values opposed in the conflict can find defenders. Are there still today defenders of mercantilism and absolutism? It should therefore be possible to solve the Deane-Lee controversy and the related contradictions which mar the history of the American Revolution. The situation was different for a long time in France. The French Revolution, threatened with the invasion of the country on all its borders turned violent and lamentably failed to bring democracy to France. As it was followed by the epic of the Empire of Napoleon I, son of the Revolution turned tyrant in spite of himself; by the restoration of the monarchy imposed by foreign powers on the defeated country; and, after several minor revolutions, by the reactionary Second Empire under Napoleon III; as France had to wait till the third quarter of the nineteenth century to enjoy a republican government, the writing of revolutionary history in France has been severely compromised. The case was different in America.

The revolutionary period itself in America was of course a period of great confusion, of divided loyalties. France, the recent enemy, would be a dubious ally. All was in ferment, in transformation: values held by people, even more than institutions. Under such circumstances, meaning would depend on the outcome. If the revolution succeeded, then it would be right. If the cause was won, the leaders would be heroes. If it failed, they would be hanged. So people saw things differently and their accounts have remained different even after the deed was done.

When values are in turmoil, human relationships are difficult. When the authorities are challenged, as much communication as possible takes place orally. What is put in writing is a minimum. Evidence is rare and sometimes it is willfully destroyed. Motivation varies and is seldom revealed. Why do people rise against governments? Why do we fight for anything? We hope to gain a better life by it. For most human beings today, better means freer, but it was not always this way. Life is a game that not all of us play by the same rules. Freer for what? For the pursuit of happiness. Happiness means different things to different people. For some, it means to make more money and have more of the pleasures of the world, or to make money and gain power on other people. For others, to be as conscious as they can become, to know and to love. For Swedenborg, an enlightened mystic of the time, when knowing and loving were in harmony, one was in heaven. The struggle between the head and the heart, that was hell. The Enlightenment held the existential commitment by which the "philosophers," the great men of the time, tried to set the world right. Action followed understanding. This perennial philosophy is based on the belief in reason and human perfectibility. There were during the last decades of the Age of Reason men who incarnated this philosophy. Not in abstraction, but authentically, in their lives.

Not all individuals carry the torch in any age. There are stragglers, those who are satisfied with the status quo and keep the old loyalties, do not question customs. For them life goes on as usual; change is invisible. The struggle appears to involve only selfish and vicious human beings. It's a competition to see who will get the power, who will get the rewards. The American Revolution has been interpreted in this manner by short-sighted historians who dismiss the natural rights ideology, who overlook the movement of ideas involved in the European enlightenment. The American revolutionary leaders knew they would be better off, were they masters of their own country. That was perhaps what Jefferson meant by "the pursuit of happiness." And in fighting for that purpose, they were, they had to be, sly, dissimulated, and cunning. George III and his government saw things this way. They believed the leaders of the rebellion were agitators, not followed by the people. They feared that the loss of British America would be a terrible blow to England. They would not let it happen. They also knew it was an unlikely event because the rebels could not win without foreign help and they knew that it was not in the interest of France to intervene, they believed that she would not dare to intervene, that England would know how to stop her, were she foolhardy enough to try. They did not mind bearing the cost of the war, because they knew they could eventually pay themselves and their friends richly at the end of the contest, with the fortunes of the rebels. The latter also knew that this was the least evil which could befall them, should they lose, but that victory would open for them infinite opportunities of wealth and power.

How many journals, kept to increase one's efficiency, were later disposed of in order to suppress whatever had been thought and done, but no longer served the writer's purpose? The founding fathers themselves were not above that. Benjamin Franklin's French diary was partially destroyed. The great pragmatist probably did away with the record of certain attempts to negotiate with British envoys. In hindsight, those pages appeared unesthetic and useless. Destroyed also were the records of the Committee of Commerce. Writing from Paris to John Jay about the opportunity he had to buy the stolen journals of Silas Deane, Thomas Jefferson remarked that he would give much "to cut out a single sentence which contained evidence of a fact not proper to be committed to the hands of enemies."[6] Whose enemies? At that time the great Virginian had no love for the unfortunate exile.

The American leaders by no means all "militia diplomats," knew how to protect and promote their country's interests. There was no love lost on their part for the recent enemy, popish France. In order to play off France against England and vice versa, they paid spies who they knew were double agents. Since the threat of French intervention was their most potent argument against the government of George III, they used

---

[6]Thomas Jefferson to John Jay, 3 August 1788, Dea 5:486.

it. The French monarchy ministers, unaware of how much they had to lose, sought to weaken both of the Anglo-Saxon countries, to make the internecine war last, and intervene as late as possible, if at all, and only if and when the Americans had proved they could win on the battlefield. The opposition party in England encouraged secret aid to the Americans, and even provided it themselves, because they hoped thereby to show the shortcomings of the royal policy, and return to power, and then perhaps wage a vengeful war against France. An American patriot, Silas Deane, was to be slowly crushed to death by this infernal machinery. That is the dark side of politics in which academic historians do not like to delve. Figaro, in a lighter vein, distilling Beaumarchais' experience, describes it as follows:

> To feign to ignore what you know, to know all that you ignore; to hear what you don't understand; not to understand what you hear; most of all to have powers beyond what you can do; frequently to have for deep secret to conceal that there isn't any; to lock yourself up in order to sharpen pens, and look profound when you are only, as they say, empty and hollow; to act a part, with more or less talent; to spread spies around and grant pensions to traitors; to soften seals; to intercept letters and try to ennoble the paltriness of the means by the importance of the objectives: that's politics, I swear to it! --Ho! That's intrigue, says the Count. --Politics, intrigue, yes; but as I believe they are somewhat akin, let someone else have at it! (BMF, 3:4).

V. Biographical Data.

1. The Caron family and Beaumarchais' early youth.

Pierre-Augustin Caron was born in a happy and cultivated middle-class family, of Calvinist origin, imbued with the work ethics, self-reliance and faith in God. His father, who as a Protestant would have been deprived of civil rights by the repeal of the Edict of Nantes, had found it a matter of practical necessity to adopt the Catholic religion in order to be able to marry and own property, the modest property which his watchmaker's craft, as well as certain commercial ventures, would bring him. The only surviving son in a family of twelve, Pierre-Augustin was expected to and did brilliantly continue in his father's craft. Before he was twenty years of age, he had invented a new escapement which permitted the manufacture of smaller watches than had been made before. He had also had to defend this invention before the Academy of Science and had done it successfully.

This craft mastery opened for him the doors of Versailles, not the court itself but the royal family. Among his many talents, charming personal attributes and social skills, musicianship was not the least designed to make him desirable there. Playing the harp beautifully (an instrument he had improved technically), he gave music lessons to the daughters of Louis XV and even composed music for them. The Dauphin, father of the future Louis XVI, showed him for eight years a special benevolence (RC, Mol 473). Slanderous envy, however, would soon and relentlessly exact a high price for Caron's remarkable successes.

The assertion often found that he was "ennobled" needs to be qualified. In France the nobility was a closed class. The beautiful British practice of raising deserving citizens to the rank of the nobility had no counterpart there. One could buy certain honorary "ennobling charges" in the so-called household of the king, which in fact never succeeded in overcoming or even denting class prejudice, the bane of the Ancien Régime. Caron did in 1760 buy the charge of "Secretary of the King," (a misnomer as the title was purely honorary), and later that of "Lieutenant general of the king's hunt," which did include the task of judging poachers and other trespassers on the lands reserved for the pleasures of the court. In order for him to qualify, his father had to cease practicing the watchmaker's craft. The honorary function of "secretary to the king" gave him the right to some of the privileges of the noblesse, for example to adopt the name "de Beaumarchais," taken from a small property owned by his wife. He was the first of his lineage, and proud of it, but others did not forget it. When the time came to show clearly what class he belonged to in the States General in 1789, Beaumarchais sat with the bourgeoisie.

2. **A Business Background.**

Beaumarchais' remarkable acceptance by the royal family led to other fortunate relationships. One of the wealthiest businessmen of the times, Paris-Duverney, asked him to obtain from the king a favor which he had sought in vain for nine years: to interest the pleasure-seeking, nonchalant Louis XV in visiting the military school which Duverney had created and was in charge of. The favor was granted, the military school was endowed, and a fruitful relationship started and continued until the death of Duverney in 1770. He became (like Voltaire before him) the friend and the associate of the humanitarian financier who gave him business training and made of him a competent capitalist entrepreneur, at a time when this species was rare in France.

In 1766 Paris-Duverney, for example, purchased the Chinon forest, which had been put for sale by ecclesiastical authorities, and associated his thirty-two year old friend in the corporation he formed for its maintenance and exploitation. Paris-Duverney sent him to Madrid on a business deal in 1764. While there, he frequented the court circles and made the acquaintance of many very important people, among whom many ambassadors and especially Lord Rochford, then British ambassador in Madrid, later to become Secretary of State.

All his life he was involved in various kinds of enterprises. Roderigue Hortalez & Co. was such an enterprise, and so were the publishing company created in Kehl (out of France) for the edition of the works of Voltaire and Rousseau, the Paris Water Company among other civic-minded projects, and finally the unsuccessful attempt to purchase in Holland 60,000 guns for the French Republic. He was engaged in many lucrative ventures which earned him a considerable fortune, a fortune much envied and disputed, which he risked, lost and remade several times in his career.

3. **The Defendant.**

Chicane would give rise to five main suits against him, robbing him of energy and time and sometimes hurting his reputation, although giving him practice in the art of dialectics. The first one took place in Spain. The second one was instituted by the Duverney heir and lasted eight years. The third one, instituted against him by one Maupeou-appointed judge Goezman, brought him fame and caused his loss of citizenship. The fourth, by his wife's heirs, lasted ten years. The fifth, on the eve of the Revolution, was brought against him by a certain Kornman. The facts in all these cases are as complicated as they are pettifogging and it took all of Beaumarchais' genius to throw light on them and extricate himself. I will not attempt to summarize them here.

Success engenders slander, especially in a closed and decadent society. The French playwright was exposed to personal attacks all his life. One of the characters of the *Barber of Seville* describes, as follows, this "singular means of doing away with people."

Calumny, Sir? You don't know what you despise. I have seen it ruin worthy men. There is no mean and paltry allegation, no horror, no absurd tale that the idle people of a big city will not adopt, if it is done cleverly. And we have here such clever people! First, a slight rumor razing the ground like a swallow before the storm, pianissimo whispers, spreading as it flies away the poisoned dart. Some mouth picks it up, and piano, piano slips it in an ear. The harm is done. It sprouts, crawls, carries on from mouth to mouth, rinforzando; then, all of a sudden, Slander rises, hissing, swelling, growing; it stretches, takes off, whirls about, uprooting, blowing away, thundering; it becomes a general outcry, a public crescendo, a universal chorus of hatred and proscription. Who could withstand it? (BBS 2:8)

His association with Duverney had been beneficial and lucrative. It had also caused the jealousy of the Duverney heir, Count de LaBlache, who started a suit against him and forced him to suffer (for eight years) the effects of the indescribable judiciary system which prevailed in the last decades of the monarchy.

The English Parliament had no other equivalent in France than the States General, which had not been called for centuries. What was called "parlement" in France was the magistrature. It was hereditary and had traditionally been one of the three influential classes (with the clergy and the nobility). The Paris Parliament had the power of ratifying the decrees of the king. When the parliament refused to ratify the king's decrees, the latter would call for a "bed of justice," and force them to obey. The judiciary retorted by refusing to render justice, going on strike. There was a continual push and pull between the king and the judiciary. In 1770 Louis XV dismissed the parliament and called upon Chancellor Maupeou to reform the judiciary. New judges were appointed and the Paris parliament was divided into six separate bodies. Judges would be paid by the government and the traditional venality was to be done away with. Chancellor Maupeou's reform, however, antagonized the princes of the royal family, as well as the people. Beaumarchais became involved in the political battle when he defended himself in a suit brought against him by a Maupeou judge. It appeared that, if Maupeou had reformed the parliaments, he had not succeeded in "reforming jurisprudence" (VHPP 498). Venality was still a way of life in the French judiciary system.

There was little at stake in the case brought against Beaumarchais by LaBlache: 15,000 francs. In first instance, in February 1770, Beaumarchais had won. The Maupeou reform, however, took place in 1771 and new judges were then appointed. A certain Goezman, a Maupeou appointee, handled the LaBlache appeal. While Duverney's former associate was successfully defending himself in court, an affair with an actress, in which he had slighted a choleric duke, and a succession of mishaps resulted in the reversal of the verdict; he was thrown into prison, and his property seized.

Then began the compensation for the tribulations imposed upon him. He discovered the weapon which would serve him against arbitrary power for the rest of his life. He defended himself by addressing public opinion, flouting the laws of the press, as his pleas were published without the required permission. They were to establish his reputation as a man of wit and knowledge. With a mixture of logic and humor, they succeeded in exposing the continued corruption of the system. They sold by the thousands and contributed to the downfall of the Maupeou parliament. The defendant was carried in triumph by the people of Paris and feted by the princes. On February 12, 1774, Prince de Conti[7] and Duke de Chartres[8] celebrated this victory by giving in his honor at the Temple a dinner attended by some 500 guests. "We are of a good enough house, I believe, my nephew and I," Prince de Conti said, "to give the kingdom the example of how to treat a great citizen like you" (RC, Mol 473). Beaumarchais' reputation as a courageous and eloquent leader of public opinion reached England and all the way to America. But at the same time, he was cut down in the middle of his life: sentenced to civil death. Misfortune brought new opportunities to the man who had adopted Voltaire's maxim "My life is a combat."

---

[7]A descendant of the patriotic and originally Protestant branch of Bourbon-Conde, of Armand, Prince de Conti (1629-68), and a legitimized daughter of Louis XIV and Mademoiselle de la Valliere, Louis Fran ois (1717-1776) was grand master of the Order of Malta. His father had been a minister under Louis XV. His grandfather, Fran ois-Louis (1664-1709), had been elected, although not appointed, to the throne of Poland in 1697.

[8]Louis Philippe Joseph (1747-1793), a grandson of the Regent, Duc de Chartres until he succeeded to his father's title and Duc d'Orleans thereafter (in 1785). "Philippe Equality" voted for the execution of Louis XVI in 1792. His former title then passed to his own son, who became King Louis Philippe in 1830. He had been repeatedly "exiled" by Louis XV, to his Villers-Cotterets home (a small town near Paris which is also the birthplace of Alexandre Dumas) for his support of the judiciary. He was guillotined in 1793 with all the other members of the Bourbon family who had not emigrated.

The defendant was adept in transmuting base metals into gold: "Everything," he wrote in 1771, "appears to me to be based on the sublime and consoling principle of the compensation of evil by good," (Mol 354). That was the case in 1774, when the great misfortune of the "blame" at once propelled him onto the public scene, where he remained for the rest of his life, and forced the banished man to move to England and discover a universe that was to change his life.

4. London, School for Politics.

Then, like many persecuted Frenchmen before him, like Voltaire, he crossed the Channel and found in England a lordly refuge. There he was admired, appreciated, invited to the gatherings of the liberal circles of the Lord Mayor, John Wilkes. There he discovered democracy in action and tasted "English freedom."

He soon became an habitue of two somewhat overlapping circles: that of the picturesque and turbulent French political refugees, on the one hand, and the Opposition to the British government on the other, some members of which constituted, with certain Americans living in England, the secret society known as the Friends of America.

The French refugees, most of them journalists persecuted in their country for their courageous political opposition, had no other way to make a living and to fight arbitrary power than to use their bitter pens to expose the abuses of the decadent monarchy. The new arrival among them, Beaumarchais, was in the same situation, except that he was more famous than most. Seizing a way to return to France and recover his civil status, as well as to help his brothers-in-exile, he offered to Louis XV his services: he would stop writings offensive to the king, which were called "libels" although they were often telling the truth. The fact that he had, so to speak, a foot in either camp, has been frowned upon by certain historians unfamiliar with the temper of the times. Was it libellous to protest against the horrors of the decadent monarchy: Louis XV's secret diplomatic service which he carried on separately from Choiseul's diplomacy, resulting in confusion and the sacrifice of some unfortunate secret agents; the king's inordinate love of women and his yielding government affairs to the current official mistress? Beaumarchais' first mission dealt with Theveneau de Morande, the "Armored Gazetteer," author of *Memoirs of a Prostitute*, which lampooned the latest of the mistresses of Louis XV, Madame DuBarry, who had caused the fall of a ministry, influenced the king in the latest arbitrary dismissal of the magistrature, and was understandably hated by the people. Unfortunately, by the time the king's agent had succeeded in solving the Morande affair, Louis XV was dead (May 1774). He had died of smallpox, a disease which could have been avoided, had he listened to Voltaire forty years earlier, instead of burning his book.[9] By then the DuBarry matter had lost its relevance (Louis XVI first act was to send Madame DuBarry to a convent). The banished playwright had secured a pension for the gazetteer, no longer in armor, but lost the opportunity to regain his civil rights.

He immediately, however, wrote a glowing letter to the new king, "Louis le désiré," the hope of the long-suffering nation, informing him of what he had done for his predecessor and renewing his offer of services. Louis XVI accepted the offer and graciously accorded to him a written proof of that acceptance, in the form of a note in his own hand which the banished man carried in a gold locket suspended by a chain around his neck. In the Atkinson affair (alias Angellucci), he ran throughout Europe in search of the libelist, meeting with bandits who did not exist except in his imagination, the hoax can probably be called a sophisticated literary revenge. When he had access to the inner sanctum of power, he tried to intervene in favor of those persecuted Frenchmen exiled in England.

Another acquaintance of his in London was Chevalier d'Eon, a former diplomat in the secret Foreign service which Louis XV maintained in order to spy on the official Foreign office. D'Eon, a virtuoso of the sword, as well as the pen, was entitled to receive a pension from the king, which pension often failed to be paid. A typical aristocrat, he had a complete disregard for money matters, that is, as far as paying his debts was concerned. Spending money, he took for his birthright. He had in London incurred a huge amount of debts, charged to the account of the French Embassy. He was a prolific writer and despised Count de Guerchy, the

---

[9]In the eleventh of his *English Letters*, burnt in France under Louis XV in 1734, Voltaire told his countrymen how smallpox vaccination had been introduced in England, under George I, against the disease which at that time was contracted by 6 out of 10 persons. The author brilliantly explained how effective it was and that it was backwards on the part of France not to try it. In fact Louis XIV's son had died of it, and Louis XV received the fruit of his injustice and backwardness. After his death, Louis XVI consented to being vaccinated.

French ambassador in London under whom he was supposed to serve, for his lack of talent and patriotic spirit. There ensued an underhanded fight between the ambassador and the Chevalier, who succeeded in having Guerchy indicted by a British grand jury in February of 1764 for assassination attempts made on his person. The incident caused major embarrassment to both the French and the British courts (Pinsseau 119). He was insanely conceited, even in the eyes of those who shared his class prejudice. His expressed admiration for the author of the Mémoires ("There is still a man left in France!"), was not sufficient to balance the effect of his scorn for the commoner.

D'Eon had critical papers in his possession, which he was using as leverage when his pension failed to arrive. As a result of his quarrel with the French ambassador, Duke de Guines, he was hounded by the French police in London. In 1775, he solicited the help of Beaumarchais, who quickly succeeded where others had failed, securing a pension for him in exchange for his papers. But in order to neutralize the swashbuckling Chevalier, and keep him from exterminating his enemies in duels, it was suggested that he should wear female clothing and assume the female sex. A dragoon captain, knight of the royal order of Saint-Louis, the unfortunate Chevalier had to lend himself to the comedy, as it was enjoyed in all social circles and staged in the newspapers on both sides of the Channel. His witty letters and the replies he received from Beaumarchais would certainly provide comic relief here, but as they are voluminous, I have decided to give only a few.

Chevalier d'Eon was a friend of prominent Englishmen who were like him Freemasons and members of the "Lodge of Immortality" in the Strand, England (Pinsseau, 119). But Beaumarchais needed no introduction in London. He was immediately received in the house of John Wilkes,[10] hub of secret activities in London, involving some of the French refugees as well as the Friends of

---

[10] John Wilkes (1727-1797), after being expelled from Parliament in 1764, frequented in Paris the house of Baron d'Holbach, where he met Helvetius, Diderot and other French philosophers. Popular with the poor people of London, he was elected Lord Mayor in 1774. He was a typical English rake but and a man of wit, courage and integrity. Beaumarchais is "in regular correspondence with Mr. Wilkes," wrote Lord Stormont on 25 September 1776. "Their letters are not trusted to the post but sent by private hands" (SF 1366).

America. The two men remained in correspondence all their lives.

An English admiral, Lord Ferrers (Washington Shirley, Fifth Earl of Ferrers, 1722-1778), played an important role in the activities of the Friends of America. He was a friend of Chevalier d'Eon, to whom he made loans secured by d'Eon's secret political papers.

Through the intermediary of Wilkes, Beaumarchais met Arthur Lee. The Frenchman was at first very much impressed by the "virtuous American." One of the four sons of a prominent Virginia family, Lee had been since 1768 residing in London where he studied law. He was interested in politics and occasionally wrote in the London press under the pseudonym "Junius Americanus." The Committee of Secret Correspondence had engaged his services in December 1775 and sent him 200 pounds with the authority to hire an express boat any time he had an urgent message for Congress. He would be reimbursed for all of his expenses. They wanted to know "the disposition of foreign powers towards us." By that time the Frenchman had already sought the American and mentioned the original scheme of Hortalez and Company to him. The famous "Peace or War" memorial of February 29, 1776, mentions Arthur Lee and clearly shows that the "militia diplomat" had craftily persuaded the politically immature Frenchman that the king of England was willing to let the colonies go; that England would make up her losses by overtaking France's sugar islands; and that it was therefore in her interest to aid the American revolutionists. He bragged that Spain had already received two American commissioners. Vergennes knew better, but Beaumarchais could not believe Lee would lie. Lee wanted to involve France into the controversy between the mother country and the American colonies. The political value of the aid interested him more than the military assistance. He persisted in not hearing the Frenchman's suggestions regarding the establishment of a trade involving tobacco returns. (See Hortalez and Co. section, below.)

The Virginian and the banished playwright had a common acquaintance in the person of Count de Lauraguais, who had been privy to Beaumarchais' political schemes, had accompanied him to England once, and served as an interpreter between the two men. (See "before September 1775" memo to the king.) Born of the highest noblesse, very talented with words, a would-be alchemist and a Freemason, Lauraguais had been several years earlier forced to seek refuge in England. Since then, he freely traveled back and forth, with perfect disregard for expenses, having dilapidated his fortune but still keeping an extravagant style of living. Like d'Eon, in spite of his Masonic connections, which ought to have given him some notion of the brotherhood of men, he despised commoners, taking his rank as a substitute for merit.

In London, the playwright was informed of many intrigues involving French exiles, major characters like the writer Simon Linguet, minor ones like a certain Texier (or Tercier) and Baron de Linsing, about whom little is known, but who elicited much concern from the ministers. Linguet (1736-1794), an energetic man of letters, historian, publicist, lawyer and editor of the <u>Journal</u> <u>de</u> <u>Politique</u> <u>et</u> <u>de</u> <u>Littérature</u>, was banished from France in 1775. His work L'Aiguillonnade, the complete edition of which was found in the Bastille depository in 1789 (Manuel 1:250), lampooned Choiseul's successor and Vergennes' protector, the duc d'Aiguillon. "The Foreign Affairs Tartuffe," wrote Manuel (1:278) referring to Vergennes, "would not have left millions to his children if he had reimbursed the public treasury the millions his reputation had cost it." In London and Brussels, Linguet published a newspaper called <u>Les</u> <u>Annales</u> <u>politiques</u>, <u>civiles</u> <u>et</u> <u>littéraires</u>. The French government feared Linguet like the devil and paid the "Baron de Thurne" (alias for Goezman) to spy on him in England. He became an Austria Councilor of State in 1786, published Memoirs on the Bastille in 1789 and wrote his last work in defense of Louis XVI. He was guillotined "on the charge of having flattered the despots of Vienna and London" (Encyclopedia Britannica). His life witnesses against the anomalies of the times.

5. Freemasonry.

It is well-known that Freemasonry played an essential role in propagating the Enlightenment ideology and facilitating revolutionary action at the end of the eighteenth century in Europe and America. It is at once a tempting and galling subject for the historian, because Masonic efficacy resulted from the very feature which makes it off-limits to him. Masonic secrecy, then an absolute requisite, was a matter of life and death. The Paris Temple, however, which was destroyed in 1812 was not a Masonic temple but the ancient monastery of the Knights Templar, which after the Templars' trial and extermination (1312) passed to the order of St. John of Jerusalem (which was now called the order of Malta), was a city within a city. Palace, market, and surrounding territory, out of bounds to the French government, harbored a printing press (Manuel 1:52). The grand prior of the Order of Malta, always a "prince of the blood," lived there. The Order had its headquarters in the Mediterranean island whose name it adopted after it was driven from Rhodes in the 16th century. In 1770 and until his death in 1776, Prince de Conti was grand prior, the same prince who protected Beaumarchais in 1774, and who had protected Jean-Jacques Rousseau earlier. It happened that the Duke of Chartres, Conti's nephew and grand master of The Grand Orient of France, also lived there. But the Grand Orient and the order of Malta were only vaguely related, and differed in their allegiances and tenets. The claim that "under the capable supervision of the Duke of Chartres, the Grand Orient, by 1776, had succeeded in unifying rival Masonic bodies in Paris, [and] had received the tacit support of the crown" (Weisberger 1986, 166) appears exaggerated. Indeed the Duke of Chartres (d'Orléans after 1785) all his life, led the opposition of the nobility against the king, for whose death he would vote in 1792. Elected Grand Master in 1771, the Duke did suppress the Grand National Lodge of France,[11] but when? According to another source, the Grand Lodge of France did not merge with the Grand Orient until 1799 (Fay, 264).

There is evidence that the Secretary of State had some connection with the Order of Malta (to Vergennes, 4 March 1779, last paragraph). One would like to know what it was and if here was any common ground between the order of Malta and Freemasonry in France at that time. Indeed the affinities were real, but so were the differences. Some lodges, obeying the Masonic pledge not to become involved in politics, were, at least outwardly, friendly to the monarchy, while others and especially those affiliated with the Grand Orient had sworn its demise. Emmanuel, Prince of Rohan, who died in 1797, was the last grand master. He was a brother to the Cardinal, Louis, the main actor in the affair of the Queen's necklace, and (like the Duke of Orleans and General LaFayette) a follower of Cagliostro. The Revolution was fatal to the Order of Malta. Its possessions in France were confiscated in 1792. During the Revolution Malta became a refuge for French emigres, while the Temple in Paris temporarily served as a prison for the royal family. The Directory suppressed the order in 1798.

There were material differences not only between the various orders but also between lodges, and within

---

[11]*Memoirs of Talleyrand*, 1:125-6. "Frivolity and dryness of heart" characterized the duke according to Talleyrand.

them, between the various degrees or ranks of the initiates. Things also evolved and changed with time and place, so that statements have to be carefully qualified in that respect. Everything that pertains to the enigmatic Count de Saint-Germain (not to be confused with Louis XVI's minister of war) or to "Count Cagliostro" remains to haunt and taunt the historian with mysterious clues. Saint-Germain, who "figures prominently in the correspondence of Voltaire and Grimm," appeared at the court of Louis XV in 1748, was forced to leave by Choiseul in 1760, and allegedly initiated Cagliostro in Germany. The latter, Giuseppe Balsamo (1745-1795) by his real name, created the Grand Orient or Egyptian Masonry, which had sworn enmity to the French monarchy, ("Lilia Pedibus Destrue").[12]

Benjamin Franklin, the Mason par excellence, started early to establish an international network. During his visits to France in 1767 and 1769, he met the most influential philosophers. As President of the American Philosophical Society (and master printer), he was able to distribute copies of the first Transactions in 1771, which greatly contributed to the enthusiasm of the French intelligentsia for America (Echeverria, 22-38). From London, he gave letters of recommendation to Thomas Paine in 1774, then from Philadelphia he instructed Silas Deane to contact Edward Bancroft in London and Jacques Barbeu-Dubourg in Paris. He also picked the Englishman who was to serve as butler to Arthur Lee in Paris. And it turned out that he had planted British spies on both of the unfortunate men. In Passy, he joined the "Lodge of the Nine Sisters," the creation of which was due to the astronomer Jerome Lalande (Weisberger, 166), a friend of Beaumarchais' companion and biographer, Gudin de la Brenellerie. Attracted by Franklin, Voltaire was initiated into it shortly before his death, in 1778. The lodge, flouting government orders, conducted ceremonies for the writer's

---

[12]The works of Alexandre Dumas, *Joseph Balsamo* (tr. *The Memoirs of a Physician), The Queen's Necklace, The Countess de Charny*, etc. although not footnoted, were based on historical research. The Latin phrase means "tramp upon the lilies," the lilly being the symbol of the French monarchy. Balsamo, alias Count Cagliostro or Baron Zanoni, and his predecessor, Count de Saint-Germain, are not entirely fictional characters. Henry Adams found more historical truth in the works of Walter Scott and Alexandre Dumas than in academic writings *(The Education of Henry Adams*, 1916, p. 434). Dumas' collaborator was the historian Auguste Maquet. In a domain where secrecy was of the essence, the novelist's intuition is the only way to evoke the truth.

funeral. The Secretary of State, having ordered the closing of the lodge, finally yielded to Franklin's entreaties and allowed it to remain open, provided the American would replace Lalande as grand master (Fay 1935, 268). Having created an ever-expanding circle of friends, Franklin devoted the greatest part of his energy in France to "making friends and influencing people." Such was his sway over the Secretary of State that he could in 1782 entertain separate negotiations with England, in violation of the treaty, and immediately thereafter obtain a new grant of money from him (Van Doren, 591-2).

Was Beaumarchais a Freemason? He shared the higher Masonic or Rosicrucian dedication to the cause of freedom, across national borders, the drive to work for the public good without expecting a reward other than the satisfaction of having participated in the progress of mankind. Many anecdotes told by Gudin seem to illustrate his adherence to mystical principles, such as the practice of silence, equipoise and patience, concentration and the courage to dare (a word often found under his pen). Many times exposed to the "tearing and burning" of his writings (as he humorously referred to the ceremony of the "pilon" by which books were publicly destroyed, described in Manuel 1:35), he had good reasons to adhere to the L.P.D. motto. He certainly yearned for the Republic, a word constantly used in his letters to Congress. He was, in fact, more imbued with Republican principles than the majority of his American contemporaries. The Encyclopedia, that incomparable testimony to the achievements of the French bourgeoisie in the arts and sciences, "the nation's eternal glory (VL15 262)" was the work of Denis Diderot, who was one of Beaumarchais' teachers. But was Diderot a Mason?[13] One historian says that he might have been for there is no proof to the contrary, the next one jumps to the conclusion that he was. If he was not, all his friends were. Yet it is noted that, generally, prominent people did not join ordinary lodges. Alexandre Dumas imagined an episode in which Jean-Jacques Rousseau declined an invitation to join. Writers teach others and need not be taught. Perhaps the literature of the seventeenth and eighteenth centuries sufficed to insure the spread of the enlightenment ideology, which was shared in essence by the secret societies of the time.

---

[13]Fay 1935, 224. Norman MacKenzie, *Secret Societies* (New York: Holt, Rinehart and Winston, 1967), pp. 168, 171.

In all probability, although he expressed "a profound respect" for the "Temple" (RC, Mol 472), and had friendly relations with most of its leaders, the versatile Frenchman did remain an outsider. He was too active, too busy, too well known to join. In a note found among his papers, undated but obviously written after the French Revolution (cited in full at the end of this chapter), he stated that he had never belonged to "any literary, political, or mystical association." Perhaps was he thinking only of France, and like Montesquieu (Fay 1935,176), had joined an English lodge. For in England, especially in 1774 and 1775, the French playwright had frequented the "Temple," where he had met key personalities, English or American, Mason or not, and in this respect, the secret society did serve as "the center of union ... among persons that must else have remained at a perpetual distance."[14]

6. Le Courrier de l'Europe.

The "Anglo-French Gazette," printed in London in French,[15] contained at first mostly translations of English papers articles. It was "the only newspaper apt to give freely to our French people just notions about your rights and the wrongs committed against you by Old England," Beaumarchais wrote Congress; "I am the one who solicited and obtained its admission into France, in spite of considerable objections." He would soon contribute unsigned articles in favor of the American cause (1783 letter to Congress, fifth and sixth paragraphs).

The principal owner of the paper was a Scot named Samuel Swinton, a former navy captain, who remained Beaumarchais' friend all his life. The paper was edited by two French refugees, Theveneau de Morande, a difficult man whom we have already met, and someone by the name of Serre de la Tour.[16]

---

[14]Masonic Constitution cited in Fay, 1935, p. 318.

[15]Although the French spelling calls for a double r today, it was sometimes spelled with one r at the time, as in English. *Courier de l'Europe, gazette anglo-française*, semi-weekly, 1776-1792, 32 volumes, can be found in the Newberry Library in Chicago (as well as BN and Bibliothèque de l'Arsenal in Paris).

[16]According to Robiquet (p. 60), Serre de Latour, also called Latour de Serre, owned one third of the paper. He had eloped to England with the wife of a French magistrate, Guerrier de Besauce. Robiquet's source appears to be Pierre Manuel, *The Paris Police Unveiled*, Paris, 1791.

After the affair of the Queen necklace, in 1784, the paper, at the request of the French court, conducted a campaign against the organizer of the organizer of the Grand Orient of France, Count Cagliostro, who had plotted with Cardinal de Rohan to incriminate the unfortunate Marie-Antoinette in that pathetic affair (Robiquet 189-205).

Beaumarchais is to be credited (or blamed[17]) for obtaining the permission for the paper to circulate (after the inevitable censorship) in France, where the first issue appeared in October 1776 (to Vergennes, 6 September 1776). As the war broke out between England and France in 1778, the copy was smuggled to Boulogne, where the paper was then reprinted. It continued to appear without interruption until war again broke out between France and England in 1793. The Boulogne editor was a Freemason, the future Girondist leader, Jacques Pierre Brissot de Warville.[18]

The newspaper, sometimes referred to as "M. de Beaumarchais' courier," propagated liberal ideas. It not only informed the French public about the American cause, but it served as a tool to forge the vocabulary needed to deal with democratic politics, an area where the French language was somewhat deficient. In spite of censorship, sometimes difficult to implement (6 September 1776 to Vergennes), it was for him personally a powerful weapon against arbitrary power.

7. **The playwright.**

The theater has been Beaumarchais' enduring claim to fame, although he considered it only as an amusement, and all of it resides in the character of Figaro, in the two comedies which display the genius of mirth. The action always takes place in Spain, in order to avoid explicit satire of French society, according to the practice of eighteenth-century writers. Figaro is for his master, Count Almaviva, a factotum, a man Friday good for any mission, as Beaumarchais was for the Count to whom most of the correspondence herein is addressed. The *Marriage of Figaro* is a symbolic rendition of the relationship between the playwright and the minister,

---

[17]The newspaper has been blamed for giving Vergennes alarmist reports (Corwin 1916, p. 14).

[18]Proschwitz 1968, 501-511. Letter from Swinton to Beaumarchais, 10 April 1778. Manuel 2:245.

the educated and enlightened bourgeois and the placid aristocrat. Contrary to certain interpretations given to the Mozart opera (whose libretto does not closely follow the play but whose music does justice to Beaumarchais), Figaro, "the most resourceful of Frenchmen," is not dishonest like stock servants in classical comedy. He succeeds in keeping his own through wit, enthusiasm, common sense, and hard work. "Everything he does to repulse injury is forgiven him as soon as it is known that his cunning aims at safeguarding what he loves and defending what belongs to him" (BMF Preface, Mol 102). In the play, his bride; in real life, France.

Because you are a great lord, you think you are a great genius! Noblesse, fortune, rank and high office, all of that makes you so proud! What have you done to deserve so many advantages? You took the trouble of being born, no more. Otherwise, a rather common man. While I, by gosh, lost in the obscure crowd, I had to display more acumen and forethought just to subsist than were used in a hundred years to govern all of Castile. And you want to joust ... (BMF 3:3)

The word "joust," which refers to medieval chivalry tournaments, is used here deliberately. Figaro sees himself as a knight in shining armor. The passage has been transposed in Le Nozze di Figaro in the "Se vuol ballare" air. If the DaPunte words do not do justice to the play, the Mozart music certainly does.

For Beaumarchais, the theater effected a sort of communion with the public. He had started with dramas involving business life, bourgeois ethics (which at the time represented true morality by opposition to the depravity of the noblesse): Eugenie, in 1767, les Deux amis [the Two Friends], in 1770. It is in the Barber of Seville, that he started, with a rare sense of humor, passing on to the public the sublimated expression of their everyday experiences, the awareness of the "anomalies of the times" (what he termed "les disconvenances sociales"), of their aspirations for freedom and justice. And he did so while making them laugh, all of them, aristocrats and commoners. When the excesses of the French Revolution rolled over the martyred country, the playwright returned to pathetic drama with his last play, La Mere coupable (the Guilty Mother). A sense of guilt permeates the play and Figaro exclaims in the final scene: "O ma vieillesse, pardonne à ma jeunesse, elle s'honorera de toi!" ("My old age, forgive my youth, it will be honored by you!") Nothing in the play can justify that feeling of guilt on Figaro's part. Guilt has been incurred by the Count and Countess, who both have been unfaithful to each other and have illegitimate offspring. The Tartuffe, the hypocrite swindler, the real criminal, is an Irish major (who has served in America) and manipulates every member of the family, until the resourceful Figaro unveils his evil schemes. Yet, the incredible and successful attempt of the lovable, superior servant to govern his mediocre master, which was the theme of the first two comedies, now seems to weigh on Figaro's conscience. As if he was no longer sure that his influence on the history of his country had been entirely beneficial.

Because the author frequently revised his plays to insert allusions to current politics, they contain many variants which in the absence of good critical editions are difficult to understand and appear to be "gaps and deficiencies of language."[19] Hence a destructive literary critique which unwittingly obfuscates the masterpieces they are supposed to explicate.

In his correspondence with the ministers, the writer can turn a compliment--untranslatable in English--in a thousand ways. (I have omitted in my translation all the closing formulas which contain those compliments.) He can write an engaging essay on any arid subject in either one paragraph, one page, or ten, even for a royal reader who does not like to read, prefers to repair clocks or look at maps. He has the most precise and extensive vocabulary, the most concise and logical sentence structure, and always a witty, understated tone. Understatement (which was a necessity in a country deprived of freedom of expression and is typical of the French literature of the time), and the fact that those democratic ideas have today become commonplace make it difficult for us to appreciate the writer's genius. Those garbled English translation, which we read under his name, correspond to masterpieces in the original French, the product of an enlightened and first-rate mind. But he adapts to his reader and to the circumstances. He is not here writing literature, although he often sketches dialogues and uses concrete language, in order to amuse while informing the ministers or the king. He is involved. He is militant. The letters addressed to the Secretary of State (before 1779) were not meant to be read in public (as was wont in those times), but to achieve results. Between the two men, during the crucial period of 1775-1777, as little as possible was put in writing. Some subjects

---

[19] Jack Undank, "Beaumarchais' Transformations," MLN 1985, 100:829-870.

had to be whispered. Hence an elliptical style which the translator must take special care not to betray.

VI. Louis XVI And his Ministers.

Louis XVI, twenty-year old grandson of Louis XV, who acceded to the throne on May 10, 1774, was in fact to see his life pitifully curtailed on the guillotine less than twenty years later. His father, Dauphin Louis (who had befriended the young Caron), had died in his thirties (in 1765), probably poisoned (Guizot 5:416). The young king, having witnessed the shameful sexual extravagance of his grand father, felt no inclination to imitate him. Married in 1770, at the age of sixteen, to the Austrian princess Marie-Antoinette, it was only after the receiving instruction from his brother-in-law Joseph II (enlightened despot and Emperor of Austria, 1741-1790), that he was able to beget an heir to the throne (in 1781).

Louis XVI never questioned his divine right to rule or the privileges of the noblesse and clergy, especially that of holding high governmental offices, to the exclusion of commoners of recognized ability. Otherwise, he had no will of his own. His brother Count de Provence compared dealing with him to trying to hold in one's hand several oily billiard balls. "His mind was weakness itself, his constitution timid, his judgment null, and without sufficient firmness even to stand by the faith of his word."[20] The fate of France depended on his choice of ministers. For prime minister, he retrieved out of retirement the old Count de Maurepas (1701-1781), probably following the advice of his aunts (the four unmarried daughters of Louis XV) and the "devots" party, i. e. the powerful religious cabal. The courtier par excellence, Maurepas' main ambition was to stay in position of power. He had served in Versailles, in one capacity or another, since the age of seventeen. The prime minister would leave three volumes of memoirs, containing mostly ditties and anecdotes.

For Secretary of State, the king and Maurepas agreed on Count de Vergennes (1717-1787). A career diplomat, Vergennes had been removed from the Constantinople embassy by Choiseul who found him apathetic. From 1768 to 1770, he lived in retirement in his Burgundy home, whence he had been called by Duke d'Aiguillon to serve as ambassador to Sweden. Strangely, his reputation

---

[20]Thomas Jefferson, *Autobiography* (Boyd 1:131).

in history was established on the prestigious policy of intervention in favor of the United States, while on all other counts he showed himself blindly reactionary. Manuel shows him as "hypocritical and intolerant" and busily persecuting writers (1:77, 184).

Wanting peace and social reforms, Louis XVI appointed as comptroller general of finance, Jacques Turgot (1727-1781), an economist, experienced administrator and enlightened philosopher,[21] a man of proven worth, the hope of French intelligentsia. This apparent stroke of genius was in fact the result of the influence of Maurepas' wife, who happened to know Turgot's family (Guizot 5:417). In 1774, the annual deficit of the royal treasury amounted to 35 million livres and the total debt to 235 million (NCMH 8:595). Turgot outlined for the king a comprehensive plan of reform. Without borrowing or increasing taxes, the budget would be balanced in time as the economic structure of the kingdom was gradually liberated from feudal shackles, and taxes rationally distributed. A civil code would be drafted and the system of weights and measures revised. Meanwhile, economy was in order and peace had to be preserved. Fate had it otherwise. Fierce opposition from vested interests triumphed (with the help of Vergennes). Turgot was dismissed in May 1776.

His successor, a certain Clugny, survived his appointment by only a few months and was himself replaced by Jacques Necker (1732-1804). A former administrator of the French India Company, Necker had recently received an award from the French Academy for his "Eloge de Colbert," a study of the statesmanship of the genial finance minister of Louis XIV, one of the builders of French hegemony in the seventeenth century. Necker was expert in finance, honest and hard-working. The fact that he was a Swiss and a Protestant, however, would soon add to the list of his enemies. Because of it, the title of Finance minister was not conferred on him, even though he exercised the functions thereof. He remained in office, on and off, until the revolution. Between 1781 and 1788, the post was occupied by a succession of mediocre courtiers, Calonne, Joly, and d'Ormesson. Recalled in 1788 Necker labored, to no avail, to remedy the financial crisis and the famine which soon propelled the bloodiest of all revolutions.

---

[21]Turgot wrote the maxim, "Eripuit caelo fulmen sceptrumque tyrannis," which was inscribed on the Houdon bust of Franklin. His Complete Works were edited by Pierre Samuel Dupont de Nemours (1808-1811).

Louis XV's efficient lieutenant-general of police, Count de Sartine (1729-1801), was appointed as navy minister. while a certain LeNoir took over the police until 1785, and DeCrosne until July 1789. Sartine had run the worst gestapo in the previous reign, and one perhaps should wonder how this qualified him for the navy. He did, however, rebuild it, going over his budget by twelve millions, so that in 1780 he was discharged at the request of Necker. The people of Paris (where everything, people said, ends up in chansons) had a ditty about him: "I combed Paris with extreme care, And wanting to comb the English out of the ocean, I sold my combs [ships] so high, That I was combed out too." After the fall of the Bastille, he escaped to Spain, avoiding the fate of his son who died on the guillotine.

VII. Beaumarchais, the King and the Ministers.

It had been the practice under Louis XIV for the king to receive memorials from his subjects and submit them to the Council. Access to the king had since become more difficult. It was through Count de Sartine, the former minister of police, with whom he had been acquainted since the Duke de Chaulnes affair in February 1773, that the banished playwright transmitted his first memorial to the newly crowned Louis XVI in June 1774. Full of hope, like all of the French people at that time, he addressed the young monarch with deep reverence: "No reign ever started so auspiciously as that of Your Majesty. . . the people adore you and have placed their hope in you. . . . I am burning to serve Your Majesty . . . to dedicate my life to your glory."[22] And to Sartine: "Whatever the king needs to know privately and promptly; whatever he wants to have done secretly and quickly--here I am: My head, my heart, my arms are at his service, and I have no tongue. Up to now, I did not want any master. But I like this one: He is young, well intentioned; Europe honors him, and the French people love him. Let everyone help this young prince to deserve the admiration of the whole world, whose esteem he already enjoys" (cited Lom 1:387).

The king did not refuse the offer and the banished patriot continued the police missions which he loathed. Politics came to the surface for the first time in the paper dated April 27, 1775, in the final paragraphs, starting with "That done, I dedicated myself to a nobler study, a more satisfying research." Concisely and

---

[22] 20 June 1774 to Louis XVI, Mor 2:50.

forcefully, Beaumarchais offers his services to the king in the area of diplomacy, the services of a man who had earned the applause of enlightened people on both sides of the Channel. He calls the king's attention to the political crisis in England, to the obvious passivity of his cabinet, and the need to employ a competent man. Citing commoners who had gloriously served in the past, Cardinal de Richelieu in France, William Pitt in England, he prayed that his merit would be recognized, and that he would be given the opportunity to serve on a high political level, that he might be appointed to a position of power. His credentials were well-known. His writings had proved the superiority of his mind. A testimony to that effect is given in Vergennes' letter of June 21st, 1775: "You are enlightened and prudent, you know men. . . . I am very appreciative of the praise you were kind enough to give me in your letter to M. de Sartine. I aim to deserve it and I receive it as a token of your esteem which will flatter me at all times."

Alas, his reputation did not extend to the king. He soon realized that the monarch, the most prejudiced man in his kingdom, did not hear him. He then allied himself with Vergennes, who in December 1775 started forwarding at least some of Beaumarchais' political papers to the king. The papers would always be handed open to the Secretary of State, who would read them before transmitting them sealed, as if he had not read them; for the minister was afraid to appear supportive of them. The letters intended for the minister were marked "for you alone." The king must have been wary, because soon a letter was marked "for you alone," which was shown to the king. From that time on, Beaumarchais constantly passed through the sole channel of Vergennes, to the exclusion of every other minister, as if he had made a pact with him to this effect. Even the letters written to other ministers were first seen by Vergennes. He had no secret for him, but the minister did not reciprocate. He kept his own counsel, questioned Beaumarchais' sources, and especially Arthur Lee, promised one thing and did the other. Seduced at first by the writer's eloquence, bright cheerfulness and wit, the minister soon would resent the superiority of the man who had first charmed him.

The long-standing controversy as to who instigated the policy of secret aid to America, which occupies such voluminous bibliography, becomes a moot question when the correspondence here presented is taken into consideration. The painstaking reasoning based on the assumed dates of certain 1776 state papers becomes superfluous.

Beaumarchais' free-lance "state papers" date from 1775. Samuel Bemis's unchallenged contention that documentary evidence was lacking to settle the question (Bemis 1965, 35) is false.

The elementary tone taken by Beaumarchais to instruct the king in political affairs, and the extreme care with which he tried not to tire him or lose his attention, show the infinite patience and good will of the man with the unfortunate young monarch upon whose weak shoulders rested the future of France. The same tone, compounded with flattery, is noticeable in some of the letters he later wrote to Maurepas. This was "a time when men of courage needed to belittle themselves when they wrote to powerful people" (9 December 1792 letter). With Vergennes, he seems, for a while, to have expected a quicker intelligence. He seems to have cultivated a true friendship with the minister, confiding in him more than has so far been suggested, sharing history books with him (a biography of Charles II of England), writing for him an essay on the kings of France. His tone, however, would eventually register irony, and the unavoidable flattery would make its appearance; for he was, to a great extent, at the mercy of the man.

There was a period of intense communication, between the two men, which lasted from June 1775 to December 1776. However, we hear only one voice directly. Letters from Vergennes, which are acknowledged, have disappeared from the National Archives. Upon the minister's request Beaumarchais must have returned them. Thereafter they must have been removed from the archives by the minister, probably because he no longer approve of their tenor. They showed him in opposition to the policy he would later adopt.

The arrival of the new commissioner, Benjamin Franklin, signaled the end of that period of trust. The crafty diplomat immediately bypassed and ignored the playwright, and behaved with Vergennes like a regular courtier, "receiving, taking and asking again" (Mol 474). The minister, seduced by the soft-spoken diplomat, soon forgot Beaumarchais' principles regarding the duties of a neutral state, the need to spare the royal treasury, and granted Franklin anything he asked for.

The news of the Saratoga victory (5 December 1777 letter to Vergennes) marked the turning point in British and French diplomacy. The free-lance statesman urged the French ministers to act and outlined a full program of action in a paper entitled "Private Memorial for the

King's Ministers," dated hereunder as of December 27, 1777. Moreover, aware of the American and British interest in effecting a reconciliation, Beaumarchais kept counter-espionage operations, watching the secret peace overtures made by British envoys to the American commissioners in Paris, and urgently informing Vergennes of his findings. The Franco-American alliance was signed in Versailles in February 1778, but the memorialist was not even informed of the negotiations.

In March, Deane heard that he was being recalled by Congress. Dismayed, the French patriot and free-lance statesman wrote for the ministers an analytical account of the Deane-Lee controversy and outlined again the policy France should follow. His advice was heeded. As suggested, Silas Deane left for Philadelphia with the French fleet in March of 1778. Thereafter, Beaumarchais restricted his concerns to domestic matters concerning French commerce and needed economic and social reforms, with no more success than Turgot before him.

VIII. Roderigue Hortalez and Company.

Such is "the tradename and signature under which I have agreed to conduct the entire business," Beaumarchais told the king of France in a rarely cited memorial dated herein below "October or November 1775." "Rodrigue" refers to the courageous Cornelian hero of the classical French play "Le Cid," who avenges his father's honor and becomes his country's defender. "Hortalez" to a French ear signified "Exhort them!" Give your countrymen the example of courage and enterprise, show them the trade route to America!

The plan described in this memorial is referred to in the 15 December 1775 paper, where the banished man, citing Grotius and other authorities, explains to the young king that there is no moral turpitude involved in the "proposed means," because nations are not subject to the same principles of morality as individuals.

This Hortalez memorial seems unknown today in France. The 1966 Beaumarchais Exposition Catalog (Bibliothèque Nationale) does not mention it, following in this respect Doniol, Lomenie and Lintilhac. The manuscript of the undated letter "to the king alone," written in 1775, had been "found in the Genet papers and typewritten for M. D. Conway."[23] The famous French ambassador who during the French revolution tried to persuade the United States to reciprocate with France, honor the 1778 treaty, and open American ports to French privateers. Citizen Genet probably intended to use it as a proof that the French nation and especially French commerce under the leadership of Beaumarchais, and not the French monarchy, were responsible for the secret help given the American insurgents. Such was also the theme of a descendent of the ambassador, George Clinton Genet, in an article published in the Magazine of American History (November 1878), which also gave the excellent translation of the memorial reprinted in the Deane's Papers. But the manuscript itself seems to have disappeared ("lost, strayed or stolen," I was told) from the files of the Connecticut Historical Society where it was supposed to be housed.

The Hortalez plan was not accepted for several months and not without modifications. It had not been accepted when Beaumarchais first approached Arthur Lee in 1775. When the main idea was accepted, in June 1776, the risks and perils, as well as any eventual profits, were largely left to Beaumarchais. The king had not been amused by the proposition that His Majesty would become a merchant, even if he would be the owner of a large and profitable enterprise of overseas trade, which was, exceptionally, a form of trade not prohibited to the noblesse. The government only promised Hortalez "a certain tolerance. . . which would be curtailed at the first sign of publicity" (1783 letter to Congress). Hence, the difficulties and contradictions encountered in the shipments of 1777, and the daily coaxing of Vergennes and Sartine. When bankruptcy threatened the firm, however, in order to avoid ensuing publicity, Hortalez had to be bailed out.

Before any such company was dreamed of, Beaumarchais had already formed "in various places which are hardly suspected," because they include England (where the Friends of America actively searched to help the American rebels), "a secret association which made me the referee and the dispenser of the means and funds we put into it together." It is because he had "come possessed with large means" (1795 appeal), that the banished man got the ear of the ministers.

---

[23]*The National Union Catalog Pre-1956 Imprints* (London, Mansell, 1969), 41:472.

The names of all the French persons who were associated with Hortalez are not known. They included merchants like John Joseph de Monthieu and a certain Hugalis or Hugaly, and the public at large, "the honest individuals" mentioned in the <u>Correspondance</u> <u>littéraire,</u> a society sheet edited by Baron de Grimm (1723-1807), cited hereunder, certainly not suspected of any sympathy for the "bold genius" he found too incredible to like.

The operations of the company are summarized briefly in the author's letters to Congress and at length in the Observations on the Justificative Memorial of the Court of London (1779). Figaro's father never suspected that the American commissioners' trusty secretary, Edward Bancroft, had been planted there to insure the leaks of his operations to the British ambassador.

I have omitted most of the letters relating to the business of Hortalez after 1778, in order not to burden this edition with voluminous and peripheral material. I have also omitted, for the same reasons, letters involving the artillery and genius officers whom Deane sent to America in 1776 and 1777 with the financial help of Hortalez. I have included on the contrary some of the letters Beaumarchais wrote to the ministers on the subject of tobacco, in 1777 and 1779. Tobacco importation was the monopoly of the Farmers-General, the tax collection agency. Out of taxes collected, only a predetermined sum was paid to the royal treasury. The Farmers-General, concerned only with their own profit, would fix the price of tobacco as low as they could. They would even for that purpose buy tobacco from England which had been seized on French ships. Without the needed reform, trade between America and France could not function and was doomed. The question was therefore eminently political. A few years later, Thomas Jefferson would try in vain to solve this peculiarly vexing French problem.

Beaumarchais received on June 10 a million livres subsidy from the French government and another million from Spain on August 11, 1776. Receipts therefor are given hereunder. But only simplistic minds will consider these subsidies as a proof that Hortalez was not, in spite of its political connections, a bona fide commercial firm. There is in this respect a profound gap between French and American or Anglo-Saxon culture. In the United States, the pharisaical proposition that business and politics are incompatible is entertained. Business, it is often alleged, cannot be mixed with politics. It is an either-or proposition. When Hortalez presented his company as a politico-commercial endeavor, when he explained that he needed to have a bona fide trade, with returns in American products, he unwittingly shocked them. Inversely, when Frenchmen visited the United States, whether they were officers or diplomats, they were also shocked by what they perceived as a lack of "personal disinterestedness and pecuniary probity" in Americans generally. They concluded that the Americans' most distinctive trait was "mercantile cupidity" (Echeverria 92). In this respect, the French thought, British and Americans were alike. It takes a superior mind to understand foreign cultures without judging them summarily. However, perhaps Jefferson may be called here to testify about French culture:

> I cannot leave this great and good country without expressing my sense of its preeminence of character among the nations of the earth. A more benevolent people I have never known, nor greater warmth and devotedness in their select friendships. Their kindness and accommodations of strangers is unparalleled, and the hospitality of Paris is beyond anything I had conceived to be practicable in a large city. Their eminence too in science, the communicative disposition of their scientific men, the politeness of the general manners, the ease and vivacity of their conversation, give a charm to their society, to be found nowhere else. (Boyd, ed. 1:159)

When Beaumarchais' representative in America, Theveneau de Francy expressed his cultural shock, his boss disregarded those comments, for he was capable of withholding judgment and seeking the causes behind the effects. But in his relations with Franklin, he seemed to have been troubled by the same phenomenon. The commissioner, who had "constantly shown him a disobliging aloofness. . . denied him the most basic civilities and never set foot in his house," explained his attitude by the desire "not to appear to criticize or disturb the work done before he had arrived by his colleague Deane." Yet, he had not hesitated rudely to claim the first return cargo from America on one of Beaumarchais' ships and argue with him in this respect. Whenever money was involved, it seemed to the playwright, Franklin was there (to Congress, 20 December 1778).

Other merchants had received a subsidy from the French government (Vergennes to the king, 2 May 1776). If Beaumarchais appeared to ask for a monopoly of American trade in his letters to Congress, it was only to insure secrecy and the efficiency of the operations. Moreover, no one heeded that request, either in France or in America. It is often overlooked besides that, after supplying Congress with the arms and munitions which enabled the American troops to win the battle of Saratoga, Hortalez continued doing business with other parties in America, public or private, for several years. The correspondence shows that the patriotic desire to develop French commerce,[24] and thereby foster a new prosperity in his own country, motivated Hortalez's efforts as much as his love for the American cause. In fact, it was part and parcel of it, as he saw it.

Silas Deane, a Connecticut patriot, representative of his State in the First Continental Congress, was, on March 2, 1776, commissioned by the Committee of Secret Correspondence (then composed of Benjamin Franklin, Benjamin Harrison, John Dickinson, John Jay and Robert Morris) "to go to France, there to transact such business, commercial and political as we have committed to his care, in behalf and by authority of the Congress of the thirteen united Colonies" (Dea 1:119). He was instructed to apply first to the French government in order to secure certain military supplies, and, if he met with a refusal, to purchase these supplies from private sources. He was authorized to pledge the faith of Congress, who promised to pay for these supplies "by remittances to France . . . as soon as our navigation can be protected by ourselves or friends" (Dea 1:124-5). He arrived in France on May 4, 1776, and immediately, according to Franklin's instructions, wrote a letter to Dr. Edward Bancroft in London and contacted Dr. Barbeu-Dubourg[25] in Paris. The first one, in the pay of Congress as well as the British government, was to be the rotten apple in the affairs of Hortalez. He was Deane's bosom friend and secretary, had the key to the commissioners' correspondence, and immediately reported to the British government everything he knew about Beaumarchais and Deane's activities.[26] This, no doubt a part of

---

[24]The importance of trade was a tenet of the French Enlightenment. Cf. Voltaire's *Tenth English Letter:* "Commerce, which gave wealth to the Citizens in England, contributed to make them free, and this freedom in turn increased commerce, resulting in the greatness of the State."

[25]Jacques Barbeu-Dubourg (1709-1779), author of *Le Petit Code de la Raison Humaine*, 1774.

[26]Paul Leicester Ford, ed. Edward Bancroft's Narrative of 14 August 1776 (Brooklyn Historical Printing Club, 1891). Boyd's statements (1959 article) to the effect that Franklin did not know Bancroft was a spy are unfounded.

Franklin's diplomacy, provided a dramatic irony the French playwright never suspected. By comparison, Dr. Dubourg was only the fly in the ointment.

On July 10, 1776 Dubourg introduced Deane to Vergennes, who referred him to Beaumarchais, and the collaboration between Deane and Hortalez started immediately.

In December 1776, both Arthur Lee and Benjamin Franklin were adjoined to Deane, as commissioners. Franklin arrived preceded by the most charismatic reputation. He soon procured a loan from Vergennes, who had no compunction in violating the principles of neutrality and forgetting what he had promised Hortalez. That was known in London immediately thanks to our friend Bancroft, and the involvement of France in the war began to appear as inevitable.

In fact, Vergennes did much more than finance the American commissioners. He offered them ships for their needs in procuring supplies to Congress (7 February 1777, to Vergennes). He repeatedly made disclosures detrimental to Beaumarchais' business. Later, he gave orders to the French ambassador in the United States, Conrad Alexandre Gerard, to write off some monies owed Beaumarchais against monies due by France to Congress for the food supplied to the French fleet in America, thereby reinforcing Arthur Lee's claim that the supplies were a gift of the king of France and deliberately taking credit for the supplies Beaumarchais and Deane had sent to America. In his accounting with Franklin in 1783, he listed the one million livres which had been allotted to Hortalez. The minister's attitude led to the "lost million" affair which was to prevent the payment of Beaumarchais' claim during his life, smear his reputation, give fuel to the persecutions inflicted upon him during the French Revolution, rob him of the opportunity to lead his country during that fateful time, and shorten his life.

IX. A "Political Opuscule" (November 1779).

The years 1778 and 1779 brought disillusionment and frustration in France as well as in America. The Spanish fleet had joined the French under Count d'Orvilliers in several bloody naval engagements, without decisive results. Admiral d'Estaing's squadron had been unable to achieve results in America, and even though he had obtained a victory in the West Indies, he had been recalled before he could prove himself. Before setting cap towards France, he had tried, without success, to lead an assault on Savannah, Georgia.

Beaumarchais used his pen to try and keep up public morale, embellishing every event which could be interpreted as a victory for French and American arms, exposing everything which could feed public resentment against Great Britain. An article published in the Courrier, decrying the British cruel treatment of prisoners of war, led to an exchange of letters with a reader. According to the custom of the times, the letter circulated among the public, in the cafes and literary salons, where people behind closed doors indulged in the forbidden activity of criticizing the government. The author was called to task by the Secretary of State (4, 6 and 8 June 1779). The incident illustrates the relationship that existed between the writer and his public, a public long used to incisive reading of clandestine, understated writing. There would be two versions of the same letter, one claimed by the writer to be authentic, the other to have been circulated by "enemies." In fact, they show how the public in France knew the art of reading between the lines, an art today much forgotten and which must be revived in interpreting the <u>Observations</u>.

When war broke out in 1778, after fifteen years of peace, the question before "the tribunal of Europe" was, whose fault was it? The "Expose of the motives of the conduct of France relative to England" approved by Louis XVI 15 August 1778 (Ang. 530 fol. 171-181), published in the European press, claimed that the French recognition of the U.S. was not the real cause of the war, but that England, faced by her colonies' rebellion, had warlike intentions regarding France and had allowed herself to exert a tyrannical empire over the seas, unjustly penalizing international maritime trade. The initiative and some of the contents of this manifesto had been suggested by Beaumarchais in December 1777 (See paragraphs 11-15). But the style of Vergennes' Expose appeared to be "little ambitious" to the French reader, if we can judge by the comments in the <u>Correspondance littéraire</u> (12:353). In fact, it was self-contradictory. While mentioning the "germ of independence" which had contaminated America, the royal government claimed that the British Court had forced its colonies to take up arms by its oppressive measures.

George III, thereupon, entrusted to the historian Edward Gibbon the task of defending his position. The Justificative or Vindicatory Memorial (Gibbon 122-147) started appearing on 12 October 1779, in several installments, in the General Evening Post. Vindication indeed was achieved. Was it sensible to claim that England, at a time when she was "employing her entire forces to reduce the revolted American colonies to obedience," (p. 128) would provoke other nations? The threat to French security was a chimerical one.

"The Court of Versailles readily forgot the faith of treaties, the duties of allies, and the rights of sovereigns in the attempt to profit by circumstances which appeared favourable to its ambitious designs. This court did not blush to sully its dignity by entering into secret relations with rebellious subjects; and after having exhausted all the shameful resources of perfidy and dissimulation, it dared to avow, in the face of indignant Europe, the secret treaty which the ministers of the Most Christian King had signed with the crafty agents of the English colonies . . . (p. 123-4).

The historian, possessed of the diplomatic correspondence of the British ambassador in Paris, did not hesitate to name "a certain M. de Beaumarchais and his partners" (p. 134), whose operations he attempted to describe.

Beaumarchais therefore presumed himself entitled to reply. He would not only eulogize the cause of American independence, "boldly promising a victory that was then less than assured;" he would also bring needed clarifications on the politics involved, his own and that of the government. He would dare "to blame the indecisiveness, the spinelessness [of the French ministers], and publicly reproach it to them in [his] proud reply" to Gibbon's memorial (RC, Mol 475c).

Shortly before November 11, 1779, the pamphleteer, saying that he was ill and in bed, sent Vergennes a paper of eight oversized pages, entitled "Faithful Expose of the Complacencies of the Court of France for that of England against the Interests of her own Commerce" (Ang. 524, fol. 409 and S.F. 2008) which suffices, he asserted in conclusion, "to vindicate the ministry of France against the allegation that they protected those delicate enterprises, a protection wrongly attributed to them in England." He slyly asked for the permission to send this piece of work to the Courrier, which Vergennes was not about to give, as shown by a gloss noted by him or at his request on the manuscript. The minister therefore gave a diplomatic answer: "Yes, but . . . but I'd like to see your work before you send it." Well, the Count had seen the gist of it. And the author rushed his work to the press of the newspaper in London.[27]

The publication created an uproar among the public. The style of the famous playwright and memorialist was unrecognizable, especially in the involuted prose of the first paragraph of the introduction. The Juvenal citation on the cover indicated a satire. But what kind of satire? The second paragraph seemed to point to the British ambassador Lord Stormont as the target. The informed reader, however, well accustomed to reading between the lines (see letter to an anonymous reader, June 1779), quickly caught the nature of the work. The pamphlet was a binary work, with two faces, an ostensible one, a masquerade meant to escape censorship, and a true one, commenting on current politics, a subject absolutely out of bounds for French writers, and directing satire against the royal government. But in order to get the full impact of it, the style had to be analyzed. It was like a puzzle. The tone shifted constantly from hyperbole to understatement. The first indicated the ostensible face of the pamphlet, the logically fallacious argument ad hominem, the farcical accusation about the faulty statements of the English ambassador, faulty because they were not complete. When the tone shifted to understatement, the reader knew that the satire was serious, hidden, forbidden and dangerous, because it was aimed at the government.

As it happened, however, the Duke of Choiseul and his cousin, Duke of Praslin, as well as the Duke of Nivernais, were startled by the general tone in which a commoner presumed to write about diplomatic affairs. They were especially concerned by the statement alleging that there had been a clause limiting the French navy in the 1763 treaty of Paris, which they had negotiated (Par. 65). They asked for suppression on that basis and Vergennes promptly concurred, although the censorship committee apprised of the work had decided to let the work circulate. In the 18 and 19 December correspondence between the minister and the writer, they both carry on an act, hiding their real feelings and intentions. Vergennes maintains that the Dukes were absolutely right in their request, and Beaumarchais affirms that the pamphlet is a worthwhile defense of the French

---

[27]The pamphlet came in three different formats: in octavo, 68 pages (at the Bibliothèque Nationale and British Museum); in 12, 64 pages (only at the BN); and in octavo, 56 pages (BM and LC).

government against the British accusation of breach of faith. The books were torn and burnt as scheduled, and the author's fall out of grace complete and irreversible.

A year after the suppression, in 1780, a diplomatic work bearing the same title, Observations etc., was published by the French government, without author's name. It had been written by Joseph Mathias Gerard de Rayneval, the distinguished publicist who had replaced his brother as first secretary in Vergennes' office, when the latter was sent to the U.S as ambassador. Rayneval's work was translated by a certain Peter Stephen DuPonceau and published in Philadelphia by F. Bailey, in 1781.[28] In library classifications, the two works have been confused. Librarians, always trying to fill in the gaps in publication data, attributed the unsigned diplomatic document to Beaumarchais, thereby unwittingly giving Vergennes' suppression a lasting efficacy.[29]

After the first edition was suppressed, Beaumarchais defiantly had the work reprinted in London, with no change other than two typographical corrections and the ironic addition in appendix of the suppression judgment and the correspondence relative thereto between Vergennes and the Dukes of Choiseul and Praslin. The text of this last edition, given hereunder in translation, is different in a few but crucial points from the text printed by Gudin and his successors in the author's so-called complete works (Mol 457-468). An order dated 4 June 1780 from Vergennes stopped the entrance of the book at Boulogne (Ang. 532, fol. 351).

Gudin (30 years later) had included the text of the pamphlet in the complete works, although mutilated and without any date or introduction, so that it was destined to remain dead letter. He had simply removed the sentence which had been the pretext of the suppression, and he had throughout the text changed spelling and punctuation in a manner which indicates that he was not

---

[28]The two *Observations* are listed under nos. 80 and 81, respectively, in Bemis 1935, p. 14. Stephen DuPonceau had come to America as Von Steuben's aide-de-camp and settled down there. See his "Autobiography," in *Pennsylvania Magazine of History and Biography*, 1939, 63:446-449.

[29]Only one historian has cited this work, Edward S. Corvin, who was admittedly confused by the various forms of what he took for the same work, p. 403-8.

aware of the satirical intent of the work. Thereafter this crucial episode of Beaumarchais' life fell into complete oblivion. The one or two French literary critics ever to allude to it, have described it as "a libel against England," or, more recently, as an account of difficulties encountered by maritime merchants in time of war,[30] both, of course, miles away from the truth.

In spite of the sui generis clandestine style of the work, which is analyzed at length in my doctoral dissertation ("Un Pamphlet clandestin de Beaumarchais, 1779, édition critique," University of Wisconsin, Madison, Wisconsin, 1971), once he is aware of its background and peculiar nature, the reader should be able to grasp its meaning. The irony was more intricate than that of any of his predecessors because the writer ran a greater risk: His name appeared on the cover and the target of the satire was the here and now.

Composed of short paragraphs, the pamphlet is easily outlined, as it is structured by various rhetorical devices, the use of symmetry, the repetition of the same words at the beginning of paragraphs in order to group them (anaphora), or at the end of paragraphs, as well as the use of key-words within the paragraphs. The fourth paragraph of the introduction indicates two main parts, one relative to the question of international law, the faith of treaties -- which the thinking reader understands is not the real subject of the work -- and the other relative to "particular facts" involving the activities and principles of the author himself which contains the criticism of the French government and conveys the serious satire.

The first part opens up with the rhetorical question, bombastically worded, "What nation is it which today presumes to smear us with the suspicion of perfidy . . ." It is answered by a negative rhetorical question, repeated at the beginning of the next six paragraphs, "Is it not that English nation. . . that same nation . . . that predatory nation, etc." which contrasts the aggressive Realpolitik of England with the pharisaic pose adopted by the English writer. Yet, the facts alleged in this parody of rebuttal, far from following the expected, logical, progressive order, are in fact anticlimactic. From the epic stance of William Pitt against the House of Bourbon, we go to the drunken

---

[30]Jean-Pierre de Beaumarchais, editor of his ancestor's Théâtre (Paris: Garnier, 1980).

pranks of a certain MacNamara in Senegal and to burlesque incidents of the naval war, pointing out the reciprocity of the ruses used on either side [6-15].

With the rhetorical question, "Who is it the author of the Justificative Memorial is trying to sidetrack in Europe" [16], starts a more serious dialectic, the panegyric of the American revolution as a fight for freedom under the English constitution [16-22].

As to France, she should have followed the dictates of Reason of State, but she did not [23-24]. She proclaimed her neutrality [25-26]. England might have objected then and declared war on France, but she could not because the constitutional issue involved in the American resistance divided the English Parliament [27-34]. Then Beaumarchais states his views regarding the rights and duties of France as a neutral State [35-41].

The transition between the two parts of the pamphlet [42-44], implies more than it states. It is hypothetical, reticent, and dramatic. "It remains for me to prove . . ." To prove what? That the ministers forgot the principles they had adopted and they betrayed the interests of the nation? Yes, but that cannot be stated if the pamphlet is to pass the censorship committee. The satire will therefore masquerade as a personal attack against the British ambassador.

The situation of maritime merchants in time of war is then humorously described [45-50], spoofing the so-called law of war.

Then [51-52] we have the author's "personal views." The rhetorical appeal is no longer to reason but to passion, to ethics. "I confess . . . that I dared foresee . . . I dared believe" that the cause of freedom would prevail. I dared give the example of trading with America. The real satire surfaces again: I confess I did not foresee the English ambassador's clout over our ministry. I was in fact relying on their protection [53], he implies. Bitterly, the pamphleteer denounces the French government "inquisition" on French commerce, while apparently putting the blame on the English ambassador [56-60 and 70]. Lord Stormont has left out a great many facts, which are forthwith given [54-60] and which show the subservient attitude of the French ministers in taking it upon themselves to stop private trade.

The French troops which according to Gibbon had been sent to America [60] by the French government, were sent by him, Beaumarchais. The proof of it lies in the fact they were not altogether welcome in America, a fact in which the pamphleteer saw "Republican pride," and it warmed his heart [64]. Such pride is, in Beaumarchais' work, opposed to "monarchical honor," i. e. the love of recognition and honors, which according to Montesquieu was the main spring of despotic governments (including the French monarchy), and which was, of course, an integral part of the culture or ethos prevailing in France before the Revolution.

The next paragraph, the climax of the pamphlet, a monologue, reminiscent of Figaro's, is in the rhetorical mode of confession. The vision of a different and better future, an era of liberty and justice for all, motivated the writer's involvement in the American cause. The paragraph ends in irony, however: The king of France is so simple, anything may happen.

Then comes the narration of the author's shipping activities and especially the story of the Proud Rodrigue [67-70], which, fearful and forgetting their promises, the ministers held back in port for more than a year [71-87]. He cites in extenso a letter written to the minister of the navy [77-84], using again the comic mask of childish spite against the English ambassador [88-90].

Switching back to a serious mood, Beaumarchais states the basic principle of natural law by which every state pursues its own interests while inflicting as little harm on others as possible. The reader knows that's not what France and England have been doing [91]. The next paragraph broaches the difficult question of continuity and responsibility with democratic governments [92], and therefore, the vanity of requiring France to keep the faith of treaties towards England.

The criticism of the French government surfaces in the paragraphs ostensibly intended to put the blame of the war on England [97-99]. The ministers have incurred the "indelible ridicule" of stopping with one hand what they had encouraged with the other. Moreover, they did not really want to help America, which they could have done with an early financial aid [100] without involving France in the war. Then comes the satire of the opportunistic and myopic timidity of the king's policy [101-103]. Why did the king wait so long before recognizing the United States? "Listen to me, reader, and weigh my words. That's the end of everything." The king was sucked into the war without forecasting any advantages for France [102-103].

The last paragraph makes an ethical appeal which the enlightened contemporary reader associated immediately with Jean-Jacques Rousseau's revolutionary work, *Du Contrat Social*. Right makes might, and not vice versa. The writer, a private individual, has dared raise his voice in the quarrel among governments, because "a man is always strong enough when he has reason on his side." Beaumarchais, before the tribunal of public opinion, claims his reward: the esteem of "the three great nations" involved, "France, America and even England."

In conclusion, in 1779, while the war drags on in America, Beaumarchais, a patriot, a lifelong champion of free speech, representative of the rising bourgeoisie, leader of public opinion, advocate of the American cause, of free trade and of all the ideas of the Enlightenment, speaks out again. He takes the militant position that the War of Independence is already won, but he accuses the royal government of nothing less than betrayal of the national interests through careless and criminal incompetence. French commerce was prevented from taking full advantage of the situation and helping America without involving France in the war. War was entered into without securing any legitimate advantage to the nation. He coined the word "lese-nation" (par. 70), which twelve years later would serve to send Louis XVI to the guillotine.

X. Epilogue.

Although the claim question today may lack in interest, it is pertinent to summarize here its settlement. Congress who had received a dozen letters from Beaumarchais during the war, had never answered any of them--except for John Jay's laudatory letter to Beaumarchais in date of January 15, 1779. The contract obtained from Congress in 1778 by Hortalez's representative, Theveneau de Francy, had never been ratified by the commissioners and was never implemented. Beaumarchais went on trading but with other parties than Congress. He tenaciously, however, pursued his claim. As shown by the 1781, 1783, 1787 and 1795 letters to Congress, he was involved into a vicious circle by which Congress insisted on having his accounts checked and would not allow them to be verified. Of this, he suffered morally more than in any other way. He fought to the end, and especially during the utter misery where he found himself in 1795. Then he really was in need, and he even thought of emigrating to America, "the only place in the world where one can breathe in peace." His reputation and the political question involved concerned him more than the money due him. It was unconscionable that, having so passionately espoused the cause of America's freedom, he would be subjected to slanderous and vague accusations based on his dealings with America, alleging that he had deceived the new republic. That was to be his fate, however, while the United States government struggled with the vexing problem of taxation and funding of public finances.

In the summer of 1787, Beaumarchais paid a visit to Thomas Jefferson, then ambassador in Paris, and asked for and received his support. Jefferson wrote to James Madison, on August 2, 1787: "A final decision of some sort should be made in Beaumarchais' affairs" (Boyd 11:664). And to John Jay: "He means to make himself heard if a memorial he sends by an agent in the present packet is not attended as he thinks it ought to be" (Boyd 11:699). Congress gave the 1787 appeal to a committee of three chaired by Arthur Lee, who promptly found that, far from owing anything to the Frenchman, Congress had overpaid him by 742,000 livres.[31]

The main obstruction to the settlement of the claim, however, was not of Lee's doing. It resulted from Vergennes' vengeance. In the summer of 1786, Congress had discovered that, in a state paper between Vergennes and Franklin dated February 25, 1783, the amount of the aid gratuitously extended by France to the United States before 1778 was shown as amounting to three million livres, whereas only two millions had been accounted for by Franklin. The "lost million" became a mystery which Congress set about to solve. Franklin suggested to Charles Thompson, Secretary of Congress, that the said million might be the million furnished by the Farmers General on their tobacco contract. Thereupon the U.S. banker in Paris, Ferdinand Grand, was instructed to ask Vergennes for clarification. Vergennes replied that the million in question had been expended by the Royal Treasury on June 10, 1776. Franklin then wrote Thompson that the "lost million" had probably been received by Beaumarchais, that it was "a cabinet secret, which perhaps should not be further inquired into." In May of 1793, Alexander Hamilton reversed Lee's decision and found the United States indebted to the Frenchman in the amount of 2,280,000 francs, subject to the clarification

---

[31]JCC 33:536, 649; 34:542-549.

of the "lost million." In June of 1794, Gouverneur Morris, then ambassador in Paris, obtained copy of the Beaumarchais receipt.

In 1805 a committee of Congress, after deducting one million livres and interest thereon, found a balance due the Beaumarchais heirs in the amount of 222,046 francs, or approximately $41,000. This sum was paid to Eugenie Delarue in 1806. Litigation continued as the heir sued for the million deducted in 1805. An interminable exchange of notes took place between the French and U.S. governments. In 1817, President Madison concluded that the million in question had been by the French government put in Beaumarchais' hands "as its agent, not as the agent of the United States, and was truly accounted by him to the French government," and that the claim was therefore due. In 1827, as the U.S. and France were negotiating the settlement of reciprocal claims arising on one side from Napoleonic spoliations, and on the other from claims incurred during the American revolution, they arrived at a general settlement, out of which a sum of 800,000 francs was paid to the Beaumarchais heirs on July 4, 1831 (HR 220).

From the political point of view, the letters to Congress offer the only overall account Beaumarchais would ever write. He had intended writing a political autobiography, until the cataclysm of the French revolution made that project appear to him either irrelevant or dangerous, or unfeasible for lack of time and strength. In 1783, the war of independence was over, the writer was not in need, and the narrative he gave of his involvement has a unique, poetic style. In 1795, the lamentable sanguinary excesses of the French revolution had taken place, giving proper weight and meaning to the French involvement in the American Revolution, if we believe the existentialist assertion that it is only after actions have produced all of their consequences that they can be judged. Then, after escaping several assassination attempts (1792 open letter), he had for three years erred along the French border, living in exile and misery in Germany. His heart had already called for time out, giving warning of the heart ailment which was to cause his death four years later.

Certainly he must have felt some responsibility for the turn of events in his country. The Frenchmen who had fought in America, defending the cause of freedom, found themselves bound in contradictions and impotent to defend the French monarchy. The clubs and secret societies throughout France took it upon themselves to hound and chase out those contradictions. They raised temples

to Divine Reason, leading to the scaffold all those who
ignored its dictates and still seemed to want to hold on
to the absurd past. As England and her allies waged war
on revolutionary France in 1792, the price of Vergennes'
and Maurepas' policies, or lack of them, had to be paid.
But Beaumarchais knew he had not had the power to really
guide the government of his country. He knew that as a
result of the entrenchment of mediocre aristocrats in
high places, revolution had become unavoidable and that
revolutions were bound to be unpredictable and bloody.
America alone among all nations did not have to pay the
price historically demanded of revolutionists. America
had, "thanks to its geographical position," avoided the
sacrifices traditionally imposed on the courageous
generation which raises the standard of revolution (1795
letter to the American people).

Beaumarchais had always passionately tried to serve
his country. He tried again, but in vain, during and
after the revolution. With the last letter herein
given, addressed in 1798 to the Secretary of State of
the Republic, Talleyrand, he submitted a political paper
regarding France's current difficulties with America.
He was then hoping to obtain from the Republic the
appointment to public office the monarchy had refused
him. In vain. He died in 1799, without having been
able to give his country his full potential. Trying to
find the reason for such enduring failure, he wrote:

Although naturally inclined to mirth and friendliness, I
have had innumerable enemies, and yet I have never stood in
anyone's way or even walked on the same path. After much reasoning with myself, I have found the cause of such widespread
hostility. Indeed, it was bound to be.

As a wild youth, I played all instruments but I did not
belong to the musicians guild.[32] The people of the art hated
me.

I invented a few mechanical devices, but I did not belong
to the mechanics guild. People talked against me.

I wrote poetry and songs. But who would have called me a
poet? I was a watchmaker's son.

---

[32]Each craft or trade had its own, self-enforced, centuries
old rules, meant to protect its members and their descendants. The
guilds transmitted the art and secrets of the trade but also
prevented competition.

Having no taste for bingo, I wrote plays, but they said: What is he meddling with? He is not a playwright, he is involved in all kinds of big business.

Unable to find someone to defend me in court, I published long legal briefs in order to win my cause in suits which were brought against me and may well be called atrocious. But they said: What is he meddling with? You can tell these are not a real lawyer's briefs. He is not boring to death. Will such a man be allowed to prove his case without our help? Inde irae.[33]

I have dealt with ministers on questions of needed financial reforms. But they said: What is he meddling with? He is no financier.

Struggling against all the powers that be, I raised the art of printing in France by superb editions of Voltaire, an endeavor considered as above a private individual's ability. But I was not a printer. They said the deuce of me. I had the machinery of four large paper mills clicking at once, without being a manufacturer. Industrialists and merchants were against me.

I have traded in the four corners of the world, but I was not a registered merchant. I had at one time forty ships at sea, but I was no shipper. I was denigrated in the harbors.

A warship of mine had the honor to fight on the line of battle along with His Majesty's ships at the battle of Grenada. In spite of navy pride, they awarded the cross to my ship captain and other military honors to my other officers and I, looked upon as an outsider, I got out of it the loss of the merchant fleet convoyed by that ship.

And yet, of all Frenchmen, whoever they may be, I am the one who did the most for the liberty of America, the mainspring of our own, the plan for which I alone dared to formulate and implement in spite of England, Spain and even France. But I was not listed among the negotiators, but I was an outsider in ministerial offices. Inde irae.

Tired of seeing all of our houses lined up and all our

---

[33]This Latin formula means: Hence the hostility.

gardens trite, I built an exemplary house.³⁴ But I did not belong to the arts. Inde irae.

What was I then? Just myself, such as I have remained, free in the midst of chains, serene in the face of peril, holding fast in the midst of storms, carrying on business with one hand and waging war with the other, lazy as an ass and always working, assailed by a thousand calumnies, yet happy within, having never belonged to any club, either literary or political or mystical; having courted no one; and hence rejected by everyone. (Lom 2:538; Mol 715)

This brings us back to the question of associations, especially the clubs and secret societies so powerful during the French Revolution, and gives us an insight into the nature of individual liberty and whether or not the joining of any group is for an individual a necessity of life. The leaders of the revolution belonged to such clubs. Had he been a member, would he have been able to better serve his country in its time of need? Would he have been spared the attacks on his reputation that plagued his life on both sides of the Atlantic? Or was it a recognition that an individual's freedom is limited by the situation in which he finds himself, i. e. by the society in which he lives (which is the theme of Jean-Paul Sartre in Les Jeux sont faits (The Die Is Cast)) and that in a closed society, free men live at their own risk.

Certainly, these reflections must have been written in a moment of depression. For the playwright had known a huge success on the stage all his life. In 1790 the opera *Tarare* (music by Salieri) had triumphed, together with the principles of liberty, equality and fraternity it extolled. The basic theme of Beaumarchais' theatre exploded in it: A man's worth does not come from his condition in life, from his birth in a certain class of society, but from his character, what he does with his freedom. What Figaro had brilliantly demonstrated in a comic vein, what Mozart's music (better than the DaPunte libretto) had immortalized, was finally expressed in the form of a mystical opera, starring Nature and the Genius

---

³⁴On a 2.5 acre lot on the Boulevard St. Antoine (now Boulevard Beaumarchais near the Place de la Bastille), he had built a mansion with elaborate garden. He moved in it in 1791. The painter Hubert Robert, who had decorated Voltaire's theater in Ferney, contributed many works. The property was put up for sale after his death. It was destroyed by the City in 1818 and the art work transferred to the Paris City Hall, where they burned during the 1871 revolution.

of Fire, Nature's lover, and the Winds, as well as a courageous soldier named Tarare, who is finally raised to the throne by popular acclaim, but accept only in the spirit of service to the people. The opera is no longer played and probably could only succeed in the decade of its creation, for an audience just rid of class prejudice and obsessed with the ethos connected therewith. On May 5, 1797, La Mère coupable was again triumphantly played at the Comédie-Française, and Figaro, "the most resourceful of Frenchmen," was enjoying the supreme union with the spirit of his countrymen, a form of ecstasy which must have compensated for the agony of his life. Yet, had he asked himself, like Thomas Jefferson, whether his country, was the better for his having lived at all, he would probably have answered: "Of all Frenchmen, whoever they may be, I am the one who did the most for the liberty of America, the mainspring of our own."

A cruel fate prevented him from extending to revolutionary France the leadership he was capable of providing, and which she so badly needed, but perhaps did not deserve. The lamentable excesses of the French Revolution cannot be erased from the collective memory of humanity, and their causes must be understood. Until the majority of the people have become able to recognize, admire and gratefully accept greatness and superior courage in their leaders, democracies will stumble and err as much as other forms of governments, and people will suffer exceeding miseries. The alternative chosen by Voltaire, enlightened despotism, deprives individuals of the opportunity to develop and evolve freely, in their own way, after learning from experience and the lessons of the past. Montesquieu, and Tocqueville after him, had warned that the spirit of equality carried to excess would cause the corruption of democracy. This seems to have already happened in the West today. Analyzing this trend as it is reflected in history, an eminent historian ironically observed: "There is a lobby against the continued appearance [of "great men"] in history. The manifest motive is to avoid anything that savors of elitism, for an elite is less than the whole. But a no less potent motive is the fatalist assumption about the course of human events: great men are illusions, mere facades for the real forces or factors."[35] If history is to emerge from its present state of "superficiality, intellectual irresponsibility and futility," which (quoting the same his-

---

[35]Jacques Barzun, Clio and the Doctors (The University of Chicago Press, 1974), 112, 2.

torian) is the result of that philosophy, it will be necessary to revert the trend. Historians will have to learn again to recognize, respect and admire the true merit, moral stature, and intellectual achievements of great men.

1775: A VISION OF GLORY AND PEACE.

This is the springtime of Beaumarchais' political adventure. Bursting with energy, hope and candor, in the following "Abstract," he broaches the political issue with the king. He has dedicated himself, he says after dealing with police news items, "to a nobler study, a more satisfying search." The letter was submitted to the king as usual by Sartine, the former police superintendent, although he is now Navy minister.

To facilitate the task of the young monarch, the writer has provided for a wide margin on the left, entitled "Abstract of the Abstract" (in parentheses hereunder) and another margin on the right for the king's comments. This paper is given here with omissions as it is found in Lintilhac, and only there.

27 April 1775, to Louis XVI
(Lin 391-5)

First[1] Abstract for the King

(My trip from Paris to London)
   I chartered a small boat for myself alone. Although the wind was quite contrary for the crossing to Dover, I had myself thrown on the coast of England, fifteen leagues southwest of Dover; and after a painful journey of seventeen hours, I landed in a village named Hastings, and headed towards London.[2]

(My search for libels printed there.)

(I receive a threatening letter containing some verse insulting the King and Queen.)

(I show myself openly in London.)[3]

---

[1]"First" is equivocal. First in 1775? There is a previous "First Abstract for the King," dated 20 June 1774, which is the first that Beaumarchais addressed to Louis XVI and concerns libels published in London (Mor 2:50-51).

[2]He had left Paris on April 8, 1775. He rowed to Hastings. (Gudin 1888, 163). This memorial was also mentioned in the Gudin biography (Gudin 1888, 166).

[3]He had been enjoined to leave London immediately if he valued his life, but he thought the best way to twart those threats was to appear in public under his own name, which was famous in all of Europe (instead of the pseudonym "de Ronac").

(I have my answer to the anonymous letter inserted in the newspapers.)

(My precautions for the future.)

On the way I found out that a certain Vignoles,[4] an unfrocked Prémontré, publishes in London a sort of scandalous newspaper, the contents of which, received from Paris through the mail in manuscript, return there through the same route. I showed the first 12 or 15 pages to M. de Sartine. You can read there everything that is done in Paris against the government; an alleged decree in verse by Louis XVI, declaring he only wants to look like a king, etc. If I am not mistaken, the prose and the verse come out of that shop. In my next abstract, I will point out the shortest way to destroy without getting compromised that vipers' nest, if Your Majesty so desires.

That done, I dedicated myself to a nobler study, to a more satisfying search. And my name alone having made me welcome by people from the different parties, I was able to learn from the good sources all that relates to the government and the present situation of England: I can draw for your Majesty's eyes a striking, faithful and instructive picture, detailed or succinct, of men and things.

I can give the soundest notions on the king, his family, his favorite Lord Butte[5], his ministers of the first and second order. I know who is in the king's party in the high as well as in the lower house. I know the present status of what they call the opposition in England. What party holds the majority in Parliament. The position, name, rank, character, credit and intrigue of all those who influence the commonweal in both parties. The effect of the troubles of the mother country upon her colonies, and of the latter upon England; what must ensue for both; the extreme importance these events have for the interests of France; what we can hope or fear for our sugar islands; what is likely to keep us in peace, or to make war necessary; finally, I can tell you things so certain and so clear that Your Majesty, with no other work but a not very

---

[4] Jean de Vignoles was a friend of Chevalier d'Eon, like him a former secret agent of Louis XV, and living in exile in London.

[5] John Stuart, Lord Butte, succeeded William Pitt as Prime Minister in 1762.

amusing reading, will be familiar with today's England, her currency, her naval forces, the skill of those who govern; so that at each political happenstance, Your Majesty can refer to my work and understand the reasons for everything and the interests that brought it about, until new combinations will force me to procure new lights.

Your Majesty may decide at will to have either a quick glance or a much more extensive view on all the matters I have just mentioned.

The only reward I would dare wish for, in giving such new proofs of my zeal for the service of my Master, would be that Your Majesty will deign not to abandon me to the resentment, the hatred of the ministers or courtiers, who certainly will strive to ruin me, should they hear that something from me has reached your Majesty without going through their channel. I know how they have already tried to discredit my past endeavors, which no other man would have undertaken, for half the amount of his fortune, and the merit of which I have tried to understate with Your Majesty rather than to take advantage of it.

But nothing will extinguish my desire to serve if M. de Sartine is instructed by you, Sire, to give me your royal word that my secret works will be for you alone, and that after they have been accepted, they will not lead to my ruin. Then I will work happily hoping that my maturity will not be completely useless to the youth of my august Master.

I would finish here this first abstract, if an unforeseen matter were not asking to be included: that of Chevalier d°Eon.

While I was working night and day in London, this unfortunate man, learning I was there, hastened to my house. I was not seeking either his friendship or his trust. He came to beg me to accept the one, forcing me to be the repository of the other.

After I had assured him I had no mission concerning him, he was very unhappy that I should not have been charged with negotiating his return to France. "I would have been back in my country a long time ago, he said, and the king would have received all the important papers relative to the secret of Louis XV, which must not remain in England."

He showed me his correspondence with M. de Broglie[6] and M. de Vergennes, and his trust finally passing all bounds, he begged me to place it at the feet of Prince de Conti[7], and to engage that prince to speak to your Majesty in his favor.

In vain did I explain to him that Prince de Conti, an upright and enlightened man, lived in a philosophical estrangement from the administration, through no fault of your Majesty, and had no desire to leave his inaction; I could not communicate this to Mr. d'Eon, who lives in the midst of a nation where this prince enjoys the highest reputation of patriotism and equity, and where he is held in such high regard that, although from an enemy nation, they have entire confidence in his word and look upon him as the pride of France. So d'Eon refused to let me go without a packet for that Prince, whose protégé he once was, as well as a letter for Count de Broglie, which only begs the latter to have no secret about him with Prince de Conti, etc.

(I do not want to deliver it without the permission of the King.)
(D'Eon easy to bring back to France.)
(D°Eon is a woman.)
(His political pretensions.)
(My reflections on this matter.)

Although one must not attach too much faith to everything that appears in the English papers, there is in that nation such a great curiosity for everything French, that the least piece of news from Paris creates a sensation. The last promotion of the Marshals of France seemed to me to have caused a furor that could be heard from the public papers. I had one of them translated for M. de Sartine.

(It is possible to turn these to the advantage of France.)

(I will expound on this in another abstract: this one is already too long. I mean to inform and not to bore Your Majesty.)

---

[6] Count de Broglie (1718-1804), one of the main secret agents of Louis XV, and a high-ranking army officer during the Seven-Year War. During the French Revolution he was the head of the *Emigres* army.

[7] Louis Francois de Bourbon (1717-1776), Prince de Conti.

I arrived in Paris on the 23rd of April, after a crossing of 24 hours, from Dover to Boulogne.

21 June 1775, From Vergennes
(Lom 1:419[8]; Mor 2:128; MS BN 248)

I am looking at the report that you submitted to M. de Sartine regarding our conversation on M. d'Eon. It is most accurate. I have consequently taken the king's orders. His Majesty authorizes you to agree to all reasonable cautions that Mr. d'Eon may demand for the regular payment of his pension of 12,000 livres, it being understood that an annuity of that amount will not be established outside of France. The main funds which should be used for this creation do not depend on me and I would have the greatest difficulty in procuring them; but it is easy to convert the said pension into a life annuity whose title would be delivered.

The article of the debts payment will entail more difficulty. D'Eon's pretensions in this respect are very high; he will have to come down, and quite a bit, for us to arrive at an agreement. As you must not, Sir, appear to have any mission with him, you will have the advantage to see him coming and in consequence, to have the upper hand. M. d'Eon has a violent temper, but I believe him to be honest and I will do him that justice to believe him incapable of treason.

It is impossible for Mr. d'Eon to take leave of the king of England; the revelation of his sex will not allow it.[9] That would cover both courts with ridicule. The attestation to give in lieu thereof is a delicate one. It can, however, be granted, provided he is satisfied with the praise deserved by his zeal, his intelligence and loyalty. But we cannot praise either his moderation or his submission and in no way should we mention the scenes he had with Mr. de Guerchy.[10]

---

[8] The text given by Lomenie, who says he left out "some insignificant passages," has been reproduced without any addition or correction by Morton.

[9] Vergennes pretends that d'Eon is a woman since that is a part of the deal offered the Chevalier.

[10] Count de Guerchy, ambassador in London since 1763, having arrived at his post several months later than d'Eon, his associate, found the latter had been lavishly entertaining at the Hotel de France and had charged his accounts with enormous debts. Antagonized by d'Eon in many ways, he tried to get rid of him by

You are enlightened and prudent, you know men, and I have no fear but that you will strike a good deal with d'Eon, if possible. If you do not succeed, it will be obvious that it cannot be done, and we will resign ourselves to the consequences. The first could be unpleasant for us, but the following ones would be awful for d'Eon. It's a very humiliating part to play, that of the exile with a varnish of treason; contempt is what he gets.

I am very appreciative of the praise you were kind enough, Sir, to give me in your letter to Mr. de Sartine. I aim to deserve it, and I receive it as a token of your esteem which will flatter me at all times. Be assured of mine and of all the sentiments, etc.

23 June 1775, Vergennes to Count de Guines
(Gai 215)

You will kindly take every opportunity to assure his Britannic Majesty of the king's feelings towards him, and his desire that the most perfect intelligence should endure between the two crowns, based on the existing peace and friendship. The principles of moderation and justice, which have so constantly informed the king's counsels and directed all his resolutions, must reassure his Britannic Majesty against all the misgivings that some restless minds, enemies of public tranquility, would like to impart to him about our views. Far from seeking to take advantage of the difficulties which England faces with respect to her American colonies, we would rather help her to solve them. The spirit of revolt, wherever it breaks out, always gives a dangerous example. It is the same with mental as with physical illness: both may become contagious. We would not want to appear so wary, however, as to cause alarm in England.

I beg you, Sir, to watch carefully the progress of the revolutions which can be expected and especially the influence which Lord Chatham will be able to gain over the king of England, should he give in to the appeal which this prince is said to have made to him. M. d'Eon might perhaps be able to procure interesting information in this respect. If you feel you can indirectly get in

---

the most violent means. Guerchy was indicted by the Grand Jury in February 1764 for assassination attemps against d'Eon. The king of England granted the ambassador a noli prosequi decree, after which he was recalled. He died in 1767. Pinsseau, 122-132.

touch with him, I know that he is not averse to being useful to you. His heart is still French, although his misfortunes and his bad temper have sometimes seemed to alienate him. He has friends among the opposition party, which is not the worse channel to obtain information.

London, 14 July 1775, to Vergennes
(Gai 230-32; Mor 2:129)

Monsieur le Comte,[11]

I have always felt that the governments' secrets were easier to penetrate than those of private individuals. Whatever a nation has interest in doing, you may be sure it will do it if it can or if its cabinet is not imbecile or sold out; for nations have among themselves no other morals than politics and no other law than natural law. That is not the case with private individuals, whose interests, hidden, hurt and restricted in a thousand ways, must be guessed rather than seen. Hence, an open commission is a lot easier to fulfill by an ambassador than a covert and mysterious affair by a secret agent; and there you have my compliment ready--made; that's already something. It would be more touching in an impartial mouth, but for the lack of a third party to handle it, I have added the job of praising me to that of doing my chores well. That's only half a fault.

Be that as it may, Sir, I think I have cut off at least one head of the English hydra. I have at your orders Captain d'Eon, a brave officer, great politician, and filled <u>by the hea</u>d of the most manly features. I am taking to the king the keys to an iron coffer, well locked with my seal, well deposited, and containing all the papers that the king needs to recover. That's how I went about it with the late king about another exile whose pen was feared. At least, while I am going to try to finish with you the job started with d'Eon, the king and you will be certain that everything remains in statu quo in England and that they cannot misuse anything against us, between now and the end of the negotiation, which I believe nearly finished.

I would leave immediately and give you all the detail of my offices and my work if I were charged with

---

[11]This address, constantly used by Beaumarchais with Vergennes whom others called "Your Excellency," will not be repeated hereinafter.

only one matter, but I am charged with four at once, and I find myself obliged to leave for Flanders with Milord Ferrers and in his ship. It would not be fair that the king and M. de Sartine should be less happy with me than the king and M. de Vergennes.

In politics, it is not sufficient to work, one must succeed, or else one gets as a salary, instead of a reward, a bitter smile and one is a poor fellow. I am therefore going to try and succeed, and I will not rest until I have informed you of the true current situation in England, which becomes more important to know every day, and as soon as I no longer have to worry about M. de Sartine's business as I do with our amazon, I will go to Versailles to receive the civic crown and permission to rest, for which I am beginning to feel a great need.

I am taking advantage of the first safe opportunity to have a letter dropped in the mail in Calais, to let you know, without it being discovered in London, that I have put in the hands of the king some papers and a creature which were about to be used against him.

I say "without it being discovered in London" because it a great puzzle game here to try and guess what I am here for. But what can they get from a man who neither talks nor writes?

P.S. Would you please hand the enclosed to M. de Sartine himself. Thank you.

26 August 1775, from Vergennes
(Lom 1:421; Mor 2:134)

Whatever desire I may have to see, meet and hear Mr. d'Eon, I will not hide from you a certain worry I have. His enemies are watching and will not easily forgive him what he said about them. If he comes here, however well-behaved and careful he may be, they will put words in his mouth, in contradiction to the silence imposed on him by the king. Denials and justifications are always embarrassing and hateful for honest souls. If Mr. d'Eon wanted to wear women's clothes, the matter would be over. That's something for him to decide, but for the sake of his own peace of mind, he should avoid, at least for a few years, to stay in France and especially in Paris. You will do with that observation whatever you see fit.

Before September 1775, to the king
(Mor 2:137-9)

Sire:

The most secret news from England hold that plans are being made to conquer the Spanish and French islands in the Gulf of Mexico.

Before informing your Majesty, I have discussed it at length with Count Lauraguais, one the best-informed men on inside English politics. He is of the opinion that not only is this news probable but the project in question has become indispensable to England in her present situation.

Thus the only thing that is not fixed is the time such a move will be made, but it cannot be doubted that it will be very soon, for the following reasons which I beg Your Majesty to weigh carefully.

England is a maritime power whose splendor is founded solely on her colonial trade.

The immense population of the English colonies of America, their manufactures of all kinds, and especially the interior communication that the northern provinces have opened with those of the south, through the Ohio and the Mississippi, have given rise to a great smuggling trade between the continent and the islands of the gulf, which the united efforts of the English, French and Spanish governments can no longer prevent.

The lively commerce of the produce of these various countries has disgusted them for the unprofitable commerce they have with Europe; hence the colonies' efforts to shake off the mother country's yoke; which threatens to destroy all of England's trade and throw them into bankruptcy.

England first tried to subjugate her colonies; but in a country where national interest is everyone's affair, people soon realized that the mother country cannot subdue her American colonies without completely devastating them; neither can she make peace with them without giving them independence; two points which make both peace and war between England and her colonies equally destructive of English trade.

The only resource remaining to England is to grab as soon as possible the Spanish and French islands; which in the flourishing state of her navy and the languid state of ours, is a thousand times easier than to conquer her own subjects on the continent, a conquest whose ultimate effect would be to exhaust England and annihilate her power. Since the 1762 cession to England of Florida and a few islands (which has given them everywhere the advantage of the wind, so important on those seas where it blows consistently), nothing prevents them from grabbing all the straits from the 11th to the 28th parallels and blocking the Gulf of Mexico so that no ship may get out without their consent.

Once our islands have been conquered and the smuggling between those islands and the continent is carried on for the benefit of the English, they will find themselves, without firing a shot, in control of the whole continent. They will remain the unique channel through which cereal, sugar, cotton, indigo, coffee, tobacco, in one word all the product of America will arrive in Europe. They will forever be in exclusive control of the richest trade in the world.

Therefore, instead of continuing the damaging war with their American colonies, or granting them the independence they claim, the greatest interest of England is to take over the Gulf islands.

Therefore they will not fail to take them, as they know no other law than self-convenience.

Therefore this information is of the utmost importance.

Unfortunately the united efforts of the French and Spanish navies do not suffice against the formidable English navy. Attempting it would expose us to lose both our islands and our ships. We are too weak on the ocean to be able to use force.

Negotiating with England is a paltry resource against such a powerful interest as the recovery of her trade. You may be sure that the nation will always force the king's hand in this matter.

To prevent a setback that would cost us three hundred millions and would render us forever unable to make war to England, we have at our disposal the sublime and secret plan Count Lauraguais whispered in the ears of Messrs. de Sartine and de Vergennes.

It is certain that if this sublime project can be implemented, it will be through this man alone, who can not only dare to conceive it but also make it succeed through genial means.

A perfect knowledge of England, her forces, her resources, her banking system, the most intimate relations with everything that carries power and influence on the government. Possessing the English language and laws better than the local scholars. Full of genius, courage and vigor, and especially having bought experience and wisdom at the price of errors and long misfortune, the only true preceptors of men.[12]

I thought, Sire, that it was my duty to get this important advice to your Majesty, and I would consider it as a crime indeed if, after the misfortune had happened, I could reproach myself that while I could have prevented it, I had been too timid to dare inform your Majesty about it.

21 September 1775, To the king
Submitted to the king, sealed, by M. de Sartine
(MS BN 317; Lom 2:92-6; Mor 2:139)

Sire,

As I trust that the abstracts I address to Your Majesty are uniquely for you will not get out of your hands, I will continue to present to you the truth on all points known to me which appear to concern your service, without taking into consideration anyone else's interests.

I slipped out of England, saying I was going to the country, and I ran from London to Paris, to confer with MM. de Vergennes and de Sartine on matters too important and too delicate to be entrusted to any messenger.

Sire, England is in such a crisis, such disorder in and out, that she would be near ruin if her neighbors and rivals were capable of taking advantage of it. Here is the faithful account of the situation of the English in America; I hold these facts from a man from Philadelphia. He has recently arrived from the colonies and had been conferring with the English ministers, who were shaken and frightened by what he had to say.

---

[12]Lauraguais had been banished by the government in 1766 and 1770. Upon his return Louis XV asked him: "Lauraguais, what did you do in England?" "I learned to think, Sire." "Oui, panser les chevaux," replied the king (groom horses), playing on the word "penser."

The Americans, resolved to suffer anything rather than bend, and full of that enthusiasm for liberty which made that little nation of Corsica[13] so fearsome to the Genoese, have 38,000 men, capable and determined, under the walls of Boston; they have reduced the English army to the necessity of starving in that city or seeking winter quarters elsewhere, which they are about to do. Approximately 40,000 men well armed and as determined as the first are defending the rest of the country, and those 80,000 men have not taken one farmer away from the land, not one worker from the manufactures. All those who were employed in the fishing industry, which the English have ruined, have become soldiers and believe they have to avenge the ruin of their families and the freedom of their country: all those who had a maritime trade, which the English have stopped, have joined the fishermen to make war on their common persecutors. All those who worked in the ports have increased that army of furious men whose actions are motivated by vengeance and outrage.

I say, Sire, that such a nation must be invincible; especially since they have so much back country available for possible retreats in the event the English obtained control of all their coasts, which is far from happening. All sensible people are therefore convinced in England that the English colonies are lost for the mother country, and such is also my opinion.

The open warfare taking place in America is less deadly for England than the intestine war which will soon break out in London. The bitterness between the parties has reached excessive heights since the king of England's proclamation declaring the Americans in a state of rebellion. This ineptitude, this masterpiece of folly on the part of the government, has strengthened the opposition by uniting them against it: they have resolved to take a diametrically opposed position to that of the Court's party in the first sessions of the Parliament. It is believed that before the end of these sessions, seven or eight members of Parliament will be sent to the Tower of London, and that is the moment they are waiting for to sound the tocsin. Lord Rochford, my friend of fifteen years, talking with me, told me with a sigh: "I am afraid, Sir, that winter will not pass without a few heads rolling, either in the king's party

---

[13]Jean-Jacques Rousseau had written a constitution for Corsica, before it was acquired by France from the Republic of Genoa (in 1768).

or in the opposition." On the other hand, the Lord mayor Wilkes, in a moment of joy and freedom, at the end of a splendid dinner, told me publicly: "For a long time the king of England has done me the honor of hating me. I did him the justice of despising him. Time has come to decide which one of us has judged the other the best, and on which side the wind will blow heads down." Lord North,[14] threatened by all this, would gladly give his resignation today if he could do so in honor and security.

[. . . .][15] The least setback the royal army will receive in America, increasing the daring of the people and of the opposition, can decide the affair in London at the most unexpected time, and if the king appears obliged to bend, I shudder to say it, I don't believe his crown more firmly established on his head than his ministers heads on their shoulders. Those unfortunate English people, with their frantic freedom, can inspire a genuine compassion in a thinking man.[16] Never have they experienced how sweet it is to live under a good and virtuous king. They despise us and call us slaves, because we willingly obey; but if the reign of a weak or wicked king sometimes has momentarily harmed France, the licentious rage that the English call freedom has never left a moment of real peace and happiness to that unmanageable people. King and subjects are all unhappy. Today, to further increase the trouble, a secret subscription has been opened in London, at the houses of two of the wealthiest merchants of that capital, where all the malcontent are donating gold to send to the Americans or pay for the supplies the Dutch are furnishing them. That's not all, they have secret ties in Portugal, in the very council of the king, for which they pay dearly, to try and prevent the Portuguese from settling their differences with the Spaniards.[17] They hope that this war will soon draw the English and the French into the quarrel of their allies, and that this new incident will even more surely destroy the present

---

[14]Lord North (1739-92), prime minister 1770-82.

[15]The omission cannot be corrected as the manuscript remains hidden in the family archives.

[16]This, obviously intended for Louis XVI, has been cited by literary critics, (Lom 2:95 and Vier 1957, 6:44) to support the contention that the playwright was not a Republican.

[17]Portugal had been Great Britain's ally since 1654, while Spain was, since the Family Compact (1761), the ally of France.

ministry--which is the constant object of all the opposition.

SUMMARY: In spite of their efforts, America is lost to the English; the war rages in London fiercer than in Boston. The end of this crisis will bring war against France if the opposition wins, whether Chatham or Rockingham replaces Lord North. The opposition, to increase the troubles, are scheming in Portugal to prevent its accommodation with Spain.

Our ministers, poorly informed, look stagnant and passive on all those events which touch our skin.

A superior and vigilant man would be indispensable in London today.

The first thing we can't avoid doing is to invite the Spanish ministry to be less difficult with their demands from Portugal. While the English ministry strive to push Portugal towards reconciliation and call to the attention of the Portuguese the fact that the domestic troubles of England would absolutely prevent her coming to their aid according to the terms of their last treaty, our intervention with the Spanish ministry is indispensable to destroy as much as possible the effect of the English opposition's intrigue and bribery, as they are making ultimate efforts in Portugal to set the two southern powers at odds [. . . .]

[. . . .] Such are the reasons of my secret errand to France. Whatever use your Majesty may make of this work, I rely on the kindness and the virtue of my Master, and hope he will not let turn against me these proofs of my zeal, by confiding in any one. That would augment the number of my enemies, who will never succeed in stopping me so long as I can count on the secret and protection of Your Majesty.

22 September 1775, to Vergennes
(Ang. 511, no. 174; Don 1:134; Mor 2:143)
For you alone.

M. de Sartine handed the manuscript to me but said nothing on the affairs. He even advised me to travel to Versailles and urge you this morning to ask for the king's orders relative to me.

But concerning my appearing to keep secret from you my work of last night for the king, I deemed it better to send you an ostensible letter [immediately following] which you may take or have delivered to His Majesty and if you are not charged by him to make a ministerial answer at least I will receive one from your kindness which will console me for my lost labors.

Please include a blank passport and if you believe I should wait in London for the king's orders, as a result of your not having had the time to decide, kindly let me know it too. Thus, everything being well understood, it will be up to you to write me in a manner obscure enough so I alone may guess the subject of your letter, if you send it to me through the ambassador.[18]

Paris, 22 September 1775, to Vergennes
(Ang. 511, no. 175; Don 1:159-60; Mor 2:143)

When zeal is indiscreet, it must be repressed. When it is agreeable, it must be encouraged. But all the sagacity in the world cannot help someone who remains without an answer about what he must do.

I had Mr. Sartine deliver to the king yesterday a small work which is only a summary of the long conference you had accorded to me the day before. It is an accurate statement of men and things in England. It ends with the offer I had made you to muzzle for the length of time necessary for us to get ready for war, all those who either by speaking out or remaining silent can hasten or delay its arrival.[19]

This must have been discussed in the Council last night, and this morning I am not apprised of it. The deadliest things for business are uncertainty and waste of time.

Must I wait for your reply here, or must I leave without any? Was I right or wrong in approaching the minds whose decisions are becoming so important for us? Will I in the future abort confidences and will I avoid, instead of encouraging them, any overtures which must influence the present revolution? Finally, am I a useful agent for my country or only a deaf and dumb traveler?

---

[18]This advice should be taken in consideration in interpreting Vergennes' and Beaumarchais' letters.

[19]This probably refers to action to be taken in regard to the Iberic peninsula. The incomplete 21 September memorial does not permit a verification.

I am not asking for a new assignment, I have too much serious personal business to finish in France. But I would have felt remiss in my duty to you and the king, as a good Frenchman, if I had passed under silence the good I am able to do or the evil I can prevent.

I will wait for your answer to this letter before I leave. If you do not reply about the affairs, I will look at my trip as null and void, and without regretting my efforts, I am going back immediately, I finish in four days what remains for me to do about d'Eon and I come back without seeing anyone in London. They will all be very surprised. But someoneelse do better, if he can. I wish for it with all my heart.

23 September 1775, from Vergennes to the king
(French NA K 164:3, year 1775:28; Don 1:136)

The work I had taken the liberty of requesting from Your Majesty had for object not only expediting a few current affairs of the department, but also reporting some overtures the "Sieur de Beaumarchais" made to me relative to England and to take Your Majesty's orders to answer him. I see, Sire, by his letter, which I have the honor to include herewith that he reported himself to your Majesty the notions he gathered in London, and the advantage we can draw therefrom. It involves a sacrifice of money, the extent of which I cannot estimate, Mr. de Beaumarchais not having let me in on this, but the payment would be due only whenever Your Majesty would feel it would pose the least risk for the duration of the peace. This matter being likely to be of importance, I beg Your Majesty either to give me your orders, or to permit me to go and get them directly from you. I have asked Mr. de B. who was about to leave last night for England, to defer till today, noon.

Paris, 23 September 1775, to Vergennes
(Ang. 511, fol. 177; Don 1:137; Mor 2:144)

I am leaving, well briefed by the king and you. Let your Excellency rest assured. It would be asinine on my part to compromise in any way the dignity of the master and his minister. Doing one's best is nothing in politics: Anybody can do as much. To do the best possible in the matter at hand is what must distinguish from the common servants the one whom His Majesty and you honor with your confidence on such a delicate point. Sureties will no doubt be needed but it is up to me to give them so that, in no instance, will they be reversible on you or the king. As to the sums of money; they must be combined according, on the one hand, to the degree of importance of my requests, and on the other, to the appetite of my players. The hungriest will cost the least, that's the rule. It is impossible for me to set a tariff ahead of time. But kindly assure the king that my life is no dearer to me than the interests entrusted to my care.

I am leaving without the passport which you forgot. But I will in Boulogne commit the misdeed of scratching and writing over the one before last, which I happen to have with me--trusting you will kindly not say a word of it to Count LaBlache, who would draw therefrom a powerful argument in the suit he must lose against me--for Count LaBlache is a terrible reasoner.

[October 1775] To the King Only
(Dea 1:100-115; MS Genet Papers, Conn. Hist. Soc.)[20]

Sire,

While reason of State engages you to lend a helping hand to the Americans, politics requires that Your Majesty take such precautions so that an aid secretly conveyed to America will not become in Europe a fire-brand between England and France.

Moreover, prudence requires you to make sure that your funds cannot be diverted into other hands than those you intend them for. Finally, as the present state of your finances does not allow you to make so great a sacrifice as events seem to require, it is my duty to submit to you, Sire, and a matter of wisdom for you to examine the following plan, whose primary purpose is to avert, by an absolutely commercial configuration, the suspicion that Your Majesty or his council may have anything to do with this affair.

The second advantage of that plan is that your Majesty's council will be able to follow your funds easily through the various changes and metamorphoses that commerce will make them undergo, from the generous hand which bestows them up to the grateful hand which will receive them; without fear that they may be diverted or lost on the way. But the principal merit of that plan is to augment the appearance and size, the substance of your aid to such extent that, by multiplying these funds by their product, a single million raised to its second circulation, will produce

---

[20]This paper has been dated either 1775 or February 1776. See Introduction: Hortalez & Co.

the same result in favor of the Americans as if Your Majesty had actually paid out nine millions for their benefit. This requires further explanation.

Finally, this plan, in execution, unites with so many other advantages the power of retarding or accelerating the course of these supplies as your prudence may dictate, and according as the situation of the Americans becomes more or less pressing, with the result that this assistance wisely administered, will serve not so much to terminate the war between America and England, as to sustain and keep it alive to the detriment of the English, our natural and relentless enemies. And should Your Majesty in pursuance of this important object, be obliged to increase the amount of the assistance, it is certain that every million spent by you to enable the Americans to defend their soil, will cost the English 100 millions, if they persevere in going 2,000 leagues from home to attack them. In other words, to sacrifice a million in order to occasion a loss of 100 millions to England, is precisely the same thing as advancing a million to gain ninety-nine millions; and, in all the calculations of the longest reign, Sire, you will never find another opportunity to make a less expensive, more practical or greater gain.

Let us consider the details of the enterprise.

The constant impression of the affair for the mass of Congress is the certitude in which they must be held that Your Majesty does not want to have anything to do with it, but that a company is generously going to entrust certain monies to the prudence of a faithful agent to furnish eventual assistance to the Americans by the safest and speediest ways, in exchange for returns in tobacco.

Secrecy is the essence of all the rest.

But the two vital points of the operation are, first, the ease with which Your Majesty may obtain as much powder as you wish, at a moderate price, and, second, the impossibility for the Farmers-General now to procure tobacco at any price whatever.

These two points granted, I intend to proceed as follows:

Your Majesty will begin by placing one million at the disposal of your agent, who will style himself Roderigue Hortalez and Company, this being the tradename and signature under which I have agreed to conduct the entire business. One half of this sum, changed into moidores or Portuguese pieces, the only foreign money that passes in America, will be immediately forwarded thither; for it is necessary that the Americans should have a little gold at once, in order to put in circulation their own paper money which, lacking this impetus, is likely to become valueless and stagnant. It is the leaven that must be added to the heavy dough to make it rise and properly ferment. From this half million, no other benefit can be derived than its return in the form of Virginia tobacco which the Congress must supply to the firm of Hortalez, the Ferme-Générale having previously agreed with the latter to purchase the tobacco at a good price. Yet, this is of small consequence.

Roderigue Hortalez intends to use the remaining half million in procuring powder, and in conveying it without delay to the Americans. Instead, however, of buying this powder in Holland, or even in France, at the current prices of 20 or 30 sols tournois a pound, the price at which the Dutch sell it, or even higher, when supplying the Americans; the real artifice of the operation consists in secretly procuring all necessary powder and saltpetre from Your Majesty's Registrars (as Roderigue Hortalez hopes to do if it pleases Your Majesty), on a basis of four to six sols a pound.

If the firm of Hortalez contracts with the Americans to forward to them powder on the basis of 20 sols a pound, and pays the equivalent to the merchants, it cannot send to Philadelphia for the remaining 500,000 livres more than 500 thousandths of powder, and this second operation will be as barren as the first regarding the gold coins, nor will it yield other profit than a payment in tobacco, confining the speculation to the same return as in the first instance. As has been stated, this is of small consequence in itself.

But if Hortalez secretly obtains powder from Your Majesty's Registrars at 5 sols a pound, with the 500,000 livres remaining he can obtain 2,000 thousandths, or 20 thousand quintals, of powder, which forwarded to America, at 20 sols a pound, will leave Congress in debt to Hortalez to the amount of 2 million tournois. The profits, returning in the shape of tobacco, sold in advance to the Ferme-Generale, will enable the firm of Hortalez to settle with the real owner, namely, Your Majesty, for the sum of two millions five hundred thousand livres; and in addition there remains to be calculated the profit on sales of tobacco, that may rise in round numbers to 500,000 livres.

The return of these various sums will place at the disposition of Hortalez an actual capital of 3 millions, with which to renew the operation, first to rehabilitate the American paper money with 1,500,000 livres in gold, and then to supply the American mortars and cannon with 60,000 quintals of powder. But this 60,000 quintals, although costing Roderigue hortalez but 15 thousand livres, will nevertheless make the Americans his debtors to the amount of 9 millions in return for both the powder and the portuguese gold received by them.

This is enough to show Your Majesty how the product of this affair, managed according to the customary principles of commerce, must increase in circulation, not in the double progression of 1, 2, 4, 8 etc. but in the triple progression 1, 3, 9, 27 etc. for if the first million gives three; these three plowed back in the business, must give nine more and these nine 27, etc. as I think I have clearly proved.

Your Majesty will not become frightened if this operation looks complicated under my pen, when you learn that no commercial speculation is run or succeeds in any simpler or more natural way.

I have treated the affair under your eyes, Sire, as a big merchant who wishes to speculate to advantage and I have explained the only secret by which a big commercial operation, drawing all its profits from abroad, by an advantageous exchange of merchandise, increases the prosperity of all the nations which have enough common sense to protect it. Quite superior to the art of the financiers who, invariably drawing their profit from domestic speculations directed against the subjects of the State, can increase revenues only at the expense of the subjects' standard of living. Thus, instead of the healthy well-being brought about by commerce, the destructive art of finance only produces a monstrous swelling like a tumor on the head, the result of penury, discomfort and the general clogging of all other parts of a sickly body.

But to return to my subject, my goal being less to embark Your Majesty on a lucrative speculation than to secure for the first input of your aid the appearance and effect of a much larger amount; the outcome of my first operation, above described, will be that the Americans will receive from Your Majesty, through Hortalez, an actual assistance in the amount of 2 millions 500 thousand livres; that is, 500 thousand livres in gold and 2 millions in powder, while your Majesty will have laid out only one million livres. And if the assets in tobacco and the sale of this return proceed as I have indicated, Your Majesty can soon recommence, by the hand of Hortalez, the redistribution of the three millions arising from the sale and profit of these returns, and begin the operation anew on a larger scale. But then, according to the geometrical progression indicated above, the Americans will have received in two installments from Your majesty a sum of 9 millions (that is to say, 2 millions in gold and 7 millions in powder) although Your Majesty, having merely invested a second time the profits of the former operation, will have actually paid out in all but a single million.

This clearly understood, it is the same to the firm of Hortalez whether it employs for the trade a French or a Dutch ship. In either case there are advantages and disadvantages that I will briefly describe.

The choice of a Dutch ship conceals more effectually the source of the supplies, but it also renders the munitions and returns liable to be intercepted by English cruisers during the long course of transportation, and thus we may be instantly deprived of all the profits of the operation.

The choice of a French ship insures safe transportation of the munitions to the French Cape, selected by Hortalez as the first depot for his trade with America.

This way, however, gives ground for a suspicion that the French government may very well favor the enterprise. But considering that proof of the fact cannot be produced, we can disregard it; for whether France does or does not assist the Americans, the English, for some time past, have been certain that we do lavish our aid to the brave rebels in America.

Supposing then, that a French ship be employed and freighted on account of Roderigue Hortalez and Company, Congress, or rather Mr. Adams, the General Secretary of Congress, will alone be informed by the American agent in England [Arthur Lee] that a ship will carry to the French Cape gold and munitions to be paid for in Virginia tobacco, so that he may send to the Cape his representative on a ship loaded with tobacco, with authority to receive the gold and munitions, to give his receipt and to transfer to the captain and supercargo of Hortalez his entire returns in tobacco, or at least, a note to Roderigue Hortalez for the proportion of the debt still outstanding.

Whereupon, the French captain will deliver to him all his cargo, and carry to Europe the cargo of the American, in such a way that if the American ship is captured during the short run between San Domingo and the mainland, no trace can be discovered of anything beyond a simple commercial transaction between Hortalez and an American merchant. The cargo of tobacco landed in France safely by the French ship may meet part of the loss, and the operation will be resumed in hope of a better result and without compromising any one.

Before closing, I want to hazard an idea suggested by him[21], namely that it would be rather pleasant to help the Americans with English money, which is very easy.

It would suffice for Your Majesty, adopting an English usage that exacts a tax of 75% ad valorem on all French vehicles entering England at Dover, to decree that in the future all vehicles and horses landing in your ocean ports shall pay a tax equal to that levied on ours when entering England.

Considering the enormous amount of carriages, horses, etc. which curiosity, folly or commerce draws hither from that country, I promise Your Majesty that were I allowed to manage this little matter on his behalf, he would no longer need to contrive how to furnish secret funds to the firm of Hortalez, but would soon have enough to enable the concern, which is really his own, to flourish in great style. And this stroke of finance is quite superior to all other speculations of this murderous science since the cost is borne by the English and not by Your Majesty's subjects; and it accords with the principle adopted by the merchant, economist and politician, Hortalez de Beaumarchais, that foreign merchandise and products ought not to be admitted into any country, unless they create a revenue equivalent to their consumption.

By putting in practice this idea, Your Majesty would have the pleasure of using for the relief of the Americans the very money squeezed out of the English, and this seems to me quite piquant, and would plant a few flowers amid the dry waste of explanations of the output, return and profits of the commercial capital of

---

[21]The translation given in the Deane Papers skipps this reference to Arthur Lee or Sam Adams: "an idea suggested during its composition" replaces what we have.

the firm of Hortalez, of which Your Majesty is about to become the sole proprietor.

After what has been said, it is not necessary for me to prove that Your Majesty will be able to restrict or expand his assistance at pleasure. The Hortalez commerce, slowed down or accelerated according to exigencies, will have that effect without raising a suspicion of the true reason of these fluctuations.

Such is the plan I submit to your Majesty for this affair, after thorough consideration and a calculation of the chances. The decision depends on your commands, the execution on my prudence, and the success on luck. It seems to me to be the most beneficial of all.

In case Your Majesty does not adopt it, I will at least have the advantage of showing once more for his service, if not very extensive knowledge, at least a zeal as active and pure as it is inalterable.

Versailles, 24 November 1775, to Vergennes
(Ang. 513, fol. 3; Don 1:251; Mor 2:149)

Instead of waiting for the king's answer, which must carry a formal resolution, would you mind writing him again that I am here, that you have seen me, trembling that, in an affair as easy as necessary and perhaps the most important the king will ever in his entire reign have to decide, His Majesty might choose the negative?

That, whatever his reasons, I beg of him not to make up his mind before he has heard me speak for a quarter of an hour and demonstrate to him respectfully the necessity of undertaking, the ease in executing, the certainty of succeeding, and the immense harvest of glory and peace that must result for his reign from the smallest seed so timely sown.

May the guardian angel of this State favorably turn the King's heart and give us so desirable a success.

In case of an order from you, I am at the Jouy Hotel, Recolets Street.

7 December 1775, to the king
[Summum jus, summa injuria]
(MS BN 319; Lin 395-9; Mor 2:150-155)[22]

Sire:

When Your Majesty disapproves a project[23], it is a general rule for all concerned to give it up.

But there are projects of such a nature and of such major importance for the good of your kingdom, that a zealous servant may believe himself justified in going over them with you another time, for fear they were not seized at first under their best point of view.

The project which I am not designating here but which Your Majesty knows through M. de Vergennes, is one of those. I have only the strength of my reasons to get it approved. I beg you, Sire, to weigh them with all the attention such an important affair deserves.

When you have read this writing, my work will be done. It's up to us, Sire, to propose; up to you to judge. And your task is much more important than ours; for we have to answer only for the purity of our zeal; and you answer to God, Sire, to yourself and to all of the great people which is entrusted to you, for the good or evil resulting from the decision you make.

M. de Vergennes writes me that Your Majesty believes **your sense of justice is involved in not adopting the proposed means.**

The objection, therefore, rests neither on the immense usefulness of the project nor on the dangers involved in its execution but only on Your Majesty's moral scruples.

Such reason to refuse is so respectable that one ought to stop short and be condemned to silence, were it not for the extreme importance of the proposed matter which calls for examining whether the justice of the

---

[22]Submitted by the author to Vergennes, unsealed. Morton reproduces the text given by Lintilhac, with the same cuts. The autograph, No. 319 in the BN 1966 exposition, belongs to the Beaumarchais family collection and is not available to research.

[23]The project of R. Hortalez and Company explained in the paper given above under the date of October 1775.

king of France is really involved in not adopting the proposed means.

It is certain that in general any idea, any project which offends his sense of justice must be rejected by a gentleman.

But, Sire, it is not the same with State policy as with citizens' morals. A private citizen may not harm his neighbor, whatever good this may bring to him, because all of them live under a system of law common to all, which provides for everyone's security.

But a kingdom is a great isolated body; more separated from its neighbors by conflict of interests than by the sea, the citadels and the barriers which surround it. Nations do not have a law common to them to watch over their security. Their only relations are those of natural law, that is to say those that self--preservation, well-being and prosperity of each state impose upon it, relationships modified in several ways under the name of law of nations, the principle of which, according to Montesquieu himself, is to do your own good as the first law; with the least possible harm to other States, as the second.[24]

And this maxim has been so rigorously established as political principle that a king governing an indigent, famished people, as he must look at himself as a stranger to any other people and a father to his own, could not keep his unfortunate subjects, lacking other means of subsisting, to go and take, even by force, what they need in the neighboring States.

For the justice and the protection a King owes his subjects are in the nature of a strict and narrow duty; whereas those he may grant neighboring States are always a matter of convenience. Whence it follows that national policies, which maintain the States, differ almost in everything from the common morals which govern private individuals [. . . .]

But Sire, between France and England, has there ever been, can there ever be a single bond capable of stopping Your Majesty? When it is proven that the peace

---

[24]"The law of nations is naturally based on the principle that the various nations must in time of peace do one another as much good and in time of war as little harm as possible without harming their own true self-interest." Esprit des Lois, 1:3. Cf. Observations, paragraph 91.

of your kingdom, the well-being of your subjects, the splendor of your reign depend solely upon your being able to curb that natural enemy, that rival jealous of your success, those people always systematically unjust towards you and who have no other principle towards you but this damnable maxim: "If we wanted to be just towards the French and the Spaniards, we would have too many restitutions to make. Our duty is to keep on weakening them." A maxim repeated a thousand times and applauded in the mouth of that famous Pitt, now the idol of the English nation, after he was refused a cavalry company for not having enough nobility or ability to exercise this slight position! [. . . .]

Thus it is with that bold people, without restraint or scruples, that you will always be dealing. The proposed plan deals only with that nation. She is the one, Sire, it behooves you to humiliate and weaken, if you do not want her to humiliate and weaken you at every opportunity. Have her usurpations and outrages ever had any other bounds than those of her power? Has she not always made war on you without declaring it? Has the last one not started by the surprise capture, in a time of peace, of 500 ships of yours? Hasn't she humiliated you into destroying yourself the most beautiful of your ocean ports, and forced you to disarm in all the others, and has fixed the small number of ships that henceforth would suffice you?[25] Did she not recently submit your merchant ships to her visit in the northern area? An humiliation the Dutch did not want to undergo, and which was reserved only for us? A humiliation such that Louis XIV would have eaten his own arms rather than bear with it; a humiliation finally which grieves the heart of every good Frenchman, especially when he sees that insolent rival attracting into that same area Russians ships, to whom they are teaching the road to our American possessions so that one day they will help in taking them away from us [. . . .]

[. . . .] If your tenderness of conscience is such that you do not want to favor even that which can harm your enemies, how can you let your subjects vie with other Europeans in the conquest of countries belonging by right to poor Indians, African savages, or Caribbeans, who have never offended you? How can you allow your ships to take away by force and force to groan in chains black men that nature had made free and who are

---

[25]This statement which passed unnoticed will be repeated in the <u>Observation</u>s (paragraph 65, note 50), and furnish the pretext of the suppression.

miserable only because you are powerful? How can you bear to see three rival powers sharing iniquitously the spoils of Poland, you, Sire, whose mediation should carry so much weight in Europe? How can you have a pact with Spain, by which you promise in the name of the Holy Trinity, to furnish men, ships and money to help her fight a war, even an offensive one, at her first request, without even having reserved the right to examine if the war you are being led into is just or if you are not helping an usurper? Your Majesty, I know, did not do or allow all these things. They existed before your reign, they will exist again thereafter; this is the way things are in politics; examples abound so much that I only had to recall a few to prove to you, Sire, that the policies which maintain nations differ almost in everything from the morals which govern private individuals.

If men were angels, no doubt, one would have to despise, even hate politics. But if men were angels, they would have no need for religion to enlighten them, for kings to rule them, for magistrates to restrain them, for soldiers to subdue them, and earth, instead of being a living picture of hell, would itself be a heavenly place. Indeed, we must take them as they are and the most just of kings cannot go further with them than the legislator Solon, who used to say: I have not given Athenians the best laws possible; but only the most suitable to the place, time, and men for whom I work.

Thus, since the sovereign law of States is politics and since politics is indispensable to their maintenance, please never lose sight of the fact that the masterpiece of good politics is to base your tranquility on the divisions of your enemies. By reserving the precious morals which makes you so respectable, for the home administration of your kingdom, you will have fulfilled all the duties of a good and great king.

Richelieu, that man brought up from an obscure state to the highest degree of power,[26] that man to whose genius royal authority in France owes so much, Richelieu in order to follow in all safety the plans of greatness his master had formed, did not think the justice of Louis XIII was involved in not fostering in England the troubles which finally overthrew Charles I

---

[26]The author is repeatedly trying to call the king's attention to precedents where commoners brilliantly occupied high offices: first William Pitt in England, now Richelieu in France.

from his throne [....] To arm iniquity against itself is the surest way to destroy it without fail. We must never forget that England is to France what the English thieves are to the citizens of their country [....] I beg you, Sire, not to be deceived by the brilliant sophism of false scruples. **Summum jus, summa injuria.**

[....] I have dealt summarily with a most serious issue lest I weaken my argument by overstating it and especially for fear of tiring Your Majesty's attention.

And if there remain any doubts in your mind after reading me, Sire, erase my signature, have this essay copied by another hand so that the low condition of the reasoner will not hurt the strength of his reasons, offer this writing for discussion to someone who has a long experience of the world and its affairs; and if there is one only, starting with M. de Vergennes, who does not agree with my principles, I will fall silent and throw into the fire Scaliger, Grotius, Puffendorf, Gravina, Montesquieu, all the publicists, and I will admit that <u>my life study</u> has been a long waste of time; since it has only led me to impotence in persuading my Master in a matter that seems to me as obvious as it is important for his interests.

[....] It's absolutely impossible to treat in writing all that pertains to the substance of the affair because of the deep secret it requires; although it is infinitely easy for me to demonstrate the safety of undertaking, the ease in executing, the certainty of succeeding and <u>the immense harvest of glory and peace</u> which the puniest seed timely sown, Sire, must give to your reign.

May the guardian angel of this State turn favorably the heart and mind of Your Majesty. If you give us this first success, the rest will follow. I vouch for it.

8 December 1775, Vergennes to Viscount Stormont
(France, 542, fol. 36; S.F. 1308)

I received the letter Your Excellency has honored me with the 5th of this month to let me know the warning you were given that the captains of a few American ships which have recently appeared in several ports of Europe, have confessed that their intent was to procure arms and munitions, and in consequence asking me to solicit the king to circulate in his ports the orders necessary to prevent the outgoing of war munitions of any kind on British ships and even on ships from other nations, destined for America.

I have, Sir, transmitted your request to His Majesty in his council. He has ordered me to reply that he will never wish for anything more than to give the king of England the most convincing proofs of his sincere and constant friendship, as well as of his desire to maintain and perpetuate the happy harmony which subsists between the two nations, and that with this view in mind, he is going to have orders renewed not to let out of his ports, either on English ships or on any nation's ships, arms and munitions of war destined for North America.

[before 13 December 1775]
"Essential Points I beg Count de Vergennes to submit to the King's approval before I leave for London on December 13, 1775,
to be answered in the margin."
(BN 257; Gai 262-4; Mor 2:155)

Does the King grant Miss d'Eon permission to wear the cross of Saint-Louis on her woman's clothing?
King's answer: Only outside of Paris.
Does His Majesty approve the gratification of 2.000 ecus which I passed to this damsel for her female trousseau?
King's answer: Yes.
Does he leave her entire disposition of all her male clothing?
King's answer: She must sell them.[27]
As these favors must be subordinated to certain dispositions of mind which I wish to impose permanently on Miss d'Eon, Will His Majesty leave it up to me to grant or refuse, as the case may be, when it is useful for his service?
King's answer: Yes.

As the King cannot refuse to give me receipt in good form for all the papers which I brought to him from england, I have begged Count de Vergennes to ask His Majesty to be kind enough to add at the bottom of that instrument, in his own hand, a few words expressing satisfaction with the manner I accomplished my mission.

---

[27]The Queen made her dressmaker available to the Chevalier and offered him a fan made with 24,000 livres worth of banknotes. The Chevalier, disregarding the king's order, kept his military uniform. On August 17, 1777, he made an appearance at court in full dragoon captain dress wear (Pinsseau 208-9).

This reward, the dearest to my heart, may one day be of great use to me. . . .
King's answer: Good.

As the first person I will see in London is Milord Rochford, and as I do not doubt he will ask me secretly what the King of France replied to the King of England's prayer which I transmitted to you, what shall I answer on behalf of the King?
King's answer: That you received no answer.

If this lord, who is still in close relationship with the king of England, still insists on taking me secretly to the King, shall I accept or not? This question is not idle and deserve to be pondered before answering.
King's answer: That may be.
. . . .

I have the honor to warn the king that Count de Guines[28] has attempted to make me suspect with the English ministers; am I allowed to say a few words to him about it, or does His Majesty wish me to appear unaware of all the covert plots which have been devised to harm me, my operations and consequently the good service of His Majesty?
King's answer: He must not know about it.

Finally, before leaving, I am asking for a positive answer to my last memorial; if ever an issue was important, this is it. I will answer upon my head, after due consideration, for the most glorious success of this operation for the entire reign of my master, without ever compromising his person, his ministers, or any of your interests. Will any of those who turn Your Majesty against it, dare to answer on their heads for all the evil which must befall France after rejecting it?

In the event we should have the misfortune to see the king refuse to adopt a plan so simple and so wise,[29] I beg Your Majesty to allow me to note down the date on which I suggested such a superb resource, so that you will one day recognize my views were right, when all

---

[28]Adrien-Louis de Guines (1735-1806), former grenadier colonel and career diplomat, ambassador in London 1770-76. He had to leave London as a result of a suit brought against him by his secretary, and an affair with the famous Lady Craven.

[29]This refers to the October 1775 Hortalez plan.

that is left to us is to regret bitterly not to have followed them.

15 December 1775, to Sartine
(Lin 390; Mor 2:158)

    I beg you to put at the king's feet my just loathing for a sort of chores, more difficult to do well than the most important political missions. It isn't because of a lack of zeal that I no longer wish to be charged with those. I proved myself in this regard. But, after the last news from England, I am afraid to return there too late; and I have too well perceived that in that sort of affair the dangers will be extreme in case of failure, and I have too well experienced that in case of success the negotiator is rewarded with all kinds of unpleasantness. I don't know what must be done today, but I indicate at least in that memorial the most certain way to prevent from now on such problems . . . .

15 December 1775, to the king
(Lin 391)

. . . . Absolutely discouraged about that frustrating occupation, I beg Your Majesty's pardon if I beg you from now on to ask someone else to do this job which brought me neither thanks, nor honors, nor profit, where I have several times barely escaped with my life, and which appears of such little importance, once the danger is gone, that one barely deigns to listen to my reports, after I have met with all kinds of unpleasantness to spare them to everyone else.

    [. . . .] A matter which must be decided without further delay.

Charles Gravier, Count de Vergennes
by Charles Wilson Peale

1776: HARD WORK AND COMPROMISE

Paris, January 1, 1776, to Vergennes
(Ang. 514, no. 1; Don 1:252-3; Mor 2:162)

It is impossible to be as touched as I am by your kindness and not be also very much affected when you appear to grow cold. I have examined myself, I feel I do not deserve it. Hey, how can you tell I have pushed my zeal too far, if you don't first review with me in detail all I have done and had to do? At my age, it would be foolish to substitute eagerness to planning in political activity.

When you have employed me more, Monsieur le Comte, you will be convinced that the first thing to do to be reassured on my operations, always is to question me on what I have done and why. The practice of men and the use of adversity have given me a wary prudence which makes me check every possibility and handle things according to the character, timid or courageous, of those for whom I do them. But the same practice of men has also taught me that the only crime of honest people is prejudice, something the best minds are not always able to avoid. In the country where you live, Sir, they neglect no opportunity to create new preconceptions against whoever makes himself useful. Don't forget, M. le Comte, that the wind which appears to blow me away from the swirl of slander is enfolding you in it more and more and that in this country of intrigues a good servant with some wits is more useful to keep than twenty Court friends to satisfy.

Our great affair is going a little astray: while we argue over accessories, I assure you they do their best to take advantage of our indolence and deal a blow on the principle; the enemies of the administration and those of the State are equally striving to extinguish in our friends the hope that we can be useful to them. It grieves me to see it, and in a few weeks, it will be too late to remedy it.

Think of it, Monsieur le Comte, I will go tomorrow night warn M. de Maurepas about it, and if around 8:00 your door is not closed to me, I will hand you the statement of funds used and the d'Eon affair balance.

The renewing of the year adds nothing to my respectful sentiments.

January 7, 1776, d'Eon to Beaumarchais
(Gai 403)

[First answer from Chevalier d'Eon to Beaumarchais, in London. This sample of the Chevalier's style is included here to give an idea of the comedy which delighted everyone on both sides of the Channel. Thereafter we will no longer pursue this affair.]

Count Ferrers'mansion, Staunton-Harold, Leicestershire.

I have known the superiority of your mind and talents for too long, and you gave me in France with the King and Count Vergennes too many proofs of your excellent heart not to be entitled to my gratitude for the rest of my days; but you will permit me to tell you that the despotic tone that you affect in your judgments since the signing of our preliminary transaction and since your last return from Paris, is unbearable to me, and makes you as impracticable as Mr. Pitt, in 1761, at the time of the negotiation of the last peace.

I would try in vain today to make you change a judgment that you adopted, either as a consequence of your natural principles, or by intimate persuasion, or by mere complacency for the interested views of some of your friends. I will therefore abstain from it. But on your side, knowing the firmness and sensitivity of my character, it would be a waste of time and effort to want to change my mind in a matter which concerns the conscience I must have regarding my personal honor. I would not, for any consideration or any sum of money in the world, want to let the public believe that I am interested in the infamous wagers that have arisen on my sex.

That is, Sir, a genuine principle of honor I have established for myself, and from which I cannot depart, as I have already warned you and had your friend Gudin warn you, before your last departure for Paris. The wits and the financiers of Paris may laugh about my scruples and my paragraph in the Morning-Post of November 13, last; they may look at the position in which I find myself as an occasion to go and plunder English pockets. That's something I will never encourage by my own actions, were I to be blamed by all of France. Let people take my principles for nonsense, or even silliness, I don't care; I'd rather be called a silly woman than a thief or a knave. On this chapter, I have raised a tribunal in my own heart, a hundred times more severe than that of the Marshals of France, the natural judges on points of honor. If these reflections are sound, they justify me; if they are false, my error will be my excuse.

Under these circumstances . . . I went and met Milord Ferrers on his land. He had been inviting me for a month to go spend my convalescence with him. I sorely needed that change of air after keeping my bed and room for almost the whole months of november and december. Besides, I still have several affairs to finish with Milord, and the burst of emotion you caused me has exhausted me.

I will therefore, take advantage of my stay in the country to open my heart to you and talk to you with the sensitivity of Miss d'Eon and the frankness of Chevalier d'Eon. I will start by commenting a little on a few sentences of your epistle, where you tell me: "You found me easy and gay in society, you experienced my frank and generous approach in business; but have I given you such a paltry ideal of my character and principles that you should flatter yourself in a serious discussion to make me take nonsense for reasons?" . . .

London, January 14, 1776, to Sartine (For you alone) (Mol 650; Mor 2:166)

I am taking advantage of the courier I am sending to M. de Vergennes, to warn you that if the information I acquired is not deceptive, all of it has branches that go out so high that there may be as much danger in taking action as harm in letting it go.[1]

This reflection of profound politics is for you alone. I will take such precautions that any idea relative to you will be pushed a thousand miles away and even, if possible, all those relative to me and the work I am doing. Besides, if you had not approved the precautionary arrangement I have just established for the future, I would not want for anything in the world to meddle with this chore any more: it looks to me like the tree and the bark of Plato, between which the prudent man should not stick his finger. Go as far as you

---

[1]Gudin, who had not accompanied the author to London, expresses puzzlement about the meaning of this letter, stating that it showed into what hornets nest he was getting there. Gudin 1888, 187-9. The matter seems to involve a lurid publication with engravings concerning Chevalier d'Eon (reproduced in Pinsseau). D'Aiguillon had not been satisfied with the settlement of the affair, wanting to know who else was involved in it.

want in your thoughts, without fearing to go too far, and you will get close to the goal.

In fact, they only want to throw things into confusion, and take advantage of the divergence to lay hold of the King; then you would certainly be lost. That's what concerns you, and touches me infinitely. As to me, I am nothing; but I see to it that the future will no longer be at my expense on the part of the malcontents. For the past, it is not in my power to prevent the resentment still prevailing against me; it will be up to the king to safeguard me, and truly that's the least which is due to me.

Enough on this matter: Don't let my mail be held up for an instant. M. de Vergennes will no doubt forward to you my large ministerial despatch.

22 January 1776, Vergennes to the king
(France 1776, no. 1; Don 1:253-4)

Sire,

I have the honor of sending to Your Majesty a communication from Beaumarchais, without leaving anything out, even what he intended for myself alone. If I permitted myself to cut out anything, I believe it would be the personalities. Facts are mentioned which I am not in a position to verify and which would be difficult to prove. What seems the most important to me is the picture of the present state of affairs and the consequences which may result. England is becoming despondent. I can easily believe what Beaumarchais suggests--that the overthrow of the ministry is not far away; in order for them to remain a little longer in office and withstand the storm , or escape the dangers which threatens their heads, nothing is left but desperate solutions. This foresight seems to warrant that of Your Majesty. But it may be easier to imagine what should be done than to indicate how.

As it will be only after I receive Your Majesty's orders that I will be able to reply to Beaumarchais, I beg you very humbly to be kind enough to order the moment when I can go and receive such orders.

[29 February 1776] To the king only
[Peace or War Memorial]
(Lom 2:99-106; Don 1:402-7; Mor 2:171)

Sire,

The famous quarrel between England and America, which is soon going to divide the world and change the system of Europe, imposes on each power the necessity of examining the possible outcome of this separation, whether it can serve or harm them.

But the most concerned of all certainly is France, whose sugar islands, since the last peace, the English have constantly regretted and coveted, which must without fail bring war to us, unless through an unconscionable weakness we will consent to sacrifice our possessions in the Gulf to the chimera of a shameful peace, more destructive than the war we dread.

In a first memorial given Your Majesty three months ago by M. de Vergennes, I have tried to establish soundly that Your Majesty's sense of justice could not be hurt by taking wise precautions against enemies who have never been scrupulous about those they take against us.[2]

Today when the moment of a violent crisis is quickly approaching, I am obliged to warn Your Majesty that the preservation of our American possessions and the peace you appear to wish for so ardently depend solely on this proposition: <u>We must aid the Americans</u>. That's what I am going to demonstrate.

The king of England, the ministers, the Parliament, the opposition, the nation, the English people, the parties in one word that tear that State apart, all agree that they can no longer flatter themselves with the hopes of bringing the Americans back into the fold or that the great efforts made today to subjugate them will succeed. Hence, Sire, the violent debates between the ministry and the opposition, this ebb and tide of opinions granted or rejected which, without promoting anything, only serve to shed more light on the question.

Lord North, afraid to steer the ship alone throughout such a storm, has just taken advantage of Lord Germain's ambition to shift the weight of the affair on his ambitious head.

---

[2]The "Summum jus, summa injuria" paper of December 7th.

Lord Germain,[3] stunned by the clamor and struck by the terrible arguments of the opposition, told the party leaders, Lords Shelburne and Rockingham: "Under the present circumstances, Gentlemen, dare you answer to the nation that the Americans will accept the navigation act and will go back under the yoke on the sole condition, contained in Lord Shelburne's plan, that they will be reinstated in the condition they were in before the 1763 troubles? If you dare answer for it, Gentlemen, you may assume the duties of the ministry and the welfare of the State at your own risks, perils and fortunes."

The opposition, inclined to take the minister at his word, and ready to say yes, is held back only because they worry that the Americans, encouraged by their successes and perhaps emboldened by some secret treaties with Spain and France, might refuse today the same conditions of peace they were begging for two years ago.

Besides, a certain L. (M. de Vergennes will tell you his name)[4], a secret agent of the colonies in London, absolutely discouraged by the uselessness of the efforts he attempted through me with the ministry to obtain from them supplies of powder and war munitions, told me today: "One last time, is France absolutely determined to deny us any help and become the victim of England and the laughing-stock of Europe through this incredible inertia? I myself, obliged to give an answer, am awaiting your final reply in order to give mine. We offer France, as a price for secret aid, a treaty of commerce which will let her enjoy, for a certain number of years after the peace, all the profits with which we have enriched England, plus a guarantee of her possessions according to our strength. Don't you want it? I only ask Lord Shelburne for the time of a round trip for a ship to go inform Congress of England's proposals, and I can tell you right now what the Congress will resolve. They will immediately make a public declaration by which they will offer the nations of the world, in order to obtain help from them, the conditions that I am offering you secretly today. And to avenge

---

[3]One of the fiercest adversaries to the American cause, George Sackville Germain (1716-1785) was Commissioner of Trade and Plantations from 1775 to 1779, and Secretary of State for the colonies until Lord North's resignation in 1782.

[4]Arthur Lee, mentioned here for the second time in a memorial to the King, has obviously sold a bill of goods to the naive Frenchman.

themselves of France and publicly force her to make a declaration regarding them which will compromise her excessively, they will send in your ports the first prizes they take on the English: then, whatever you do, the war that you dread so much will become unavoidable for you, because either you will receive our prizes in your ports, or you will send them away; if you receive them, you are sure to break off with England; if you send them away, Congress will accept the peace proposal from the mother country; the Americans outraged will join their forces with those of England and overtake your islands, proving to you that the fine precautions that you were taking to keep your possessions were the very same ones that were to deprive you of them forever.

"Go, Sir, go to France and give them this picture of the situation: I am going to shut myself up in the country till you come back, so I will not be forced to give an answer before I have received yours. Tell your ministers I am ready to follow you there, if needed, to confirm these declarations; tell them that **I hear that Congress has sent two commissioners to the court of Madrid for the same purpose, and I can add thereto that they have received a very favorable answer.** Is it the council of France's glorious prerogative to be blind on the glory of the king and the interests of his kingdom?"

There you have, Sire, the awful, striking picture of our position. Your Majesty sincerely wants peace? The way to keep it, Sire, is the object of this memorial.

Let us admit all possible hypotheses, and let us reason together.

What follows is very important:

Either England will have in this campaign the most complete success in America; or the Americans will throw them back with losses.

Either England will take the decision, already favored by the King, to let the colonies go their own way and separate in peace; or the opposition, taking over the ministry, will answer for the Americans to get back into the fold provided they are granted their 1763 status.

There you have all possibilities together: is there any of them that will not give you instantly the war you are trying to avoid? Sire, for God's sake, deign to look at it with me:

1. If England triumphs over America, it can only be at the cost of an enormous expenditure in men and money; the only compensation the English count on for so many losses is to take over on the rebound the French islands, to become in this manner the exclusive merchants of the precious commodity of sugar, which only can repair the damages of their commerce, and this capture make them forever absolute owners of the illegal trade the continent is doing with those islands.

Then, Sire, you would be left with the only choice of starting too late an unfruitful war, or to sacrifice to the most shameful inactive peace all of your American colonies, and to lose 280 millions capital and more than 30 millions revenue.

2. If the Americans win, they are immediately free and the English, desperate to see their standard of living diminished by three-fourths, will be the more eager to find a now indispensable compensation in the easy take-over of our American possessions, and you can be sure they will not fail to do so.

3. If the English believe themselves forced to give up the colonies without fighting, which is the secret wish of the King, the loss being the same for their standard of living and their trade being ruined, the result for us is similar to the previous one; except that the English, less weakened by this amicable surrender than by a bloody and ruinous campaign, will be the more able to grab our islands which they will no longer be able to do without, if they want to keep a foothold in America.

4. If the opposition takes over the ministry and makes peace with the colonies, the Americans, outraged against France whose refusal alone would have forced them to yield to the mother-country, threaten us today to join their forces with those of England to take over our islands. They will reunite with the mother-country even only on that condition, and God knows then how the ministry, composed of Lords Chatham, Shelburne and Rockingham, whose dispositions for us are public, will be happy to adopt the Americans' resentment, and they will make on you the most relentless and cruel war.

What must we do, therefore, in this crisis to have peace and keep our islands?

You will keep the peace you desire, Sire, only by preventing it between England and America, and by avoiding that one of them triumphs completely over the other; and the only way to accomplish this is to give aid to the Americans, such as to balance their forces with those of England, and nothing more. And rest assured, Sire, that the savings of a few millions today may before long cost France a great deal of blood and of money.

You may be especially sure, Sire, that the preparations only of the first campaign will cost you more than all the help asked of you today, and that the paltry saving of 2 or 3 millions will be sure to cost you before two years have passed more than 300.

If it is held that we cannot help the Americans without hurting England and without bringing over us the storm I want to avert, I will answer in my turn that this danger will not be incurred if you agree to the plan I have so many times proposed, of secretly aiding the Americans without being compromised, imposing on them as the first condition that they will never send any prizes into our ports, and will not do anything liable to divulge such aid that the first indiscretion of the Congress would make them lose instantly. And if Your Majesty has no abler man to employ, I take it upon myself and I vouch for the treaty, without any one being compromised, persuaded that my zeal will sooner make up for my want of ability than another's ability would make up for my zeal.

Your Majesty can see that success here entirely depends on secrecy and speed; but one thing infinitely important to one and the other, would be, if possible, to obtain the recall of Lord Stormont, who because of his relations in France is in position to inform and does inform England on a daily basis of all that is being said at Your Majesty's council.

That may be extraordinary, but that's the case; the opportunity of the recall of M. de Guines is most convenient.

England demands an ambassador: if Your Majesty took his time to appoint a successor to M. de Guines and would send to England a simple *charge d'affaires*, a man of known ability, at the instant Lord Stormont would be recalled, and whichever minister they would appoint in his place, it would be a long time before he would be in a position to do us as much harm as Lord Stormont does. And once the crisis is over, the most futile or ostentatious of our lords could be sent safely as ambassador to London; the job then having either succeeded or failed, the rest would be of no import.

Your Majesty may judge by this writing whether my zeal is as enlightened as it is ardent and pure.

But if forgetting the dangers one word escaped from his mouth can occasion to a good servant who knows and serves only him, my august master lets it be understood that he is receiving this secret information through me, then no authority could prevent my being destroyed, so powerful are intrigues and cabals at your Court, Sire, to do harm and to ruin the most important undertakings. Your Majesty knows better than anyone else that secrecy is the soul of efficiency and that in politics a disclosed project is an abortive project.

As long as I have been serving you, Sire, I have never asked you, and I will never ask you, for anything. Grant me only, my Master, that I will not be prevented from working for your service and my whole life is dedicated to you.

16 April 1776, to Vergennes
(Ang. 515, fo. 320; S.F. 1323; Don 1:407-11; Mor 2:177)

I am taking advantage of a safe way to get this dispatch to Mr. Affiery and giving my mail to Mr. Garnier[5] in exchange for a packet from him. I will write M. de Sartine on Friday to thank him, as well as the King, for having furnished me the means of sleeping soundly in London. Certain that you will pass on to him my big dispatch [which follows immediately], I put down the pen for I have been writing and copying myself for eight hours and I am worn out.

The principles of French neutrality are established in the following letter: England has no right to demand that France order her merchants to stop trading with America. Vergennes will applaud, and later he will yield to the threats of the English ambassador, who had better proofs that foreseen that the trade included arms.

London, April 16, 1776, to Vergennes

---

[5]French diplomatic agent in London, not of the rank of ambassador. De Guines had not been replaced except by Garnier. This seemed to agree with Beaumarchais' advice. However, it did not bring about the recall of Lord Stormont.

(Ang. 515, no. 76; S.F. 1322; Mor 2:177-182)

While England is gathered in Westminster Hall to witness the trial of the old adulterous and bigamous Duchess of Kinston, I am going to report to you on a rather serious conversation I had with Lord Rochford.

Last Sunday, while sending me tickets for Westminster Hall, he asked me to go see him. After the usual compliments, the conversation becoming more and more lively, he told me: "Sir, having a proof of confidence and friendship to ask of you, I am first going to give you one by showing something I have not shown anyone."

That something, M. le Comte, was a letter from the king of England, written to him, but full of kindness, familiarity, and full of the most tender attachment by which this Prince is asking him to accept the viceroyalty of Ireland that Lord North is supposed to offer him on his behalf. The King adds: "I need a very sure man in that island; in the present state of affairs we must fear that Ireland will follow the steps of America. The only grace I ask of you is not to take your secretary with you there, that wretched knave Bloker, who has been in France with the Duke of Harcourt and has kept there dangerous relations. He caused the Duke of Harcourt to be hated in Ireland, etc.

"That is what the King wrote me yesterday," Lord Rochford told me. "I am sorry he feels that way against Bloker whom I like, but everything concerning France worries us today. [Whence I conclude, Sir, that they are concerned about us in England.] If they grant me the condition that I will have to spend there only six months out of the year, the deal is done. I am expecting something from Lord North. But I must not fail to read you the last sentence of the king's letter, because it concerns you personally: 'Don't forget what I recommended you. You will report only to me.'

"It's about news received from, Bristol. A ship carrying letters from the Congress and merchandise for a merchant from Nantes named Montaudoin, with order to exchange the merchandise for war munitions of all kinds, was taken right to Bristol by a captain faithful to his King. The letters prove that this correspondence has been going on for a long time and their language indicate it may very well be protected by your government. This event plus the fact that two French gentlemen[6] have

---

[6]Pliarne and Penet who were in relations with the merchant Montaudouin.

been negotiating secretly with the Congress on behalf of your ministers [They pay us in London more compliment than we deserve], which gentlemen have hidden relations with some people in London, have singularly alarmed our Council.

"A few misinformed people have even tried to connect you with that connivance, but the King is so little impressed that it is with his permission that I am discussing it with you. What do you think of all that? I know that you are here to finish with that fellow D'Eon, about which affair I don't want to believe anyone but you, and I informed the King as you know.

"Before answering you, Milord, regarding me, I said, permit me to start with the American ship, not according to any instructions received from our ministers, but according to my own light.

"I had already heard, Milord, about the arrival of the American ship in Bristol and I was no more surprised about its being loaded for a Nantes merchant as for one from Amsterdam, Cadix or Hambourg.

"The insurgents need munitions and have no money to buy any in Europe. Therefore, they must venture to send merchandise of their own to exchange them and all ports where munitions can be found must be equal to them.

--But, Sir, France has given orders in her ports in this respect, has she not? Haven't we the right to expect the Nantes merchants will be punished, as we will ask your ministers to do?

--Milord, you permitted me to speak to you frankly, I will do so inasmuch as I don't have any mission and will not compromise any one. Why should our administration take sanctions against the Nantes people? Are we at war with anyone? and since we are at peace, our ports are open to all the merchants in the world, are they not? Before you ask France to account for the Nantes merchants, you should start by asking a preliminary question, rather strange, as follows: For a quarrel involving only Englishmen and in which we have nothing to do, has England the right to restrict our trade? What treaties oblige us to open or close our ports to merchant vessels according to the wishes of Great Britain? Indeed, Milord, I can hardly believe you dare raise such an incredible question, the answer to which could have consequences it is in England's interest not to provoke, especially when the noble principles of the king of France are solidly proved by the neutrality he has assumed; although everything seems to invite France to

take advantage of your intestine disputes to recover from England all that they took away from us during the last war.
--But Sir, the Americans are rebels and our declared enemies.

--Milord, they are not ours.

--And when we are at peace with France, does she have the right to favor them?

--To favor them! By God, Milord, that's all you could say if we prevented you from running on all the insurgents' ships on the open sea, because they would be carrying merchandise for our ports or coming therefrom. Who keeps you from taking action against them? Cruise all over, seize them anywhere, except under the cannon of our forts. It is none of our business. But to demand that we worry our merchants because they have trade relations with people we are at peace with, whether we look at them as your subjects, or as a free people, a people you are fighting against but which you dare not, you, ministers, to bring to trial before your own nation, really, that's a little strong! I don't know what our administration would think of such a demand, but I do know I would find it more than out of place.

--I can see it, Sir, you are red with anger. (In fact, M. le Comte, the fire had gone to my face, and if you disapprove my showing so much heat, beg your pardon, I will answer that my opinion was involved, not yours.)

   --Milord, I resumed gently, as an Englishman and a patriot, you must not disapprove that a good Frenchman should be proud of his country.

--So I do not resent it, Sir, but at least you will agree that your ministers cannot help but deal severely with the Frenchmen who go and negotiate with Congress on behalf of your government.

--I do not believe any part of this news, Milord. Some Frenchman may have dealt with them on his own for private assistance such as merchants may furnish by way of trade. And that's no doubt where the Bristol ship started to correspond with the Montaudouin firm of Nantes. But if you can get the names of those alleged agents and acquire the least proof they pretended to be agents of the government, I believe I am so certain about the principles of our ministers in this regard, and even those of the King, that I can assure you they will be disowned and even punished, if they can be arrested." (You see, M. le Comte, that I am playing straight. Too bad for those who are caught in London or elsewhere.)

This declaration put us back in good terms, the lord and me. "Now, I said, Milord, I am going to tell you about my being here. The d'Eon affair is no longer my business. Whether he goes back to France or not, no one cares. His decision in this matter is his own and does not concern me. You are going to ask me what brings me here?

--No, Sir, for I already know what you will answer.

--I see, Milord. My letters were opened.

--My friend, we are old hands at politics, you and I, and we know people write what they please.

--Agreed, Milord, but if one can write what he pleases, one does not act that way. It is no idle banter that the King of France and his ministers are charging someone with the supplies necessary to the service.
--Are you really charged with anything?

--I have no secret for you, Milord. Here is what the King has granted me. Then I showed him the ministerial letter M. de Sartine wrote me about supplying Portuguese coins for our American colonies. He read it several times very carefully, and as it appeared to him likely enough to be true, he told me: That was a good deal when those coins had currency in England, but since they have not been legal tender for two years, why does it bring you here?

--It's that it is more convenient for me, Milord, to deal in London, where I know everybody, than in Lisbon where I know no one, and that I am concerned with profit as much as with doing an honorable job. (So, M. le Comte, I was right to insist on this precaution with M. de Sartine before I left, and right again to have seen several bankers in London as soon as I arrived. I've learned last night that information was checked with the exchange where I had entered into a real deal about this object.) Let's resume my conversation.

--Now, Milord, I added, I must congratulate you on the part of the King's letter which concerns you personally. And if you accept the viceroyalty, I hope you will remember your old friendship for Mr. Duflos, whom I recommend to you again. I hope you will put him in charge of your household in Ireland, as you did in France. (This Duflos, M. le Comte, is a Frenchman I had long ago given to Lord Rochford, which Frenchman is absolutely devoted to me, and through whom you will always have sure information about the most intimate household of the viceroyalty. I am a little like Figaro, M. le Comte, and I do not lose my head for a little noise.)

We are to meet again, the Lord and I, after he has reported to the king regarding our conversation. All I know is that tomorrow there is a council at St. James about the Bristol ship. But the King of England has been well briefed. I hope I said enough so you will not entertain any dishonest proposition about that.[7]

I must not forget to let you know that the Dutch merchants have threatened to attack the ministers before the grand jury of England regarding the three Dutch vessels heading for America which were captured and taken to Deal and Dover. I know moreover that the ministers afraid the grand jury would decide against them and that this would bring up a more important issue (for you suspect that this Jesuitic move comes from our friend Wilkes), the ministers, I say, have secretly agreed to pay for the whole load of munitions these ships were taking to America, and agreed that if others were taken, the munitions would be kept in England but the price would be paid to the Dutch merchants. For no one wants to go to court with our friend Wilkes (advice to the reader, M. le Comte). I hold this from good source, although not from my lord, as you can guess.

(Other advice to the reader.) One of the schemes the Dutch captains are using is to get two commissions, one ostensible and the other secret. They make use of one or the other according to the need.

Besides the Hessian troops have left. The English are waiting for them. They have pledged allegiance to England on March 22.

---

[7]He means: You will not heed the English ambassador's suggestion to punish anyone.

"O! le bon billet qu'a LaCh tre!" Ninon Lenclos[8] would say.

The Americans presently have 12 vessels from 22 to 44 guns, 12 to 15 pieces, and more than 30 of 12 pieces, which constitutes a navy almost as respectable as that of England. Thus, for the past two and a half months, the English have captured only the one ship that went to Bristol, which is quite remarkable.

The king's guard who pursuant to a secret counter--order, were being held back, according to news brought by a ship that spies in an Irish port, have received order to embark. They started to yesterday. They are leaving tomorrow. That's all for today, M. le Comte. I have emptied my bag.

I am counting on your kindness not to forget my recommendation for Aix. It would not be fair for me to be judged in the south when I am 300 leagues north. A word from Miromenil will suffice. This news will relieve my worries.[9]

Receive my regards etc. I am waiting to hear from you. Count Lauraguais is still in the country.

London, April 19, 1776, to Vergennes
(Ang. 515, fo. 532; S.F. 1325; Mor 2:184-5)

Excuse my stupid distraction in dating my letters the 12th, last Tuesday the 16th. It needs to be corrected only in my long letter, because the 12th contradicts several later facts mentioned.

The public papers in this mail will let you know the last scene at the opera between Baron de Linsing and Texier.[10] This Texier story is a tissue of extravagance

---

[8]Woman writer (1620-1705) whose salon was frequented by free-thinkers. She bequeathed 1000 Francs to the young Voltaire, to buy books with. Marquis de LaCh tre was a minor writer, author of memoirs.

[9]The LaBlache suit was coming up for trial in that Provence city. Miromenil was minister of justice. The defendant was asking for an extension of time.

[10]Also spelled "Tercier." Jean-Pierre Tercier, a career diplomat, directed the secret correspondence of Louis XV. Dictionnaire de Biographie Nationale states that he died in 1767 of a heart attack, in Paris. There are, however, indications that

from one end to the other. However, this Texier is still another man persecuted by France, whom a group of aristocratic women consider it honorable for them to protect publicly. M. de Lauraguais, back this morning from the country and more than compromised in Texier's last paragraph, is supposed to put an end to all that printed exchange by a short and precise account of all the facts, bidding his brave adversary a Medea's goodbye.

The most curious of all is the rumor spread by Texier with all the partisan women friendly to the late ambassador, that the latter is sure to return and that such is the reason why no one has been named to succeed him. To accredit the rumor, the ambassador, who had announced the sale of all his belongings, has sent a counter-order, so that thanks to the audience he has received from the King of France, about which people are really talking here, he is expected to come back with laurels on his head and the embassy in his pocket.

I realize I have not done enough for my security by showing Lord Rochford my accreditation on the coins for our islands, and that I must take more care to give this occupation of my time in England a greater authenticity. Mr. de Lauraguais himself claims that will not suffice. But until I see the need to reinforce my props, I will rely on the rumors I have spread among tradesmen and on my connections. I have no more doubt than the Count that I am being followed, but as long as M. de Sartine sees eye to eye with me, I believe I have nothing personal to fear.

News from the last ship

South Carolina, who had only mumbled up to now, finally spoke out as clearly as the other colonies. She has her little fleet of three vessels, well equipped; 6000 troops in good order and more than 200 guns forming batteries around the town of Charleston, which the people don't want to see burn down like her Massachusetts sister. A certain DuMenil de St. Pierre, a Norman by birth, a good gentleman by profession and bad wine-grower by pleasure, heading a little colony he called New Bordeaux, where he grows grapes which do not ripen and mulberry trees that die from the cold, has raised a

---

he reappeared in London, where he communicated with Chevalier d'Eon. When, in 1774, Count de Broglie settled with the new king the accounts of Louis XV's secret diplomatic corps, a pension was given to Tercier's son. Pinsseau, 72, 85-88, 90, 92, 100-106, 162.

regiments of French, Danish, and German refugees, which he offered to the city of Charleston, his neighbor. They refused him as holding his concessions from the English government, and as having already forsworn his first country, France. I bet that Norman's offers, perhaps reiterated before Congress, have caused all the talk about the Frenchmen allegedly sent by our government. If I can find out, I will use it well with the Lord I am indoctrinating. Meanwhile, I will always say what I think about it.

April 26, 1776, from Vergennes
(Ang. 515, fo. 393; S.F. 1329; Mor 2:185-187)

I have placed under the eyes of the king the letter you sent me on Tuesday the 16th and not the 12th of this month. His Majesty much approved the noble and frank manner in which you countered Lord Rochford's attack regarding the American ship on its way, they say, to Nantes and led to Bristol. You said nothing that His Majesty would not have prescribed you to say, if he had been able to foresee that you would have to formulate an opinion on a subject so removed from what you are charged to do. If they have no other evidence than what has been made public in the English papers, which has been handed me by M. de St. Paul, one must admit they are jumping to conclusions. Far from seeing the proof of any connivance on the part of the correspondent Montaudouin, the shipper is so unsure he can count on this resource that in his instructions to his captain, he recommends to him to exchange his cargo for a certain quantity of arms and powder, or if he cannot procure the latter to take instead some saltpeter, and failing all that, to bring back the value in money.

By his tone, Lord Rochford would seem to argue from the point of view of a treaty which would bind us to make England's interest our own. I do not know any such treaty, and there is no example of it in the behavior of England, when she had a chance to harm us. Let us only recall how they behaved towards us during the troubles in Corsica, the assistance of all kind poured there without any sort of caution. I do not cite this example to authorize us to follow it. The king, faithful to his principles will not take an unfair advantage of England's situation to increase her difficulties, but he cannot cut off the protection he owes to the commerce of his subjects. It is through friendship for the king of Great Britain and not as a result of any agreement that the king proceeded to forbid in his ports the shipping of war munitions for North America, but this order cannot be made more general. If those facts are smuggling from the point of view of the English who have the misfortune of being at war against their colonies, they are matters of trade with us, who do not participate in it and nothing prevents the English from taking care of them themselves if they fear that the americans will find a way to procure them. But it would be against all reason and propriety to claim we must not sell any of these articles to whomsoever because they might pass second-handedly into America. Moreover, the English have enough forces at sea to intercept the ships who can attempt to introduce in this are merchandise said to be contraband. They have no reason to complain we hinder or obstruct their cruising. They may even be assured we will not claim any of the American ships they may seize, provided they don't make bold to arrest them in view of our fortresses and under our guns.

M. de St. Paul talked to me about the snow Dickenson, but with much less feeling than Lord Rochford with you. He was far from suggesting that the merchant Montaudouin should be punished. He was mostly concerned about that noble ambassador who presented himself before Congress on our behalf. If we were in a mood to wish to enter in correspondence with the insurgents, we would have no need to send anyone for that purpose to America, and if we sent anyone there, we would choose him capable of making himself less visible. I do not know anything about this alleged French gentleman whose return is announced. Could it be some ruined merchant or some merchant representative who seeing an opportunity to make some money, has gone and offered his services to the Congress to establish a mercantile correspondence? The English ministers being better informed than we are about what goes on in our ports, I would be obliged if they would let me know who this pilgrim is. I will welcome a conversation with him, and if it is proved that he presented himself to Congress as a French emissary, he certainly will be chastised. The king is not inclined to permit such a criminal abuse and every time you hear valid complaints, Sir, you will not be compromised in making sure that justice is done.

Receive all my compliments, Sir. After I have assured you of the approval of the king, mine must not seem interesting. However, I cannot deny myself the satisfaction of applauding the wisdom and firmness of your conduct and assuring you again of all my esteem. I did not neglect your commission for Aix, the Keeper of the Seals assured me everything will be held in suspense until you return.

No news from our amazon? [Chevalier d'Eon] It would be surprising for her to be in England and not contact you.

26 April 1776, from Vergennes
(Ang. 515, fo. 395; Don 1:417-8; Mor 2:188-9)

I have received, Sir, on the 21st and 23rd your personal letters of the 16th and 19th of this month. My last mail having been sent on the 20th, I did not have any safe opportunity to write you and I don't think the post would be one. It is not that our letters cannot be read there. There is no conspiracy between us, but I am beginning to think that governments so praised for their freedom are much more touchy than ours. I cannot keep from laughing to myself at the ballyhoo about the Dickenson adventure. I see nothing in it more interesting than the profit that will go to the capturing crew, unless it is that Lord Rochford, your friend, who feels forlorn away from the affairs,[11] grabs at every little circumstance and blows them up to create for himself a secret ministry. The King approves your not rejecting the overtures this former minister may make to you. You are prudent and sagacious, I would have no misgivings even if you had a commission more important than the one M. de Sartine gave you. It's a good thing you had it, however, since it enabled you to dispel the huff caused by your frequent trips to London. You have to admit that those Englishmen are well below women, if they can be frightened for so little.

I handed your letter to Mr. de Sartine. He read it before me and promised me that my mail would carry his answer. I hope he will not refuse anything you asked for. But should he not be sufficient to reinforce your props to cure Lord Rochford's suspicions, what could he do? You are not in relations with proscribed people, and besides you have no practice that can compromise you.

I don't care if Baron de Linsing and Texier carry their battle in the newspapers, but I very much wish that Count Lauraguais would stay away from this kind of fencing. The latter man especially is not an athlete worthy of him. I will not tell you whether M. de Guines wishes and hopes to return to England. But I do him too much justice to think he would want to use the channel of Texier to spread a rumor about it. Besides I don't

---

[11]Lord Rochford ceased to be Secretary of State in the fall of 1775.

know exactly what he is doing. I have not changed my way of thinking since you left, and you know that I was not involved in his recall, and do not want to get involved in its consequences.

We have not yet been advised from Germany about the departure of the first Hessian division. Obviously, ships were not available. Should they be delayed a little, they may well arrive at destination at the end of the season suitable for their operations.

I have only to thank you for the news from America you are kind enough to pass on to me. If North Carolina joined the colonies, that's an incident which may well change the campaign plans. England is powerful but perhaps not enough for what she has started.

London, April 26, 1776, to Vergennes
(Ang. 515, Fo. 389; S.F. 1328; Mor 2:189-94)

I am taking advantage of a safe opportunity to talk freely with you about the only important affair today: America and all that pertains to it.

I reasoned at length, the evening before last, with the man you deemed advisable to keep from coming to France [Arthur Lee].

As he arranged the interview, M. de Lauraguais briefed me on all that had told each other in my absence, and in the same manner told him everything that had passed between the two of us, before taking me there.

That man appeared to me to be astounded rather than surprised by the denial of his announcement brought to you from the south.[12] He can't imagine where the error comes from. But he believes he is well informed, because it is in their interest not to deceive him. Perhaps, also, Congress has sent those commissioners to the Spanish possessions in America, or to their fleet commanders, instead of all the way to Madrid.

He expects to hear further on this at any time. The news have arrived in Holland, whence they will be forwarded to him by the safest channel. In twelve days I will know what to tell you. Meanwhile he keeps on asking me if we don't want to do anything for them, and

---

[12]That is, from Spain, where according to Lee, two American commissioners had been received by the court.

without idly repeated how important their success is to France--for he does us the honor of thinking we agree with him on this point--he tells me evenly: We must have arms, powder, and especially engineers. You are the only ones who can do it and have a great interest in doing it. We mostly need a few engineers. I answer him that the last article is exceedingly difficult, because you cannot send men without giving them a commission. Men talk, we would be compromised. Merchandise does not talk. Well, he says, give us the money and we will get engineers elsewhere--Germany, Sweden, Italy etc. you will not be compromised. There we are, M. le Comte, what can I say?

Since the arrival in Bristol of the ship intended for the Montaudouin firm in Nantes, on which I have heard the many arguments which you have, our man has asked me to forward secretly to this firm the letter included herewith. I am sending it to you, you may send it on without adding a word, recommending it covertly.

The Americans besides are doing as well as can be. Troops, fleet, food, courage, all is excellent. But without powder and without engineers, how can they win or even defend themselves?

Are we willing to let them perish rather than to lend them one or two millions? Are we afraid this money will not return, one way or the other, once the war is finished?

You can see, M. le Comte, how frightened the English are at the most absurd piece of news which seems to come from France, and conclude therefrom on the state of their affairs.

Colonel St. Paul brings to London a false and ridiculous piece of news, about an alleged new treaty between France and Spain: instantly the stock market plunges.

They spread here the silly rumor that the French have taken Jamaica, and although every one says that's impossible, and laughs the best they can, that does not prevent the stock exchange from falling.

The least scare concerning us has this effect on the exchange.

Thus when Lord North said yesterday, in the Commons, that the intelligence between France and England was perfect, inasmuch as "it was much more necessary to the French than to the English," the whole Parliament had the common sense[13] to laugh in his face.

And when he added that, in spite of Dr. Price's[14] reveries, the nation never had been so prosperous, the whole Parliament had again the good sense to laugh in his face.

But laughter was replaced by indignation when the opposition started speaking. And without going into all that was said yesterday in the commons, because it was sent to you undoubtedly, I cannot help taking in consideration all the debates carried on there.

Feebleness and fright, that what is seen there. The minister, always hassled about the intentions and deeds of France, cannot answer one word. Why do the French have 7,500 men on Bourbon Island?[15] No comment.

Why, another asks, are the Spaniards at Hispaniola with nine men-of-war, by which they probably protect the trade from the continent. No comment. Governor Johnson rises. Why do the Spaniards, besides their American fleet, have in Cartagene and Cadix two fleet ready to set sail? And how can you answer nothing, when I am certain of the oncoming war between France and England. Absolute silence.

Charles Fox nods, saying: What forces do you intend to us against a fleet of 45 American privateers, good sailors, active, valiant soldiers, protected by tornadoes and ten ports, protected by 20 foreign men-of-war, always ready to help them with munitions, protected by two powerful nations, soon ready to assist them openly and to recognize them as allies? No comment.

Why, Mr. Barré says, is Lord Howe, who was supposed to lead the fleet, not leading it? No comment. The Commons orator, seeing the minister speechless, spoke but without answering Mr. Barré's question which the latter asked again heatedly. Then Charles Fox, in an inspired manner, questions the ministers' honor, and

---

[13]Doniol and Morton are in error here, giving "bonheur" instead of "bon sens."

[14]English philosopher, author of <u>Observations on Civil Liberty and the Justice of the War with America</u>.

[15]Former name of la Réunion, in the Indian ocean.

giving the answer himself, "it's been a chimera for a long time, he said, it's gone and completely absent from England's public affairs." It is clear, M. le Comte, that the one who keeps silent here, does so because he has nothing to say in reply. Fear and anger on one side, weakness and confusion on the other. That's the true picture. And you will be even more convinced of that truth if you recall the nature of all their treaties with the Germans, and most of all if you examine the nature and the rate of the new government loan.

For each 100 pounds sterling lent to the government, one will get a note of 78 pounds sterling and three sweepstake tickets worth 10 pounds sterling each for a total of 30 pounds sterling, which amounts to a profit of 8 pounds sterling to start, and by the gains of the stock market they have already gone up to 11 pounds sterling, before delivery. Add 3% interest, which the government will pay on the 78 pounds sterling. That makes an interest rate of 14%.

These proofs of difficulties are unquestionable and when it is demonstrated that they certainly cannot carry more than one campaign at this horrible price, is it true, M. le Comte, that you will do nothing to bring the Americans up to par with their enemies?

Will you not have the virtue of showing the King once more how he can win, without firing a shot, in this one campaign? Will you not try to convince His Majesty that this wretched assistance they ask for, and which we have been debating for one year, is to give us the fruit of a great victory without having incurred the dangers of battle? That this assistance can make up, in our sleep, for all that the shameful peace of 1763 caused us to lose, and that the Americans' success, reducing our rivals to the status of a second rate power, gives us back our first rate status and gives us hegemony on the whole of Europe?

What greatest view can occupy the king's council? And what will your argument lack in strength if you bring up the opposite consideration of what an American defeat can cost us! 300 millions, our men, our ships, our islands, etc. For really, their forces once reunited against us, their troops in fine fettle and made more audacious by such a huge success, it is too certain that they will force war upon those same Frenchmen who could, for two millions, forever plunge them in a peace as shameful as ruinous.

In spite of the risk I run writing you from London such daring things, I feel twice as French here as in Paris. These people's patriotism reawakens mine. It even seems that the precarious and dangerous situation I see myself in, because of my being suspected and constantly watched, fires up my enthusiasm.

However, do not neglect, M. le Comte, to entreat M. de Sartine on the matter of my security. That's the least which is due me. The king and he were kind enough to provide for it. But the same merchants, bankers, brokers, gold dealers etc. who, secretly contacted by the ministers, have testified that I was negotiating with them a currency exchange, soon will not fail to answer that this is a deception, eyewash, if they don't see me pass from the order to the purchase. Two suspected Irishmen have been arrested. I wish to be in a position to defend myself without committing the king or yourself, in the event the same thing happens to me, until His Majesty is willing to own me or it becomes absolutely indispensable. Till then I am a piastres or moiadores merchant.

Even in that capacity, well certified, I will know how to defend the nation against the administration and will win the case and court costs. But another suit! I am tired of them, I swear to you. I hope (against Mr. de Lauraguais's advice) they will not go so far as to arrest me, when they see me pursue effectively a trade matter avowed by the nation.

By the way, what happens to Mr. de Lauraguais is really no more than a cat in his feet, and because he has close relations with Lord Shelburne and other members of the opposition, Lord Mansfield and the ministers have his cowardly opponent, Texier, backed up by women, in order to cause him such difficulties that he will want to return to France, for these people cannot suffer to have near them clear-sighted persons, still even less those who have a binocular aimed at their most secret actions. The public papers probably told you that Lord North has brought up in Parliament the amount of expenditures for last year, amounting to 9 097 000 pounds sterling, and as to cope with present needs he had in hand, he said, 9 118 444 pounds sterling, including, in advance, the three matters of the Bills of the Exchequer, creation of slush funds and of the 3% loan, which I mentioned earlier, for a total of 6 300 000 pounds sterling. So that the balance at hand to force America back under the yoke is 21 444 pounds Sterling. The rest will go as events permit.

Such, at the time I am writing you, M. le Comte, such is the state of England, America, Parliament, the public funds and that of the most devoted of your servants, myself!

I forgot to tell you that they insisted in Parliament on the question of whatever happened to an observation frigate sent in front of Brest to follow the fleet that would come out of it. And that on that matter as on the others, Lord North remained silent. Please confer with Mr. de Sartine about it.

London, 26 April 1776 to Vergennes
(Mor 2:195; S.F. 1328)

After I closed my package, I received news, which I am going to dictate because I am too tired to hold the pen. It has been confirmed that General Lee has taken all weapons away from shaky people in New York, where he leads an army of 20 thousand men.

The ship in question arrived at Merroy, Ireland, and brought many letters which were intercepted by the government. That ship, the Poly, Captain Montayne, had been confiscated by Customs officers for carrying hemp and hemp seed procured in America, but after a representation was made to the Lord Lieutenant, to the effect that it fell under the exceptions provided in the confiscation act, based on its departure from Europe as well as the nature of its cargo, the ship was released. Its arrival was known, but its name and the presence of intercepted letters have not yet been made public.

A great many of the convoy vessels dispatched to America have been thrown on the coasts with two detachments of the 45th and 56th regiments. This mishap and the American prizes have caused a shortage of wholesome victuals in Boston and first necessity items are hard to find. The same situation prevails in the city and in the camp of the provincials led by General Washington, who came close to being revoked for his failure to make any assault on Boston during the whole winter. That's how things stand there.

Some of the letters are from Arnold (Lieutenant of Montgomery),[16] who has not been taken but is wounded in the left leg. Montgomery was killed, together with 60

---

[16] Benedict Arnold (1741-1801) was with Richard Montgomery, a general of the Continental army, who captured Montreal in September 1775 and was killed on November 13.

of his men, and 300 taken prisoners. General Carleton[17] lost only 88 men in this attack. Arnold has led a troop he has gathered close to Quebec in retrenchments where they cannot be forced out.

The reason why Lord Howe refused to go to America is that he does not want to go unless he is given the power to negotiate a reconciliation with the Americans. This appears to have been granted to him by the ministers but the king did not agree, insisting on absolute submission, as if it were possible. Lord Bute is waiting behind the curtains, whether or not someone backs him up.

In his speech in Parliament, Lord North compared the present situation with the first campaign against the French in Germany, which was followed by the most glorious conquest. He blamed the present lack of success on the sluggishness of the nation, which allowed all the energy progressively to rest with the friends and defenders of the country. He predicted he would soon be ready to prove what he had stated and he pledged that when the nation would get together and stand up, and would no longer be put out of tune by outcries and predictions based on the weakest reveries or on the treachery of the enemies of the State, there no longer would prevail the animosity of a few individuals, who, through lies and iniquitous actions worthy of the worst punishment, had dared trouble the peace of their countrymen.

Lord Littleton and Lord Carlisle are both asking to be sent to Spain as ambassador, Lord Grantham[18] being on the verge of being recalled. They say that Lord Carlisle, son of Lord Gower, will take it away. The duke of Malborough is supposed to replace Lord Stormont, whom Lord Mansfield would like to send to Ireland. You know what I wrote you about Ireland, but that's still a secret.

The Amazon, Diamond, Lark and Richmond, four frigates of 32 cannons each, are being outfitted in Chatham and are ready to set sail for America. Captains Fielding and Jacob, two of the skippers, left last night to join their ships.

---

[17] Sir Guy Carleton (1724-1808), Governor of Quebec.

[18] Thomas Robinson, Lord Grantham, served as British ambassador in Madrid from 1771 to 1779.

Lord Germain has been working for a month on a plan for America which he will set before the House. It is predicated on continuing the war, more vigorously than ever.

Troop movements are supposed to have taken place in Sweden, which gives some concern to the ministers, certain as they are that Sweden has been put down. The existing treaty between England and Russia binds them so tightly that war in the north cannot be waged without the consent of Great Britain, who is neither willing nor able to split her forces.

2 May 1776, Vergennes to the king
(HR 220:15; Wha 1:229)

Sire,

I have the honor of placing at Your Majesty's feet the paper which authorizes me to supply a million livres for the use of the English colonies, if you deign ratify it with your signature.

I likewise enclose, Sire, the draft of the reply which I intend to make to Beaumarchais. Should Your Majesty approve it, I beg that it may be returned to me without delay. It shall not go forth in my handwriting or that of any of my clerks or secretaries, but in my son's, which cannot be recognized. Although he is only fifteen years old, I can vouch for his discretion.[19]

As it is of consequence that this operation should not be detected, or at least imputed to the government, I propose, with Your Majesty's consent, to call hither the Sieur Montaudouin.[20] The ostensible motive will be to ask him to account for his correspondence with the Americans, the real one, to charge him with the transmission to them of the funds which Your Majesty is pleased to grant them, directing at the same time all the precautions to be taken as if he advanced the funds on his own account. On this head also, I take the liberty of requesting the orders of Your Majesty. That being done, I will write Marquis de Grimaldi; I will

---

[19] 2 May 1776 Vergennes to Beaumarchais, which follows hereunder, is in the handwriting of Vergennes' son.

[20] French merchant from Nantes, already in correspondence with Congress (16 April 1776 to Vergennes) and who is receiving encouragement to extend credit to the Americans.

inform him in detail of our operation, and propose to him to double it.

Versailles, 2 May, 1776, from Vergennes
(Ang. 516:2; S.F. 861; Don 1:385-6; Mor 2:197)

   I received on the 1st of this month the letter you wrote me the 26th of last month. It is as easy to talk well as it is difficult to act well. That's an axiom everyone in administration will certify you, including the British ministers. Those whose part it is to reason look at a matter from a single point of view, grandly deducing the advantages to be gathered therefrom, but if they could have a complete view, they would soon realize that these advantages, so exalted in their speculations, would in fact turn out to be a source of harmful consequences, deadlier one than the other. I have long been in the orchestra seats before I arrived on the stage. I saw there people of every class and every sort. All of them were challengers and critics: nothing was done properly according to them. A few of them, judges that they were, came to a position to be judged themselves. All of them, almost, took up the errors they had so severely condemned, so true it is that there is a kind of force of impulsion or inertia, call it what you please, which always brings men back toward a common center.

   This preface is not meant to refute your foresight, which on the contrary I praise and approve. But do not believe that it is necessarily rejected when it is not promptly grasped. There are gradations it is prudent to follow, and in spite of your ebullient qualifiers, every sleep is not lethargic. Although the way I am using is sure, I don't trust it enough not to restrain the desire I have to tell you all I think thereon but I am relying on your sagacity to guess it. Think it over and you will find me closer to you than you thought.

   Let's drop this metaphysics and pass on to real matters. Is there anything so sound and brilliant as the way Lord North depicted the flourishing state of England? If he was as truthful there as when he denied the rumor of those 14 000 Frenchmen transported by air to America, we must envy England the inconceivable luck of finding prosperity where others usually find ruin. I used to have a great esteem for the country where you are, but not to the point of considering as ordinary a levy of sixteen millions Sterling. I conceive that a lot can be done with paper, because it is easy to produce in quantity; that's all right as long as it is supposed to represent what it is worth; its value may even increase a hundredfold through an active and easy circulation; but whenever an event affects confidence, whenever clogging and stagnation ensue, I ask Count Lauraguais what becomes of the edifice and whether it isn't a card castle soon to be blown away by the wind. That has not happen, they will say. I agree, but does it mean it will not? They want to prove it by the figures from 50 to 80, and then to 140. But if this progression has no bounds, where can you found a solvent caution? You can say what you please about England's wealth, I compare it to a swelling. I prefer France's plumpness in spite of her dieting a little. Everything is real here, fertile lands, precious metals, ringing cash. Credit may be lacking without hurting any of that.[21]

Is the snow Dickenson still in the newspapers? Never has such a puny adventure caused so much noise. I want to get all the facts on the Montaudouin brothers' correspondence. But I am already sure and the published letters witness it, that they never had suspicious relationships in the country whence the letters came. I know they are honest merchants, with a good reputation, enjoying a great credit and most trustworthy.

Thanks a million, Sir, for the news you passed on to me. It was seen and appreciated.[22] I expect we will soon hear most interesting things and we will know at last what will become of Quebec.

I forwarded the letter you recommended to me. If there is an answer, you will get it.

You know, Sir, my friendship and attachment for you.

P.S. I will not write to Count Lauraguais since you let me expect he will be back soon. Give him my regards and tell him I hope he will not shut himself up in Montacanisi[23] before paying a little visit to his friends. I can't wait for the Texier affair to be at the bottom of the Thames, where that financial hero

---

[21]Note Vergennes' mercantilist attitude. France did not have a bank. Finances and credit institutions were chaotic. All attempts at reform made by Beaumarchais (and others) will meet with the complacent opposition shown here by the minister.

[22]Seen by the king, of course.

[23]Lauraguais' residence in France.

himself should be. If it's a cat in the legs they are throwing at Count Lauraguais, I will admit your serious Britishers are clever in little tricks.

I am assured you will be authorized to start the gold coin shipments, but maturity dates should be rather delayed. As to me, I am afraid of them because their cost is very high.

London, 3 May 1776, to Vergennes
(Ang. 516, no. 5, fol. 11-12; S.F. 862; Mor 2:203-6)

I have too little time in front of me to do anything but acknowledge receipt today of your packet of April 26, containing a long letter from you, a more private one, and two letters from M. de Sartine, which Mr. Garnier handed me this morning, the day he sends his mail to Calais.

Besides, there is little going on here except the news of the Boston evacuation. The news arrived three days ago. The evacuation happened on March 17th. The English general's and the officer's letters date from the 24th, on board the ships leaving for Halifax, without having destroyed Boston, without having removed their guns, and without being bothered while embarking by the local people, who no doubt are glad to see them go.

The government, at this news, take on a look of approval, mystery and even intelligence. They would like it to appear as a scheme ordered by the ministers. But it does not work. It is too obvious that it is the want of victuals which prevented the English from staying in Boston any longer. It reminds me of last winter in France. When my news told me the English were suffering all kinds of shortages, Milord Stormont would answer, with a sublime imposture,[24] that the king's troops were taking it easy, their feet on the logs, drinking punch, while the rebels were starving in the cold snow. Everything turns up finally. Then it's so embarrassing.

That evacuation, General Lee's entrance with 22 000 men in New York, whence he sent away all suspected people, and those Hessians who you tell me are still at home, although they are supposed here to have left a long time ago--all of that confirms what I bade you in my last mail: that the Americans are doing well on all

---

[24]This expression will reappear in the <u>Observation</u>s, par. 62.

counts, except for powder and engineers. Ah, M. le Comte, powder and engineers, please! I don't believe I have ever wanted anything so much.

Milord Rochford told me again this morning that he is turning down the viceroyalty because Lord North does not want to lose the fruit of the 200 000 guineas he spent in order to establish Ireland's present form of government, by allowing the viceroy not to live there continually, a condition without which Lord Rochford would not accept the offer. It's too bad. We could have learned directly from Ireland all the interesting news about that island. It might have been useful.

Count Lauraguais is now back in his place after being forced to go out and use the newspapers against Texier, but only, as he himself says, until he encounters an angry protector of that man, of a condition such that he could fight him without shame and avoid the ignominy of always having to face an opponent below him.

I don't doubt Mr. Garnier will send you the last episode in which he was forced to take part. But as he handled himself prudently and with dignity, and the Count with firmness and nobility, and Milord Holdernesse, who is the reason for the incident, with all due respect to the information sent by you on Texier, and finally since this lord has kicked the man out of his house--we can hope that all that fuss will finally, to use Rabelais' charming expression, endure into nothingness.

But I think any ambassador immediately succeeding M. de Guines would have had to be bothered by this upon his arrival in London, for either he would have to eat everywhere with Texier or he would not eat at all, and had he given explanations, he would have met with the same fate as Count Lauraguais. Duke Dorset came to my house on his way back from Garnier's, to obtain some explanations from me about Texier, which I gave him without any passion or animosity, but forcefully and truthfully, as I always do.

I thank you kindly for your help in my Aix affair.[25] I thank you also for the honorable encouragement the king's approval and yours have given me in my work. That's what I call success. And if anything could increase my enthusiasm, it would be the sweet

---

[25]The appeal of the LaBlache suit had been postponed.

reward of your kindness, which fills my heart with gratitude.

Truly, M. le Comte, a little exaltation in the heart of an honest man, far from making him less efficient, will give life to everything he touches and allow him to achieve more than he would have dared to undertake from his natural ability.[26] I feel that exaltation, which I must be prudent enough to direct for the good of the king's affairs. Keep me your kindness, M. le Comte.

I am still not saying a word about our heroine [Chevalier d'Eon], because she is raving on and I would get angry if I listened. But her brother-in-law has arrived. He is a peaceful man and if my heroine is not a detestable and ungrateful creature, he will bring her back to reason.

I told Milord Rochford this morning, that Lord Mansfield wanted very much his nephew Stormont to obtain the viceroyalty he was turning down. He replied: "A Scot! Can you think of it!" That's really funny. Their ministry is full of them. England offers a microcosmic picture of the universe, where general harmony is founded on the continual warring of all beings against one another. No other country in Europe can compare.

I am at His Majesty's feet, in the posture of his most respectful and grateful subject.

Enclosed is a letter from Count Lauraguais.

London, 8 May 1776, to Vergennes
(Ang. 516, no. 18; S.F. 864; Mor 2:206-9)

I would not send you the detail of the evacuation of Boston, which you will have soon, if I did not have very private news, and if all of this did not lead to certain reflections which are my only concern here.

What I had guessed eight days ago has been confirmed by the scores of private letters received in London from General Howe's packet. By dissimulating, the government saved themselves only the first embarrassing moment. It is obvious today that General Howe received no order from the Court, and that he was driven from

---

[26]This is the Rousseauan, preromantic aspect of Beaumarchais' personality. He believes in passion, in emotions.

Boston by force, on the one hand, and by want, on the other.

But here is something else. Far from having received orders or assistance, General Howe had been without news from England since October. This fact appears as incredible to me as to you, but the proof is unquestionable: the March 24 letter from General Howe, giving notice of his leaving, is addressed to Milord Dartmouth, who since last October is no longer Secretary of the Colonies. And the Court is forced to admit today that all they have been sending to Boston since that time has had to stopover in Antigua without being able to go through.

There even are in London a lot of wagers, five to one, that the first notice received from the fleet on its way to Halifax will come from . . . Ireland, because the winds constantly blow in that direction in this season.

Imagine what would become of the troops with victuals for 15 days only, four rations to six men! I knew that through indiscrete statements made by members of the private council, especially Lord Littleton; and Count Lauraguais, who heard it from General-Admiral Keppel, just confirmed it to me.

Here is the detail from Boston: On March 2, the attack started with a battery set up on the heights of Philips-Form. The 3rd, another battery joined in, on the Dorchester corner. The 5th, General Howe put six regiments to sea to attack that second battery. Contrary winds prevented him from getting close enough.

Two successive attempts were also prevented by the winds. Finally, General Howe, seeing he could no longer withstand infernal firing, began parleying. Messages having been exchanged for several days, during which the gun-fire and bombing had been suspended, General Howe blew up the William castle, attacked by the provincials as well as the city. This precaution saved the fleet, as this fortress commands the harbor. He destroyed a part of the small arms and had his troops embark hastily, without being able to retrieve either cannon or mortar. The cause of this hasty embarking was the news that, as the William castle was being destroyed, the provincials had decided on a general assault.

On March 17th, the English fleet, composed of 140 sails, that is to say scores of cargo ships and few vessels of the king, set sail for Halifax. The provincial fleet ran after them and captured ten to twelve of the worst sailers. The rest is now where it pleases God and the winds.

These news, which are far from insignificant, had kept the king's council in session last Thursday until after 3:00 a.m. The king himself had left only at 1:30 a.m. The opposition triumphs. And what a triumph! Englishmen against Englishmen, are they not?

However I see catastrophe impending and I am not the only one to. Chevalier Ellis, of the king's party, could not stand Lord North's asserting in Parliament that everything was for the best. "I don't know, he said rising, what it is that makes the noble lord try spreading a confidence that he no longer possesses, any more than anyone else in the council. I believe everything is at its worst etc." This speech, by a royalist and a worthy man, prodigiously impressed the audience.

In the last five days, four packet boats left from England: one for Halifax, the others for New York, Rhodes-Island and Quebec. The ministry really is at bay, and although the papers claim that the first division of Hessians has left from Portsmouth, it was still unsure two days ago whether Lord Germain would not go to that port to urge or force the Hessian general to set sail, which he does not want to do until all his troops have arrived.

I say the time is near when the Americans will be masters in their own country, and the nearer because General Lee, after he left seven thousand men in New York, has set out with the remaining fifteen thousand straight ahead for Quebec.

If the Americans have the upper hand, as everything leads to believe, are we not going to be sorry, M. le Comte, we did not yield to their entreaties? Then, far from having acquired, as we could have at little cost and without risk, rights to the gratitude of these neighbors of our islands, we will have alienated them forever. They will have won without us and they will make a good peace, against us. They will avenge themselves for our cruelty towards them.

Hey! What's two or three millions advanced without being compromised? For I can swear to you on my sacred word to see to it that they receive, even through Holland, all the assistance you want, without risk and without any other authorization but the one now existing between us.

Perhaps even for us to look as if we were trying will suffice, as I know that the Virginians have an abundant manufacture of saltpeter and that Congress, since South Carolina has joined, has decided that the powder which was manufactured only in Philadelphia would be made on location.

Moreover, the Virginians have seven thousand trained troops and seventy militia soldiers, plenty of iron, and they manufacture almost as many weapons as the rest of America together. But some engineers, engineers and powder, or money to get them! That's the result of all my conferences.

I am therefore awaiting news from you and from M. de Sartine. I beg you both to realize that only the bank of London trades in gold and knows exactly to the very penny what competition I give on those matters. Their grumbling about it must be the basis of my security. If you hear me, you will conceive why it is so important for me to be recognized as a genuine gold merchant. That's what I reported to M. de Sartine.

I had this letter taken to Calais by someone reliable and devoted to me.

10 May 1776, from Vergennes
(Ang. 516, no. 26, fol. 68; S.F. 866; Mor 2:209-11)

I have received the letter you sent me the 3rd of this month. You are hard to please if you don't consider the evacuation of Boston as important news. Although I don't know how and why it happened, I can't believe General Howe abandoned this stronghold wantonly and without necessity. I am not asking you what the ministers think or say about it. Most certainly they will try to keep a straight face in a bad game. That's their part vis a vis the public. But I am not convinced they are the happier for it. It was in Boston that they were to take the greatest part of their forces and from Boston that they were going to strike the greatest blows. Probably the insurgents were not generous enough to leave them open doors. They'll have a new campaign plan to make at the moment the operations should start. The result of that event that you look upon with such indifference may very well be that, even if the campaign is not totally lost, it will lag and they will do well to save themselves a few advantages they can use against the insurgents another year. I don't know if those lack anything for their defense but I do know they were clever enough to get from a neighbor of ours a huge quantity of munitions of all kinds and, whatever precautions may be taken everywhere to intercept the aid, they won't lack any as long as they are able to pay as well as I hear they have done so far. If you ask me where their mines are, I'll tell you ingenuously, Sir, I do not know; but they must not lack any resources when merchants are so eager to serve them.

I praise God that Count Lauraguais is rid of Texier. What an unworthy opponent! Had I been within reach, I would have spared nothing to keep him from entering the lists with that kind of man. Only in England can such people find support. That does not give me a wonderful opinion of the country in which you live. As Texier will not die of shame for having been unmasked, he will no doubt produce some jarring news to try and rehabilitate himself. Make sure M. de Lauraguais pays no attention to those, and does not go back into the lists after he has gotten out so honorably.

I can't understand anything in the conduct of your heroine [d'Eon]. Her semester is due and she does not pick it up. Perhaps she thinks her devil-may-care attitude will unsettle us. My mind is made up. I have exhausted whatever seemed to be due to the misfortunes of her sex. It's up to her to enjoy the happy lot assured her. No longer up to me to go any further.

You may count upon my friendship, Sir, etc.

London, 11 May 1776, to Vergennes
(Ang. 516, no. 43, fo. 144; S.F. 870; Mor 2:212-14)

You were certainly close to me, as you say, when I thought you were very far, and you put my sagacity quite at ease, by the tone with which you gave me to guess what you were saying quite clearly.[27]

I beg Your Excellency to forward the enclosed reply to my friend Hugalis.[28]

All the quarrels here have for eight days been turning upon the <u>quo modo</u> [the manner] of the Boston

---

[27]This banter refers to Vergennes' letter dated 2 May 1776.

[28]11 May 1776, to Hugalis (Morton 2:211), is an ostensible letter to fabricate some evidence of the purchase of Portuguese coins by private individuals wishing to speculate. The address, "Your Excellency," indicates a tongue in cheek tone.

evacuation. The opposition and the ministers are at each other's throats on that.

The doctors are discussing the reason for the patient's death. Let's leave them arguing around that big coffin. The couriers are getting here, one after the other. Day before yesterday, at 4:00 a.m., one arrived from Ireland, in the lieutenant's yacht. It is supposed to come from General Howe, swept onto the coast of Ireland, in accomplishment of the prophecy. The council met without delay.

One ship, named Elizabeth, Captain Figuice, has arrived since, with news relative to the distress of the fleet coming back from Boston.

Another ship, also named Elizabeth, Captain Campbell, has also arrived since at Dover. It comes from Philadelphia and has brought more than 700 letters. Tomorrow all the American papers news will be in the English papers. The truth is beginning to come out.

Lord Howe finally left Plymouth yesterday, on his vessel the Eagle, to join the fleet waiting for him at Portland and to set sail on Tuesday.

Last Monday, when Lord North asked the House for a one million sterling credit on behalf of the king, Colonel Barré, after a forceful and bitter preamble, demanded that General Howe's dispatches be put on the table before everything else. A debate of several hours ended in a refusal to show them: 174 for the king against showing them, 56 only for the opposition. Speaking for the opposition were Lord Cavendish, Mr. Hartley, Mr. Burke, General Conway, MM. Bing and Sawbrige, the Lord Mayor. On the other side, Lord North was seconded by Mr. Littleton the uncle and Mr. Ellis.[29]

Here is how General Conway sounded: Suppose the war were just, although I believe it to be infamous; suppose that our brothers' blood ought to be shed by our hands, is this a way, by God, to make war? Do you ship two thousand leagues away food that is needed right now by the unfortunate you are sending it to? Do you choose

---

[29]Edmund Burke (1729-1797); Henry Seymour Conway (1721-1795), not to be confused with General Thomas Conway; Isaac Barr (1726-1802), and Lord John Cavendish (1732-1796). David Hartley (1721-1813) was in constant correspondence with Benjamin Franklin and would later try to persuade him to abandon the French alliance, "the greatest stumbling block in the way of making peace."

the worst season to ship it? Do you send mercenary soldiers, sold by their princes, which soldiers can only strengthen the enemy by joining there the people from their own country? Do you set their departure for the 25th of March, when half of these troops, who run down the treasury of England, will not arrive before the end of May? Let's suppose they leave in the middle of June, they won't be in America and fit for marching at the most in September, cold and feverish in that country, and the campaign will be over for us before it is started. And you call patriots and enlightened ministers those who direct such absurdities! No, there is no more decency nor honor in the council of the king who governs us.

Mr. Burke gave the lie to Lord Germain who was stating that General Howe had neither parleyed nor capitulated. --Show your letters and I will get mine out, and the nation will know which one of us is deceiving the people.

Lord North, apparently dumfounded, blurted out this absurdity: That it was no more consequential for the success of British arms to move six thousand men from Boston to Halifax, than to get them out of Halifax to reinforce Boston. He was booed and Mr. Burke answered with utmost scorn: "Then, Milords, look upon General Washington's attack as a godsend, because if heaven had not within fifteen days dropped quails and manna to our troops in Boston, they would all have starved to death. But we must hope that Halifax, better equipped by our noble care, will furnish them torrents of milk and honey, since Halifax is the promised land of that campaign; and when the expenditure we made to take Boston and give it back has been shown to be over 1,700,000 pounds sterling, and last year each soldier has been costing the State more than 220 pounds sterling, you ask for money while promising success! etc. Such is the tone of the daily meetings, M. le Comte, in that tumultuous Parliament.

Today, the Duke of Manchester made a motion in the House of Lords to ask for the communication of Lord Howe's letters and to make the ministers accountable, on their heads, for the success of the war. They are still debating at this hour, 10:00 p.m.

The Lord Mayor accused Lord Sandwich and the admiralty, before the Parliament, of having loaded some of the king's vessels with contraband for America; and although there were only 36 voices for his motion, he proved a fraudulent exportations of colors, fine fabric, gauze, etc. The house had not adjourned at 3:00 a.m. There are 27 witnesses to be heard.

The minister was advised that Georgia, while declaring for the Congress, burnt ten vessels in one of the local ports, Savannah: nine merchant vessels and one frigate, the Nedhy. The loss of their cargo, destined for london, is estimated at 120 thousand guineas.

He has also received the sure information that the Americans have at least twenty privateers at the mouth of the St. Lawrence for the purpose of intercepting any assistance to Quebec, while Lee is marching towards it the whole day long. The privateers are to destroy anything they cannot keep.

There is a rumor among the opposition that Admiral Hopkins has taken over the isle of Providence and that he looking askance to the English islands. It was his fifteen sail fleet that had been seen near Jamaica. The ministers do not know where to turn. They are so upset that they did not prevent the American ship from putting in at Dover and flooding the country with news which dismay them.

I received last night with great pleasure your letters of May 4th.[30] Thank you very much indeed for the contents and the form. I hasten to finish this letter to send it to Garnier before he closes his packages. Will you do me the favor of having this letter copied for me. It is too late for me to do so before the mail leaves.

London, May 1776, to Vergennes
(Mor 2:215)

I am including with my long letter this private word for you alone. I hear from sure sources that Mr. Frenchman [Lauraguais] who appeared to me to be an essential relation in England, is absolutely devoted to Turgot. I believe you ought to know it.

Far as the Superintendent of Finances [Turgot] is from anything which does not concern domestic affairs, it is up to you to decide whether it would be fitting to place in London someone who shared M. Turgot's views rather than yours. On this important object you must take no one's advice but yours.

---

[30] These letters are not extant.

They worry a lot here about a certain long conversation Count d'Aranda[31] is supposed to have had with the king, and about alleged ministry changes. My heroine did tell me the other day: "I will not hurry. When my friend, Baron de Breteuil,[32] is a minister, I will get fairer treatment than from the present one." Her friends, she says, have arranged all that in France and have advised her. I hope that was unfounded advice.

London, 17 May 1776, to Vergennes
(Ang. 516, no. 43, fol. 144; S.F. 870; Mor 2:216-7)

I received last night your letter dated the 9th of this month,[33] as well as that of Hugalis, included therein. I needed no new urging to use prudence and push foresight as far as my lights will allow me, in whatever you seem to desire sincerely. I see, from the terms of Hugalis' letter, that my plan didn't even cross his mind. I will take pride in it only when two persons have approved it, the king and you.

Since your letter of the 9th, you have received some from me which prove to you amply that I do not attach less importance than you to the evacuation of Boston. It is so important indeed that I have regretted telling at someone's house, when the news was announced, the following bad joke, which was retained too much: "The English had the Boston disease. The Americans procured them an evacuation, which, far from being beneficial, is but a deadly bloody flux." The next day, the newspapers printed: "The case of Boston is not an evacuation, but a bloody flux." I was not mentioned fortunately. That will teach me to turn my tongue seven times.

The news of the 12th from France, is getting general attention, but the reaction in the high public is sad and even gloomy. They say Choiseul is going to recover his position and consequently, war is imminent. I don't know why they can't dissociate the idea of war

---

[31]The Spanish ambassador in Paris. He was a Freemason and organized a Gran Oriente in Spain in 1780. John Robison, <u>Proof of Conspiracy</u>, 1798.

[32]Louis-Auguste LeTonnelier, Baron de Breteuil (1730-1807), minister under Louis XV, ambassador to Vienna from 1775 to 1783. The Choiseulists, meeting at the salon Guémenée, were renewing their efforts to replace Vergennes with their leader.

[33]Letter from Vergennes of May 9 is missing.

from the name of Choiseul. I would bet the stock exchange will fall tomorrow. What gives the English such a keen apprehension against Choiseul is the honor given to Mr. de Guines and the choice of Mr. de Clugny,[34] known to be creatures of his. They are already sending Guines to Vienna and bringing back hence Breteuil, to set him behind your desk. That's a perfect arrangement, they say. We heard about it a long time ago.

To the devil with prognostics! I don't believe a word of it, and I would not talk to you about it, if I did not know that overworked as you are, you only see in your position the happiness of being useful to a good master, without paying attention to the intrigues, true or not, which put people in places around you.

Once more, I don't believe a word of it, but I am sorry to see these people acting as if they knew ahead of time all the secrets of the French cabinet. It gives an air of gossip and flightiness to whatever is done in France. At least, M. le Comte, you are the only one I let in on this nonsense, which has, however, a lot of repercussion here where the ministers believe Choiseul always made war or prepared for it in order to maintain himself in place.

Eight days ago, a packet boat from Virginia dispatched by Lord Dunsmore brought to the government news so bad that they announced that the trunk had fallen into the sea during a storm. Admirable cunning! Superior genius! Yesterday, another ship arrived from Canada. They fired a gun without entering the harbor. A small craft went out to the boat. A man jumped in it and the ship sailed away. This man ran all the way to London. But the purpose of his dispatch is unknown. Hence the current refrain: "The news must be very bad for them to be so mysterious about it!" I plan to leave on Tuesday morning.

Beaumarchais has been in touch with Arthur Lee for almost a year. The following letter is the first one exchanged between the two men. The last one is dated July 18.

---

[34]For Comptroller General of Finances in replacement of Turgot.

London, 23 May 1776, from Arthur Lee
(Wha 2:96; Dea 3:295; RG 76)

Monsieur Hortalez,

Be persuaded that Count Lauraguais cannot in any manner embarrass you. I pray you to consider, in your arrangements at the Cape, that the want of tobacco ought not to hinder your sending out your supplies to the Americans, for tobacco is so weighty an article that it will greatly impede the sailing of the ships, and the essential object is to maintain the war.
[Signed "Mary Johnston," written by a woman's hand]

Paris, Friday, 24 May 1776, to Vergennes
(Ang. 516 fo. 181; S.F.871; Mor 2:218)

I am arriving, very tired and worn out. My first thought is to request an appointment from you. It's 3:00 a.m. My black servant will be in Versailles when you get up, and back in Paris when I get up. I hope he will bring me the news I have been awaiting most impatiently, the permission to go assure you etc.
I sign because I am so tired you might not recognize my handwriting.

Paris, 5 June 1776, to Vergennes
(Ang. 516, no. 89; Mor 2:219)

I will have the honor of seeing you this afternoon, in order to conclude before I leave the matter of my funds, or rather your funds.

I had not yet finished the arrangement for my piastres [moiadores or Portuguese gold coins] with M. de Sartine, and that delay would have given me a competitor in my purchases in London, which would have caused the price to rise to my detriment. I made him see it and all has been settled.

I would like you to be kind enough to obtain for me a short interview with M. de Maurepas. I will whisper to you the purpose of it and you will be free either to ignore it or to know it, as you choose.

Paris, 6 June 1776, to Arthur Lee
(Wha 2:97)

I received your letter of the 23rd of May. I will perform my promises in the way I pointed out. I am about to send to the French Cape, on the island of San Domingo, a ship loaded with merchandise to the value of twenty-five thousand pounds sterling, besides cannon powder and stores; but this last article will arrive but in small parcels, on account of the risk. On your part, do not fail to send a ship loaded with good Virginia tobacco, and let your friend send in the ship an intelligent, discreet and faithful person, with powers to receive the money or merchandise and powder and to make the remittances in tobacco, which I can no more do without than your friend [code for Congress] can do without what I send to him; in a word, let him give his notes to my house for what he shall not be able to pay in tobacco, and make certain and solid arrangements with my agent at the cape for the future.

The captain, on his arrival at the cape, must inquire of the first magistrate, who is the merchant intrusted with the affairs of Roderigue Hortalez & Co., and he will introduce him to the correspondent of your humble servant.

Paris, 10 June 1776 [Receipt]

I have received from Mr. Duvergier, pursuant to Count Vergennes' orders dated the 5th of this month, which orders I have handed him, the sum of one million for which I will be accountable to M. de Vergennes. [signed] Caron de Beaumarchais

12 June 1776, to Arthur Lee, alias Mary Johnston
(Wha 2:98, dated 26 June 1776; Mor 2:219)

I refer to my previous letter of June 6, whose provisions I ask you to follow. The difficulties encountered with the ministers have caused me to form a company which will handle the assistance in munitions and powder to your friend without delay, in exchange for returns in tobacco at the French Cape, and always under the name of your servant

[signed] Roderigue Hortalez & Cie.

Versailles, 13 June 1776, 6:00 p.m., to Vergennes
(Ang. 516, no. 90; Mor 2:220)

The purpose of my little trip to Versailles was to beg you to obtain from M. de Maurepas a private interview for me before I leave, on Sunday at the latest, provided I have obtained from M. de Maurepas the interview, the day and time of which you will kindly let me know; the place, I know, is always Marly. It involves the secret affair about which we talked for such a long time the other day. But as it is top secret, even for you who have agreed to ignore it, I beg you to obtain this interview for an important affair whose purpose is unspecified. When you pass his orders on to me, I would be obliged if you could send back my little essay on the kings of France[35] and my letter from England which I cannot answer without having it.

I have the book, translated from English, on the history of Charles II[36] and I will hand it to you when I return to Marly. I plan to go through Versailles and report to you on my interview as agreed.

I have not yet given you my letter in ciphers [which follows immediately infra] because it is to leave only tomorrow in your London mail. And now that I am in Versailles I realize I foolishly forgot to put it in my secret portfolio. I will be punished by not seeing you tonight. You will receive it with a French translation tomorrow in your morning mail.

As you communicate with M. de Maurepas several times a day, I hope to receive his orders and yours on Saturday morning and to offer you my thanks on Saturday night, after I have seen him.

London, 14 June 1776, from Arthur Lee [Mary Johnston]
(Wha 2:97; Dea 3:296; Mor 2:221)

I have but one moment to thank you for your letter of the 6th of June, which I received safe this moment. I will do my utmost to answer your wishes; but I advise you, as I advise my friends, to consider always that the communication of sentiments [tobacco] is difficult, and for that reason we ought to do all in our power, without insisting on a certain and immediate return. [In ciphers] Consider, above all things, that we are not transacting a mere mercantile business, but that politics is greatly concerned in this affair. I have written on your account to our friend Vrayman.[37] I will write you more by next mail.

---

[35] The essay has not beeen located. The two men are studying history together.

[36] Charles Stuart, king of England, of a character similar to the kings of France, Louis XV and Louis XVI. The history of the great English revolution should have proved instructive to the minister.

[37] The manuscript seems to me to read Vrayman, true man, and not "Grayman" as printed in Morton. Could it be a cipher for Lauraguais?

16 June 1776, to Vergennes
(Ang. 516, no. 121, fol. 351; S.F. 876;
Mor 2:223 incomplete)

Here is the letter corrected.[38]

Mr. de Lauraguais, before he leaves for Normandy could very well go to Versailles and even to Marly to show to you and Mr. de Maurepas how displeased he is about your inaction. He is the one who told me an American commissioner had seen Mr. du Chatelet, and he will not fail to talk to you about it. I kept a negative attitude with him regarding any kind of action in favor of the Americans, based on the king's principles and the danger the insurgents would boast about our aid and bring about a general quarrel.

I am leaving[39] in two hours and will come back to offer you my respects in fifteen days, if nothing stops me.

21 June 1776, from Arthur Lee
(RG 76; Dea 3:297)

The army of England in America consists of forty thousand men, and their fleet of one hundred ships, of which but two are of seventy-four guns. Their officers, both sea and land, and engineers are good; they are well supplied with artillery and stores. Consider then, Sir, how difficult it will be for the Americans to resist such forces if they are not assisted by France with officers, engineers and large ships of war. You may send them out without the least risk. Ten French ships of war dispatched secretly, and to the Cape or Martinico, and joined with the American fleet, might scour the American coast and destroy the whole English fleet, dispersed as it is at present. Thereupon the land army, deprived of succour, would be easily defeated. And by this stroke the English navy would be mortally wounded. Do you feel that this will kindle a war between the two nations? But how will England be able to support a war without fleets, without colonies, without seamen and without resources? On the contrary, if you suffer

---

[38]Which one? Did the corrected letter please the minister? Did he fail to send it on to Lee?

[39]For Bordeaux and other ports where the business of Hortalez is being started.

America to fall again under the dominion of England, the latter will forever be invincible. Adieu.

Bordeaux, 21 June 1776, to Vergennes
(Ang. 516, fol. 368; S.F. 878; Mor 2:222)

Arrived yesterday in this city, my first concern is to write you today, for tomorrow's mail: that I have already arranged everything, that I am writing M. de Sartine, that I am sending him the various requests for his orders, which I beg you to help expedite, suggesting to him to let me have them as soon as he has signed them. I would like this matter to be answered by return mail.

I have the honor of including herewith a note which I beg you to hand to or to send yourself to the person you sent me to in Marly.[40] I believe I found a way to accomplish a great thing he considers as almost impossible, but which he seems to desire infinitely. You and he will probably be grateful that I thought over this project which can honor your humanity and which must bring glory to your persons and your administration.

I ask that no decision be taken for or against the great object of the last memorial of M. de Malesherbes[41] until I have conveyed my ideas to him when I return.

Kindly send the packet of orders from M. de Sartine in care of the Hotel des Princes, in Bordeaux, which I will not leave until I have received and accomplished them.

A little seal under the envelope of the letter which I am sending you open, before you pass it on. I will always proceed in this manner.[42]

---

[40]Dalsème and Morton suppose this person was the king. Why not Maurepas?

13Lamoignon de Malesherbes (1721-1794), member of the Academy of Sciences and the French Academy, was in charge of the king's household between 1775 and 1776. He had already resigned when Beaumarchais made this pressing appeal. Head of censorship until 1768, he had saved Diderot's papers. He tried to defend Louis XVI before the Convention and died on the guillotine in April 1794 with his daughter, son in law and grandchildren.

[42]This paragraph and the preceding one are missing in Morton.

I have just heard that I can levy, without harming the service, five hundred quintals of powder at <u>Chateau Trompette</u>. Consequently, I am including herewith a petition to Count Saint-Germain on this subject. I beg you to have it answered quickly and positively. That's the part I will use first. You will be most kind to let me have this order with those of Sartine, which should be all be addressed to the same names used for the requests, and the whole under envelope addressed to my name at the Hotel des Princes, in Bordeaux.

Paris, 3 July 1776, to Vergennes
(Ang. 517, no. 4; Mor 2: 223-4)

I have just arrived from Bordeaux and I would have given the news in person if my carriage had not broken down eight miles from here. I left it there together with all my clothes. If Mr. de Sartine's packages have not left for Bordeaux, I will receive them from his hands myself.

I have done all my business or rather that of the king to my greatest satisfaction, about which I will report to you in the morning. But I very much regret that my brother-in-law,[43] in an excess of indignation, has gone and bothered you about the stupid thing they have done to me here while I was away. What does this have to do with you, who never did anything like that to anyone and whose actions have been so beneficial to me. You can believe I know everything the <u>quare</u> [the why] and the <u>quo modo</u> [the how]. They felt it was better to get rid of me than to employ me. The truth will out and then let anyone blush who needs to![44]

If the Sartine packages have left, it will only be overabundance, and at any rate there will not be a minute lost. If you were kept from seeing me tomorrow, the carrier of this letter is supposed to wait for your orders.

I did not go to Aix, for one must run to what's most urgent and I never employ anyone else when I can perform by myself.

---

[43]Miron, husband of one of his sisters.

[44]The Parlement had rejected his application for an extension of time in which to appeal the sentence of 26 February 1774. It was granted after his case was pleaded by the attorney Guy Target, 12 August 1776 (Gudin 1888, 189-194).

Versailles, 13 July 1776, to Vergennes
(S.F. 1339; Mor 2:224)

I beg you to hand this draft of letter to M. de Maurepas the first time you see him. As I have become a time merchant and as it is a precious commodity, I waste as little as I can. And as your mediation is always infinitely dear to me, the first thing that occurs to me is to beg you to accelerate, by handing this to Maurepas, the invaluable effect of his kindness and yours.

M. de Saint Germain to see.
The artillery to decide.
The Spanish Ambassador to tap.
And your servant to protect always.

13 July 1776, Barbeu-Dubourg to Vergennes
(Ang. 517, no. 26, fol. 57; Don 1:490 incomplete)

Your Excellency,

I saw M. de Beaumarchais this morning, and seeing I was authorized by you, I conferred with him freely. Every one knows his wit and his ability and no one recognizes more than I do his honesty and discretion, his zeal for whatever is noble and good. I believe he is one of the gentlemen the most qualified for political negotiations, but at the same time the least qualified for business. He loves luxury, he keeps young ladies, I am told, he has the reputation of a money killer and there is no merchant or manufacturer in France who does not consider him as such and who would not hesitate in doing any business with him. I was therefore astounded to learn from him that he has charge not only of consulting with you but of concentrating in himself the whole and the detail of all the commercial operations, export and import, war munitions as well as ordinary merchandise, from France to the united colonies, and from the colonies to France, the management of all business, the regulation of prices, the contracting powers, engagements to take, recoveries to make, debts to pay, etc. I agreed with him that the result would be the advantage of carrying all these operations a little more secretly, but I argued that by taking over this immense trade and excluding therefrom people who had gone to such expenses, endured so much fatigue and run so many risks for a year for the service and on the request of the Congress, he would only give rise to cries of monopoly and really inflict a wrong on those people who deserve better. He told me this would not inflict any loss on them and put forth all his eloquence to prove it to me from a to z. I confess these particular reasons would not suffice to balance that of the necessary secrecy in such a critical conjuncture, but I may be allowed to suspect there are other ways, even better ways to insure that important secrecy, because certainly M. de Beaumarchais, in spite of his genius, would not be able to dispense with hiring at once many employees, always less discreet than the merchants whose main objective is to hide their speculations from everyone. But I come back to my first and main reflection and beg you, Monseigneur, to ponder it carefully. There may be one hundred, a thousand persons in France, much less talented than M. de Beaumarchais, but better able to carry on your objectives by inspiring more confidence in those they will have to deal with, either Frenchmen or Americans, in towns, ports, manufactures, etc. I have advised MM. Deane and Bancroft to talk little between themselves and even to change their names; and I will tell everyone, including Lauraguais and LeRay, that I have not seen them again and that they obviously were sent back suddenly and without fanfare.

16 July 1776, to Dr. Dubourg
(Ang. 517, no.42, fol. 107; S.F. 882; Mor 2:225)

Until Count de Vergennes showed me your letter, Sir, I was unable to grasp the true meaning of the one you sent me. This gentleman "who neither wants or can take it upon himself with me" made no sense. I can see now that you wanted to take time to write the minister about me. But to obtain true notions from him, was it necessary to give him some false ones? Hey, what do our affairs have to do with my being well-known, a big spender, keeping girls, etc. The girls I have been keeping for twenty years, Sir, are your very humble servants. There were five of them, four sisters and a niece of mine. In the last three years, two of these kept women have died, most regrettably. I no longer keep but three, two sisters and a niece; which is still rather lavish for a person like me. But what would you have thought, had you known I was keeping men as well? Two nephews, very young, rather pretty, and even the most unfortunate man who fathered such a scandalous philanderer?

As to luxury, it's even worse. For three years, finding lace and embroidery too plain for my vanity, have I not been conceited enough to insist on the most beautiful plain muslin on my wrists? The most superb black cloth is not too beautiful for me. Sometimes I even went to silk, when the weather was warm. But pray don't go write these things to M. de Vergennes, you would ruin me with him.

You had your reasons to write him about me, although you do not know me. I have mine not to be offended, although I have the honor of knowing you.
You are, Sir, a gentleman, so eager to do a great deed, that you felt you could permit yourself a little bad one in order to succeed. That's not exactly gospel morals but I have seen many people making do with it. It's in that spirit that the Fathers of the Church, in order to convert the pagans, would sometimes take liberties with quotations, holy slander, which they would call between them "pious frauds."

Enough pleasantries. I am not angry, because M. de Vergennes is not a small man and I can rely on his reply. I grant that those I will ask for business advances may distrust me, but for those who really care for the common friends who are involved here, let them think twice before turning their back on an honorable man who offers to do all the favors and advance all monies useful to those same friends! Do you hear me now, Sir?

I will have the honor of seeing you this afternoon, early enough to find all of you still together. I now have the honor of being your most humble and obedient servant, doing business under the name of Roderigue Hortalez & Cie.

18 July 1776, to Arthur Lee
(RG 76)

I have received two letters from you, dated June 14 and 21, after I returned from Bordeaux where I had gone for our common affairs. I will answer them as soon as I travel to London, in the near future.

Count Lauraguais is leaving for England. In spite of what Dr. Dubourg might have told you, do not confide in him. That is absolutely forbidden to me.

Paris, 18 July 1776, to Vergennes
(Ang. 517, fo. 119; S.F. 883; Mor 2:227)

I have the honor of sending you my letter to Mary Johnston [Arthur Lee], so you may kindly put it in your packet. I plan to inform you tomorrow morning about my conferences with the Doctor. He started in a hostile mood and ended confiding in me. And since it is my rule to walk always under your eyes, I am sending you, so you may laugh for a moment, the copy of what I replied to his dinner invitation, when he wrote you I was keeping women. The good doctor, seeing I was not angry, decided to talk to me freely. Thus, the Turkish women, unable to deceive their husbands, find pleasure in loving them.

I am mailing this for fear your courier will leave before I arrive in Versailles.

Ogreman [d'Eon's brother-in-law] came to see me. But, according to what he told me, I felt he would need a new little lesson from you about his sister-in-law before he leaves. They are still asking for one hundred écus[45] and his entire annuity insured in England. I will tell you all he related to me about that.

---

[45]One ecu equals three livres. Ten livres equal one pistole. Twelve deniers equal one sou. Twenty sous equal one livre tournois or francs.

Now starts the cooperation between the Connecticut patriot and Hortalez. Unfortunately, Silas Deane is accompanied by the double agent Edward Bancroft, paid by Congress, by Deane and by the British government. The "devil" has entered into Hortalez's affairs. In Versailles, frantic frustration and doubts about Hortalez.

Paris, 18 July 1776, to Silas Deane
(MS Conn. H.S.; Dea 1:144-5; Mor 3:9, dated 14 July)

    I do not know, Sir, whether or not you have someone available to translate French letters dealing with confidential matters. I will not be able to do it freely with English letters until someone arrives from England, who will serve as interpreter between us. I can inform you, however, that having been for a long time desirous of helping the brave Americans to shake the yoke of England, I have already attempted in several ways to open a secret and sure commerce between the Congress and a company I am organizing for that purpose. Either by way of our islands or directly, I will manage to supply the continent with whatever the Americans need and can no longer procure from England. I have approached in this regard a person in London who claims to be devoted to the interest of America, but our connection since I returned from England having been difficult and in the form of a ciphered correspondence, I have not received any answer to my last letter, in which I tried to set down the basis of this great affair.

    Since you, Sir, have a character which can be trusted, I ask for nothing better than to resume with you, in a more secure and consequent manner, a negotiation which can only be considered as having been tentative with anyone else. My means are not extensive as yet, but they can increase infinitely if we succeed in establishing together an agreement based on suitable conditions and exact execution.

    I cannot grant to Mr. Dubourg or anyone else but yourself, Sir, the confidence necessary to freely talk about the trade I plan. But after you have compared the nature of the offers which you will receive all around with the disinterested zeal which binds me to the American cause, you will feel the difference there is between dealing with ordinary merchants, on the hardest conditions, and the good fortune of meeting a generous friend whose pleasure it will be to prove to your nation and to you, their secret representative, Sir, how devotedly, I am, Sir, etc.

20 July 1776, from Deane (Paris, Hotel Grand Villars)
(Dea 1:153-4)

In compliance with your request at our interview of yesterday, I send you enclosed copies of my Commission and an extract from my Instructions, which will fully satisfy you of my being authorized to make the purchases I have applied to you for. To understand this extract it is necessary to inform you that I was ordered to make my first application to the Ministers and to procure the supplies wanted of them, by way of purchase or loan, and in case the credit or influence of Congress should not be such under the present circumstances as to obtain them from that quarter, I was instructed then to apply elsewhere. My application to the Minister, and his answer I have acquainted you with.

With respect to the credit which will be required for the goods and stores which I propose to engage of you, I hope that a long one will not be necessary. Twelve months has been the longest credit my countrymen have ever been accustomed to; and Congress having engaged large quantities of tobacco in Virginia and Maryland, as well as other articles in other parts, which they will ship as fast as vessels can be provided, I have no doubt but very considerable remittances will be made within six months from this time, and for the whole within the year. This I shall in my letters urge Congress to do, but the events of war are uncertain and our commerce is exposed to be affected thereby. I hope, however, that at least such remittances will be made you, that you will be able to wait for whatever sum may remain due after credit we shall agree on is expired, having the usual interest allowed you.

I send you also an invoice of the clothing and of many of the articles of furniture and stores necessary for our army, in which I cannot be so particular at present as it will be necessary to be hereafter in case you undertake, but as the articles for the uniforms can at this time be ascertained as well as ever, I have made out the detail of them.

Though my instructions speak of but 200 Brass Cannon and of arms and clothing for but 25,000 men, yet considering the importance of these articles to America, I shall, if to be obtained, venture on a larger quantity. The probability of some part being taken, with other circumstances, will I think fully justify me therein. But it is improper to add on this subject until you resolve whether you will undertake, and on what terms---which I presume you will do.

As soon as you shall have obtained a translation of this and of the enclosed, I will do myself the honor of waiting on you, and in the meantime, am with the utmost respect and attachment, etc.

Paris, 22 July 1776, to Deane
(MS Conn. H.S.; Dea 1:154-6; Mor 3:10)

I am going to repeat to you, Sir, what I had the honor of telling you last Saturday, so that the conditions I am asking for will be more fixed in your mind. My means for helping the united colonies are not as extensive as the desire I have to do so. It will take an uninterrupted circulation of returns for my shipments to put me in a position to renew my first efforts and to spread their effect on larger amounts of money. Moreover, it would be impossible for me to follow exactly the order and the description of the supplies you need. Not all of them can be had as easily and as quickly. My engagement cannot, for the present, go beyond doing my best to approximate your requests. Having your invoices under my eyes, I will make the orders but the objects will arrive to our ports unevenly, and the totality may not be completed until after several shipments have gone.[47] We also agree that the American vessels which will land on our coasts will be loaded with whatever the warehouses in the port will contain without choice of troops divisions, since any apportionment can be done exactly only after all these goods have arrived in America.

We also agree that the first ships which will arrive loaded with goods from your country will begin the circulation of returns to my benefit, so that I will be able to have those goods sold and thereby increase both my means of action and the confidence of my friends who will invest new funds in my business.

We also agree that the stores which the risks of the sea, or such other perils, will prevent me from directing straight to the continent will be sent to our islands in the gulf; and that for another circulation of the same kind as the European one, all the American ships which can land there with goods from the continent, or which can pick up in those warehouses the

---

[47]The next sentence was left out in the printing of the Deane papers.

stores I will have sent there, will take them away and will do a kind of cabotage from our islands to the continent and from the continent to our islands, so as to strengthen our trade as much as possible.

As to the value of the return merchandise, I plan to base it on the exact worth of their sale in Europe, all expenses deducted. I will give for the net sums I obtain receipts on account; and I promise you, if your principals are faithful to these conventions, as I hope they will be, always to use these return funds for new advances.

One year is rather long for the balance due, but as the current situation does not permit us to contemplate a shorter term, I accept it without making it a condition of our agreement, and of course, nothing will be subtracted on all subsequent cargoes arriving in France, which we destined in advance for the satisfaction, in whole or in part, of the debt that you are contracting on behalf of your country with my company.

Regarding the prices to be affixed to the goods from Europe; they will depend on the amount of care, efforts and expenses involved in getting them to their authentic destination which is the continent. As I believe I am dealing with a virtuous people, it will suffice for me to keep on my own an exact accounting of all my advances. Congress will choose either to pay these goods at their usual value, at the time of their arrival, or to receive them according to the purchase price, the delays, the insurance, with a commission in proportion to the efforts, which cannot be fixed today as it is impossible to foresee the kinds of obstacles and hindrances we will have to overcome, or the costs involved. I mean to serve your country as if it were my own, and I hope to find in the friendship of a generous people the true reward of my endeavors, which I am devoting to them with pleasure.

You may, therefore, Sir, do me the honor to come and arrange the detail of these things with me. I am asking from you all the discretion which you feel we need, in order not to attract the attention of the English Ambassador, and not to alarm our ministers through that Ambassador's complaints, which would give us some strange difficulties. What you and I have to do in first priority is to slip between everyone's fingers and not cause anyone to squeal while we do our business.

22 July 1776, Deane to Conrad A. Gerard[48]
(Etats-Unis, 1, no. 40, fol. 136; S.F. 573; Dea 1:159)

Inclosed I send you a copy of the Article of my Instructions which was the subject of our last conference. I have not as yet had the pleasure of seeing Monsieur Beaumarchais, but am so confident from the character I received of him from you that he will be able to procure for me the articles I want, that I shall apply to him in preference to any other person; and I imagine through him the stores mentioned in my instructions may be procured with the utmost secrecy and certainty.--They will amount to a considerable sum, and as the colonies expect, and are willing to give a commission for negotiating the business, this concern may turn very well to his account, without his having much trouble in the affair.

24 July 1776, Deane to Beaumarchais
(Dea 1:159-61; Mor 3:12)

I have considered the letter you honored me with the 22nd, and am of the opinion that your proposals for regulating the prices of the goods and stores are just and equitable. The generous confidence you place in the virtue and justice of my constituents affords me the greatest pleasure, and gives me the most flattering prospects of success, in the undertaking, to their, as well as your satisfaction, and permit me to assure you the United Colonies will take the most effectual measures to make you remittances, and to justify in every respect the sentiments you entertain of them. But at the same time, as the invoice for clothing only, and without the incident charges, amounts to between 2 and 3 million livres, and as the cannon, arms and stores will raise the sum much higher, I cannot, considering the uncertainty of the arrival of vessels during the war, venture to assure you, that remittances will be made for the whole, within the time proposed, but in that case, as I wrote you before, I hope that the interest on the balance will be satisfactory.

With respect to cargoes sent from America either to France or to the West Indies, designed as remittances for your advances, I think there can be no objection to their being sent to the address of your house in France, or to your agents when they arrive.

---

[48]Vergennes's clerk and future French ambassador to the United States.

I find that cannon, arms and other military stores are prohibited and cannot be exported, but in a private manner. This circumstance gives me many apprehensions, for I cannot have those things shipped publicly, I cannot have them purchased openly, without giving alarm, fatal perhaps to our operations. In this case various deceptions and impositions may be practiced. You know that the Ambassador of England is attentive to everything done by me and that his spies watch every motion of mine, and will probably watch the motions of those with whom I am connected in this situation, and being a stranger in a great measure to your language, I foresee many embarrassments, which I know not how to obviate, and such as I fear may greatly perplex even yourself, notwithstanding your superior knowledge and address.

Two things, you will agree with me, are as essential as even the procuring of the cannon, arms etc., first that they are good, and well laid in, and that they be embarked without being stopped and detained. The fate of my country depends in a great measure on the arrival of these supplies. I cannot therefore be too anxious on the subject, nor is there any danger or exposure so great, but what must be hazarded, if necessary, to effect so capital and important an object. I pray you to consider this subject, and to give me your thoughts upon it.

I called on you this morning with Dr. Bancroft to have conversed on this subject, but found you was [sic] to Versailles. Permit me to urge your early attention to this subject.

Paris, 25 July 1776, to Vergennes
(Ang. 517, fol. 159; S.F. 885; Mor 2:232)

I am getting back from Bordeaux the order Count de St. Germain [minister of war] and the refusal of M. de St. Paul, Artillery Commander at the *Chateau Trompette*, as well as that of the artillery guard at Blaye, to deliver powder to my correspondent in Bordeaux, until Mr. Hortalez himself comes and signs the affidavit to replace it. In vain was it answered that Mr. Hortalez had signed an affidavit with Count de St. Germain himself. They persist in saying they have their orders on this matter.

In order to remove those eternal difficulties, I am sending you back St. Germain's letter with the model of the order he must give in Bordeaux and in Blaye for the delivery of the powders. Barring that, it is absolutely impossible for me to proceed.

I have received none of the letters from M. de Sartine. I am going to send him a similar model of order for the different ports; and we will start over on new expenditures.

I saw Mr. Deane this morning and we parted quite happy with each other, counting on meeting again on Sunday. He will bring me the statement of his needs and I will do my best to satisfy them.

He asked me not to tell the doctor [Dubourg] that he had seen me, because that doctor wanted to give him suppliers among his friends. I certainly will not, I told him.

Have you tried to get me the cannon I am asking for? What do 100 pieces of 4 matter on the 1700 pieces at least of this caliber that fill the King's warehouses? The matter of the coat of arms [of France on the cannon] is cleared up. They will be removed safely. Do I have to go the foundries? That would be even more dangerous. That's the only matter which bothers me and it is the most pressing of all. If my other business calls me tomorrow to Versailles, there will be no hope yet for me to get an answer from you on these matters. I will nevertheless have the honor of presenting you the respectful greetings of your most devoted servant.

I think there is no need to send you St. Germain's letter to Hortalez. I am enclosing herewith the model only for the ministerial order to the artillery commander, etc.

What about the Spanish ambassador! I am going to need him now.

Paris, 26 July 1776, to Vergennes
(Ang. 517, fol. 174; S.F. 886; Mor 2:233)

It isn't because I didn't wish or need to, that I did not have the pleasure of presenting my respects to you the last few days. But I am stalled by the Keeper of the Seals' cavilling about forms; and the difficulties they put in my way are the hydra's heads. All these obstacles tire out M. de Maurepas and exhaust his good will, and I suffer and I am without [civil] status.

Tomorrow I think I will be able to take bring him a counsel's opinion on a subject which did not require any, on a formal declaration of the king about an item they contest as obsolete, and a new form of letters patent, although those I gave them were done under the chief magistrate's eyes. There's no end to it. The rehabilitation keeps me awake and working at night. The press of business more than devours the time of day, which grief and contradiction render more exhausting.

How quickly harm is done, how slow good is! My just hopes are destroyed four times a week, and for nearly two months I have been unable to procure valid orders for our ocean ports. During the ten days I was in Bordeaux, I lost in Paris two considerable law suits, and it's been one hundred days I have been working to set up an essential undertaking which everything seems to deny my zeal for the king's service! Patience!

More nonsense! They are trying to suppress the discount bank [caisse d'escompte][49] before it is opened. It is a shame thing which a sensible man, a good Frenchman cannot bear without indignation. This might considerably damage M. de Maurepas' reputation. I have written him to that effect today; and to keep in all matters my secret pledge with you to think aloud in your presence, M. le Comte, I entrust to your good judgment the rapid reflections this news suggested to me. Lift one side of the envelope, read my letter, and put a little wax under that side before passing it on to M. de Maurepas. Thereafter, find a way to switch the conversation to this matter and if you share my opinion, let your thunder be heard against the infamous thing they are preparing today. Your reflections will hit harder than mine. Let us join together to keep him from yielding on a matter of interest to the State and to himself.

My trust in your intelligence and my respectful attachment to your person are without bounds; it is with those sentiments I mean to pay my debt to you.
- - -
Please send my letter on to M. de Maurepas as soon as you have read it.

I hope I will have the good fortune of paying my respects to you tomorrow, Saturday.

Paris, 26 July 1776, to Deane

---

[49]Gudin (1888, 197) says that the parties who wanted to see banking organized in France asked Beaumarchais to intervene with the ministers. Many still had bad memories of the Law bankruptcy some fifty years before and opposed such reforms.

(MS Conn. H.S.; Dea 1:162-4; Mor 3:13)

We will talk about your gratitude and that of your country, Sir, when the service has been done. We are now only trying to get it done. The reward I will value the most will be to be looked upon as a true friend of the noble supports of your freedom. As to the monies due, only in equity will they be assessable, according to the testimony that you will be able to give your constituents, regarding the activities, the zeal and the resources we have used to overcome every obstacle.

Don't try to look for cannon or other arms. You are too new in this country to succeed in procuring any of these objects. They cannot be found anywhere, of the good quality you need, except in the King's arsenals and warehouses. I may be able to find some to buy, in toto or in part, among the surplus of what is needed for the service--but I cannot do it without extreme precautions, by disguising the buyer's name, their use and their destination. Several persons are going to handle this secretly on my behalf. I will do whatever is necessary, including giving bribes, to know the quality and volume of the artillery we can procure. Do not worry.

But it seems to me impossible, in case I can fulfill your requests, that such a train of artillery leave without conductors, or even officers, for with such a peaceful people as the Americans have been till now, everything pertaining to military tactics must be unknown, and the science of using artillery being the most difficult part of it, you must not hesitate in following Mr. Arthur Lee's first plan, which I talked to you about, and which consisted in sending engineers and officers, and especially artillery men. If you are in agreement, I will secretly entice the best men, especially among the officers of fortune[50] who cannot be promoted except on merit and must work harder than the others for advancement. One of the most important conditions for our success will be that once arrived in the ports, the men, the arms, the munitions and the stores will find there ships ready to embark them on--for that's where too often starts the noise connected with secret embarkations. That's where the enemies keep their spies, and your main concern must be that each object will be far from our coasts whenever the notice arrives and gets to our ministers' ears.

---

[50]Military higher ranks in the French army were reserved to the noblesse of France. Officers of fortune were sometimes foreigners who hired out their services.

What cannot be done during the day will be done at night. We won't try to save money, the only thing that can make up for lack of power or authority.

If you will answer for the American ships, I will vouch for the European supplies, and nothing will leave from France for the service of our friends (excuse me for taking the liberty of talking about them this way), unless it has been tested and found to be of the best quality.

27 July 1776, from Deane
(Mor 3:14-15)

I received yours of yesterday morning and have given its contents that attention which so important a subject calls for, and on the whole I find no other method which appears probable but that proposed by you. I see the advantages to be such that I have ventured to give up the objections which I had at first and should still have under any other circumstances than the present. Your opinion has great weight with me on the subject, and your knowledge of men and their connections is so extensive and just that I must depend on you for the choice of proper persons and such whose talents may be of service to America and whose connections here may help to facilitate effectually our operations.

I hope that by the time the stores and goods shall be transported to the ports, some American vessels will be arrived on which they may be embarked, but as I cannot expect there will be a sufficient number I shall write to my correspondents to see if I can procure the vessels wanted; possibly I may engage some of them of my Friends here.

Dr. Bancroft sets out this day for London; if you have any commands, he will gladly receive them.

Paris, 2 August 1776, 7:00 p.m., to Vergennes
(Ang. 517, fol. 89; Mor 2:234)

I am carrying out an hour too late the sad errand you assigned to me. Prince de Conti died an hour before I arrived at his house. He lost consciousness, as I told you, last night at 2:00 a.m. and did not recover it. At 9:00 a.m. in the middle of his sleep, he was taken away mercifully. You know my grief.

I can't keep from telling you that while we were together this morning, Dr. Dubourg, that cruel babbler, was at Mr. Gerard's house with Mr. Deane whom he drags with him everywhere. He said he had come to separate his rights and mine, proposing to Mr. Gerard to leave me the political part of the American affair as well as all the prohibited goods and supplies, reserving for himself and his company all commercial operations, etc. . . You may judge what impression all that rambling, my name, politics, the Americans, must have had on Gerard, who certainly knew nothing about that.[51] I felt like beating that doctor up when he came out, but I restrained myself and turned away without a word. It's up to you, M. le Comte, to deliver us from that deadly scatterbrain. I would give up everything, were I obliged everyday to put up with such contradictions. Make up as you can for his indiscretion with Gerard, and as to that fool of a physician, I recommend him to you on your behalf and mine.

Versailles, 11 August 1776

I have received from His Excellency, Count de Vergennes, an acknowledgment for one million livres tournois which Mr. Duvergier had given the Spanish Ambassador, with which acknowledgment I will obtain from the royal treasury the said sum of one million tournois, for which I will account to the said Excellency, Count de Vergennes.
[Signed] Caron de Beaumarchais

Paris, 13 August 1776, to Vergennes
(Ang. 517, fol. 177; S.F. 889; Mor 2:235-6)

Mr. Deane advised me last night that his London correspondent informs him the English ministers know about his being in Paris and that orders have left for Milord Stormont to remonstrate with you forcefully about it. Deane is told that the English papers quote him about his alleged relations with the French ministers, etc. Deane says he is being tailed by a spy, but he begs you to believe he never committed the least imprudence. He assures me he never opens his mouth when he meets any Englishmen. He must therefore be the most silent man in France since he can't say ten words in front of Frenchmen. He is told also that Milord Rochford has left for Paris, has probably been here since yesterday or the day before. I am going to find

---

[7]Deane and Dubourg had been in communication with Gerard from the beginning. For letters between Vergennes and Dubourg, see S.F. 566, 570, 567, 880, 881, 882, 884, 887 and 888. The commissioner and the minister both kept it secret from the trusting playwright.

him, eager that I am to find out what commission he is probably charged with. You can therefore expect Milord Stormont's remonstrances, M. le Comte. I am not worried about what you will answer.

I forgot, the night before last, upon leaving Count de Maurepas at 9:30 p.m. to go and ask you on his behalf to write the Comptroller General that if his secret order had not left for the ports, he should hold it. Since M. de Sartine is sending an express, it is useless to multiply the number of people involved.

I thank you for not having me do this tiresome errand myself. M. de Maurepas told me this had just been arranged between you. I have such pressing affairs in Paris, and they are going so poorly as soon as I leave, that I thank you from the bottom of my heart for not asking me to abandon them at the height of a crisis.

I never saw M. de Maurepas as gay as he was when he left the council. That looked like a good omen to me. "God keep you in that mood, M. le Comte, I told him, and let us make hay while the sun shines. That's a fine job." I was not referring to the council but to what he had told me that morning. He appears to feel the way you wanted him to. Come on! If all is not well, all is not bad, either. That's the motto I feel like adopting from now on.

Receive the expression of my gratitude and please do not forget my poor bronze guns.

I have just received the letter for M. de Clugny and the one you honored me with. I am sending for Mr. Deane. He will here in an hour. If Mr. de Clugny is in Paris and I have to see him, it will be done today. And if I have to leave for Bordeaux, although I hate to do it, I'll be on my way as soon as the letters patent are registered. With secrecy, courage and speed, there is nothing in politics one cannot overcome.

I beg you to solicit with M. de Maurepas the prompt expedition of my letters patent.[52]

Friday, 16 August 1776, to Vergennes
(Ang. 517, no. 128; S.F. 1347; Mor 2:237)

You may be surprised you did not hear from me since your last two letters. My only excuse is that I could

---

[52]The paper giving him back his civil rights.

not find one hour to take care of it. Work in the city and in the office has been so pressing I could hardly breathe. Here are your letters and copies for the Spanish Ambassador I am sending to you. File closed. Plus, M. de St. Germain's letter and note. I saw the Comptroller general, the Farmers General, Mr. Deane. Everything is set. Mr. Deane is convinced that the vessels in question have come only to give him some funds through the sale of their salted fish. A new commissioner from Maryland, a friend of his, has just arrived from Holland.[53] He hurried to bring him to me. These gentlemen are sending some mail for Congress through Bordeaux by a shallop, an excellent sailer. We are agreed on the pay for a general officer, artillery or engineer, and all lieutenants and people necessary to that service. That's the fruit of several conferences in my office between him and Mr. du C.[54]

As a result, the two commissioners, the artillery man and the courier are dining at my house tomorrow. Each one will bring the work he has done for the Congress: some their dispatches, the other the assurance he will leave with the officers who are going; I, the letter containing the whole plan of active, reciprocal and perpetual trade between the firm of Hortalez and Congress, in a handwriting other than mine.[55] Finally, the courier will get firmly into his head all that he is taking with him, so that in case there is a need to throw everything into the sea, he will at least be able to give his message verbally when he arrives.

Resolved that all ships coming from America into our ports will be addressed to Hortalez and that the cargoes requested by that house will have priority on all others.

I will bring you the copy of my letter to Congress. Something surprising is that neither Deane nor I have received any direct news from those five ships, although I have a letter of August 10th from Bordeaux telling me three American ships are in the harbor, two warships and the third undecided as to what load it will take. They are supposed to be waiting for ships which left after

---

[53]That was William Carmichael.

[54]Tron on DuCoudray, artillery officer of the highest rank, about whom we will hear further.

[55]Hortalez to Congress, 18 August 1776, follows immediately.

they did, from New London, and from which there is no news. How, then, did Count de Maurepas get his?

I will send you as soon as possible my applications for artillery to Count de St. Germain. I will have to confer with him for the detail and especially about guns from Charleville I have to ask him for and which will later be replaced. My applications for artillery will not go until I have settled exactly what I want and where I want to take them, Strasbourg and Metz are so far, Holland alone can receive it and the Rhine carry it. Moreover, I will make an arrangement with the general supplier of artillery carriages and convoys to pick it up. I am meeting this morning with M. de la Porte for the salt. But so many things that must go forward together, without counting the textile manufactures, are forcing me to hire new employees. This politico-commercial affair is growing huge and I would drown in detail, I and the few clerks I have hired until now, If I did not get some help soon. Some will travel, others will reside in the ports, others in the manufactures, etc. I promised tobacco to the Farm and I am asking the Americans for it. Their hemp will also sell pretty well. At last, I am beginning to see clearly in my affairs.

The only business I can't understand and about which I have no news is that of those letters patent, although judges, lawyers, friends, relatives, even newspapermen, hurry to ask me if that's only a false rumor. They've scamped the suit that was killing me in three days in the council, and after six weeks I cannot have the first document necessary for the hearing that is to resurrect me! M. de Maurepas tells me every time he sees me: "It's done, it's all over." Last Sunday these letters were supposed to be with M. Amelot to be sent; I was to receive them on Tuesday. Friday is here, but not the letters. At the end of the court session, this three-day delay makes me lose three months because of the vacation.

I am not angry but very sad to see my civil status still equivocal and its return uncertain.

This is the first of a dozen letters addressed to Congress by Beaumarchais, who is ready to run arms and other military equipment, together with artillery officers, to embattled America. But British intelligence watches in every port and the deed is not done yet. It will be the end of the year, just as Franklin arrives in France, before the first ship, the Amphitrite, is ready to sail.

18 August 1776, Roderigue Hortalez & Cie
to the Committee of Secret Correspondence
(MS BN 327; Wha 2:129 (Eng.); HR 220:24-5; Mor 2:241-4)

The respectful esteem I have for that brave people who defend their freedom so well under your leadership makes me want to share in this great endeavor by forming a powerful commercial house, for the sole purpose of serving you in Europe, there to meet your needs of all kinds, to see to it that you obtain rapidly and under concession all the goods, cloth, canvass, powder, munitions, guns, cannon, even some gold for you to pay your troops--and in general everything that can help you sustain the honorable war which you have undertaken.

Your commissioners, Gentlemen, will find a reliable friend in me, a sanctuary in my house, money in my till, and every means of facilitating their public or secret operations. I will remove whenever possible any obstacle that European politics might oppose to your wishes. Right now and without waiting for any answer from you, I have procured for you about two hundred pieces of brass cannon, four-pounders, which will be sent to you at the earliest opportunity, two hundred thousand pounds of cannon powder, twenty thousand excellent guns, some brass mortars, bombs, cannon balls, bayonets, plates, cloth, linens, etc. for the clothing of your troops; and some lead to make musket balls.

An artillery and engineer officer of the greatest merit, accompanied by the lieutenants and officers, artillerymen, gunners etc. he deems necessary for your service, will leave for Philadelphia even before you have received my first shipments. That's the best gift, gentlemen, my attachment could offer you. Your commissioner Mr. Deane and I have agreed on the treatment we felt suitable for this officer, and I have found this commissioner's powers sufficient to warrant this officer's leaving under the commissioner's engagement towards him, the terms of which I have no doubt Congress will comply with.

The secrecy demanded by some of the operations I undertake for your service, also requires you to resolve absolutely to address all of your ships and the orders they carry, constantly and directly to my house so as to avoid gossip and waste of time--two things that are deadly in this business. I will receive from you notice of the cargoes carried by the ships you will send to our ports. I shall choose, in return for what I have sent, so much of their loading as will be suitable to me when I have not been able beforehand to inform you of the cargoes I wish, and I will help you unload, sell and dispose of the rest.

For instance, five American ships have just arrived in the port of Bordeaux, laden with salted fish. Although this merchandise, coming from abroad, is prohibited in our ports, as soon as your commissioner told me that these ships were sent by you to help him make his purchases in Europe with the money proceeding from the sale, I did everything necessary to obtain from the Farmers-General an order for landing it without any repercussion. I could even, if need be, take this salted fish cargo on my account, although it is of no use to me, and see that it is sold or used in order to simplify the operation and lessen the difficulties encountered by your merchants and commissioner.

I shall have, Gentlemen, in each of our ocean port a correspondent who, when your ships have arrived, shall wait on your captains and offer them every service in my power. He will receive their letters, bills of lading, and transmit the whole to me, even the things you would like to be forwarded safely to any country of Europe. After I have conferred with your commissioner, I shall see to it that they go safely on and the replies will also get to you through me, so that you will be spared a lot of anxiety and delay.

I request of you, Gentlemen, to send me before next spring, if you can, ten or twelve thousand hogsheads, or more, of Virginia tobacco of the best quality. It should be clear to you that I trade with you in Europe, that I make shipments from, and take returns in European ports. Although my house is well established and I have allocated many millions to your trade alone, I could not operate if all the dangers of the sea, going and coming back, were not entirely at your risk.

Whenever you choose to receive my goods in any of our windward or leeward islands, only let me know and my correspondent will be waiting for your orders there. Then you shall have nothing else to pay over the price except freight and insurance. But the risk of being captured by your enemies will still be borne by you, pursuant to the explicit contract I will make with your commissioner.

This commissioner should receive, as soon as possible, full power and authority to accept deliveries, receive my accounts, examine them, make payments thereon or enter into engagements which will bind you, as the leaders of the brave people to whom I am devoting my work; in short, power to deal with me continually about your affairs.

In spite of the overt opposition which must be shown by the king of France, his ministers and all the French administration agents, for everything that infringes on foreign treaties or the ordinances of the kingdom, I dare promise you, Gentlemen, that I will do my utmost to clear up difficulties, soften prohibitions, and in short pave the way for a trade which my advantage much less than yours made me undertake with you.

What I have just outlined above, Gentlemen, is only a general agreement, subject to any augmentation or restriction which future events may require of us. One thing can never vary or diminish; it is my loyal desire to serve you in every way I can.

By my signature, you will recall that one of your friends in London has for a long time told you of my good will and attachment for your interest. Look therefore upon my house, Gentlemen, as the center of all operations useful for your service in Europe, and myself as one of the most zealous partisans of your cause, the soul of your success, and with respectful esteem, etc.
--
I would like to add here, in conclusion, that every American ship which will not be directly armed or loaded by you, will be entitled to my good offices in this country; but that yours alone addressed to my house will have priority.

I must also warn you, Gentlemen, that about the nature of our relationship, it is advisable for you to use discretion even when reporting to Congress. Everything that goes on there, in your great assemblies, is known to the king of England, I don't know how.[56] Perhaps some indiscreet or treacherous citizen is giving in St. James Palace an exact account of your deliberations. In times of great exigency Rome had a dictator; and the more concentrated the executive power is in critical situations, the more effective it is and the fewer leaks there are to fear. It is to your wisdom, Gentlemen, that I address this remark; if it seems as just to you as it did to me, take it as another token of my ardent zeal for your rising republic.

---

[56]This reveals excessive candor under the circumstances.

19 August 1776, from Silas Deane
(Wha 1:132)

Since the stores and goods have been engaged and getting ready, I have made inquiry of several merchants respecting the charter of vessels for America generally, without mentioning what their cargoes should consist of, and have written in the said way to some of my correspondents, and in the whole I find I shall not be able to provide them so early as is necessary at any rate, and I fear not without making their destination and object too public. You will recollect that I mentioned my apprehensions on this subject some days since, and now propose (if consistent with your other engagements) that you would take the procuring of the vessels necessary on you, at least so far as to be security for the payment of their charter.

It gives me pain to put this additional trouble and expense on you, but I know that you think that nothing within your power is too great to be undertaken for the service of the United Colonies of America, whose grateful acknowledgments must equal, though they can never exceed, your generous exertions in their favor at this critical and important period of their affairs.

These vessels will return with cargoes on your account, which, with what will probably arrive from other remittances, will enable you to proceed to the greatest extent in executing the great and liberal plan you have proposed.

I shall do myself the honor of waiting on you tomorrow morning on this and other affairs.

29 August 1776, to Vergennes[57]
(Ang. 517, fol. 251; S.F.895; Mor 2:245)

I had the honor of seeing Count de St. Germain yesterday. The error came much less from him than from M. DuCoudray, who had the good faith of admitting it. I saw to it that it will not happen any more. M. le Comte you are no more courteous and helpful to me than Count de St. Germain was yesterday. That will tell you I was

---

[57]Another letter to Vergennes the same day (Ang. 517, fol. 247; SF 894; Mor 2:246), not included here because it concerns mostly the d'Eon affair, announced the arrival of Francy: "My secretary has just arrived from London, and Mr. Deane and I do chat together as quickly as our mutual curiosity warrants it."

pretty well received. When he learned that I was that very same courageous unfortunate man whose defenses he read in the newspapers, he said, with so much pleasure, he went into the most flattering detail, found in me the friend of his old friend Duverney, and a conversation of two hours, he asked me to stay for dinner. But the unfortunate who run to try to solve their lawsuits hardly have time for dinner. I left him; but I may hope I have one more protector. If everything is not well, not everything is bad!

I have drafted a letter apt to repair the error made on the artillery. I showed it to him. He thought it was necessary. That will be your reply to his letter. Excuse me, Sir, if I took the liberty of acting as your secretary, but I've been attached to you a long time by all kinds of titles.

If you approve the letter, it only needs a signature.

6 September 1776, to Vergennes
(Mor 2:250)

I have just been judged "deblamed" amidst general applause. Never has an unfortunate citizen received more honors. I hasten to let you know, begging you to present my heartfelt gratitude to the king. I am so overjoyed I can hardly hold the pen to describe to you the respectful sentiments with which I am, Sir, your very humble and obedient servant.

Please pass on to Messrs. de Maurepas and de Sartine my very happy news.

I am surrounded by 400 people who clap their hands, kiss me and make an infernal noise which sounds to me like a superb symphony.

6 September 1776, to Vergennes
(Mor 2:252)

I have the honor of introducing to you the owner of the Anglo-French paper named <u>Courrier de l'Europe</u>.[58] I

---

[58]Contemporary spelling is "Courier." The collection at the Newberry Center in Chicago has vols. 1-26; 1 Nov. 1776-29 December 1789. London, E. Cox. Semi-weekly "gazette of gazettes" written in French. The collections at BN and Biblioth que de l'Arsenal in Paris together offer 32 vols. On 8 October 1776 the paper was authorized to circulate in France after censorship in Boulogne.

had the honor of telling you how sorry he is about that bad paragraph which was inserted without his knowing it. He apologizes on his editor's behalf for this imprudence. His intention from now on is to limit that gazette, for all articles relative to France, to the strictest decency. He submits his paper to whatever censorship you please. The copy coming from London will be examined and corrected as you see fit and will not go to the printer until it has been found to be acceptable. With these precautions, M. le Comte, I don't think there is any inconvenient in favoring this branch of foreign literature which can amuse curious Frenchmen. Since most of the articles are taken from English newspapers, we will be up to date on English mores and London anecdotes.

15 September 1776 to Committee of Secret Correspondence (HD No. 220; Wha 2:146-7[59])

In writing this letter I imagine that you have been informed by my first one[60] of my active zeal for your interests. I therefore suppose you will acknowledge me as one of your friends and faithful servants. These titles I adopt with pleasure, as I believe I have deserved them. In addition to what I have offered you in the way of goods, I will presume, if I may, to offer you also something to think about. Living in Europe, I am better than you are, able to grasp the hidden considerations which give motion to the nations in this part of the world. Above all, I am persuaded that if you have shaken off the yoke of one of them, it is only to become a better friend for the rest. I will therefore venture to reason with you upon your present situation. However arrogant and self-confident your enemies affect to be, your Declaration of Independence has thrown them into consternation. As they no longer hope to bring you back artfully into the fold, they are beginning to fear they will not be able to force you into submitting. Their shattered finances, lagging

---

Abbot Aubert was the first censor.

[59]Wharton gives only a portion of the letter, in English. I have not been able to locate the French original. However, the English is transparent: it lets you read the French behind it, while it does not really translate the French into equivalent English. This is a translation problem which only comparative stylistics can solve. I have tried to improve therefore on the translation given in Wharton.

[60]The letter of August 18, 1776, to the same committee, above.

commerce, exhausted strength, plainly indicate that this is the last effort they will be able to make against you, and if you are brave enough to withstand the present campaign, it is almost certain that it will be the last one.

But, while you are fighting in America to free yourselves from their yoke, there are developments in Europe which may be used to hasten your deliverance. The blunder made by Portugal in closing their ports to you, with more imprudence than arrogance, seems to be a godsend in your favor of which you cannot too soon avail yourselves. For a long time Spain has been resentful of Portugal, so that, were I presiding your committee, Gentlemen, I would not hesitate in arguing that you should declare war against Portugal, and immediately thereafter send a fleet to Brazil. This bold and sudden step would be very beneficial. First, it would put Spain on your side and perhaps even cause her also to declare war upon Portugal. Henceforth you would become the allies of Spain, since our enemies' enemies are more than half-way our friends. Have no doubt that Spain would open her American ports to your warships and grant asylum to your privateers, receiving the prizes they may make on the Portuguese. If your declaration is fortunate enough to draw Spain in openly, as I have no doubt it would, such a diversion would soon force the English to divide their efforts in going to the aid of Portugal, unless they decide to give up this quasi--colony as well, which is not likely. Then if you gathered your own forces, you would have an immense advantage upon them. And you would be even more successful if Spain went into it openly. For France has to come to the aid of Spain with ships, troops and money, whenever Spain is engaged in a war, according to the terms of the Family Covenant, and therefore England will have to lend to Portugal a more considerable assistance. Then England won't be able any more to prevent France from opening her ports to you without reservation and permitting you to obtain there, by way of trade, plentiful supplies of every sort.

--What can we do, the French minister would say to the British Ambassador. The King, our master, is going to the aid of Spain not because he wants to make war but because he has to comply with treaties. If he wanted to make war, what would prevent him from taking this opportunity to make war against you? And if he does not want to make war to his rivals and almost enemies, why should he provoke others to make war against him? See what happened to Portugal, do you want us, in closing our ports to them, to provoke the Americans with whom we have no quarrel, to pounce on our American possessions or seduce them into separating themselves from us and uniting with them? Do you want them to lay waste our islands with their many cruisers, which are holding fast against England? In order to oblige the English, are we going to fall into the absurd situation of making war to the Americans on the one hand, and helping Spain against Portugal on the other, in concert with the same Americans?

This, Gentlemen, is what our minister would say, and I believe nothing could be replied. Who knows how far things would go in Europe as a result of such confusion of various and remote interests? All this may and probably will come about if you declare war against Portugal. This is the second opportunity I have taken to convey this suggestion to you. It seemed to impress your commissioner who always knows a good proposition when he sees one. I do not doubt he will also write you to this effect. I am therefore of the opinion, Gentlemen, that you cannot consider this proposition too soon and take a decision worthy of your courage.

18 September 1776, to Deane
(Mor 3:15-16)

If you will do me the honor, Sir, of coming to my house today for supper, the person I mentioned the other night will be there and we will start discussing the terms of the boat charters which will be offered to us. If they are such as I was led to believe, I think you must not hesitate. My guarantee being the first condition required, the deal must be negotiated at my house. Let me know if you will come so that I may tell the person in question and ask him to bring the proposal he has prepared.

As to the officers and their pay, I am still of the opinion that if you believe they can be of service to Congress, a little money more or less should not matter. The choice is a good one, and you cannot engage good people to leave their country, if you do not offer them more advantages than they would have staying at home. The very idea of bargaining appeared to repulse the leader.[61] Perhaps M. de Bellegarde would have been more modest; but it would be difficult to take him away from his present post, and besides the man we have is younger

---

[61]Tronçon DuCoudray showed the characteristic typical of French noblesse, in that he considered money questions below his dignity.

and more energetic. In ventures such as this one, spirited people seem to me to be the best choice. This affair must also be decided at my dinner. I will have to bend backwards to cope with the charters. Thereafter, you had better pray that the wind will blow toward us a few tobacco loads, for I will be broke.

If you have any news from America, bring them to us, please. We need to know that people there are true to the cause of freedom, to keep up our own enthusiasm.

21 September 1776, to Vergennes
(Ang. 518, no. 50; S.F.1384; Mor 2:253)

I have just sent to Mr. d'Ogny [Postal Superintendent] Mr. Swinton with a letter which Mr. d'Ogny will send on to you probably in the morning relative to the arrangement of postal costs for his English packages. As to the reading which will serve as censorship for each Courrier, have you decided anything? or would you have the package come to me, and that I give you an account as we go? The man seems to want it that way. I neither ask for it nor refuse it. It's up to you. There is more important.

We are looking very far for whoever has blown up the munitions affair, and I have just heard that the doctor is always doing public work on the subject. Baron de Rullecourt who has just left my house and who, in parentheses would like to lead to the insurgents a well disciplined corps of 600 men he has at hand, was sent to Mr. LeRay de Chaumont[62] or a Dubourg, his choice. He went to the former and found the latter there. They assured him that not only the French ministry would find it excellent for him to pass to that service, but that he would be given in writing in his pocket the assurance of this consent. If while we are closing the door on one side, they open the window on the other, the secret is bound to escape. Those babblers must be silenced, who like LaFontaine's dog do nothing and hinder those who do. Let them commit themselves if they choose but not the ministry!

I am asking you, M. le Comte, what's this Baron de Rullecourt and if I can put him quietly in touch with

---

[62]Jacques LeRay de Chaumont, wealthy high government official and Freemason friend of Franklin, who contracted to supply military stores for the Americans and would later be in financial difficulty because of it. After the arrival of Franklin, the Commissioners lived in his beautiful Passy property.

Deane. I did not tell him anything. Only promised to see him Tuesday morning. That Doctor wants to be included, no matter what the cost, and his agent is that Penet[63] whose prohibited shipments you are supposed to stop, to make an example of it. It would not hurt if you imposed on him again the law of rest, for it appears the Valcroissant and the Planta etc., etc. who find my door closed turn around in that direction. I hasten to let you know my discovery, while asking for your continued, precious kindness.

- - - -

I am going to drop by Count de St. Germain's to tell him nothing has changed on the moves from the land arsenals to the warehouses in the ports and to please avoid making any changes on the orders given. If I don't find him in Paris, I will leave something with his Swiss at the arsenal.

Pass on to M. de Maurepas the circumstance of the Dubourg and LeRay de Chaumont meeting and the necessity to silence them.

25 September 1776, to Vergennes
(Ang. 518, fo. 170; S.F. 898; Mor 2:255)

I am even more unfortunate than Cassandra, whose prophecies no one believed because she always announced calamities. I announce only good things, and I am told that I am taking for real the flights of my overheated imagination. I predicted the Americans would win and be soon rid of the English, and people ridiculed me. I predicted that if there was action in New York and the loss was even on both sides, the difference of situation would increase it a hundredfold for the English, and people shook their heads. I said that General Burgoyne, in bad terms with Carleton, could not pass the lakes for more than four months, and people doubted it. Let's prop my conjectures with a few news freshly arrived.

Nantes, 22 september 1776. By ship arrived two days ago and come in 26 days from Nantucket, Rhode Island, we received important advice that

1. Congress is still in Philadelphia and is not contemplating leaving.

---

[63]Penet & Cie (partner of Pliarne) of Nantes also contracted to supply Congress with arms in the winter of 1775 (Dea 1:181, 195-6, 412).

2. The Americans have declared their independence on July 4 and have not wavered since then.

3. Sir Peter Parker after being defeated in Charleston in South Carolina, has sent those of his ships that had been so mistreated to the western islands to be repaired, and has sailed with the others to join General Howe in New York.

4. General Dunmore, having been defeated in Virginia, was forced to flee on board a war-ship and abandon his post on Gurin Island. That a small ship arrived at Glasgow the 11th of this month brought the news that he was forced to evacuate Virginia and retreat towards General Howe.

5. The Americans have taken over the two important forts of Crownpoint and Ticonderoga. They are waiting there for Burgoyne who is master of Montreal but cannot advance because he lacks boats to pass the lakes which are going to freeze up while those are being built.

6. On August 12th or 13th, there was a very bloody scrap in New York. General Howe being camped on Staten Island in view of His Excellency General Washington, who was on Long Island, and having resolved to attack General Washington, made a pretense of landing his troops on one side of the island while landing them on the other. These took over a hill and surrounded the American army. The two sides having thus opposed each other for some time, the American generals realized their troops were going to be butchered in that sort of blockade, if they did not do something to regain the advantage. They summoned their soldiers to pounce, sword in hand on the English and go through their ranks; which they did with an awesome courage, and then attacked these troops from behind, disrupted and forced them to retreat to their ships. The loss is about equal on both sides and amounts to 11 thousand men, both English and American. But the latter have taken prisoners three generals, 15 major officers, several artillery officers, and a great many English soldiers.

7. It is not true that the provinces of Maryland and the county of Sussex on the Delaware have declared for England, as reported by the English gazette. On the contrary, the thirteen united colonies which comprise the whole people have all declared for independence; as Florida is counted for zero, as well as Nova Scotia, because of the very small number of their inhabitants.

That's the news, M. le Comte. You will kindly pass it on where advisable, while expecting the abstract of a very lengthy memorial which I am writing for the commissioner on the past, present and future of his country. He is expecting two other commissioners with new instructions, and it will soon be time for you to say either yes, or no. I'd go hang myself right away, if it was the latter. But I hope in the wisdom of the king's council sufficiently to look forward to a long life in the service of my master.

I am sending the news bulletin to the Spanish ambassador.

I forgot to copy the following from the same bulletin: we learn by the same ship that no peace negotiation is expected as a result of the powers given Lord Howe. He had made a few such attempts when he arrived by publishing declarations to this effect but he was laughed at and Governor Cook of Rhode Island, among others to whom he had sent a declaration, answered him with a copy of the Declaration of Independence.

Bravo, bravissimo.

14 October 1776, to Vergennes
(Ang. 518, fol. 265; S.F. 899; Mor 2:258-60[64])

I recommend to you the contents of the enclosed letter[65]. We don't know the reason why the Bilbao administration arrested the American ship in question. It would be consequential for the Americans to hear that one of their privateers was mistreated by Madrid. Then they would be sure they have nothing to hope for from France or Spain, a proposition the English try desperately to give credit to. That alone could make them agree to a truce or an open negotiation, and perhaps a total reconciliation with England, who taking advantage of such a gross mistake on the part of Spain, would not fail to blow up the event and build a golden bridge for the Americans to unite with the motherland. The remedy to this wrong is to send a messenger to Madrid to recommend that whatever the cause for arresting that ship, the court sets it free, or at least does not take action against it, until a total success of the Americans in New York teaches the Spanish court that it can safely offer its assistance to a brave people who

---

[64]The first sentence has been omitted in the Morton edition.

[65]It is probably the following letter to d'Aranda.

no longer need it; or that a military defeat induces them to make a trophy of that unfortunate ship at the court of England, like weak Cleopatra who offered to victorious Cesar the head of Pompeius who had given himself up to her. They may beat around the bush, abandon the Americans to their own courage, fail to help them smash our only enemy, as long as we are believed to be ready to do it, and that saves face partially for us--but to arrest a brave privateer! To tear the veil that made the Spaniards' intention at least equivocal! In honor, there is enough to lose one's mind from grief and fury!

Pardon, M. le Comte, if I yield to the pain I feel. Poor France! A thousand years will not give you back the moment you are wasting! Once that moment is gone, you will be the laughingstock of all the sensible people in Europe who will take the pen to tell the story to our children! Write to those cruel Spaniards, I entreat you, M. le Comte! By God, if they don't want to help, at least let them not do any harm. Is it too much to ask of them?

Every time I consider that we have in our hands the destiny of the world, that it is up to us to change its whole system, and I see so much good, glory and benefits escaping from us, I regret having no influence on the resolutions of the two courts' councils and not to be able to multiply myself to prevent harm on one side and concur to the good on the other. I know your patriotism too well to be afraid I will offend you in giving vent to my anxieties.

I plan to be at Fontainebleau on Thursday at the latest. Till then I will not sleep unless I have finished the finance paper I promised M. de Maurepas. No bankruptcy. It would be an infamy when we are at peace. A better organization in tax collection, by itself, ought to allow us to fight a war which events make unavoidable and which we flee from only because we are afraid we won't have the wherewithal to sustain it.
--
Reading this over, I find myself carried away by such a strong feeling that I beg your indulgence, writing for you alone.

14 October 1776, to Deane

(MS Conn. H.S.; Dea 1:316; Mor 3:16)

I am sending you the freight contract for the 1600 barrels, or more if necessary, on the conditions agreed to between you and Monthieu. I will not disguise the fact that I tried to get out of having to pay for you half of this freight in advance, because my finances are becoming straitened; but unable to do so, I have to yield. A guarantee for the whole on my part, and half in advance, are the conditions without which we will not obtain any ships. As soon as the contract is signed, I will whisk away as fast as possible not only the bundles of goods and weapons--which can be done without notice---but also the artillery pieces, which are worrisome because of their shape that nothing can hide or dissimulate in route. I'll try, however, to have them take a detour, at a slightly increased cost, so that they can be floated on a river, which would save us from the inquisitive looks which are beginning to follow us. But money, cares, hard work, they will count for naught if we succeed in embarking the goods, and if the cargo fortunately arrives at destination, that will be compensation enough.

You will please bring this contract back to me tomorrow when you come for lunch. If you did not make any changes, we will sign it.

No news from the continent. No tobacco. That is sad. But there is a long way from sadness to discouragement. You can always count on the zeal and attachment of etc.

[End of October 1776] To Count d'Aranda, Spanish ambassador
(Mor 2:260-2)

After expressing to your Excellency some surprise that the Court of Madrid has left unanswered the memorial that M. de Vergennes gave us on the reciprocal situation of the two courts relative to the funds destined to the affair whose agent I am honored to be--I am going to give you a sensible man's views on the plan to follow in this affair in order to avenge Spain and France from England and forever take away from this predatory power the possibility of disturbing the two united powers' possessions and trade, while insuring the United States of North America peace, freedom and the perpetual alliance of the two nations whose aid and friendship they are seeking today.

Although these are only a private individual's views, if they were agreeable to the two courts and it was decided to take advantage of the unique opportunity presently bestowed by fortune, they will be, I promise you, presented in the most official form.

Outline of a treaty of alliance between Spain, France and the United Colonies of America.

1. The thirteen united colonies will be recognized by France and Spain as independent States and will be treated as such. Possession of the portion of North America ceded to Great Britain at the last treaty will be guaranteed to them.

2. The United States will guarantee to France and Spain all their possessions and rights in the various parts of America, north and south of the equator and all the islands that these two powers possess in the American seas.

3. If France or Spain, singly or together, were to take over the western islands now owned by Great Britain (to compensate for losses sustained during the last war, which was started by England in violation all treaties and the law of nations), the United States will help these two powers and guarantee them the possession of these acquisitions.

4. Fisheries on Newfoundland, Cap Breton and neighboring areas known as cod fisheries, will be free to the French and Spaniards and the citizens of North America, but no one else. Each of the above-mentioned nations will have its own islands or possessions specified for handling and drying fish, salt it, with such provisions that there could not be any misunderstanding on the subject.

5. There will be absolutely free trade in those islands between France, Spain and the United States, and they will agree to protect one another against outsiders.

6. To strengthen this alliance, it will be decided that every English ship found on the coasts of North America, including the islands, within a certain distance to be agreed upon, will be regarded as a good prize, in peace as in war. Access to the North American ports will be forbidden to English ships. This article shall not be modified except with the consent of each of the three contracting parties.

7. During the present war between the United States and Great Britain, France and Spain will send and maintain a fleet in North America to defend the coasts and protect the trade of the United States. And should French or Spanish possessions be attacked by the English or their allies, the United States would have to assist them as much as possible.

8. Such are the ideas I am submitting to the two courts. But I have to add that if time is wasted in deliberations, no one can vouch that the United Colonies, vexed by the two courts' indifference, will not accept the peace overtures which England will soon propose to them.

9 November 1776, to Vergennes
(Ang. 519, fol. 68; S.F. 903; Mor 2:262-3)

Upon arriving in Paris this morning, I found a letter with the following news in black and white:

Dover. I hasten to let you know that the English have at last taken possession of New York on September 14. They lost only 17 men, the Americans 400, and they lost them as they were retreating. They had set the city on fire, which the English were able to put out. General Howe has arrived. They don't say where Washington's army is but only that the British have not been able to involve him in a general battle. Impressment continues with utmost violence in all British ports.

That's my news. It seems to me that it is their inability to use artillery which causes them to lose ground. They have courage but no science. It is most important not to let anything stop our artillery company and engineers, which would soon give them other means of retrenching and defending themselves.

Don't you agree with me, M. le Comte? I saw poor DuCoudray last night. He was quite discouraged and writing a letter suggesting to give up everything and leave him in France. It appears Duke de Lorges is causing all that mess. It was agreed that he would go to San Domingo with all the baggage. He mentioned it to de Lorges who talked about it and spoiled everything.

12 November 1776, to Vergennes
(Ang. 519, fol. 86; S.F. 904; Mor 2: 263)

I will be at your Excellency's on Friday at 8:00 a.m.

If I was not sure I was complying with your views in wishing that you do the utmost to remove obstacles which delay my progress, I would not be clumsy enough to talk back, instead of giving in. But I know you are as annoyed as I am with whatever crosses my objective. That's what consoles me and helps me bear patiently with a job which would be sickening and completely unrewarding if it did not please you. For there is a long way from where I started, with the meager assistance I have received, to where I want to be. My goal is to have the Americans rely on us through a beneficial trade, finding in France all the advantages they lost by breaking up with England. This great cause enthuses me, but what a long way, my God, between what I am doing and what should be done! The Spanish ambassador would say: "God, he is a Bourbon . . ."

Do not take my impatient remarks as insubordination, M. le Comte. It's only zeal. Kindly observe that if I am to go to San Domingo, it was rather useless to transport the artillery from Dunkirk to Brest, when the ship expecting it is bogged down in LeHavre. Is that port less French than Brest? Is it not a waste of time and money to leave me with a freighted ship which no longer knows what to do--unless before you leave for Fontainebleau, you are kind enough to have St. Germain send an order for 2000 quintals of powder to be delivered to me in LeHavre and Nantes, with which I could leave, under the protection of God and your little fleet? All the warehouses are bursting with goods and the war minister is a long way from having taken from the registrars all the powder he has coming. As much in Marseilles, and I will be satisfied, because at least I won't be useless and my ships will be loaded with enough to pay for their outfitting.

Could you also, in talking with M. de Maurepas, find out if it is safe for me today to do my work with M. Necker? If he believes I may confide in him, I'll do it effectively. For all their doubts cannot changed a proven truth, and the sophism of the apparent lack of luck to today's financiers, compared with what I claim is being levied on the people, cannot stop a man who reasons and has become convinced. What is involved indeed? Is it not to find out whether or not such sum is collected from the people, when another one is going to the king? When I have proved the major premise and demonstrated unquestionably that sum is being levied, what do I care about the negative reasoning of the financiers' luck?[66] That's skinning the eel by the tail, and a good logician as I believe I am, cannot be stopped by such futile objection. Let's prove that more than 630 millions is being levied. When that is established, we will try to find out how the least of those 25,000 sucking pumps bleeding the people, are yielding 60%, 100% and up to 300% of the price of the job. Then we will prove no one in France is well-fed except that miserable vampire called finance, etc., etc. and we will have reasoned properly.

Why can't I be trusted a little more? Is anyone better intentioned than I am? Have I acquired the reputation of being a sensible man only to see it go at the first important point I try to make?

You may believe, M. le Comte, that I am often sick at heart when I see how everything is going, or rather not going at all.

21 November 1776, to Vergennes
(Ang. 519, fo. 194; S.F. 906; Mor 2:265)

I am not happy with all that comes out of your department. Since M. de St. Germain's answer, which you showed me, I have gotten the most accurate information on the powder in the king's warehouses and I found there is 19,200,000 and some pounds in weight. You must admit some malevolent devil must be meddling in my affairs, when the moderate amount over the 19,000,000 is refused to me! When I computed the quantity of barrels I wanted to ship, I then had, besides the stores, all the artillery agreed upon, its gear, etc. The total mass required six ships. I limited myself to five, two of them at LeHavre, one in Nantes and the other two in Marseilles. Following uncertainties and counter-orders, I presumed that in lieu of the artillery which prudence is holding back, powder at least would not be denied to me. You know why I cannot apply directly to the administration. If the war minister was really short of powder, it would be better for him to ask for a supplement than to have me see too many people and be found out by all those suppliers. But with 19 and close to 20 million pounds of powder, is there the slightest reason to let my ships drag unloaded in the harbors, imposing enormous outlays on me?

---

[66]The financiers in question are the tax-collecting Farmers-General.

The king of our affair is also the king of the artillery, is he not? And all these difficulties from one department to the other are distressing to the person who has to get things done, to hide, to proceed without ever receiving any help from anyone. If I was asking for a personal favor, I would lose patience. I will lose it if you don't help me. You may be sure you won't hear anything from me whenever your cooperation is not absolutely necessary.

I am sending you a letter from Nantes, which seems sure to me. I am including the French translation, asking you to return both to me, when you have read the French version and M. de Maurepas the English.

We are not in as bad a shape as they say in London, since we are fighting well and are inflicting on our enemies great losses they are forced to hide.[67] Their whole tactic is to deceive France with false news, and make us forget our true interests.

I beg you, M. le Comte, to confer effectively about the powder with M. de St. Germain.

1 December 1776, to Congress
(HR No. 111; Wha 2:209-10[68])

As to me, Gentlemen, I am too sincerely attached to your cause and I esteem you too much to hesitate and to wait for your ships to arrive in this country, loaded with your own produce as payment for our merchandise. Trusting in your commissioner's powers, a copy of which he handed to our ministers, I have procured from our factories all that I thought might be useful to you in your present situation and I have started to send supplies to you by the ship which carries this letter, with a brief account of what it contains for your use, as I expect to send you my invoices, attested and signed by Mr. Deane, by another ship which will take to you another supply of munitions, whose invoices will be sent by a third ship, and so on.

But Gentlemen, no matter how eager I am to help you, I do not have enough friends to allow me to double and treble my advances to you, if you do not send me in

---

[67]"We" means the Americans. Beaumarchais already associates himself and Vergennes and all of France with them.

[68]This is only an extract, given in translation. I have not yet been able to locate the original.

return, on my own ships, your remittances in products of your country to pay for the supplies I am sending you.

What I call my ships, Gentlemen, are French vessels which I hired for freight, according to a contract passed between a shipowner and myself, in the presence of Mr. Deane, since the ships which you had promised a long time ago have never arrived. I am enclosing a copy of that agreement.

Now, Gentlemen, please send me remittances either in excellent Virginia tobacco, or in indigo, in rice, etc. My advances in this shipment must soon be followed by a second one as considerable, which amounts to about one million tournois.

2 December 1776, to Vergennes
(Ang. 519, fol. 252; S.F. 908; Mor 2:266)

I saw day before yesterday the Spanish Ambassador and warned him that the commissioner of the United Colonies was about to transmit to him copy of the Declaration of Independence and wanted to know if His Excellency would appreciate his doing it in person. He appeared to me to want to consult with you on this matter. I assured him this transmittal by Mr. Deane did not require any reply; that it would contain only the declaration and expression of thanks for the safeguard granted the American ships in the Spanish ports. I am sending you the literal translation of Mr. Deane's letter. I intend to send privately this translation to Mr. d'Aranda, so that he won't need to consult anyone to know the contents of the original which he will certainly forward to Madrid.

I am taking the liberty of including herewith a letter for M. de Maurepas. All those who surround him deliberately pursue and would like to hurt me. But how, M. le Comte? In spite of all kinds of humiliations, I attend to the job with self-assurance. Barring a firing shot that would stop me, those who come will find someone to talk to.

My zeal and disinterestedness will ground my defense. Besides, I am following the law like President Jeannin.[69] I have no important papers in my house; everything is safely stored. But it is not to suppress

---

[69]A judge and minister under Henry IV, the great king praised by Voltaire.

them that I hide them, it is, on the contrary, so that they may be used to defend my conduct when it is attacked.

I am sorry for the matter that I was not in London; I am pleased for myself.

The harm done to the Americans on the lakes, the English boasted about so much, consists only in the taking of a few boats which were trying to locate the English fleet. Will there ever be a good soul to demonstrate to all of Europe the impudence of that nation? I would do it, if my pen wasn't repressed. On the other hand, the English are more clever than I reckon, for they know how to confuse us at the very instant we should act.[70]

I don't know what DuCoudray is doing at Versailles. He has been there since Friday. He was only waiting for two or three mailings by M. de Sartine, but I have not heard from him for three days. Everything is ready to go, everything is waiting. I am on needles. Who can be holding him back? The ship is at anchor in the harbor. Why can't I discuss everything and handle everything? Nothing would be held back and my ship would already be in America.

The news I send to M. de Maurepas are taken from Lord Germain's private letters. This is for you alone. It's my secret.

After being so successful, Carleton is back in Quebec. What a beautiful campaign!

Versailles, Saturday, 9 December 1776, to Vergennes
(Ang. 519, fol. 288; S.F. 910; Mor 2:267)

M. de Sartine will transmit my memorial to the King today. He is afraid that, in spite of the urgent manner in which the subject is treated, it will not sway Mr. de M. (Therefore, that minister is into the secret.) I too am afraid of that. Not that I think he will reject the thing for itself, but because of the man behind it. Think this over.

I have asked M. de Sartine to be sure to have this read to the king and to try to make him appreciate it, before the time of the objections has arrived; and whenever that time is there, to send me directly to M.

---

[70]The end of this paragraph was left out by Doniol and Morton.

de Maurepas, enjoining me afterward to report to the king on the manner I discussed the matter and persuaded or failed to persuade this minister--but I believe I know how to get his ear. A personality is a cruel curse in state matters. Whatever may happen, M. le Comte, the expression "la Mobile" which you used, has just given me a bright idea, which I hasten to pass on to you.

Spain is no less acquainted than we are with the usefulness to be drawn out of this beautiful machine. But how shall we make sure of Spain? How shall we convince her? How can secrecy be preserved with so many persons involved? Finally, how can we negotiate with the intensity and speed required? Here it is.

See that the king makes up his mind. I'll handle Spain and England. Have the king make up his mind, and I am on my way to London. I stay only fifteen days. I return. I skip over to Aix where the pretext of my suit brings me already closer to my goal. I plead. I win, and immediately I get on a boat for Barcelona, and from there on to Madrid. I can take care of my business in 15 days, as I know everyone there, and at last, I get back to Paris to get some rest. This idea has the following merit: (1) You will know exactly, upon my return, what to expect about the real intentions and possibilities of that country; (2) You will be able to use this plan yourself to object to the king's or rather M. de M.'s objections.

What can be objected, if Spain adopts a plan that should never even have raised one question in Versailles, and if she joins in financing this inexpensive enterprise?

That's my whole secret, M. le Comte. Yours is to make use of it cleverly in favor of the project with which I have no doubt that you agree.

But since I am explaining myself in this letter in a frank manner which is not due to everyone, I won't ask you to burn my letter, but to be kind enough to send it back to me with your answer.

I did not promise you to do my best in politics, but to do the best that can be done. You can judge if I intend to keep my word.

10 December 1776, Vergennes to Superintendent of Police Lenoir
(Etats-Unis 1, fol. 91; Don 2:94)

We hear from all directions that several individuals claiming to be officers are spreading in cafes, shows and other public places the rumor that they are being sent by the Government to the insurgents, and that they are being encouraged to enlist. These rumors deserving urgent attention, it would be interesting, Sir, for you to be kind enough to recommend the police officers to pay special attention to the matter and to arrest those claiming to be on their way to America. You will inform me of your arrests, as well as the minister of the department involved. It would be very appropriate for the search to be done publicly and severely enough for the public to see that the Government has no part in these maneuvers, the publicity of which is supremely disagreeable.

16 December 1776, to Vergennes
(Paris, Monday, 6:00 p.m.)
(Ang. 519, fol. 343; S.F. 911; Mor 2:269)

Just out of my carriage, I am succinctly reporting to you what I have done since my last letter.

Having left Paris on the 6th of this month, forced to go to LeHavre where embarkation difficulties multiplied ad infinitum, I succeeded, after working for seven days, in arranging both men and things. On Saturday, at noon, by the best wind possible the ship Amphitrite did set sail. As all the men became certain they were going to San Domingo, after hoping otherwise, they started crying out for money. One officer even turned in his commission and headed back for Paris. All the others asked that, above and beyond the six-month gratification I had paid them, they be given their pay until the first of January ahead of time in letters of exchange drawn on San Domingo.

The request not being exactly unfair, and desiring mostly silence and peace, I gave them all what was coming to them up to that time, in letters drawn on San Domingo. You have no idea of the work involved in that new deduction; but it had to be done. Thereafter I made sure that no one carried in his trunk or pockets any incriminating papers. And after the visit on the ground, I went along with the ship for two leagues, whereupon I recommended the Captain again to make sure this point was well understood. A hiding-place was worked out in the ship during the night for the indispensable papers, which only the Captain and DuCoudray know about.

During that time I had conveyed to London my desire to have a secret conference, the danger for me to go there, and the need for them to send someone to me at LeHavre. Instantly a small boat loaded with coal was dispatched to London, with a man disguised as a sailor, on whom I am told I can count. But while he was getting there, I received from Nantes the news that Mr. Franklin had landed there.

Knowing as I do this country of gossip and idleness, I trembled that when this famous man arrived in Paris, he would be greeted by so many that there would be some indiscretions. I hastened to write Mr. Deane to go greet his friend, and keep him locked up until I returned, and not to let him speak or give any letter to anyone before I had talked to you, M. le Comte, and taken your orders. Saturday night, when I returned to LeHavre I did no more than meet my Englishman, ask him to follow me to Paris as soon as possible and I traveled back night and day so as not to keep Mr. Franklin prisoner too long.

In fact I made such haste I arrived ahead of him. He will be there only tomorrow. Reassured on this account, I now take time, in spite of sleepiness that overcomes me in spite of myself, to write you this. My ship has gone, with 130 men on board. The English who have a royal ship of 60 guns in the Channel and who visit everything under our nose may examine this one. None is more in order: sent to Mr. d'Ennery by the Minister of the Navy. To touch it, they would have to break glass and declare war. I don't think they'll try.

If I had not gone to LeHavre myself, this unfortunate ship would not have left for fifteen days! My secretary stayed behind me in that port to send on its way the second ship of 250 tons, named le Romain. For although the Amphitrite is 480 tons, it has so many passengers and the gun-carriages are so encumbering, there was no room for all of the load. The rest will leave between next Saturday and Monday. The ship from Nantes in 12 days, etc.

During that time my secret envoy from London is making his way after me, not to Paris, but he will stay in St. Germain, from where he will write me. Between today and that time, Mr. Franklin will have arrived, I will have gotten your orders and I will be free to do some errands with my Englishman, about which I will report to you later.

As tomorrow is Ambassadors' day, I will postpone till Wednesday morning the honor of seeing you. Don't worry, M. le Comte, I have my eye on everything and except for the idle talk of Paris, which neither I, nor the king, nor Heaven, can stop from going around, I vouch for everything. The commotion caused by Mr. Franklin's arrival is inconceivable. This courageous old man allowed the ship to make two prizes on the way, in spite of the risk to his person. And we, Frenchmen, we would be afraid! Let's be prudent so we cannot be taken with our hand in the bag, I told my captain, but don't let them insult you, and have the whole crew sign your affidavits. Pardon, M. le Comte, my scribbling. I've been riding for 40 hours through diabolical roads and I can't keep my eyes open. But I thought this letter had to go. My messenger will await your answer and your orders. I'll jump into my bed and stay there until he returns.

17 December 1776, to Deane
(MS Conn. H.S.; Dea 1:423-4)

I am back from Le Havre, Sir, where I drank to the dregs the chalice of my mission. All we were able to do was to send the Amphitrite away before the minister's embargo arrived. I had more than one hundred men who worked for two nights, and three-fourths of the provisions had to be taken in the road in barks. It was an awful mess. What was meant for one ship, was stuffed into the other; and part of what was meant for this one, was left for the other, as the goods were to be disposed in a certain order and distance from the sides of the ship, which we were too rushed to follow. Well, the Amphitrite at least is safe. The other two boats have been stopped and are going to be unloaded publicly, in spite of my entreaties and efforts. I will tell you, however, that the rigor and publicity of these unloadings is affected, so that I still hope to be able to reload and leave, as soon as the complaints have been appeased by our public proscription. I am going to start by having the ships' names changed; the rest will be done at night, with little noise. But what a loss, money into the sea! Every blunder, every obstacle has to be removed by dint of a great many gold Louis. I would be ashamed of it, if I did not know we cannot do otherwise.

I received your letter through Mr. Eyries.[71] You gave a piece of news which interests me infinitely, and the arrival of Mr. Franklin, who is held in great esteem in this country, can only help American affairs. I beg you to tell me frankly if the reunion of several agents changes the powers of the first agent, and if I will have to start over with the new commissioners what I have done with you. Or will your mission remain the same? I cannot receive better advice on this subject than from you. Be kind enough to advise Mr. Franklin, as soon as he arrives, about my character and my activities. Whether I must deal with him again regarding my shipments, or whether your mission remains intact and continues, it is fitting for him to know how diligently I have served his party. If he is the man I think he is, it is from me he will receive the first and surest information regarding political matters. I am only a private person, but no one knows better than I the shifting sands on which you and I are walking.

They say Mr. Franklin made one or two prizes. Is he bringing funds, or hopes for future means? That is going to become essential for us to continue our shipments.

It might have been better if I had received the news of Mr. Franklin's arrival a day later. Mr. DuCoudray, who heard about it as he was getting on the boat, seemed to be worried. Perhaps he would have wanted his future treatment to be confirmed by this new agent, but I reassured him. How could he be unwelcome, coming with such supplies?

I salute you, honor and love you.

29 December 1776, to Vergennes
(Ang. 519, fol. 403; S.F. 1404; Mor 2:271)

I received this morning a letter from Mr. Durival.[72] It's the first one, M. le Comte, that comes to me from you through another's hand. But that is right at this time. I know the power of circumstances and I will make the best of it. But if this continues after

---

[71]"The most finished of villains," according to Deane, he chartered vessels to carry goods to America at exorbitant charges (Dea 1:48, 2:176 and 5:206).

[72]A secretary in Vergennes' office. Note Vergennes' change of attitude at this point in time.

I have talked to you with an open heart, I will be mortified. The accounting Mr. Durival wrote me about, has been ready for a long time. I must hand it to you in order to avoid a trial in writing. I will present myself in your office only in the evening and that will be the day that I will spend giving (where you know) an infinitely serious accounting.

It will not be long before you come out from under the cloud and are more convinced than ever that I am etc.

1777: MORE HARD WORK TOWARD SARATOGA

7 January 1777, to Vergennes
(Ang. 521, fol. 27; S.F. 912; Mor 3:27)

My friends, who have no ships of their own nation, assure me that M. Gerard has given them, on your behalf, permission to use French ships they have chartered to transport the various cargoes which French merchants are eager to procure them.

They are writing to M. Gerard by my postilion to confirm to me that permission. I would like to receive it from yourself and beg you kindly to confirm it to me by return mail.[1]

The news of the English squadron at Belle Isle [Newfoundland] is false; although that fleet may have indeed left from England.

The Amphitrite, after sixteen days of very bad weather, was forced to put in for a while at Lorient [French port in Brittany], in order to take on board live provisions, what they had having drowned in the storm. That news comes from M. DuCoudray who asks for secrecy and plans on leaving in a few days.

Tomorrow, by your messenger, M. le Comte, I will give you interesting detail. This one does not allow me time to go on.

7 January 1777, from Vergennes to Gerard
(Etats-Unis 2, no. 15; Don 2:313)

You must have a letter from the Americans, who claim you gave them permission to transport their goods on our ships, those at the Havre, I suppose. M. de Beaumarchais writes me on the same subject and indicates he wants to have this permission from me. I shall certainly not give it to him, although I have it in writing.[2] Fortunately, M. de Sartine has been put in

---

[1] That would be an obvious and dangerous breach of neutrality.

[2] Lomenie cites this letter (2:137) (minus the first sentence) and states: "This appears to indicate that ... each minister, when they had to take a decision, asked for an order written by the king himself. I do not see any other way to explain M. de Vergennes' sentence." The point is that Vergennes is deceiving the trusting Hortalez. He is forgetting the principles agreed

charge of this job. I am going to send him [Beaumarchais] on to him [Sartine]. Proceed in the same manner in your reply without throwing off the masks.

8 January 1777, from Deane
(Dea 1:451; Mor 3:28)

As we may, probably in a short time, send means to forward the stores at Nantes and LeHavre, I can but mention to you a circumstance which gives me some uneasiness, and which I conceive it to be your interest as well as mine to remove. Certain busy persons have hinted that the arms and other articles were not good nor well laid in. Now, though I have no more doubt of the falsity of these reports than I have of the ill designs of those who propagate them, yet to remove even the shadow of suspicion on this subject, I propose having an inspection made in a way that will be at once satisfactory and without making the transaction public. To effect this, I will, if agreeable to you, prevail with Mr. Carmichael, whom you know, to go to LeHavre, and with Mr. Williams, the nephew of Dr. Franklin, who is a merchant, and on whose judgment full reliance may be placed, to Nantes, to examine personally the state of the arms and stores, and to make their report how they find them.

I propose farther that Mr. Carmichael stay at LeHavre until the Seine shall be dispatched, and Mr. Williams at Nantes until the stores from there can be got to sea, if it can be effected in any season.

If this proposal is agreeable to you, the gentlemen will wait on you to receive any orders you may have, and set out tomorrow, or the next day at the farthest.

11 January 1777 to Hughes Eyries, LeHavre
(Mor 3:30-31)

All things considered, Sir, we deem it advisable to make the expedition of the ship presently loaded, for San Domingo, through Brest, then off towards the high sea at Ouessant [island off the coast of Brittany, near Brest], and then follow the road. Two things must be noted.

There have been no complaints from the neighbor, as you think! But only many covert observations which would become deadly if you lost another instant and took

---

upon.

the time to send notices to the landings in the other world, especially now that the good season is over. The ship, once visited, certified good, must put to sea without wasting any time, like the last one and may God keep it in the same manner.

The person who hands you this letter is responsible for bringing back proof that your ship was rightly or wrongly accused. As I am convinced that some rascals of your town have played this trick on you, make your proof as clear as you can, and we will thereafter do justice to these gentlemen.

Recommend everything to the wise DeGoy [ship captain] whose merit I value infinitely. Leave the Seine alone, if the other ship suffices. Watch the packing. The first one to leave put in again, they say, only because the packing was bad and the provisions worse. I do not believe it, and I sent someone to Lorient to make sure. I am told it has sailed away again. God be praised. All of that gave me much sorrow. Have this ship addressed directly to Count d'Ennery, referring him to the letter he has received from Mr. de la M. by the Amphitrite, which announced the arrival of this one.

In this mercantile business, one must deal with the ministers as little as possible; make use of them without compromising them, and not ask for too much; for, not only are they snowed under, but they have so many people to spare that, before you get their consent, you have to go through a lot of "yes" and "no" and waste a lot of time.

Go ahead, and most of all, don't forget the eleven cannons without carriages. Mr. de Mistral [French Navy superintendent at LeHavre] has received from the minister the secret order to act in agreement with you, and I am warning you that these eleven cannons have been granted to me and that I take them on my own account. Let Mr. de Mistral take them on his own, ask for them like the others to Mr. de Selon and give them to you. There will be no difficulty thereupon in that country, for it is not the thing, it's the publicity that annoys them. Go therefore noiselessly, promptly, and let your captain procure, however he can, a coastal pilot.

The bearer of this letter will also hand you secret instructions. Same precautions, please, as for the first ship. Every loss of time is deadly, and unfortunately that's the commodity they here are the least miserly about. If these eleven cannons cause too much trouble, after exhausting all means, let's keep them here and join them to those in Dunkirk which I hope to obtain as soon as I have nothing else to fear for these.

You are wise, you hear me. When a ministerial embargo is taken off, one must run as to a fire--for fear another one may come back.

Be very considerate to the bearer of this letter, but do not expose him too much to the curious idlers. Let Mr. DeGoy say he is going to Brest, or say nothing. Above all, let him control, if possible, these young people's tongue. Those are all my prayers, advice and orders. Give my regards to the Mrs. and rest assured, my dear Captain, that if you do a good job here, I will not forget it at the proper time and place.
--
If on the road, M. DeGoy met a good American privateer, and contrived to be taken as a prize to the continent by this honest pirate, you know we would not think less of the [American] captain's and M. DeGoy°s gallantry. That idea comes from me. See for yourself.

At the moment of departure, change the name of the ship. Let the expedition be done under the name Amelie.

13 January 1777, to Vergennes
(Ang. 521, fol. 28; S.F. 914; Mor 3:32)

Don't apologize, M. le Comte, for talking to me about an account to be checked concerning sums allocated for England. Don't I know as well as you do that accuracy is a must in money matters and that one cannot conform to regulations too soon and too often in the country where you live?

I have no excuse to make, however, except for not having made myself clear when I handed you the other night the bills and note which M. Durival took (I thought this note sufficed in order for you to do your accounting for the year); and except for adding that on the first suggestion from you, M. le Comte, the balance would be paid in silver or paper in London, where you told me you had to pay. As I have considerable funds there myself, I am handing you two bills payable there in two months for my balance of 1685-17-4 Sterling. That's what we call in business gilt-edged paper, equivalent to gold in Paris as in London. If that is not convenient, M. le Comte, when you send them back to me with a money order payable on sight by whomever you want in Paris, the sum will be paid out by my cashier, for I do not have a single louis I can sacrifice to you in gold and the sum in silver is not portable to Versailles.

But in checking the settlement of this affair, I hope you will notice that I have not taken any deduction for my expenses, travel, crossings, stays in London, errands, work, etc. for the past two years, whether in this affair or any other. This is not the proper time. Later, I will be able to remind you that I owe to the State my zeal and my work, leaving it up to your equity to solicit the king for the reimbursement of my expenses, without any salary or reward. Today I limit myself to an accountant's accuracy in remitting to you what I have left over from the king, with the faithfulness of a banker.

The stupid carelessness of our French officers having forced me to send my English secretary to Lorient, I cannot send you the translation of my purchase of M... 's small annuity. When he returns from Nantes, you will receive it, together with the 2000 pounds relative to it.

I am very ill with a cold which sticks my lungs to my back, and the most humiliating contradictions having added to it a fever of impatience almost deadly for an active man who has nothing to reproach himself, I write, I cough, a dry heat is eating up my blood, and I suffer in body and mind.

Ah! M. le Comte, Everything is going badly. What are we doing about it? I did not write the long explanation I had announced, because all that is better said than written. You must, however, be aware that the memorial in question will not be forthcoming. Everything is changed. Serious complaints have been received from M. de Ch[aumont] who was being served, and this furious resentment caused the raising of other batteries, the mechanics of which you will not mind learning.

I am enclosing with the letters of exchange a receipt which you will kindly send back to me with your signature.

27 January 1777, to Vergennes
(Ang. 521, fol. 127; S.F.915; Mor 3:39)

Although I believe I cleared myself with you for the contemptible indiscretion I had been accused of, I did not rest until I found out where so much wickedness comes from. For I do hear every day such impossible things about the King's ministers, I have to suspect some devil is again cavorting in my business, to scramble and ruin everything. I know now more than I would like.

Alas! M. le Comte, while you suspect such a proved servant of the King, of M. de Maurepas and yourself, of having made an adolescent's mistake, you cannot see what they dare, in trying to remove you from office and replace you with one of their friends. You don't hear what they say about you and M. de Maurepas, although they don't make any secret of it. You must, however, both of you, know about that. But for the past three days I have been in bed from grief, fever and fatigue; I ache all over. I feel a little better this morning, but not sufficiently to write at greater length. I will see M. de Sartine tonight, if I can move about, for, while evil advances with giant steps, good drags on like a turtle.[3]

28 January 1777, to Francy
(Lom 2:139, Mor 3:43)

We must say like Bartholo, "the devil is into my business," [BS 2:3] and remedy as we can the wrong done, while seeing that it does not happen again. Hand the enclosed letter to M. DuCoudray. I am sending it open so that you can answer his objections, if any, on my behalf. Let the Captain see the enclosed order, which as owner of the ship, I am giving him, and get his word of honor that he will comply to it entirely.

I received yesterday a letter from my nephew, along with yours. As childish as the others, my nephew seems worried about getting back on board the Amphitrite. You know I have no tolerance for this childishness, but recommend him to M. de Conway and Chevalier de Bore. Order the captain to receive on board Marquis de la Rouerie, who has been especially recommended to us. Give the captain the general and secret route plan and what he must do in following his true destination. If circumstances beyond his control obliged him to put in at San Domingo, make him and Conway agree not to stop there but to write Count d'Ennery from the roadstead to advise him that he is directing the Amphitrite there only for fear of adverse encounters and that he will take from him a fictitious order for France, so as to be covered in case he meets with the English between San

---

[3] "Le bien se traine à pas de tortue" and not "se trame" as printed by Doniol and Morton.

Domingo and his true destination. You know we are in agreement with the precautions taken by the ministry in this respect. We can count on that.

As soon as the Amphitrite has left, you will go through Nantes, where I am afraid, however, you will find the Mercure gone, as it is ready to set sail. Good day, my dear Francy. Come back to Paris soon. Enough running around for this time. Another kind of work awaits you here, but I will work with you. Bring back this letter.

30 January 1777, to Vergennes
(Ang. 521, fol. 133; S.F. 916; Mor 3:45)

When one writes to a minister one respects and cherishes, one is quite embarrassed to find words to describe a deed such as the one that chokes me. Let us try, since we must.

After Mr. Deane had shown me, for a month, a foul mood, repeating there was something obscure and inconceivable in the delays of the ships at LeHavre, I finally asked for an explanation for his offensive tone. He replied that tired of not knowing whom to blame, he had sent you a memorial written by Arthur Lee, and that Your Excellency had assured Lee that "for a long time there had been no obstacle from the ministry, and that if I told him there was, it could only be some piece of roguery or some swindle from me or M. de Monthieu." Pardon, M. le Comte, if after swallowing one disgusting thing after the other without complaining, this one sticks in my throat and strangles me.

Your Excellency will kindly take a look at the four letters included herewith, written by me to M. de Sartine, on the 3rd, 18th, 22nd and 29th of January. They will inform you how things are really going, if it is possible that you do not know it, and you will tell me thereafter how much longer I must keep silent and sacrifice myself.

This stroke floors me and makes me wish that my whole conduct as watchman and faithful servant be promptly examined with the utmost rigor. I cannot take a moment's rest until you grant me this grace. Read my letters to M. de Sartine and you will imagine how I feel.

Briefly, the ministry gave orders to stop everything at LeHavre on December 14th, 1776, and on January 30, 1777--which order was not changed in spite of all my efforts.

-- Return to me my four copies, please, after you have read them, if you deem it useless to keep them.

1 February, 1777, to Vergennes
(Ang. 521, fol. 67; S.F. 1422; Mor 3:46)

Thank you very much for your kindness in reassuring me. I have strength against everything, but none if you are dissatisfied. Do not ever judge me until you have listened to me. That's the one favor I ask of you. I know too well that people make requests of you and then attribute to you an irresolution which is far from your character. Later they bring to me images of displeasure, and they put words in your mouth, to impress me more.

I will not believe people any more. I am conscious that I am doing my best, an even the best than can be done. In the midst of obstacles, a small success will pay me for my great efforts. I already feel lighter by half, since yesterday's letters announced that three of my ships have left within three days, one from Lorient, one in Nantes, and the other from LeHavre. But without cannons, I don't rate any gratitude. Mr. de Sartine is sending for me tonight. Would to God that with a stroke of a pen, Sartine put a stop to the perpetual and unbearable reproaches I receive without complaining.[4]

3 February 1777, to Vergennes
(Ang. 521, no. 70; S.F 1423; Mor 3:48)

When the ministry sent DuCoudray back to his regiment in Metz, it was no doubt in order to stop the noise and punish that officer's indiscretion. I did not have anything to do in this decision, which came to my attention a long time after the order had gone out. I had refrained from complaining personally, although I had very much resented his behavior. Today I have to advise you that, instead of going straight to Metz without passing by Paris, as required by the order, according to what M. de Maurepas told me, that officer is in Paris, writing memorials and purporting to justify his shenanigans, making a lot of noise and most of all doing me some harm.

As soon as I heard he had arrived last night, I went to see M. LeNoir [chief of police] and told him

---

[4]I have omitted the next paragraph which concerns only the d'Eon affair.

that Count de Vergennes and de Maurepas wanted to know in what hotel DuCoudray was staying. As he gave another name, I asked M. LeNoir to have tailed Chevalier de Barberin, whose address I gave him, as that artillery officer is the one responsible for directing DuCoudray's broadsides against me.

We'll know before tonight, through Barberin, where DuCoudray is staying. LeNoir promised me he would send him to you right away. You imagine, M. le Comte, what harm can result from DuCoudray's turbulent behavior. Already his friends are up in arms and the clubs are taking sides. Already St.Germain and Montbarey [war ministry] have received memorials. M. de Gribauval [Head of Artillery] is running around, and I, poor thing, am the intended sacrificial victim.

If that officer was of a kind one could openly talk about, I would only laugh at the efforts of that ambitious man. But how can one believe that you will allow this propaganda in Paris, after you got the Americans rid of that inept spokesman DuCoudray? It was my misfortune to make his acquaintance, and the misfortune of the Americans to have preferred him to M. de Bellegarde. That of the ministry would be to let him make in Paris the commotion he is preparing. As to me, I will consent to lose my head in this matter, if I cannot proved I have been as prudent and cautious as possible in this affair. But I am accountable to the ministry alone and not to the public.

You have been informed, M. le Comte. Will you please confer with M. de Maurepas. Whatever you decide to do, it would not hurt anything if you had M. Barberin requested by M. LeNoir to please mind his own business.

4 February 1777, to Vergennes
(Ang. 521, fol. 168; S.F. 1424; Mor 3:50)

At last I received the delivery, and this morning I am sending an express to Amsterdam and Flessingues. It's a pity the Dutch have to reap the first harvests of all enterprises, and that can only grieve a man whose whole purpose is to tighten as much as possible the close and exclusive link between America and France.

No matter. A more important object is not to let the Americans out of work for lack of good munitions, for if ever that nation resumes its bond, or chain, with the mother country, that will be out of spite and rage for having been unsuccessful in making us move in their favor, and it will be deadly for France. By the size of our speculations and the liveliness of our trade[5], I am sure this blow would ruin for twenty years the trade of all our ports and that is not a small consideration in the political balance of the king's council's resolutions. I am writing a short paper on this subject to be submitted to M. de Maurepas. God grant that this trade will prosper. The English are becoming so eager to buy out the votes of the leaders of Congress, nothing is too expensive for that purpose. Let's see that France's inertia does not accomplish that fatal miracle; it is up to her.

If you are serious about having DuCoudray sent back to Metz, it would be fitting, M. le Comte, for you to let me know at the earliest; for his fifteen officers, who have all refused to embark without him, need to be instructed by me on what they are supposed to do, and they cannot be swayed except if they know for sure, one way or the other, what is going to happen to their insane leader. They will become quite mild and obedient as soon as they are certain that their general[6] is back in the French artillery corps as a simple member of it.

Kindly send the packet herewith to its address after you have sealed it.

8 February 1777, from Deane
(Mor 3:51)

It is true that, at the request of the Chevalier de Chastellux and of the Duke of LaRochefoucault,[7] I signed a letter simply attesting that M. DuCoudray has the reputation of being a good officer, and had been very well recommended. I refused, however, to sign, until these two gentlemen had given me their word of honor, that no use would be made of it in France, and even that

---

[5] French commerce had doubled in that period (Tocqueville 1856, 274).

[6] That was the title agreed to between DuCoudray and Deane.

[7] The Duke of LaRochefoucault d'Anville, a Mason and influential friend of Franklin (Fay 1935, 256, 259), who later translated *American Republican Writings*, was assassinated in August 1792. His cousin LaRochefoucault-Liancourt, a social reformer, thereafter assumed the title. The future Marquis de Chastellux, officer and minor writer, went to America with Rochambeau in 1780. Like LaFayette, Gerard and later LaLuzerne, he became a member of the *American Philosophical Society* (Echeverria, 52).

nobody should see it, and that as soon as DuCoudray should have it, he should depart as best he could.

You are not ignorant of what has followed. His conduct on this occasion confirms as well as a thousand witnesses could do, my first suspicions about him. The strange, ungrateful and perfidious conduct of this man strangely mortifies and embarrasses me, and I wish with all my heart that I had never known him, so I wish likewise that he may never in his life see America, and if I were master, he certainly never should see it. I hope that the time will soon come, when I shall be able to explain myself clearly on the whole matter. Meanwhile, as he has been bold enough to ask you to obtain for him permission to depart, this letter will prove to you how sincerely I desire the contrary. Mr. Carmichael, who is perfectly acquainted with the way in which I have been used, and with my views, will give you, on all this, a fuller explanation.

10 February 1777, to Vergennes
(Ang. 521, no. 86; S.F.1431; Mor 3:54)

It's after I thought it over carefully, after I read the letter from Deane, of which I am sending you a translation, after I received this morning all the detail of DuCoudray's behavior, that I beg you to look upon his going to America as the greatest misfortune that can happen to that unhappy nation.

The terms of madman, traitor and evil, which Deane applies to him in his letter, are the result of his distressing experience with that officer.

If these considerations are such as to move you as well as M. de Maurepas, you will want to know that DuCoudray has returned to Nantes and my secretary encountered him near Angers. There is time for you to decide: no ship is ready to take in on.

There was a fire in my house last night, which prevented me from finishing a memorial relative to my last news, and quite important to the cause I have espoused.

You will see that I list Mr. DuCoudray's passage to America among the greatest dangers which may threaten the secrecy of the ministry's involvement in my operations.

I am not mentioning his follies, the most obvious of which is his returning to Nantes in spite of orders to go to Metz, because his friends have led him to hope they would arrange everything in Versailles. Where are we, then? Great God! Every one thinks he is the master here.

While waiting for the memorial which I hope I will finish tonight, I beg you, M. le Comte kindly to pass this letter on to M. de Maurepas as well as the translation of Mr. Deane's, and to take the swift decision which befits your wisdom. But I warn you that either in Paris, in Metz, or in America, your secret will certainly be compromised as soon as DuCoudray is able to talk about it. I have said what I had to and will no longer mention it. it's up to a wise ministry to foresee and prevent any harm as certainly indicated as this one.

That man's indiscretions are much worse than those which were feared with Hopkins[8]. And that is much more serious than you can imagine until you have read my memorial.

I am sending you this letter by express.

10 February 1777, to Theveneau de Francy
in care of Pelletier-Dunoyer, Nantes
(Marsan, 4-5; Mor 3:53)

If you are through with the business I recommended to you in my last letter, my dear Francy, leave and come here. I would like to be sure whether DuCoudray has taken away or has left with someone his officers' commissions and money. For him to have left with everybody's belongings would be absolutely inexcusable.

People here say that, to escape the ministers' anger, he has sneaked out of Paris and gone to Bordeaux where he hopes to get on a ship, under a different name. This plan of his may well have the same success as the others.

Be that as it may, be sure to let me know how everyone is feeling, and especially Mr. Lenfant[9] who has

---

[8] A native of Maryland, Hopkins was serving in the French army as a brigadier-general. With high expectations, in August 1776 he approached Deane about serving in America. Dissatisfied with Deane's attitude, he spread rumors to the effect that the commissioner was eager to bring about a reconciliation with England (Dea 1:287-8).

[9] Pierre Charles Lenfant, the future American architect of Washington.

been especially recommended to me. He wrote me and appears to be in great need. You could leave him a few Louis, if there is no way to figure out what happened to his salary and bonuses. At least for as long as we are in the dark about those.

We are taking across people of good will, but without publicity. For noisy or indiscrete people, they will not be missed, should they remain in France.

Come back as soon as you can.

11 February 1777, to Vergennes
(Ang. 521, fol. 248; S.F. 918; Mor 3:55)

I did not mind giving your note to M. de Sartine, since, having the honor of being well known to him, I did not fear that he would distort the meaning of my request. But that minister, having no authority on M. DuCoudray, advised me to take your note to M. de St. Germain. Pardon, M. le Comte. M. de St.Germain is the friend of M. de Gribauval, who is the enraged protector of DuCoudray. Everyone knows how hostile this officer is towards me. As I have set for myself the rule that I would never give any explanations concerning the reasons, wise and compelling, why this officer must not leave, and why he should be prevented from talking, I can be accused of persecuting a man, whom, on the contrary, I have helped to promote in very good faith, as long as I thought it was not prejudicial to the service. It is not within my character or principles to take revenge of anyone. One would have to spend his life in that despicable occupation. But they would certainly accused me of it, if M. de St. Germain told his friends I have carried your orders to him.

Since the idle people of the Court and the science academies feel they are entitled to discuss and direct the politics of France, you cannot be too careful about the presentation of certain things. It's difficult enough to avoid being blamed by those who, knowing neither what is being done or why it is done, always want to substitute their guesses to their ignorance.

Kindly advise M. de St. Germain, therefore, M. le Comte, since the orders must come from that minister, that it is necessary to stop the steps and the tongue of an indiscrete man. Or rather, if you'll excuse the bold idea, don't give him any reasons--that's the only way to avoid the gossip that always result from intimate conversations.

M. DuCoudray's route goes straight to Nantes.

18 February 1777, to Vergennes
(Ang. 521, fol. 311; S.F. 1435; Mor 3:57)

I told you so: I cannot bear the idea of your being displeased. I saw last night your angry letter to M. de Sartine. Let him dispatch his shipments, you say, and not hold them back in order to obtain new assistance, which we absolutely do not want to give him.

To that, I reply that none of my shipments has been delayed for that new stunt, alien to my daily operations. I reply that my fifth ship, bigger than all the others, is going to leave within 15 days, improbo labore; and by this tireless work, I ask for nothing better than to astonish M. le Comte de Vergennes, whose patriotic ideas I have for so long taken pleasure in serving!

If he scolds me when I have committed some indiscretion, whenever I substitute my interest to the interest intrusted to me, whenever I stop for a moment to concentrate on the most serious of all affairs, I will not grumble. But if I see him angry, when after I have combined the most powerful ideas with the knowledge of current events, I have respectfully proposed to the king the surest and simplest ways to prevent a peace between America and England and to postpone for at least one year the war that is unavoidable for France; if I see him angry because I suggest a slight sacrifice, at a time when England is throwing millions Sterling through the window to take all the soldiers Germany has to give, and send them to America; if he disapproves for a good servant to observe that two millions are always well allocated when they spare three hundred millions and thwart all of England's plans; I will have painfully to conclude that it is the worker who fails to please, and not the work.

Should the king reject my views, have I nevertheless done my duty by submitting them to him? Have not my work and my wide relations made the American affair almost as personal as it is for those who are at the helm of State. And when I propose safe means of removing war away from France, am I pushing my own ideas? You know my ideas on that subject, M. le Comte, and that my memorial to the king is but a complete sacrifice of my opinions to government's views,[10] which I respect and serve without being able to understand them. What did I do to annoy you? I have so little desire to be known as the minister's agent that I warned you twenty times that people would try to get from you some proof of it, and why it would be dangerous for the Americans to obtain such proof.

You can judge now, M. le Comte, what honor, what profit, I seek to draw from having become the factor of the thorniest of commercial enterprises, and scold me if you have the courage.

Everyone crosses this enterprise and does it harm in his own way. Ah! If proofs were wanting! They swarm in my papers. I manage the affair alone painfully, through contradictions and humiliations of all kinds.

When you see what one man alone has been able to accomplish, then you will regret that you caused him grief, that you denied him the one salary he ever asked for, not to be judged without first having been heard.

If I have desired a prompt and precise answer from the king, it's because four shiploads gathered, paid down on in all the manufactures of the kingdom, cannot remain in suspense for eighty-five days, and that one must either promptly ship them away, or miss the deal and let them be dispersed. If you call my ideas chimerical, there is nothing left for me but to wish I was wrong on the deadly consequences of the economy you have adopted.

I have the honor of bidding you that "the goat is back in london and is returning to France secretly in 7 or 8 days." [The goat, M. de la Chevre, is d'Eon's messenger.] You can decide whether, at this critical time, you want to find out, at Calais or Boulogne, for whom he takes such frequent trips.

19 February 1777, to Deane
(Dea 1:491; Mor 3:59)

---

[10]Which memo to the king? It appears to be missing. At any rate, this is an essential revelation of the use of Beaumarchais' pen by Vergennes to couch his own ideas in foreign policy, even when they differed from those of the memorialist: such as the idea of weakening both of the nations at war, and the idea that war was inevitable for France.

All those examinations, inquisitions, visits of arms and merchandise, Sir, no doubt served a useful purpose, since they were thought to be necessary. They at least served to destroy the malicious suspicions, feigned to be entertained on the goodness of my supplies--i.e., in good English, on the probity of Monsieur Hortalez. But was it worth the waste of time? And now that I can but be praised by every one, and that my cargoes are known to be excellent--should I dare ask you, Sir, by what right you have become so difficult regarding my engagements when you have so far failed to fulfill any of yours toward me?

Hold this line of reasoning, I beg you, with your colleagues, who can criticize so well what they don't know and who deny the most simple civilities to their country's most useful friend. I am talking freely to you, Sir, because I am getting embittered at heart.

The Mercure and the Seine have left, one from LeHavre and the other from Nantes, at a season when they could go straight to the continent--but when the ministers, whom I had to deceive about the loads and destination of the two ships, hear about it, will they be easier on those as they were on the others?

I would not want to risk a rich cargo like that of the Thereze, by sending it, in the long-days season, straight to the continent. The Amelie and the Thereze will therefore, if you agree, go to San Domingo. I am embarking on the Amelie M. Carabasse, my correspondent at the Cape, with orders to precede there the Thereze's arrival and to buy three or four Bermudian boats, which must act as shuttles between the Cape and the continent, with my cargoes in various sections, and the returns which they will receive when they hand the cargoes to the Congress commissioners, until the time when Congress will have its own vessels to fetch the goods at the Cape warehouse, which I will endeavor to keep always full, if acceptable returns are promptly made.

Don't feel annoyed if I am out of temper. I cannot avoid it when I see that I am the only one here who works for the good of America, that I have exhausted myself in money and in work, without being able to know by now if anyone but you appreciates it at all.

20 February 1777, to Vergennes
(Ang. 521, fol. 317; S.F.919; Mor 3:60)

The man with the letter from Poland has just left my house. I believe it indispensable that I let you know promptly information you cannot obtain any other way. Let's leave aside my alleged indiscretions. I will know how to vindicate myself when the need arises. But if you are not convinced intimately that these few lines are the effect of the true attachment I have vowed to you, no tact is needed, just refuse to see me. If you still believe in my loyalty, you can see it confirmed. I can be at Versailles so late in the evening that no one will see me.

I am sending a messenger who will bring me back your decision.

P.S. According to letters of the 15th, neither Philadelphia nor General Lee have been taken, but five English ships are at Lorient, led by the privateer who brought Mr. Franklin.

24 February 1777, from Deane
(Dea 2:12; Mor 3:61)

I have been for some time past very apprehensive of the risk in sending ships direct to the continent of America at so late a season and with such valuable cargoes; they must, if they go direct, arrive on the coast of America in the midst of the cruising season of the enemy's ships, and as the ship Theresa has on board between sixty and seventy thousand livres of goods, purchased by the Commissioners jointly, independent of the cargo furnished by you, I have consulted my colleagues on the subject and laid before them your proposal of sending her by the West Indies. They are fully with me in opinion that it will be the safest, and best way, and as the season is so far advanced, and as this route will take a much longer time for the goods to arrive on the continent, they join me in urging that the utmost dispatch may be made.

28 February 1777, to Congress
(Whar 2:276-7) [extract]

I have the honor to fit out for the service of Congress, by the way of Hispaniola, the ship Amelie, loaded with field and ordnance pieces, powder and leaden pigs. As the season is too far advanced for the ship to go directly to your ports, I have charged Mr. Carabasse, my correspondent at the Cape, to transfer the whole load on Bermudian or even American ships, if he finds any upon arrival in that port, and to transmit it to you as soon as possible.

This is the fourth ship I have addressed to you since last December; the other three have steered their course directly toward your eastern ports.

The first is the Amphitrite of 480 tons, Captain Fautrel, loaded with cannon, muskets, tents, entrenching tools, tin, powder, clothing, etc. having left from LeHavre on the 14th of December, 1776.

The second is the Seine, from the same port, Captain Morin, 350 tons, loaded with muskets, tents, mortars, powder, tin, cannon, musket balls, etc.

The third is the Mercury, 317 tons, Captain Heraud, from Nantes, loaded with one hundred thousandths of powder, 12,000 muskets, the remainder in cloth, linen, caps, shoes, stockings, blankets, and other necessary articles for the clothing of the troops.

In my letters of August, September and December last, the duplicates of which have been delivered to you by the chief officer of the men who went over for your service in the Amphitrite, I have requested you to see to it that my ships might not wait long for remittances. I am making the same request in this letter, my plan being to send you uninterrupted supplies and such as may be of greatest use to you. I hope you will, on your side, be as prompt as possible in loading again and sending back my vessels to me.

1 March 1777, to Sartine
(Mor 3:62)

When one has so many ships built, many nails are needed. Part of those are made of wood and are called tree-nails. The best tree-nails are those of high Touraine. You can see I am here praising my own tree-nails. My jobbers for the Chinon forest[11] have therefore the honor to propose to you, herewith, a contract for 900 thousand of these excellent tree-nails. I had sent it to Mr. Potties who sent it back to me, for the double reason that you must be the first to see it, and that he doesn't want to hear about it anymore.

I beg you, Sir, but not with joined hands as I do when great matters are involved, to submit this contract to the approval of M. de la Frenaye, who will return it to be signed if my tree-nails do please him.

---

[11]That forest of 3500 hectares was exploited by a company controlled by Beaumarchais since 1766.

The same jobber, Carre, who is handling a contract for marine wood for you, begs you to order that a passport be sent to him for the floating of that wood, at no costs, as much on the Loire, as the Cher, the Indre, and the Vienne, which surround his exploitation. This passport is given to all suppliers.

I am not including herewith the paper which requires Mr. de St. Germain's signature, so as not to tire you by asking for so many things at one time.

2 March 1777, to Vergennes
(Ang. 522, fol. 4; S.F. 1439; Mor 3:63)

I am not addressing to you the enclosed letter, as I believe you are already aware of its contents. I only beg you to read it, you alone, and pass it on right away to M. de Maurepas, after you have sealed it.

Mr. DuCoudray has left for San Domingo. From the ship, he sent to the American Commissioners a memorial against me, which they have been considerate enough to forward to me right away. The gist of this memorial is to persuade them that he did obtain from the government all the assistance that passed through my hands, and that only my vanity as a merchant to appropriate the merit of this operation has denatured it.

Monster that he is! he writes: "M. DuCoudray having taken with him on that ship (Amphitrite) only about the fifth of the cannon he had obtained from the government, and the agents from whom the departure depended having been changed, (these agents, that's I; the loads are indicated but as coming from the government) he felt that he should go to Paris, for the sake of these new agents as well as for the sake of the affair whose success mattered to him as much as to them, if not more."

There you have his trips justified according to him: he was the agent of the ministry and Beaumarchais' trade is nothing but a mask. He said it. He wrote it. So, his purpose is to destroy even Mr. Deane's remonstrances in America and to give himself for the savior of the State, through his efforts to obtain assistance from the French government.

And that man is going over! And the king's orders will be eluded in Metz, Paris, Nantes, and San Domingo! And everyone will be compromised. It's infuriating.

7 March 1777, to Vergennes
(Ang. 522, fol. 15; S.F. 1445; Mor 3:66)

I won't talk to you about the situation of the English in America, because if you have other data than those given by the English court gazette, as I am sure you do, you know that this situation is very unfortunate and that the English are cornered, partially quartered on New York island; that there were three and not two main engagements; and in twenty small encounters the English have been licked, as on those three remarkable days when the Americans took back all the Jersey territory; that a corps of 6000 men out of Connecticut took over King's Bridge; and that all souls in the country have been uplifted by these successes.

While not talking to you, I've just told you everything. If you already knew it, repeating it won't hurt. A surfeit of pleasant things delights the heart. What does not delight mine, is that I missed the five loaded ships in Lorient. They had been sold when my agent arrived. I confess to you the sin I wanted to commit, because I am very sorry others committed it instead. The five ships and their loads were sold 90 thousands pounds and were worth 600 thousands.

In spite of the orders given by you regarding the American privateers who bring merchandise in our ports, the Farm keeps on quibbling, so that several ships a little while ago went on to Bilbao for relief. That's not the route I wanted to teach them, you know that. I have complained to M. Robin. But since Mr. Clugny's death, the Comptroller General has not recommended this matter and Mr. Robin claims he needs a new order. Do me the favor, M. le Comte, of writing to Mr. Taboureau to give me a private audience, when I will ask him for what is becoming so necessary to obtain now that my returns are about to arrive. Let me be the bearer of your letter, unless you find a moment tomorrow or Sunday to ask him to grant me an interview very soon on this matter.

The last ship I am loading, and which is ready to leave, bears the name "Count de Vergennes." Although that name is very sweet to me and seems a good omen for a superb cargo, the name of the ship is not in my lease and if you mind the connection the English might make between the name and the use of the ship, only say one word and I will have it changed, although it is hard for me to debaptize it. That ship gone, I will have at sea the Amphitrite, the Amelie, the Mercure, the Marquis de Chalotais, the Seine, the Concorde, two Bermudian vessels while waiting for the rest, and "Count de Vergennes" whose name remains only with your approval.[12]

Never has a commercial business been carried with more vigor in spite of all kinds of obstacles standing in its way. God grant it a successful outcome!

The most gratifying of all is that I am certain I have grasped your ideas and put them to execution with nobility and promptness.

8 March 1777, to Vergennes
(Ang. 522, fol. 47; S.F. 1447; Mor 3:68)

Another letter, you will say, he will not quit! Hey! how can I quit, M. le Comte, when new objects keep exciting my attention and vigilance? I have to inform you of everything! A private secretary of Lord Germain's has arrived here, via LeHavre, secretly sent to Deane and Franklin. He is carrying peace proposals. The highest reward awaits him if he succeeds. England's offers to America are such that a commissioner may send them to Philadelphia in all honor.

The doctor has been trying to send Deane away from France. I am doing my best to keep him here. This Republican alone can with his male firmness counter the insinuations of all kinds practiced on the doctor. I really should tell you all this, which it takes too long to write. I shall, when you order me to. Peace or the continuation of war depend on too little for you to refuse to influence so easily such a great event.

Linguet is something else to think about! Can anyone be so bitter? He really is a decent sort of man, embittered and actuated by intrigue. What he is writing will give M. de Maurepas some grief, will displease you, will give the death blow to Mr. d'Aiguillon, and an unspeakable joy and pleasure to all the enemies of the present administration. Perhaps it is too late to do anything about it. Perhaps it is possible yet to stop everything without being compromised. Whatever you may think about it, I offer you, I offer M. de Maurepas, to try in a way which may be more efficacious than the official one. I used to like Linguet. His eloquence charmed me. He seemed to value enough my own character. See, M. le Comte, see with M. de Maurepas. You know how discreetly I have rallied meaner ones. It is horrible for such upright and good ministers to be disparaged by

---

[12]The approval was refused.

such a sharp-edged pen. It is painful to see France deprived of such an eloquent man. He is the most vain and irritable of writers. But he is weak as a child with any man who knows his secret. See. Whatever is honest, I can do it. I must do it for M. de Maurepas and yourself. Hey! If you trust my loyalty, speak up! that will make me twice as effective. No one will be compromised if I put that tiger in chains, and no one will either, if I fail. It's that little rascal of a goat [d'Eon's man in France] who spreads copies of that letter. Other copies came in from Holland. Hey! What is all the ado about anyway? A literary critique. Unfortunately, some faces are showing a triumphant pleasure. Do you feel like chatting about it? Would M. de Maurepas like to hear me, to get together? On all these points I await your orders.

Monday morning. Yesterday, you, or Mr. Gerard, saw Mr. Deane. While he was in Versailles, someone was with me, informing me. England's proposals are good and acceptable. People in America have been led to expect an alliance with France. Should they be disappointed in this respect, should you fail to answer the question which will be asked of you, peace with England is decided and soon will be concluded. Military success do not suffice a great people. They do their best today to subsist, but rest assured they cannot go any farther without you, or without a reconciliation. That's what proved to me yesterday.

I have several proposals to make you and M. de Maurepas. You wrote me, based on my last memorial, that I see things in black. You may be sure, however, that had Philadelphia been taken, they would not have waited for another moment to speak to you as they did to the Dutch, and you might have answered in the same manner too.

If you saw Prince Marsan yesterday, he must have assured you that we have become unbeatable on Mr. M.'s plan. Go to war whenever you want to. The King will have 150 millions at his disposal eight days after he has adopted us.

22 March 1777, to Vergennes
(Ang. 522, fol. 130; S.F. 1489; Mor 3:73)

Supposing always that you do not intend to let America perish or make up with England for lack of the assistance needed to keep up the fight, if you can procure it for her; supposing also that my work and my ministry have not ceased to please you in that district;

I have found the way for you to back up the Americans without having to disburse considerable sums, which you do not have, but which America cannot dispense with.

If you look on me as the importunate solicitor for that nation with the ministry of France, perhaps I have vested myself with this job as an occupation as noble as it is useful to the interests of my country. But since I did not do it without your secret consent, you've got to listen to me today, you've even got to help me--if you are not just to drop a plan which is without risks.

Mr. Deane has come several times to treat this great affair with me. His own thesis is that the government must guarantee the loan they will get. But as long as you affect to be neutral, that's not possible.

My own plan can be outlined as follows:

1. It is to organize a company of French and foreign merchants, many of whom have already given me their words.

2. To contribute to the capital, for my portion, the mass of the monies owed to me by the Americans; and to have my company share in advance the profits of the first returns--conditioned upon everyone investing in the business as much money as I will prove I have invested.

3. That all that can be useful to America and be taken in kind in the King's warehouses, without harming the service, will be granted to me without ado, without my contracting to replace in kind or to pay within a term similar to the one we are imposing on the Americans.

4. That you will furnish to me a way, unknown to the Americans, of extending my present credit, as needed for me to head such an enterprise, which is as easy as inexpensive to do.

5. That you will give me the means of offering my stockholders something to attract them with. But as the hope of profits on trade with the Americans appears rather uncertain and unattractive, I will indicate to you one means which will not hurt the deficient royal treasury, and that I cannot dispense with if I want to be fully successful.

There you have, M. le Comte, in few words, the outline of my business which as you can see, is only the extension, adroitly carried, of what I have been doing for a year now.

I do not, however, in spite of that, contemplate lending to the Americans the two millions Sterling they are asking for, but I would lend them seven or eight millions of French currency; and biding our time for the rest, while practicing a shuttle of shipments and returns, we will at least, while waiting for events to happen, supply at least the strict necessary to that brave nation, which it would be absurd and cowardly to abandon when it has a burning desire of becoming our ally.

If you won't draw back on what you can do without being compromised, I give you my word to succeed on everything else.
For fifteen days, I have been overwhelmed in the meditation and correspondence required by this business. Today I am in a position of negotiating secretly with you and Mr. de Maurepas. Any evening you want, I will await your orders.

But while I am negotiating with you, I warn you that they are negotiating here covertly with Mr. Franklin, something of which you are probably unaware and which I am sure Mr. Deane has not told you, convinced as he is that his colleague will not be swayed, and not wanting to hurt the good reputation enjoyed by this colleague. But I, whom experience has made suspicious and who am accustomed to draw conjectures from what strikes me--I have concluded, by what I get from London and by the faces of the English ministry, that Deane is looked upon as a formidable obstacle to any reconciliation plan, and is to be withdrawn from this country, whatever the cost may be.

That's what induced Lord Germain and Lord Temple (who will before long replace Lord North), to compromise Silas Deane in the John the Painter affair,[13] through a leap-frog process. They want to make him hateful to the English, unpleasant to the French, and make him loathe Paris. But our news carry such a positive announcement of the ministry's intentions, that my guesses have become facts. They are planning to have Deane removed

---

[13]John Atkins, alias John the Painter, accused of setting fire to a rope factory in Portmouth, England, alleged that Deane had paid him to do it.

from France and make him the scapegoat for their insane undertaking in America. I reassured him and promised him that his safety would be secured so as to prevent any kidnapping. I promised him he would be able to sleep peacefully in this protecting and neutral country.

Pass this letter on to M. de Maurepas and let me have your orders for Versailles.
--Included is a letter from Deane to Gerard.

24 March 1777, from Deane
(Mor 3:76)

I find myself obliged to urge you to give most prompt and serious attention to the idea I communicated to you some days ago, on a subject of a loan for America. Without this help it is impossible for us to answer for events, the outcome of which is nevertheless of most infinite importance. Relying on your capacity and your zeal for the cause of the Americans, and knowing how great and generous is the interest you take in it, I am glad to persuade myself that you will neglect nothing at this critical moment, when, unless aided by some essential encouragement sent from Europe, our very successes will force my fellow citizens to accept the conditions which are about to be offered them.

For my part, nothing is farther from my thoughts than to see my country again if ever it is dependent in any way on England. I have always had the pleasure of seeing that your sentiments are in accord with mine on the subject of America and the real satisfaction of receiving from you most important aid on all occasions. You are also at this moment yourself interested in redoubling your efforts, for if a reconciliation takes place at any price, England will immediately turn her resentment and forces against France, which she does not dare to do now, and which she will never be able to undertake if she finds herself separated from America forever. One of our proverbs says: "A friend in need is a friend indeed." I will make no reflection on it, but be assured that without aid, and without substantial aid, it will be impossible to continue the war against Great Britain and her allies any longer; it cannot be expected. I am quite sure that the very thought of our subjugation affects you sensibly; for my part, I will not think of it, desiring not to live a moment after so great a misfortune. I shall see you tomorrow morning, when I shall further enlarge on this subject, which is of the utmost importance and extremely urgent.

30 March 1777, to Maurepas
(Ang. 522, fol. 278; S.F. 1499; Mor 3:81)

My discretion in not making myself importunate about small things, will perhaps give me the right to insist on important ones.

I must have badly explained my ideas on helping the Americans, since you appear not to adopt them. The fear of giving you too much to read often causes me to discard detailed explanations and achieve a conciseness which may be obscure. But I know nothing is done through writing and I need to be heard in order to be understood, and this critical time calls for putting the head and the arms together, for a meeting between the leaders and the workers.

You will better feel the necessity of it when you have read the two different writings which I have forwarded at the same time, one from England and the other from the American commissioner. First see the insulting English paper, knowing that Lords Germain and Sandwich had it printed.

Those are not the despicable allegations of a Linguet. That's is the bitter and terrible lesson from an enemy which, while telling us ironically what we ought to do, takes pleasure in insulting us by showing all of Europe that we have not done it.

Next, see Deane's letter, and consider a good Frenchman, a zealous subject of the king, a good servant to Mr. le Comte de Maurepas, who respects him and would like to honor his administration with all the nations of the world--consider whether he can sustain at once your constant refusal to give him a hand, the compelling entreaties of America at bay, and the insolent triumph of militant England.

M. le Comte, spare your servants the sorrow to see it reproached to your memory some day, that you could have saved America at little cost and did not do it; taken it away from the English yoke and bound her to us through trade, and you neglected to do it.

Listen to me, I beg you. You mistrust your powers and my resources too much, and I fear especially that you fail to value highly enough the power that your age and your wisdom give you over a young prince whose heart is well formed, but whose politics is still in the cradle. You forget too often that this untried and firm soul was more than once bent and brought back a long way; you forget that when he was still the heir to the throne, Louis XVI was invincibly opposed to the magistrates, whose recall, however, honored the first six months of his reign. You also forget that he had sworn he would never be vaccinated against smallpox, and eight days later he had the smallpox mark on his arm. No one doesn't know that, and so no one excuses you for not using of the most beautiful right of your position, the right to cause the great things you have in your soul to be adopted.

If you find too bold the liberties I am taking, please recall their bright motivation, and you will forgive them to my loyalty.

I was not just playing, M. le Comte, when at the beginning of our relationship I told you: I will never have any true happiness if your administration passes without having accomplished three of the most beautiful achievements which may give it glory-- the humbling of England through the <u>union of America and France</u>, <u>the restoration of finances following Sully's plan</u>,[14] which I set at your feet several times, and <u>civil existence rendered to the Protestants</u> of the kingdom by a law which, without appearing to deal with them, will on the contrary legally replace them among all of the King's subjects. Those three matters today rest in your hands. I only want the honor of having often reminded you of them. What accomplishments, M. le Comte, what successes could crown your noble career? After actions such as these, there is no death: the dearest possession of man, his reputation survives everything and becomes eternal.

Listen to me, then, for the Americans' sake. Consider that their commissioners await my answer before they dispatch a messenger who will carry encouragement or desolation to the Congress. On what I shall say to them depends whether they will accept or reject England's proposals; and I am vouching once more that these proposals are good and acceptable. Do not make my efforts fruitless for want of cooperation on your part, and let my reward be the honor of have obtained your approval.

---

[14]Sully (1560-1641), Henry IV's trusted Protestant minister, famous for his competent administration which restored the French economy after the Wars of Religion. His financial program included liberalization of trade and removal of tax abuses.

30 March 1777, to Vergennes
(Ang. 522, fol. 276; S.F. 1500; Mor 3:79)

I took your advice and let the week go to the cares of the other world; but I hope you will approve it, if I return to the charge today on the affairs on this world, for I can see your patriotic zeal through the veil of circumspection which enshrouds your style.

Read my letter addressed to M. de Maurepas and send it on to him sealed, together with the English paper and Deane's letter, whose translation you may keep, but whose original you will please send me back. I am encouraged greatly by the gratitude of this gentleman speaking for his nation. See M. de Maurepas thereafter, and if you will only obtain the conference, I will find in my heart enough fire on this great affair to warm his up about this great affair.

Really, that English paper is of an insolence to spit in its face, but you have to admit that the substance has some force and truth to it. But if my ideas or such others like them are not adopted, I know the Americans' situation through their mail and it is impossible for them to finish the whole campaign without a powerful assistance.

I respectfully salute you and recommend to you that affair in the bitterness of my heart.
- - - -
I was going to close this packet when I learned that M. de Maurepas was in Paris. I sent him my letter, Deane's and the English paper and asked for an appointment. I got it last night at 8:00 p.m. You can tell by the tone of my letter how devoutly I pleaded my cause. He kindly went into some detail with me, and seemingly carried away by the force of my reasons and the breadth of my views, he said: "We must discuss this with M. de Vergennes. How much do you ask to set you up only? Of course, we cannot enter into their proposal of a public bank." Little money, I told him, if you give me the means of increasing my credit; and a lot of money, if you do not adopt my thrifty plan. I added that I had been pleased to see through your letters' circumspection your approval of my views, at least in general. "We must see him, he replied, and decide."

Back me up, M. le Comte, please. I am sending you copy of my letter to M. de Maurepas, so as never to depart from the duty of complete trust which I imposed on myself towards you.

The Westminster Gazette is being copied. You will have it tomorrow. I need no more now than your kindness, an appointment in your office and to work with you in Mr. de Maurepas' office.

3 April 1777, to Vergennes
(Ang. 522, fol. 300; S.F. 1506; Mor 3:83)

Your observation on the Westminster Gazette caused me to make another one apt to either confirm it or destroy it, for there are only too many bad Frenchmen in London. It's to have my translator check its English. However, he assures me that the style and vocabulary are idiomatic and that some articles have been taken verbatim from <u>Common Sense</u>, In fact, no ship was called Hazard or Trudaine, and Panchaud, the banker, is rather poorly indicated by the gazetteer. My name does not appear, and "LeRey de St. Chaumont" is mentioned for a powder contract. It all rather looks like ideas taken at random and based on hearsay. See the whole article that I have crossed. Moreover, whichever hand it may come from, the conclusion certainly states that it was published by order of Lord Germain.

We now feel sure enough that Mr. Schmitz [Smith], that lord's secretary, is presently in Paris at Lord Stormont's, whence he executes the secret orders of his master relative to the conciliation proposals with America.

He is disguised under a chaplain's wig, while little Mathy, a real chaplain, pretends to be giving up the church and to yield his position to the newcomer, if his stay in France is not too injurious to him. I am on the right track, the rest won't escape me.

Commotions, as you put it M. le Comte, only serve to ruin everything. But making abstraction of the tribe named artillery officers, noise can be avoided and everything can chime in. Provided the Americans do not become certain that the ministry is contributing, there is no danger of compromising it. To retain English forces in Europe through respect for ours, destroy their excessive feeling of security through some mysterious motions of our vessels, to keep within neutrality, to lavish our help on the Americans, who cannot make war without it now. To prefer for that purpose the way of trade, because it is doubly good, inasmuch as it displeases the English and teaches our sailors the road to America without compromising the ministry--there is enough to exhaust the English forces, at least in this campaign, without weakening ours, and such is the whole of my ideas.

I will be there on Saturday whenever you indicate. I do hope I have excited a little M. de Maurepas' soul, but I count on your wisdom still more than on my eloquence.

On the other hand, I am beginning to see that Mr. Deane is getting somewhat discouraged as he is losing hope to prevent his country from making what he calls a big blunder, if he does not receive the assistance he keeps on asking me for.

Herewith a packet from Mr. Deane for London.

6 April 1777, to Vergennes
(Ang. 522, fol. 354; S.F. 1508; Mor 3:86)

I just left the Spanish Ambassador whom I had not seen for a long time. I painted for him the truest picture of the reasons why it is important to assist the Americans efficaciously; their urgent need and the even more urgent danger that they will make up with England when the mail arrives which is to be sent to them shortly from France, should they receive no help nor encouragement. I conveyed to him my ideas on the need for the French and Spanish fleet to make mysterious and combined moves, which would, without compromising the two powers, effectively retain in Europe the forces of England, would prevent the king of England from completing the raising of the loan--as a result of the shrinking of the private funds and the fall of the stock market, and would cause the Americans to hope that those moves are taken in their favor, which would increase a hundredfold their courage and their strength. That if, in the meantime real supplies did arrive, I would vouch the English campaign would fail again and that I was planning, if he approved of it, to go and talk the Spanish ministry into providing some assistance, which joined to whatever I could steal from France, would give the means of sustaining the great edifice of American successes until next December--and especially to prevent reconciliation.

He replied to me: Personally, you know what I think and what I want. But as Spanish Ambassador, I cannot tell you either black or white.
--Hey! Why is that, Sir?
--Because the French minister has not mentioned a word about it to me.

--But, M. le Comte, it is with his consent that I am talking with you about it.
--In an affair and at a time as important as these, Sir, I must learn from the minister that he approves your views before I may reply anything to him.
-- M. le Comte, the minister will talk to you whenever you want, because I am going to send to Count de Vergennes a summary of our conversation.
--Sir, I will go tomorrow, Tuesday, to Versailles, although it isn't ambassadors' day. Your ministers are friends of mine and must be at ease with me on any matter. Have them talk with me about it. Otherwise, I won't say a word. They know very well that we ask for nothing better than to act in concert.

The rest of the conversation was only a general recapitulation of all that's going on, of which he even took some notes concerning England. He gave me an appointment for Wednesday morning. The only point, M. le Comte, which needs attention right now is my light mission to Madrid. I say light, because it will be short, because if you realize its importance, it can bring you accurate information on the Spanish cabinet and its dispositions.

If I cannot get any assistance for my friends out of them, you will know once and for all to what extent you may count on or mistrust whatever comes therefrom. M. de Maurepas says I do not believe in Spain. In fact, I don't very much. But my visit in that country, two serious conversations with the new minister [15] a few meetings with Mr. d'Ossun [French Ambassador in Spain], two or three dinners with Pieri, the favorite butler, will let you hear when I return whatever you need to know on all of that.

I have many other things to impart to you after I talked with Mr. Deane for three hours yesterday. But I am writing you from a strange house, and have hastened to inform you of what I said and did at Mr. d'Aranda's [Spanish Ambassador] so that you may take it as the <u>punctum vita</u>e for your conversation of tomorrow.

11 April 1777, to Vergennes
(Ang. 522, fol. 397; S.F.1514; Mor 3:89)

My meeting with d'Aranda was as inconsequential as his with you last Tuesday. He only told me that, as he had no opportunity to broach the question with you, he

---

[15]Floridablanca had just succeeded Grimaldi.

planned to see you again Friday morning. He seems to hope that you will have to break the ice or it won't be broken. Nothing is more detrimental to business than protocol.

I don't know if Mr. d'Aranda is being diplomatically discreet, or if it is an ambassador's parade. But as I am interested in the real thing and not in ceremonies, I beg you, M. le Comte, to be kind enough to broach that essential question with him.

I must tell you, as a consequence of my duty as a Frenchman and my obligations toward you, that d'Aranda is eager to know whether the insurgents have proposed to our minister advantages distinct from those they offered both crowns. He assured me that any information I could give him would never pass his lips. Everyone is looking for number one, and in the woods of politics the corruptors are no better than the corrupted. You know, M. le Comte, that this advice is for you alone, and that without mentioning the urgent need not to let America fall into the claws of England--which requires a prompt decision and imminent assistance--you must be eager to know how you stand with Spain.

Mr. Forth, a friend of Lord Mansfield's,[16] is back in Paris. He carried a very urgent letter to my secretary, begging him to let himself be corrupted. It's the same thing everywhere. He showed it to me. Forth is to come this morning to see him. I will show him the opened letter he brought to my house yesterday and ask him why he does not apply to me directly for this noble offer. I am rather curious to see how he will cope with my persiflage.

But, my God! In the midst of all that waste of time, I see my poor friend Deane writhing with worry and the future of America wavering, although they have been successful. We have talked over the matter of the fleets moving about. He agrees that this coup would give the last blow to the English campaign and would encourage and uplift everyone in America. Oh! What a hateful thrift, which can thwart such high purposes for so little money!

I am not saying that for you, but I am overwhelmed with grief by what I see and foresee.

---

[16]Uncle to the English ambassador in Paris, Lord Stormont. Parker Forth was an agent employed at the embassy.

15 April 1777, to Vergennes
(Ang. 522, fol. 405; S.F. 1517; Mor 3:92)

I was sorry to learn yesterday from Mr. d'Aranda that your second meeting had not been more successful than the first, and that the matter in question had not been broached.

--You perceive that as long as the question is not mentioned to me, I cannot utter a single word about it.

Although I do not perceive that at all, I had to agree with such powerful reasons. God bless the Americans and the commerce of France! People will never believe that for twelve days, a decision on such important issues was postponed on the only ground that the first word spoken about it should come out of this rather than that mouth!

--But at least, Mr. Ambassador, you could without being compromised, tell Mr. de Vergennes that I had seen you, by his own authorization; that I have become so pressing about the American affair and the assistance to be furnished, that you thought you had to discuss it with him.

No comment.

He says it is up to M. de Vergennes to mention it first. And if you do not, M. le Comte, deal incisively with this puerile obstacle and tell plainly to Mr. d'Aranda that I wrote to you about it, the three of us will be hanging for three months on the noble thread of such a grave difficulty.

If I am doing my job--as M. de Maurepas kindly put it the other day--in presenting, without cease and from all points of view, the implications of such an urgent issue, allow me to remind you, M. le Comte, what you know better than I, that to waste time, to keep silent, to remain undecided is much worse than say no. To refuse is to act: one knows what to do. But nothingness cannot produce anything.

Thus the English ministers who claim they are very well acquainted with the mentality of the French administration, have ordered their ambassador to speak loudly and proudly in Paris, about how well the English are doing in America. According to him, it is too late to help that nation whose reconciliation with England has been resolved, fixed--he almost says signed. Somebody alarmed by this news wrote Mr. Deane to find

out if it was true. He writes back on the same letter:
"It's not true. It's pure Stormont." However, shall I
say it, M. le Comte, I am afraid that "pure Stormont"
has gotten to Mr. de Maurepas. He told someone, a few
days ago: "It's too late." But if he would recall how
many times in the past eight months he thought it was
too late, and how many useful decisions were delayed
because of that mistaken notion when there was plenty of
time, he would change his mind. Besides what good is
it, to switch constantly from "it's too early" to "it's
too late." Ah! M. le Comte, there is always time: but
the more of that precious time one wastes, the less
there remains to make up for the harm done in wasting
it.

I really don't know by what magic I have been able
to sustain my friends for the last fifteen days and
prevent them from sending distressful news in the mail.
I have to give them courage by showing courage. They
suppose I have some resources when they see me unruf-
fled. But every morning I receive a note, and in the
afternoon someone comes to ask again the morning's
question.
--Have you any news from Versailles? Do you believe, M.
de Beaumarchais, I should kid my unfortunate countrymen
any longer, and make them entertain a hope I do not
share?
--Wait, is my trite answer.
--Alas, I cannot wait much more to write the truth. My
orders are so positive in this respect, I tremble for
the consequences.

Such is the life I lead, M. le Comte, furious to
see that the arrogant English have prophesied about us,
and that we are fulfilling such prophecy.

If the fear of a commotion, supposedly coming from
me, stopped the ministry and turned them against my
arguments, if I had to stoop to justify myself in this
respect--I would say that it is on the known character
of men, on their constant behavior that they must be
judged, not on vain or treacherous allegations. As long
as I can do the work alone, my secret is safe. If the
indiscreet behavior of the Amphitrite officers and their
chief, even more insane than the rest of them, has
leaked the destination of that ship: what could I do
about it beyond what you did? I can challenge any one
in this country, starting with the ministers themselves,
to quote only under what name, what cargo, in what port,
and for what destination, I have expedited all my boats.
And if, in spite of all the spies that surround me, not
much is known thereon, it would be quite unfair to make

me responsible for others' wrongdoing, and use that as a pretext for refusing my requests, with such deadly consequences. I have become openly a merchant so that I would not be taken for a negotiator. And if they seek to know where I took the capitals for my business, the part taken by the ministry in my operations is well masked by the associations of all kinds which my house affects to contract with all the merchants who hazard any shipments to America.

So, M. le Comte, when everything is set up, when the first efforts of such a large concern have proved successful, when my deep contempt for all the society gossip has confounded the babblers, and when I can answer for the happy consequences of an enterprise so well combined, will you refuse to cooperate with it again? My active perseverance will not stimulate anyone? I offer to attempt to influence the Spanish minister, to multiply myself so to speak in doing it very swiftly; this mission depends on a meeting between you and the Spanish ambassador, both of you agree, and after twelve days, nothing has even started! For God's sake, for the honor and the interests of France, do not postpone this decision any longer, M. le Comte. Have another conference with M. de Maurepas. <u>No affair is more important and as urgen</u>t.

As I close this letter, I receive one from Nantes, in which I am told that sailors are being denied to the merchants, and my ship is held back just as it was leaving. They ask me to obtain from the minister of the navy a covert and secret permission to employ ten sailors only, the rest of the crew will be composed of ordinary seamen, etc. I beg you, M. le Comte, to arrange promptly with M. de Sartine whatever this ship needs in order to sail. Let him write to the marine commissary in Nantes to give permission to Mr. Pelletier DuNoyer to take and embark on the Comte de Vergennes, previously called Thereze, ten leading seamen, which with the four others who are on the boat and a sufficient number of ordinary seamen will allow it to sail. It has been stalled in Paimboeuf for twelve days. On my side, I will write to Pelletier as soon as you give me the go ahead, and another obstacle will be removed.
I enclose herewith a note for M. de Sartine, if you deem it advisable. I plan to go myself take your orders on so many matters Thursday night, if you do not let me have them before.

I recommend the Americans to your memory and their advocate to your kindness.
--

The time of your mail has passed while I was writing. I am sending a man on horseback.

4 May 1777, to Vergennes
(Ang. 523, fol. 23; S.F. 1526; Mor 3:102)

My silence on your last letter[17] may have given you reason to believe that I accepted defeat. But, in asking your forgiveness for the frustration the reply from on high has caused me, in spite of the care you took to announce it to me. I assure you I don't consider myself as beaten, but only as refused and harshly refused.

I know that a man charged with an unpleasant task must endure unpleasantness. It's my lot, and whoever is disgusted with disgusts does not deserve the slightest success. But truly, by the way I am being treated, you would think I was some pestering protege who asked for personal favors[18] rather than a useful worker employed for the common cause.

But if everything is not well, everything is not bad either. Fortune, or luck, which has always served me better than men, brought into my hands yesterday a piece of news which relieves my sorrow and brings hope back into my soul. A letter of March 6th, written from the harbor of the Cape, tells me that Amphitrite and Seine,[19] my two first ships, have arrived safely in Charleston, South Carolina. I hasten to pass this on to you, so you can rejoice in it for my sake, if the cause of America has become of no import to you and you do not want to rejoice for its sake. I am no longer worried about my other ships: only these two carried heavy munitions.

I will have the honor tomorrow night to present myself at your house and at that of Count de Maurepas, under the auspices of those two ships of mine. I must explain myself what was misinterpreted in my last letter, and destroy the unfortunate impression made by the word "corsair."

---

[17] This letter is missing.

[18] The last twelve words have been omitted in Morton.

[19] In a letter to Vergennes, 8 May 1777 (Mor 3:108), which concerns mostly the d'Eon affair, this news was corrected. The Seine had gone to Martinique.

The Thereze, previously named "Count de Vergennes," a ship richly loaded, finally set sail by the best wind from Mindin, on the estuary of the Loire, on April 26th. But, as a result of the constant contradictions I experience, an enormous package which was to be put on the ship, was delayed by two mail deliveries at the Paris post office, in spite of my precautions and recommendations. I have no doubt but that everything was opened up and copied. It would be a small evil, because the ministry is not compromised in any way, but the considerable evil is that such an indiscretion can exist in France, and that an important package is delayed shamelessly from Monday to Friday, and that a ship should have to leave without its letters, after having waited for them for four days, and having risked ten times to see a turn in the wind which must blow it away. See where this leads: those who receive this ship will not know what use to make of its cargo, and the ship which carries the papers of the first one may be delayed three months or it may go under, and the silly curiosity of the gentlemen of the post office has put at risk more than one million of precious goods. If you or M. de Maurepas, M. le Comte, do not give me a royal order [cachet] to remedy this abuse, every time I have an important package I will have to send a messenger. It's disheartening, but that's the way everything goes. Here is what my correspondent from Nantes writes: "I am mortified indeed that I was unable to include the last package you had given me for Mr. Carabasse, as it arrived to me only Sunday, when I should have received it on Thursday. I will inform you by the way that every letter you have written me up to now has been delayed by one or two mail deliveries. I do not know why." My correspondent doesn't know why but I do. Curious people who want to know everything in order to divulge everything are behind these maneuvers. And the traitor you are looking for is closer than you think.

    I have discovered other maneuvers which I will tell you about tomorrow.

    Herewith two letters for London from Mr. Deane.

4 May 1777, to Deane
(Mor 4:312)

    I've just received a letter from M. Pelletier of Nantes (from Mindin), dated the 29th, informing me that the Thereze has sailed away on the 27th with the best wind. Another ship on its way. I am not worried about this one as I was about the others, because neither the load nor the ship papers were simulated. The English will have either to inspect it or open the fire on it, which will trigger the war.

The Happy remains in Marseilles. What I can load in Dunkirk as freight, I will and will take advantage of every opportunity for all of the merchandise that's still on its way to our ports from the heart of our manufactures. But I am at the end of my rope to find any more money. I am told that the commissioners have received some. I have not found out yet from whom or how. Do you think you can make a better use of it than by putting me in a position to continue operations as necessary to your success as mine are?

I even heard that they have selected a banking house in Paris. If I believed the gentlemen from Passy have so insulted my house as to give the business of Congress to some stranger, I would not cease to serve America because it is as much a stranger as I am to this incredible step, but I would have no more to do with people who appear to do their best to do their country a disservice. I am not putting you in that category, Sir, but I believe you are not energetic enough in checking all the wrong they are doing me.

I am no less, in spite of these reproaches, with attachment and sincere esteem, Sir, your very humble and obedient servant.

---- My postilion has the order to deliver this letter to you on his way to Versailles, but has no time to wait for the answer. You'll let me have it whenever you come for dinner, any day you please.

Beaumarchais, in financial difficulties, is helped out by the minister, who cannot do otherwise since the quandary stems from government action, and he knows how resourceful the Americans' advocate can be in defending himself. The sun shines when, on the first of July, the news of the arrival of the first ship is received.

2 June 1777, to Vergennes   (Mor 3:116)

If I have not thanked you since Saturday for your all kindness, I hope you will not doubt my gratitude and will attribute to difficulties in fulfilling all my engagements my delay in thanking you.

Because of your kindness, I can breathe until the 15th. But as this day draws near, the resources I used to complete my May 31st payment are going to need replacing and I will be strangled again.

That's the most serious part of my work with M. de Maurepas. It is too essential for me to handle anything else. Besides, to slow down such things is less hard than to pay; and your advice will always be as powerful on my mind as your kindness is sweet to my heart.

9 June 1777, to Vergennes
(Ang. 523, fol. 232; S.F. 1547; Mor 3:120)

Back from the country, where I went to lock myself up for two days to finish a job I could not have finished in the city noise, I found your letter of yesterday.[19]

Your considerate kindness fills me with gratitude. The feigned fitting out of Dunkirk is only a wise precaution on my part. Convinced that there can be no move made in this port which the English won't learn about, I am taking advantage of the season when I cannot and will not do anything, to send to Brest everything I have in Dunkirk.

Brest is a port further from them. The movements of munitions are more frequent and natural there. It is not in the season when I would be free to embark that I should get those things out of Dunkirk. *Parturient montes. . .* I have taken steps so that my intervention will not appear in that transportation.

---

[19]This letter is missing too. The present letter is erroneously dated June 2 in Morton.

Thank you again and remember me in your prayers for the 15th.

12 June 1777, to Francy
(Marsan, 5-8; Mor 3:124)

It's 1:00 a.m. Vaillant just handed me your letter. He will leave again tonight. You ask for explanations. Hey! Can't you see from where you are that they are curious up there about our forced labor? I got sure notice of it through a good friend. I found him in my house last Sunday when I returned from the country. They will not forgive you, I was told, for overriding orders, etc. Instantly, I see that they have written Versailles and the secret is out. I send Vaillant out in the middle of the night, hoping there is still time to change the order, and I send you the one Vaillant is handing you, so that I may use it to justify myself if need be, and not let them take away from my friends the only true helper they have here, by letting myself be crushed for the lack of a ready excuse. While he is taking this order to you, your letters arrive successively and I learn that it is too late and the ship will be gone before the arrival of my messenger. I am downhearted, and grief suddenly inspiring me, I go visit Mr. Deane. I show him the extreme difficulty my loyalty to them puts me in. I propose he takes everything on his own account. He thinks it over. He agrees.[20] We set everything up, and I write him ostensibly to reproach him about my learning, after I gave positive orders for Brest, that they have loaded for Martinique. I question him about that.

He replies ostensibly that he did send an express order to Hodge[21] and to you to expedite for Martinique, as much a French harbor as any other. That I claim to be their friend and am always delaying shipments which are needed for the campaign etc. The letter is clear and proud: it's good. I therefore write on high, complaining about Deane. I ask justice to the minister between Deane and me, and in the middle of that debate, Vaillant arrives.

---

[20]Who was doing the interpreting in this heavy conversation with Deane? Probably, our friend Bancroft.

[21]William Hodge, Jr. who had been sent to France by the Secret Committee of Congress in October 1776. He owned a privateer based in Dunkirk (Dea 1:302).

I am sending him back to you. Proceed along this line: You know now. Deane did everything; he wrote both of you that he was in agreement with me, although that was not the case, and except for the whining and scolding less to be feared than a deadly disgrace, Marie Catherine may go get f.. at Martinique. The devil is cause she had not left before Vaillant arrived. However, I won't hide from you my fears. Advice from on high last Sunday read: "I hope you have no part in that beautiful expedition. Those who are behind it need not embark victuals. Their ship won't go very far." However, the form of the expedition reassures me a little in the event of a prize. But imagine my anxiety, knowing that the English are cruising in front of your harbor, when I imagined that within a few days we would get the news the ship had been taken, and then, anger rising as high as it can, I would find myself lost, without recourse. Take in the sentence quoted above, please, and since the ship has not left, check the papers secretly to see if anything should be changed so that it will not risk any danger in route.

Unloading is the worst. I wish now it had left. Besides, everything that's not loaded on that ship must be loaded on the next one, and don't address it to one place or another until I tell you. I will do it obscurely because the post office will handle it. Be sure that in case this one is taken, the minister will not be in a position to protest. That's the point. You know that an imprudence caused the difficulty of the Seine.

Thank Mr. Emery[22] for me. I have felt like fainting twenty times this week. You wanted me to write you in detail, and I was choking. I told myself: he will think whatever he pleases, but he will do what I want.

What a condition mine is! Don't think I can ask the minister for anything today for the second ship. We must take a smaller one or load this one only half way. However, if I can find old copper, I'll tell you. Find out through Mr. d'Ostalis how much there is in Dunkirk, so I can check if his statement is the consistent with mine. I am going to dine while Vaillant is sleeping. If I think of something to tell you, I will add it this afternoon.

---

[22]Emery, Father & Son, Dunkirk merchants (Dea 2:181).

Bring my letter back and see to it that no one knows Vaillant made two trips. I am going to Versailles tomorrow night. The order will leave Saturday.

So, to summarize: You received my order, but you had already received one from Mr. Deane and you had acted in consequence, as you thought we were in agreement. My counter-orders arrived too late. All this is a summary of what I am saying here; over there, it is indifferent to you. Ship away in secret, or very fast at least, by the time Vaillant gets there, without it being obvious that his arrival actuated you. And for the rest, may God watch over it! You will get ostensible news from me, all regarding this detail because of the post. Be sure to get the spirit of it.

1 July 1777, to Vergennes
(Ang. 523, fol. 358; S.F. 1558; Mor 3:139)

If something could console me for all the disgusting setbacks I encounter, it certainly would be your kindness for me, as constant as it is obliging. As I was about to let the Anonymous go, I learned that ship really did not deserve any name, being, as you put it, the most worthless buggy.

Right away, I gave order to unload; reserving for later the question of who must pay for damages. It seems to be it must be whoever deserves to be blamed for it. I will clarify this better after the ship is left in the harbor, before it does any crossing, in the exact condition it was when purchased and refitted. This strong action on my part will cause some embarrassment to those who were involved. But I have no pity for foul deeds. Their statements amounted to 35,000 livres. just for refitting.

But I have just received a news which distresses me much more. I read but I cannot believe I am not dreaming. M. de Bouill , the new commander at Martinique, notified the merchants "that the Courts of France and England have agreed that the English will have the right to search French vessels coming from our islands, and seize all merchandise coming from the American continent." Everyone was startled by this incredible news, and I am floored. From that moment on, it's all over and the American ships have nothing to do anymore in our waters. So, the English have been empowered to be the exclusive customs agents on the ocean. And no one in France has been notified of this murderous convention! And already many a fortune is altered by such seizures, to which no one would have exposed himself, had it been possible to guess such a convention existed between the two crowns! But that's so impossible that while I am reading it, I cannot believe it.

It is not to you that I will speak about the deadly consequences of this convention: you must have had your hands tied to sign it, if this can really be true. I am in despair.

I have made my June 30 payment yesterday, by selling at a loss all the commercial bills I had. That's such a bad moment to pass that a million arriving the next day would not repair the harm done the day before by the lack of only 30,000 livres. Yesterday I had to pay 184,328 livres de rigueur, and 21,864 livres, 8 sols and 4 deniers left in arrears from my payment of the 15th, on which I cashed in only 200,000 instead of 221,304. 8. 3. Therefore I lack for yesterday's payment and the next 490,168. 16. 7, with the loss on my paper resources, for my three last payments, which I must repair to be even in my business.

I beg you therefore to let me have a warrant for 500,000 livres, after which I'll take a trip, but since the place of my trip is not indifferent, I'll have the honor to discuss it with you.

I thank you for the use you made of my letter of the 29th.[23] God grant that it be effective.

1 July 1777 (afternoon), to Vergennes
(Ang. 523, fol. 345; S.F. 1559; Mor 3:141)

I have just received the good news that the Amphitrite, after a tiresome crossing of eighty-five days, has arrived in Portsmouth, seventeen leagues north of Boston. The whole crew was at the end of their strength and courage. They are fine. It's Captain Heraut, commander of the Mercury, and back from Boston in 23 days, who mailed this good news after he arrived in Nantes.

The Marquis de la Chalotais got into Charlestown, accompanied by three other French ships on May 4th.

I also hear from letters from the Cape, of May 18th, that the Am lie's cargo arrived in that port, has already left from there, divided between several American and Bermudian ships, bought on my account at

---

[23]This letter is missing.

San Domingo. The officers who were at the Cape also left on the schooner Catherine, expedited without artillery but only with a load of one hundred casks of rum, for the port of Dunkirk, which will shield those officers from danger in passing to Boston.

I will have the honor of bringing you news of the condition of the armies as of June 4th, but all in all, everything was well and no move on the part of Howe.

I am distressed by the confirmation of the unfortunate announcement made by M. de Bouill upon his arrival at Martinique. It seems sure that France conceded to England the right to stop and seize any French vessel coming from the islands, which should be loaded with merchandise from the continent. What extremity may have led you to sign such a convention?

And the French merchants add this reflection: since the English often go to our colonies for clandestine deals, and take out of there some merchandise--if our French ships meet some of them with sugar, coffee, cotton, recognized as coming from our islands, they will therefore by way of reprisal, since the government abandons them to their enemies, be able to seize them and look at them as good prizes, although stopped on the high seas.

I will not pass on this second proposition. I'll just deplore the first one, but I will not believe it until I hear it from your own mouth, M. le Comte.

Please pass my news on to M. de Maurepas.

You see, by those details, that if we do not do well, at least we do quickly. But I do fear there will be gunshots between the merchant vessels of France and England, who are at peace; since the one purports to be authorized to cut the throat of the other's trade, and the latter is in no mood to comply with the kindnesses the French administration is showing to the good Englishmen, at the expense of all the French commerce.

19 July 1777, to Vergennes
(Ang. 524, no. 14; Mor 3:156)

I am sending you a brief I have just received from Dunkirk on the Godelier woman's complaints. They were going to print three memorials and start a suit. Some prudent person sent this memorial to me, asking for my advice. I cannot be a spokesman in this and I am asking you advice. It is serious enough to reverse many an allegation and even cause a great noise, if desired. I am enclosing a poster, which may have been sent to you already. It shows they wish to make us pay for all the blunders they make overseas. Oh! If they made peace with America today, how they would make war to us tomorrow! We must therefore, neglect nothing to keep that peace from happening. You know that better than I do. But how can I keep from mentioning something that's always on my mind.

Besides everything is in good shape over there. They tell me that DuCoudray[24] was sent by Washington to Ticonderoga to defend the fort. Although this man is crazy-headed and mean-hearted, I believe he will do a good job. He errs not out of ignorance, but out of reckless ambition.

As orders to stop and unload the ships continue to dart out of Versailles, Hortalez retaliates with Beaumarchais' talented pen. Two letters to the Navy minister will remind him of his duty to protect French trade and of the rights of France as a neutral State. He also writes two letters to America, one commercial, the other political, redolent of the Declaration of Independence, to encourage them to fight on. On December 5th the sun will shine bright as Beaumarchais brings to Vergennes the news that "on October 17th General Burgoyne surrendered at Saratoga!"

9 August 1777, from Deane
(Dea 2:101; Mor 3:175)

You are well acquainted with my having paid M. Eyries a sum of money on account of MM. Morris and others in Philadelphia, to be employed in the purchase of a vessel, as well as with whole of the proceedings of that affair, which I need not repeat here. You are also sensible of the necessity of speedy settlement with M. Eyries. I must therefore pray your kind assistance in bringing this transaction to a final settlement as soon as possible, and that you will conduct the affair in the manner most conducive to that end. The necessary papers

---

[24]During the Summer of 1777, DuCoudray was repaying Beaumarchais with a 27-page declaration to Congress to the effect that he, DuCoudray, had been the instigator of French secret aid to America. A copy of that paper was given by James Lovell, interpreter for Congress, to Francy who forwarded it to Beaumarchais in his letter of 31 July 1778. A short excerpt of this defamatory writing is given in Morton 4:161-2.

relative thereto I send you herewith, by which you will see what monies I have advanced to M. Eyries, also M. Eyries' promise to be accountable to me therefor. I must rely on your friendship and that you will act for me in this affair. As for yourself, I have wrote [sic] to M. Eyries, acquainting him my procedings.

28 August 1777, to Sartine
(S.F. 1663; Mor 3:185; *Observations*, 77-84)

Based upon questions asked from our agent M. Chevalier in Rochefort by the port authority, we feel that only one of those prying and prowling Englishmen, who are all over our ports, could have sounded the alarm in such an untimely fashion and caused your Highness, by ways most familiar to them, to plan an unprecedented inquisition into the affairs of French merchants.

Milord, the King's vessel Hippopotamus was for sale; it was, obviously, so that someone would buy it. We bought it, paid for it, we are having it repaired at great expense, and we do not think that is contrary to the laws of commerce or such as to make us suspect of wanting to thwart the pacific views of the government.

But if a vessel of such caliber can only be intended for high ventures, is it not natural, Milord, that we should put this ship in a position not to fear, in time of peace, to be harassed, shot at, visited, searched, insulted, looted, perhaps even seized and confiscated, in spite of the regularity of our papers (as has happened to so many others), if there is found amidst the cargo an ell of cloth whose color or quality happens to displease the first Englishman who runs into us?

After he had promptly insulted us and caused us to lose the fruit of a good mission, perhaps he would be able to get away scot-free, by simply replying to you, via the English ministry, that "the captain was drunk," or "it was a misunderstanding." But your Highness knows that, if such a trite and banal excuse is enough to appease the wrath of the French government, the useful merchant, whose job it is to entrust his fortune to the waves, on the faith of treaties, remains nevertheless ruined, in spite of the compensation he was promised but which can always be easily set aside.

Meanwhile, Milord, the maritime merchant, of all the King's subjects, the one that treaties must especially take into account, is also the one who needs a more immediate protection. If you look upon all the estates of society, Milord, you will see that the administration, the tax collection office, the military, the clergy, the law, the terrible finance, and even the useful class of farmers, all draw their subsistence or their wealth from the interior of the kingdom. All live off the fat of the land. The merchant alone draws from the four corners of the world in order to increase the wealth of the country. In ridding you of a useless surplus, he goes abroad to exchange it, bringing you in return the spoils of the entire universe. He is the only bond that binds together and unites all the nations of the world, which their different customs, cults or governments would tend to isolate, or to set at war.

Therefore, if henceforth the merchant is obliged to report in advance his business ventures, whose success always depends on speed and secrecy, and which are subject to various political events--he no longer enjoys any freedom, any security, any possibility of success, and the universal chain is broken.

Your Highness will realize that we make these observations not in order to avoid obeying orders; but only because we think that the establishment of an inquisition over the private affairs of merchants, as a kindness to the rivals of French trade and natural enemies of the State, is a use of authority subject to terrible consequences, the least obnoxious of which is the disheartening of merchants and the end of competition, without which nothing is accomplished.

When our agent M. Chevalier, under his own name, became the highest bidder and purchaser of the Hippopotamus, you were kind enough to assure him, Milord, of the first royal freight for the colonies. We beg you to keep your promise. This is the best way for you to ensure the true destination of our ship. We believe that this alone, Milord, contains within itself all the explanations your lordship may desire.

7 September 1777, to Deane
(Mor 4:313)

I let Mr. Williams do what he pleased in loading on such a puny ship as *M re Bobi* some merchandise of mine, because I must lend myself to everything that appears to facilitate the transport to America of so many objects now being tossed about from one port to the other and often from one ship to the other, when an order from the War Ministry has arrived to get it unloaded publicly.

I have had containers made up in such a way as to completely hide anything packed therein which must be loaded again at the first opportunity. I will try fortune once more, or misfortune: The latter seldom fails to come when one seeks the former.

I have since then sent on its way to Carolina the ship Hardy from Marseilles. It's true that as an agent of the general congress you are not involved with this shipment. But you know that Carolina is in as great a need as the other confederate States, and it is based on your good recommendation of Mr. Rutledge, president of its particular congress, that I have made this new sacrifice.

I am reminding you of these matters--not to reproach anything to Mr. Deane for my present situation, as I have too good an opinion of him to believe he would not help me out if he could--but only to prove to him that I will not be stopped by anything when an opportunity to ship arrives. The Happy, the Marseilles ship which has been held back so long by the authorities, will soon be on its way. I had it loaded at night, a little at a time, during the past two months, but after the English ambassador repaired to that port, he obtained once more that it should be unloaded. That was done at noon, causing a great uproar. What my friend should know is that I managed to have it loaded again. I left in the port some old artillery destined to be melted down, the bulk of which has hidden the new nightly reloading of the Flamand. That ship will no longer be named Happy; the name befits it too badly after the last two months. Finally, it is believed to be free of artillery and I am allowed to send it off to San Domingo.

I am advising you that I am sending M. de Francy to America. He will depart on the Flamand. There has been an infernal obscurity in the way the gentlemen in Passy have behaved toward me. I want to find out the reasons why I have not heard from Congress for a whole year. Unable to do it in any other way, I am giving Francy full powers of attorney. He will declare openly what i have been doing. I know this drastic decision may displease a few people, but I will henceforth disregard all the small considerations for which I have so far had too much regard.

I hope Francy will carry with him the strongest recommendation from you. I am counting on it, as you can count on the true feelings with which I am, for life, Sir, your most humble and very obedient servant.

10 September 1777, to Congress
(RG 76)

Gentlemen,

    I have the honor of sending to you Mr. de Francy, the supercargo of the ship the Happy (Captain Landais), and my personal representative in America, charged with procuring returns for the cargoes of the ships Mercure and Amphitrite which have arrived to you, returns for the Seine and Marie-Catherine which were addressed to Mr. Bingham of Martinique, and those of Am lie and Th r ze arrived at the French Cape in care of Mr. Carabasse, my correspondent, which were distributed on four smaller ships bought by the said Carabasse and forwarded to Congress, not mentioning those which will arrive to you by the first vessels I will be able to launch on the ocean--which constitutes a mass of advances so considerable that I could not proceed further, however attached to your interest I may be, if I did not promptly receive some of the returns which I have been expecting in vain for a long time.

    From a glance at the large disbursements, not including interest, commission, or benefit, which Mr. de Francy will submit to you, and which with the insurance amount to some 250 thousand pounds Sterling, I hope, Gentlemen, that in the abeyance of my general account closed by Mr. Deane and myself, which I will forward to you on the first available vessel, you will not hesitate in paying out to my agent Mr. de Francy a sum sufficient for him to purchase immediately in Virginia enough tobacco to fill the two or three vessels which I am going to send from Europe, so they may be loaded upon arrival and in a position to sail back promptly.

    While your commissioners are exerting themselves in vain to obtain a loan in Europe, I have just found in some countries close to France a resource of several millions which is entrusted to me and of which I would already have received the first million if my ship Amphitrite was back. Such is the time appointed by my lenders for the delivery of the first monies they are entrusting to me. I must repeat to you what I have many a time told your commissioners, your cause means so much to all the honest people who know that I have espoused it, that had you been more exact in sending me the returns which had been promised by the month of February, my credit alone might have sufficed to fill your needs, but your delays, the difficulties and the fear to be punished by the English are holding back the good will of all my friends, which would have been fired by your returns.

Where public opinion is concerned, Gentlemen, enthusiasm must be fed by success. The first returns arriving to me will perhaps increase tenfold my ability to furnish you with supplies. If this is wrong, it's because it would be too conservative, and this sort of commercial success alone can bind politics to your cause. You may be sure that the man who speaks to you in this fashion knows well the ground he is walking on.

Finally, so that the Republic may know exactly what it can depend on with me, I charge Mr. Francy to give you the choice, Gentlemen, to pay me in France either on exact invoices with insurance, arrears, expenses and contingencies, and a moderate profit or commission; or to leave everything to my risks, both going and coming back, and figuring my account in America, give me a profit on the cargoes which have arrived, such as to compensate me for advances, delays in payment, insurance cost, commission, etc. and allow a decent profit, such as a merchant speculating on America could expect after he had arrived in your country and sold you his cargoes.

I am adopting this frank manner of proceeding, Gentlemen, because it seems to me to be the most suitable to someone avowedly a friend of yours, of your principles, in love with your success, admiring your courage, and a zealous partisan of Liberty, which, exiled from the whole earth, is going to find at last among you an asylum.

I am with the most respectful dedication
Your very humble and very obedient servant
Roderigue Hortales & Cie

10 September 1777 to The Secret Committee
of Correspondence of Congress
(MS Laurens Papers)[25]

---

[25] Microfilm 6, South Carolina Historical Society. This memorial was published by Brian N. Morton under the title: "Roderigue Hortalez to the Secret Committee: An Unpublished French Policy Statement of 1777" (*French Review* (May 1777) 875-890). In this article (which was awarded the Gilbert Chinard award of the French Institute in Washington), Mr. Morton attributed the authorship to Vergennes. I did not agree with his reasoning. An exchange of letters between us was published by the same review.

[1]   Will you allow, Gentlemen, a friend of your country, a man entirely devoted to the interests of the noble America, a man who has proved his loyalty to you, to reason with you on the present state of your affairs.

Three great considerations come to mind:

America is at war in order to sustain its freedom and the independence it has just declared.

England, realizing too late that it has underestimated the courage and strength of the Americans and that the war presently carried is ruinous to it, and cannot but end up in a less unfavorable peace.

France, finally, in suspense between these great events, and tarrying too much, according to you, before making up her mind whether or not to take part in the quarrel.

[2]   Such are the facts. Let us look at the causes and see what good or what harm can result from the violent conflict of these three entities. Let us see especially if the apparent indifference of the French nation must bear on the reunion of the two States which separated based on reasons which have nothing to do with her.[26]

[3]   When France, at the last peace, yielded to England the possession of Canada; when Lord Chatham predicted in London that this cession would cause England to lose America, and when the jealousy of all the provinces was aroused by the privileges granted to Canada and the cares of a monarchical administration which seemed to threaten freedom--then grumbling and unrest began to rise in America. Finally, when injuries and usurpations on the part of England caused the Americans to sound the alarm and throw the yoke of England, restricting the meaning of the word *motherland* to the limits of the continent--had France anything to do, Gentlemen, with that rupture? Was it consulted on the consequences of that separation?

[4]   For a long time the fire of discontent had been smoldering all over and soon, with the Stamp Act of

---

[26]These paragraphs are reproduced, with certain modifications, in the *Observations on the Justificative Memorial of the Court of London*, paragraphs 17, 18, 19 and 20.

1765, spread from Boston to all the other cities. The bloody uprising in Boston which led the inhabitants to demand the recall of the governor and lieutenant-governor of Massachusetts-Bay, and the affair of the snow of Rhode-Island, which forced the English to repeal the Stamp Act and recall those two officers--these were the first mark of your self-confidence, the *punctum vitae*[27] of all the vigor that you have shown since then, and France had not the least part in all these great events. The tea tax, the transfer of important cases to Europe, the installation of tribunals appointed by the Court, and a thousand other outrages against your freedom made all the citizens take up arms and finally form that great body which has become so fearsome to the English because of its wisdom and its credit, the Philadelphia Congress.

[5]   Soon the Cadets' uprising, General Gage's hostilities in Boston, the tea proscription in the colonies, the English ships sent back to Europe, obstinately brought back to America, their cargoes refused and burnt by the Americans, briefly the complete rupture between the colonies and the motherland, the arming on both sides, the Lexington and Bunker's Hill affairs, the treachery of the English in arming the slaves against their masters in Virginia, and even worse in counterfeiting the paper money in order to discredit it, a kind of poisoning theretofore unknown, and all the ensuing horrors -- have led America to throw the English yoke, publish her independence and fight for it.[28]

[6]   But in all of that, Gentlemen, France always remained an outsider, she did not foment your difficulties, she was not consulted on their consequences, and only the interest that you presumed she would have in supporting America in order to weaken England, is the great Reason of State which led you to come and solicit her help. Therefore, if her own interest is the only reason you have the right to claim in begging her to intervene in your quarrel, her own interest is also the sole reason which must engage her in refusing or granting, pressing or postponing her assistance.

---

[27] Beaumarchais likes this latin expression (the heart of the matter). Cf. 6 April 1777 to Vergennes.

[28] The preceding paragraphs are inspired by the Declaration of Independence. The next one states the French national interest.

[7]   According to this principle, one cannot help but **openly** blame your privateers and the liberty, I daresay scandalous, with which they bring their prizes and sell them here without any regard for our treaties or respect for the interests of the Prince who gives them asylum in his ports.[29] They act in this respect as if they had been asked to force our hand regarding war, by accumulating under the eyes of the English so many infractions to our treaties as to give France the look of weakness or piracy, equally unworthy of her, if her administration did not once in a while take action against them.

[8]   Indeed England does not deserve any of the consideration that France shows her. England's continuous breaches of faith would justify the protection France might grant to your noble efforts in America, if her interest led her to do it. But it appears to me neither good reasoning, nor decent, for the Americans to base entirely upon the conduct of France, their decision to continue the war for their freedom, or to make peace in order to regain their tranquility.

[9]   Even if all of Europe, Gentlemen, refused to assist you in the least, and even if the English, taking advantage of your isolation, pillaged your houses while subduing your cities, you would still have an immense country, honor and freedom. Don't you share my feeling that it is better to live without ease in the woods like savages[30] than to bend down your head under the English yoke and to return to slavery?

[10]   Let us therefore consider what it involved today. Is it in the interest of France to conclude a public alliance with the Americans, or ought she not limit herself to the secret supply of all that America needs to maintain its budding independence? Or else, an indifferent spectator, ought she to await the events while strengthening her navy, accumulating her forces and her wealth to take advantage some day of the weakening of both the English and the Americans, when, exhausted by each other and weary to fight, having

---

[29]The Reprisal, Lexington and Dolphin are notorious examples, cited in Gibbon, p. 137.

[30]It was believed in France that the Americans were a virtuous people, simply because they lived in a state of nature. Rousseau declared that man was born free, society everywhere had put him in chains.

finally reunited , you will decide together to compensate for your losses by overtaking her possessions?

[11]   This last alternative, the least generous of all, may be however the safest for her. For what must happen if France chooses any of the other two?

[12]   Either the English will subdue America and forcing her back under the yoke, they will rally her soldiers and privateers in a bloody war to punish us for intervening in a quarrel where we could not have any other interest but to harm them; or else the Americans will finally succeed in chasing the English from the continent and will enjoy their freedom peacefully. But what is that freedom they want to acquire, if it is not mostly the right to trade freely with other nations besides England? And the first nation with which they should trade, which one is it but France? Therefore, by not openly taking side for America, for fear of a relapse of the latter into dependence, France is avoiding a useless war, to say the least. And if America obtains freedom of trade, she cannot make use of it without benefiting France first. Therefore, in considering things calmly, France might believe her best interests lie in waiting for the events, at peace, without neglecting to put herself in condition to fight back the first enemy who will attack her.

[13]   Moreover, who knows if Europe would calmly look upon the balance of power being destroyed by the sudden lowering of England and the house of Bourbons' aggrandizement by an alliance with the American continent? Who knows if, in order to restore this chimerical balance, all the Northern powers would not join England's alliance and seek on that continent to punish France for having tried to extend herself on the other? A powerful self-interest, Gentlemen, makes you too much overlook the political considerations which an enlightened ministry such as ours are obliged to weigh, even though they would like to help you, if they could do so safely.

[14]   From your far-away optical point, you see things only as they relate to your own interest. Our ministers, in the center of the events which relate to them by each radius of the circle, are often obliged to shirk a pleasing offer, in order not to attract on the State entrusted to them a bevy of troubles they could no longer cope with.

[15]   You are probably right in saying that it is in the interest of France to help you in order to weaken

England's power. But what man will dare decide if France must start by allying herself with the Americans, being uncertain whether or not they will make peace with England; or if she must not wait to be absolutely sure, seeing the vigorous and constant defense of the Americans, that they will never make up with England?

[16]   That's the hub of the whole issue. America says: Help us and we will never make peace. F r a n c e says: Prove to me that you will never make peace, and I will help you.

[17]   Whence, Gentlemen, perhaps comes the necessity for France to adopt the middle way between an open declaration and the absolute refusal of any assistance and that's what I would also like to establish as the basis of our hopes and of your success.

[18]   Let us put aside the question whether or not all our mysteries and restraints will prevent the English from overtaking our colonies the minute they have totally lost or regained theirs--which is one of the strongest arguments you use in trying to persuade us to declare ourselves in your favor. Let us leave it aside, because, everything considered, we would perhaps still have to conclude that we would do better to remain neutral while managing and increasing our forces, in order to fight against an exhausted adversary, should he imprudently attack us, than to weaken ourselves by provoking him as we send you our fleets and armies, without being quite sure whether that will suffice to prevent a reconciliation between England and America. Which would lead many a politician to prefer for us to an open alliance the middle-road decision to assist you without publicity, but effectively--I mean fulfilling all of your needs--and that's what the French administration could entrust to the zeal or the greed of the merchants.

[19]   I would therefore like to see our administration replace the affected severity with which it checks our business with you, by a certain connivance on the nature of the cargoes we would send; even that it should help us with its funds to facilitate our undertakings, and that on your side you should be more exact in sending us returns without which we can do nothing. The French merchants, soon taking advantage of the overseers' neglectful watch, would bravely fetch your merchandise across the ocean and would carry to you in abundance all that is needed for you to maintain your newborn independence. What would the result be? Either the English will prudently act as if they have not seen

anything and you will have assistance without France being compromised, or the English in anger will take the first hostile steps towards us. Then the natural right of self-defense making legal the use of all our forces, no Prince in Europe will be able to look upon the king of France as an ambitious man who provokes war in order to aggrandize himself at his neighbors' expense. For, by common consensus, war becomes just when it is necessary. That is also the moment when we can become your ally openly, with the approval of the whole world--instead of the universal blame which we would incur if we appeared to be excessively ambitious and the aggressors at a time when England's difficulties have reached their utmost.

[20] The moral significance I want draw from this short dissertation, Gentlemen, is that: (1) It would not be honorable for you to waver in the important decision you made to maintain your independence, without the help of a foreign power, on whose help you relied only accessorily (and who, politically, ought not to give a first example of encouraging such enterprises, since she has colonies to preserve) and who perhaps should, before recognizing you, wait until she is forced to do so by an open rupture of the English, for which you will soon be the pretext or reason. (2) From the general dispositions of this country, it seems to me you are less likely to obtain the open alliance of France by threatening to make up with your enemies[31] (the very possibility of this event causing her to be wary about taking any hazardous step) than if, by continuing to solicit her secret friendship and assistance, you succeed in convincing her that no hardship will ever lead you to renounce the independence which you have declared, not in a seditious and tumultuous manner, but with poise and method; and if, while making do with that help as effective as it is veiled, you leave it up to England to postpone our alliance with you by closing their eyes on what they don't want to see, or to hurry it up through hostilities which France is determined to fight back.

---

[31]Such a threat is made in Deane's letters to Beaumarchais of March 24 and 27, 1777 (Dea 5:555-556). The commissioners in Paris were secretly meeting with English envoys to discuss the possibilities of peace. Even though the greatest part of Franklin's Paris journal for that year was destroyed, some evidence remains. See *Franklin's Autobiographical Writings*, ed. by Carl Van Doren (New York, Viking Press, 1945), p. 429.

[21]   Those are the reflections, Gentlemen, suggested to me by the apparent rigor of our administration and the threats of an imminent peace between you and England. May they not displease you and engage you in giving the strictest orders to your privateers to respect our ports and not to place us in the unpleasant necessity to take action against them! And mostly, may they lead both of our nations, through the careful road politics forces us to tread, to the most firm and durable alliance! It is the sincere and constant wish of the one who has the honor to be with the most respectful devotion, gentlemen,
     Your very humble and very obedient servant,
     Roderigue Hortalez & Cie

19 September 1777, to Sartine
(Mol 654-6; Mor 3:192)

[1]   In replying to you on the sad embargo planned for my Rochefort ship, I don't want and must not dissimulate anything, since this affairs concerns the interests of the State as much as mine.

[2]   Lord Stormont complained, I am told, that a ship that the king has just sold is destined for the Americans. How does he know? He is only assuming it, based on some uncertain inferences. But the limit of audacity perhaps is for him to dare make this assertion before the king's ministers, who know, as I secretly told them, that this ship never was destined for the Americans, that it is rather outfitted against them since I plan for it to go and fetch me promptly and as an order, returns which have been kept away from me too long by my debtors' indolence or penury? Here are the facts and how I see them.

[3]   America today owes me five millions. Through recent experience, I see that the only returns suitable for me are *tobacco*. An ordinary ship can only bring back at the most only three hundred hogsheads, which, all outfitting and laying up expenses deducted, would barely yield in France one hundred and fifty thousand livres. According to this exact computation, in order to recover here the sum of five millions in tobacco, I would have to outfit thirty two ships, run thirty-two times the risk of being taken on the way there, and as many times coming back, and waste at least three months in waiting, without counting the thousand and one contradictions I would experience while proceeding to these thirty-two outfittings.

[4]   I had to look, therefore, for another means of honorably fulfilling my views. Too many enemies, Sir, you know it, are conspiring to my ruin, for me not to try every permissible means to come off with honor. For, if success attracts the envious, success alone can knock them out. This is what I am attempting today in outfitting a vessel of one thousand tons, with which, in one trip, I intend to go pick up and bring back the fifth or perhaps the third of what is due me, without fearing for it to be taken en route: for this ship warrants respect. So, if it suits the peaceful views of the government that no French vessel should try to pick a quarrel with anyone, the same interest also requires, does it not, that the most important merchant vessels look so good that any brutal Englishman should look at it twice before insulting it?

[5]   As to my cares, my precautions, here they are. My supercargo is already on his way to purchase and store in the port of Williamsburg or Annapolis, in Chesapeake Bay, as much tobacco as my ships will be able to hold. The order has already been given at the Cape not to let go any of my ships which will arrive there, but to have them wait for my Rochefort vessel, in order to load together and be convoyed on the way back. For since the Seine was lost, they have also seized the Anna, on its way from San Domingo, and led it to Jamaica. If I did not complain about it, it's because I found little consolation coming to me from everyone here.

[6]   Already, the rendez-vous of all my ships, the last one to leave from Marseilles in particular, and the rallying point for those which are at Charlestown or in the northeast is fixed in this same Chesapeake Bay. As soon as the sea ceases to be tenable to the English cruisers, my Rochefort vessel will take to it in order to convoy all my ships, and bring back their cargoes. Whether I can be allowed to follow a plan as carefully combined for the past six months,[32] or such plan is ruined by a stroke of the pen, makes the difference between my total ruin and my most brilliant success.

[7]   If my vessel is laid up, where shall I find the means of outfitting any others? Who will pay me back the ten thousand Louis this one costs me? Who will

---

[32]Six months, i. e. since April, when Beaumarchais purchased from the French government the man-of-war "Hippopotamus" rebaptized "Proud Rodrigue."

reimburse me for the purchase and transportation of the bundles I brought to it from all parts of the world and which comprise its cargo? Who will give me back the fifteen thousand Louis I am paying today for fifteen thousand guns that I have just sent? And the costs of my last outfitting? And my purchases from Virginia, which will spoil on the docks, where they failed to be picked up on time? What about my weak ships which will be seized on the way back, because, counting on giving them a formidable convoy, I neglected to put them in a position to defend themselves! One million, Sir, yes, one million could not repair such disorder, as I wrote you last week. Will Lord Stormont pay me for these damages?

[8]   You can see that the Americans have nothing to do with all this. But I, who cannot send any counter--order anywhere, I have so much to do with it that, if you stop my ship, I see myself immediately ruined, dishonored, good only to hang or drown: I give the choice for a pin.

[9]   After I have spoken to you openly, as charged with secret affairs, I must, in my capacity as a French merchant, assure the king's ministers that before they let my Rochefort ship out, its known outfitters will give their submission, if need be, to come back within six months to French ports with merchandise duly expedited from San Domingo, to which place this ship is going to carry the troops which were promised to them. The secret connection between this maritime trade business and politics are so well masked, Sir, that one can very well disregard it and have no consideration for the false alarms of the most indiscreet of ambassadors. Moreover, the outfitters will agree to be on their guards so that if during crossings this ship was obliged to give a good beating to those who come to insult it, that will be done so legally that the outfitters will feel entitled to ask you besides, when they return, to avenge them for the insults they have received.

[10]   Such a promise, such an engagement, suffices, I believe, to reassure the French ministry, and especially to muzzle the English ambassador.

[11]   Now, if the king's ministers would realize that it is, to speak plainly, shameful for France that the royal tobacco farm has to pay up to one hundred twenty livres per quintal for it, or do without it, while there is a glut of it in America; that if the English war lasts another two years, the king, because he was honest enough to remain neutral, is apt to see

the thirty-two million revenue of his tobacco farm compromised, because it pleased the English, who can no longer supply us with this produce, insolently to forbid us to buy it from the only country in the world where it is grown; if, I say, the king's ministers are willing to think it over, they will agree that this insolent English tutelage throws us a thousand miles away from the neutrality which we affect. This even seems so bizarre to everyone that in London itself people joke about our lack of spine.

[12]   It may be fitting here to state neutral rights better than has been done to this day. Permit me, Sir, this short digression: I believe it to be of extreme importance.

[13]   Milord Abingdon, one the most enlightened men in England, has just published a writing, which he signed with his name,[33] and which he would seal with his blood, he says, just as readily. In that writing he establishes clearly that the English and not the Americans are the only true rebels to the common constitution, and that's what I believe proved unquestionably, ten months ago, in Paris, to the two English orators, Fox and Littleton, as I had the honor of telling you then.

[14]   Milord Abingdon, a bolder man than I, in conclusion of his work suggests openly that the opposition should withdraw from Parliament, entering on the record as the cause of their *secession* (a new word he created to refer to this national insurrection) that Parliament and the prince have by far exceeded in that war the limits of their powers; above all, that Parliament, being composed of the representatives of the English people, should not have played the odious farce of the servants-masters, sacrificing their constituents' interests to the ambition of the prince and ministers; that in the event of such an abuse, the people have the right to recall such a poorly administered power, because the decision to make war in America belongs only to the people in their capacity as supreme legislators and first founders of the English constitution. In that writing, Lord Abingdon does not spare anyone. But let's pass to the application of such principles to the present situation.

---

[33]Willoughby Bertie Abingdon (a member of the House of Lords and a Friend of America), *Thoughts on Mr. Burke's Letter to the Sherifs of Bristol on American Affairs* (Oxford, 1777). Gudin 1888, 204.

[15]   If even in England, it is doubtful whether the Americans are more rebellious against the constitution than the English, *a fortiori* a foreign prince, like the king of France, indifferent and neutral in all that, may be excused from examining the issue which divides the two nations. Such is the position of the king.

[16]   Following this principle of indifference and neutrality, the king of France, had to write his chambers of commerce, as he did, Sir, through your own hand, that **his ports being open to all nations for trade, the merchant vessels of North America will continue to be admitted there with their cargoes, and will be allowed to take in return any permissible merchandise.** Thus, foreign quarrels being indifferent to you, you rightly opened your ports to the American ships as to those of any other nation. But from this unquestionable principle, it follows that, as it would be contradictory for France to open her ports to English, Danish, Dutch, Swedish, etc. vessels, while forbidding French merchants to go trade in London, the Baltic Sea, the Zuyder Zee, etc. so, **while receiving American ships in her ports on the same footing as those of all other nations,** France cannot, without contradiction, deny French merchants the liberty to go and do business in **Boston, Williamsburg, Charlestown** or **Philadelphia,** for everything here has to be equal.

[17]   Such is, Sir, the principle of neutrality, and such are the consequences France must draw therefrom relative to her commerce. Everything which departs from this is irrelevant and would only involve a tissue of contractions and absurdities.

[18]   If, as a result of your treaties or in order to show consideration to your warring neighbors, you are willing to prohibit arms and munitions in the trade with America; if you do more, if you allow the English to be the tutors of the merchants which they will catch transgressing this regulation, it does not suit me to enter into the causes for this inimitable condescension. But rice, tobacco and indigo are not munitions of war. Through what subversion of principles are they forcing you to include them in your prohibition? Why can't you just answer England that you are a free and neutral power, that you need those goods, and that you have the right to buy them anywhere they are sold? I dare not repeat here what they say in London about this; nor what they say about the alleged negotiations of the honest

Parker Forth[34] in France, or what he himself publishes about it. One would have to blush only to think about it, if all that was true. But those vain rumors do exist, and their wretched success at Ticonderoga, which they blow up, has made them so insolent that they no longer try to veil their threats and their contempt for us. "The first step the French take towards the Americans, they say, we'll know how to punish them for it through a sudden war. But, they add, they won't dare try it as we have properly warned them." That's what they write me from London, and I am dumfounded when I am told to lay up a merchant ship which carries no war munitions, has no connection with politics, simply because the English suspect it to be going to fetch tobacco in America. Oh! France! Where is your dignity?

[19]   In conclusion, Sir, it is the incontestable right of the king of France, as a neutral power, to trade freely with America. To receive Americans in our ports while giving up the right to go to theirs, would amount to a puerile and ruinous contradiction. If the King gave up the right to buy tobacco in America, he would soon run the risk of losing his best tax-farm, doing a favor to the English, in a manner the more damnable because they will never be grateful for it. In order to avoid all future fuss regarding my merchant vessel, its outfitters will submit to returning within six months to France with return cargoes duly taken at the Cape. Finally, I will be thoroughly ruined if, in spite of my reasons, this ship was laid up, which was never destined for the Americans, whatever the English ambassador may have thought. I have no more to say, as I know the king remains the master of it all, even to drive me to despair, if my argument fails to appear to his council as elementary, as strong, as proved as it appears to me, and if unfortunately they will not see the immediate connection between that ship and the greatest political events which should occupy the government.

30 September 1777, to Vergennes
(Ang. 525, fol. 40; S.F. 1707; Mor 3:201)

You frightened me last night, but at last reassured me. Thank you. How could I diverge from your patriotic views? I know them too well to do it.

Mail from Congress has just arrived. It left America August 10th. It says that Mr. Howe's fleet was

---

[34]British agent employed at the Paris embassy.

encountered on August 7th, at 35 degrees latitude, that is, lower than Cape Hatteras in North Carolina. That seems impossible or crazy to me. The packets have not yet been opened. You will not have to wait a minute as soon as I get them.

When I said last night that you saw my letter to the Congress[35] and my last memorial, you did not reply anything? Has not Mr. Sartine, whom I insistently asked to do it, not handed it to you? Upon your negative reply, I will immediately have it copied[36] and send it to you.

1 October 1777, to Vergennes
(Ang. 525, fol. 42; S.F. 1708; Mor 3:203)

I have the honor of sending you the news from America. The most recent ones had to be thrown into the sea. The only interesting part is what confirms your suspicions and mine regarding the Gulf of Mexico. But I have to repeat myself: It cannot be or the Council of the king of England have gone crazy.

I forgot to tell you the other night that our commissioners have the power to deal with all the European powers, including England. I was told this morning that Mr. Franklin was only waiting for a reply to make up his mind about leaving or staying here. I infer therefrom that the British are urging them to come to an agreement. But wherefrom that reply? It can only be from London. It's not in him to double-cross us. He looked very pensive this morning and Mr. Deane told me he was saddened by the death of Johnson and the loss of the Lexington; but what tormented him the most was the uncertainty about what he must do pursuant to a reply he is expecting. Mr. Franklin asked me a lot of questions on your dispositions, and I, eternal conciliator, sustain courage with hope, and deal with him as the commissioners with Congress, and as the latter with the American people. It's a hope chain, of which I hold the first link. I'd prefer it if you did. It would be stronger. While the wind blows my words away, yours are so weighty I realize you must be thrifty with them.

---

[35]The letter to the Secret Committee of Congress of September 10, 1777, given above.

[36]The main argument Morton uses to deny Beaumarchais' authorship is the handwriting. Here is the explanation.

My news from America

The ship Independence, Captain Young, arrived at Lorient with two English prizes, left from America on August 10, saw the English fleet on the 7th sailing southerly in spite of a contrary south-southwest wind. His dispatches from Congress date from July 14 but the newspapers up to the first of August criticize the officers in charge of the defense of Ticonderoga. The people's attitude is still the same. The hope given them that France will come to their help keeps up their courage and resentment against England.

Another vessel, left from Delaware on August 16th, Captain Grimm, also arrived at Lorient, tells us he had grave news from Congress, but chased by the British and about to be captured, he threw them out overboard. He asserts that part of Howe's fleet is back in New York, after showing up for three days (from the 2nd to the 5th of August) in Delaware, that the remainder of the fleet sailed south. If it had entered Chesapeake Bay, as it was believed it would, Philadelphia would have heard from them three days later. The captain left that town on August 16th. The only news from the fleet came from a French captain arriving from Martinique, who swore he had met an English fleet of more than 200 sails, more than 100 miles off the coast, sailing south in spite of the contrary wind. Which agrees with Captain Young's report except that he estimated it at more than 300 sails.

Since, beyond Virginia there is not a single port, nor bay in which war ships can put in, I conclude this fleet is not headed for Charlestown but for our islands. This is supported by their position 100 miles off the coast, which they sought only in order to avoid the currents which drive north.

The Philadelphia newspapers of July 30th say the English had not left Skenesboro, their first position after capturing Ticonderoga, and that the Americans were at Fort Edward where they are received considerable reinforcements. On August 16th there was no news of any English move in the north. Captain Grimm claimed the Hessians have arrived in New York with the fleet and are working on the ships. The English army may be about to rebel, it is feared.

The Lexington, Captain Johnson, on its way from Morlaix to America, was captured by an English cutter at about 45 degrees of latitude. All the officers, including the Captain, were killed, except one who suffered a broken leg. The dispatches for Congress were thrown overboard during the fight.

11 October 1777, to Vergennes
(Ang. 525, fols. 97 & 99: S.F. 1721; Mor 3:206)

My very humble respect as I leave, and the most ardent prayer that I may keep a small portion of your kindness. I have the honor of sending you today's news. We finally know what to believe about this great project.

I strictly limited myself within the prescribed conditions and all that concerns my ship has been done. I am on my way and will be absent for a month. Work costs me nothing when it involves the most honorable of projects.

I salute, respect and love you.

My last news:

Two American frigates, 32 and 20 cannons, arrived at Lorient, had left Portsmouth on August 22 in order to cruise and without intending to come to France. The only news they bring is that a corps of two thousand men, Indians, Canadians and English, who left from Montreal and came down Lake Ontario under Sir Johnson,[37] was beaten by the Americans at Fort Stanwix, three hundred men and the leader having been killed, and the rest having fled. They were planning to get to Albany from the west while Burgoyne got there from the north. It is hoped that these failures, as well as Mr. Arnold's joining the Ticonderoga troops, will stop Burgoyne's plans.

Private news from London state that General Howe, finally arrived at Chesapeake Bay, in Charlestown, has gone up to Nottingham, from which he is sending troops to North Pennsylvania to try to destroy the large stores at Carlisle. That his army is to try to stretch a formidable line from the men and fleet in the Bay to those who are to go up to Newcastle in Delaware, so as to separate Pennsylvania from Maryland, whence he hopes to get his provisions for winter. Mr. Washington came down to cover the country and Philadelphia. The action will therefore take place in that area.

---

[37]John Johnson, an American loyalist, who had fled to Canada the year before.

Marseilles, 17 November 1777, to Robert Morris
(Mor 4:315)

   This letter will be delivered to you by M. Perrier, co-captain of the ship sent to you by MM. Ricard and Merle, merchants from the port of S te.

   I am taking this opportunity to send you my regards and advise you that, if you have not yet heard from us by the Flamand, which left Marseilles loaded with objects most important to the Republic, you will before long see it arriving in Boston. In spite of all the obstacles thrown in my way, I am not losing any time to prove to you how truly attached to your cause I am.

   M. de Francy, my representative who is on board the Flamand, has the mission of going over every detail with you and the Secret Committee of Foreign Correspondence. Your friend, Mr. Deane, the man the most essential to your affairs in France and the man the republic should maintain here in the interests of the cause, knows M. Francy's merit and discretion. He will update you on a lot of things impossible to put in writing. He is thoroughly acquainted with the country where I live and work for you.

   If you can be of any help to M. Perrier, who is delivering this letter, you will oblige me as well as him. He is a good seaman and came to me well recommended.

   We are told that Philadelphia has been taken and Mr. Washington defeated. We don't believe any of it. We know that whenever the English Parliament comes back, rumors are always spread around to calm down the people and counter the opposition's attacks against the war. At any rate, even if it were true that Howe has taken the town, he would have only won, in my opinion, the space on which that city is built--only a few acres, well-improved, and lost until they are recovered by the Americans. What would it change in the cause of freedom? Nothing, as long as there remain men, courage and virtue.

   I salute you, Sir, until a new effort on my part, which will not be long in bringing you more from us, proves to you more and more that I am, with all attachment to your cause and respect for those who defend it, your most humble and very obedient servant,
Roderigue Hortalez & Co.

--Please forward that letter to M. Francy if he has arrived safely to the continent.

3 December 1777, from Sartine to Vergennes
(Ang. 526, fol. 131; S. F. 1750)

I have received your two notes, Monsieur le Comte. Thank you. I made use of the first.

Lord Stormont is easily carried away, but about the munitions, he may be wrong on the quality but he is not badly informed on the fact itself. I wrote and will write again as a warning. Beaumarchais appeared to be dumfounded yesterday, at my house. I did not have the time to talk with him. He claims he is going to see you tonight: he has come a long way.

I will expect the Ambassador's memoir regarding the Anna Suzanna. We must see what he alleges.

I have nothing new to tell you, Monsieur le Comte, and conclude in assuring you again etc. I will see you tomorrow before dinner.

3 December 1777, to Silas Deane
(Dea 2:265; Mor 4:316-18)

When I arrived in Marseilles, Sir, I learned about the Amphitrite's arrival in Lorient. I was far from imagining its cargo could be disputed to me; I am told, however, by MM. Berard Freres of this town that MM. Franklin and Lee have written to prevent its being turned over to me, saying it is addressed and consigned to them for the discharge of their debts in Europe. As I am not in direct relations with these gentlemen, I cannot answer them anything but I must send them back to you, and to you I must turn to ask of you, and beg you to tell them, if you know in the whole world any property which belongs more to anyone than the meager Amphitrite cargo belongs to me. Coming back from my advances to Congress, on the same ship which carried them to the continent, a ship for which I paid the freight both going and coming back, and first payment on a huge debt accumulated over the past eighteen months although it was supposed to be paid off within a year.

I am asking you, Sir, for an explanation of your colleagues' behavior. Is it possible for what I am telling you here and the grounds of my claim to be either unknown, incomprehensible or indifferent to them? If they do not give me prompt satisfaction, I will not only have this cargo seized but all of the ships from

251

Congress arriving in our ports, and if these gentlemen think they can, without any risk for the honor and credit of their constituents, injure, insult and wrong me publicly in Europe, I will denounce them to the Congress myself and reveal all the wretched schemes employed to try and disgust me from serving them in my country. Such schemes must have gone very far since I have not heard one word from Congress in answer to all my letters, except one letter from Mr. Langdon who acknowledges receipt of my ship and its cargo. What came to me in those gentlemen's packets probably was intercepted: but the truth will come out some day and will be vindicated. Meanwhile, Sir, I am claiming the Amphitrite's cargo, and as it is far from being sufficient to get me out of difficulty, I will ask you and your colleagues to make me an additional sizeable payment. I have no doubt they are in a position to grant my request since they have been making payments for things supplied to them well after my advances and certainly on less generous terms.

My poor Amphitrite Captain Fautrell, as a reward for obeying me against the ministerial orders, has just been jailed. I had assigned him a 2 000 ecus bonus for his trip. This incident will force me to augment it as a compensation, and there again is one of those incidental expenses I do not know how to classify or how I will get back.

I am going to write the gentlemen commissioners of America a letter I ask you to support to the best of your ability, for the sake of your country, your honor, my needs, justice and all the sentiments with which you know that I am, Sir, your most humble and obedient servant.

3 December 1777, from Silas Deane
(Dea 2:264; Mor 3:216)

I received yours of this morning. It is really hard that Captain Fautrel should suffer an imprisonment, instead of being rewarded by the services he had rendered; still harder on you to be deprived of so trifling a remittance as the cargo returned on the Amphitrite, after the immense sums advanced by you in the service of the United States. This is what I can never approve of. The cargo must be restored to you, and I am sure, will be on your stating the case to the commissioners. As to assisting you by other payments, it is not in their power, the money at their disposal being greatly inadequate for the purposes for which it was originally advanced and for which they stand engaged.

You will, I think, do me the justice to believe that nothing in my power will ever be wanting to procure returns to be made proportionable to your very great disbursements of money and expense of time in the service of my country. But until its affairs take a more prosperous turn, I dare not rely on anything. May that soon be the case!

After Saratoga, the political context is changed. America has demonstrated her ability to sustain with her arms her Declaration of Independence. It is time for France to recognize the new nation, before a compromise is reached between England and America.

By a masterful political paper addressed to the ministers on the 27th, Beaumarchais will prepare the way for the negociations of the French alliance with the new United States of America. The procedure suggested will be adopted and some of his language repeated in Vergennes' declaration to England of March 14, 1778.

5 December 1777, to Vergennes
(Ang. 526 fol. 141; S.F.1754; Mor 3:217)

God punished me yesterday for not following your advice of the day before. I did not believe myself ill enough from my fall caused by some runaway horses in the "passage de la Chapelle" as I was leaving M. de Maurepas'-- which took away from me some of my blood and strength at a time I need them so much. Yesterday morning I went to Passy with a messenger just arrived from Congress and spent the morning there, comforting my heart with the excellent news, which were announced to you simultaneously. I was coming back to Paris, taking Mr. Grand along, in a light two-horse carriage, when the careless postilion ran over some large stones in Paris and we turned over so outrageously[38] that Mr. Grand has a broken shoulder and I bled profusely by the nose and mouth. A peace of broken glass jabbed into my right arm. I was quickly bled at the foot. I almost had broken neck vertebrae. The black servant who accompanied me had a broken back.

---

[38]This adverb was misread by Doniol and Morton "avantageusement" instead of "outrageusement."

So there I am laid up, but sicker in mind than in body. My postilion is not killing me, M. de Maurepas is. The charming news from America[39] spread a balm on my wound however, and some God whispers in my ear that the King will not let such auspicious events be marred by a total desertion from the true friends of America. I am therefore the voice that cries out of my bed for them: *De profundis clamavi ad te, Domine, Domine, exaudi orationem meam.*

Although you received yesterday the Boston Gazette, I am sending you the abstract which I made myself and want to pass on to the Courrier de l'Europe[40]. It's only fair for me to give back to them in England with my sentences, all the stabbing their ambassador gives me here with his.

I salute, respect, and cherish you, and am going to sign, if I can, with my wounded arm the assurances of etc.

P.S. I hope you will kindly communicate to Mr. de Maurepas the summary of news included herewith. If either of you did not approve of it, I will not send it. I am still spitting blood, although I have no fever.

Very positive news from America

A ship dispatched by Congress, from Boston, on October 8, disembarked in Nantes a messenger carrying packages saying that: On October 17th, General Burgoyne surrendered at Saratoga, with an army then counting 5,752 men. The very generous capitulation granted him by General Gates includes the honors of war, the delivery of their artillery to a nearby fort, and being escorted by militia to Boston where they will embark, after pledging they will never again bear arms against Americans in any country. The number of royalists killed, wounded, prisoners, deserters, or lost from the 17th of september up to and including the capitulation of October 17th amounts to 9,213 men.[41]

6 December 1777, to Vergennes
(Ang. 526, fol. 187-8; S.F. 1758; Mor 3:220-2)

---

[39]No less than the news of the Victory of Saratoga.

[40]This article did not appear in the Courrier (Prostchwitz 1968, 190).

[41]For the rest of this news abstract, see Mor 3:218-9.

While I work myself to death here for the interests of America, a letter from Lorient arrives and I see that MM. Franklin and Lee have taken over the modest cargo of the Amphitrite and given orders to remit the monies from it to them alone. Mr. Lee takes as a pretext for this injustice that you told him "that you took on your own account all of the matters of my shipments, that you would make a deal with me and that I would never require any payment from them." I was so revolted by the absurd pretext they are taking to rob me of this cargo that I had it stopped right away at Lorient in the hands of my correspondent, who is also theirs.

I take the liberty of sending you the letter I just sent to the three commissioners, although Mr. Deane, the most honest man I know, perfectly agrees with me. I thought I should let you know this little trick of theirs, which appears to me to tend to despoil me and compromise you. I hope you will not disapprove of the noble and proud manner in which I countered this absurdity, on which they will not fail to try your mettle. I am not worried about that.

P.S. I have nothing broken in my body and no fever. So I hope to be up very soon.

6 December 1777, to the American Commissioners
(Ang. 526, fol. 187-8; S.F. 1758)

I have a letter from Berard Brothers of Lorient, which confirms to me that you gave them positive orders to sell the Amphitrite's cargo and give them the monies therefrom to you alone. My state of health does not permit me to go into detail, but this cargo belongs to me and I claim it entirely. Mr. Dorsies[42] of Charlestown addressed it to you **in error**, and it is even a greater error on your part to think you can dispose of it to my great loss. Mr. Langdon, of Boston, in acknowledging receipt of my ship Amphitrite informs me that he has an order from Congress to send it to Charlestown so that it may bring me back suitable returns. The munitions and merchandise I have embarked on that ship are in themselves one of the least of my claims on the Republic. When I offered my services and my friendship to Mr. Deane, he assured me returns would cross my ships on their way and arrive shortly. A year has passed and nothing has come, although I accumulated

---

[42]John Dorsius, a commercial agent of Congress.

all kinds of shipments and dedicated my care, my work, my time and my energy to the service of the budding republic.

As to the sentence attributed to Count de Vergennes regarding the munitions, artillery and guns, which I paid with my own money, you will never make me believe, Sirs, that such a wise minister could have suggested anyone that he would take these matters on his own account, he would make a deal with me, and I would ask you for no payment. These matters do not concern anyone but myself and have nothing to do with the ministry, except for the covert protection I have always begged for, which has too often been denied me, which caused me immense losses.

Therefore, when the totality of my claims amount to several millions, invoices for which have been sent to Congress, it would be indecent for you to wrangle about the first return, as modest as the one brought by the Amphitrite, especially at a moment when my zeal for the Republic and my trust in its honesty caused me to go well beyond my means and my situation to be straitened. I will not stand for it.

While waiting for your answer, Gentlemen, I had the whole cargo stopped in the hands of Berard and made them my guarantors for the least appropriation in favor of anyone. I hope you will write them immediately to hold at my disposal either this cargo, or its sale money, for which I will give you receipt on account of what is due me, and not to insist on the previous orders you gave them in my absence. I will not insult you by fearing that, when the armies of Congress deal so generously with their enemies in America, their commissioners in France are tempted to do a flagrant injustice to the man the most dedicated to the interests of the Republic.

I beg Mr. Deane to send me your reply at the earliest.

7 December 1777, to Vergennes
(Ang. 526, no. 17; S.F. 1763)

Your honorable and sweet benevolence will console me of anything. While thanking you for the advice you are kind enough to give me, I can assure you that I have not been too "vivacious" in the letter, of which I sent you a copy.

I cannot write it out but you will be more surprised than I am, because you are less acquainted with the people in question, when I report to you all that went on. I have always made a great difference between the honest Deane with whom I have dealt, and the insidious politician Lee and the silent Dr. Franklin.

The news from America have set in motion all the idles head of the country. The English[43] in the cafes and the at the shows don't know where to hide. But that's not half as curious as what's going to happen in London when these various news hit. I am waiting for details with a pleasure equal to all the grief they have tried to give me.

I thank you for the interest you are kind enough to take in my health. I am getting up today for the first time, and tomorrow, in spite of contusions, pain and weakness, I will start going about my business outside.

11 December 1777, to Vergennes
(Ang. 526, fol. 69; S.F. 1768; Mor 3:223)

Although I can hardly use my right arm, I'll have to force myself to use it anyway in order to impart to you the very private news I received last night from London. Everything has been in such fermentation since the Burgoyne news and the nation is so furious, that the crisis seems to have arrived that will sweep away the deceived king, the insolent ministry and the most corrupt of Parliaments. Everyone is coiling up and disavowing the actions of the ministry. The opposition triumphs and secret meetings are on the increase. Ireland is ready to move, if you give them the word.

What is the true moral significance of this crisis? It's that between the two nations, French and English, the first to recognize the American independence will gather all the benefits therefrom, while such independence will certainly have gloomy consequences for the rival left behind. This says it all and all will be accomplished in this moment.

As to details, if in spite of grimaces and pain, my poor aching body can stand the tossing, and if you have the time and desire to see me today or rather tomorrow, my postilion will wait for your orders.

12 December 1777, to Vergennes
(Ang. 526, fol. 210; S.F. 1770; Mor 3:224-5)

---

[43]The Frenchmen who were partisans of England.

Do not be surprised by the vivacity of my news and the sluggishness of yours. In that as in everything else, an energetic individual often finds a way where official policy only finds obstacles. You will recall that my mail and even my person always passed, while your ambassador's packets were being held back. But I am not the only one to have news. All those who sent to London to speculate on the stock market and sell, based on the Burgoyne defeat, already know that before their agents arrived the news was already known in London and annuities fell to 77 St.

You can therefore be sure that as long as you do not have a French packetboat, your politics will always be enslaved to the English news. No one knows better than you what troubles must be taken in order to achieve a little good. This idea of a packetboat, so simple and so important, which would not cost the king anything, and against which absurdities have been heaped--I had set it up so it could operate without outside help. You were for it. The Boulogne royal solicitor whom I had determined to come and follow up this affair, and for whom I had requested a conference with Mr. D'Ogny, was so badly treated by him that he ran away, and confessed he was disconcerted to see such a patriotic project being so rudely rebuffed.

What a country, where the slightest private interest suffices to thwart the most important views! Let's pass. Here is an abstract of my news, which you have already heard in part.

Lords Temple and Malborough have returned to the House in order to reinforce the minority. Temple had stopped going and Malborough was for the king. The twenty voices which were supposed to join the opposition at the beginning session and which had broken their words, have been invigorated by the last news. Cavendish, Barr, Burke, Crawford and several others, have debauched forty voices from the king's party in the House of Commons. Wilkes is promising twenty-eight others. He, Sawbridge and others from the city undertake to have the mob manifest at Westminster as soon as all these opposition voices are sure of. Besides, several members of the House of Lords have set their wives after the Queen to recruit her into the league opposed to the ministry. Lord North heard it and twice offered his resignation to the king who as yet did not want to accept it.

Lord Chatham, after he made his motion in the House, has received through Mr. Sayer two very important letters from the king of Prussia.[44]

Lord Shelburne and Mr. Townsend told Mr. Pitt that nothing is so easy as to burn Brest and that's where they must start. Indeed their means appear to me as easy as it is simple: I will tell it to you.

Mr. Smith, Lord Germain's secretary, wrote to Mr. Heinson[45] in Paris, that he was about to come to broach something with the Commissioners. And Wilkes, who knows about it, is going to denounce this step in Parliament. They are all saying that your severity for Americans in Versailles is a sham, and that you compensated the American privateers for the two ships in Nantes.

Finally, they add with me that I will be the only victim publicly sacrificed to England. *Bene sit!*[46] That you and M. de Sartine had an understanding on this point with the Commissioners and Lee wrote it to Lord Shelburne. *Bene sit,* once more. But I really do not believe it. Nevertheless, M. le Comte, if it could be useful to the King's affair for me to consent to that in advance, this consent would let all of Europe know that this sacrifice itself could have entered my plans, etc. etc. etc.

The rest of my news is detail, and good to hear although boring to read.

13 December 1777, to Vergennes (For you alone)
(Ang. 526, fol. 238; S.F. 1773; Mor 3:226)

I don't need to dissimulate my pains with you: Your kindness and good sense encourage me.

In vain do I turn over in my head the orders from M. de Sartine and Mr. de Maurepas, the current state of

---

[44]Frederick II, the Great (1712-1786), typical enlightened despot, who ruled from 1740 on, had been a friend of Voltaire. He was at that time allied to England.

[45]Joseph Hynson, American spying for the British in Paris. George III thought he "as well as any other North American spy is encouraged by Deane and Franklin and only gives intelligence to deceive" (S.F. 249).

[46]This Latin phrase, of course, means: Let it be! The Morton edition prints "Bene fit" in error.

events, and what I must do to obey. All of it implies so much contradiction that I am at a loss. My mind is at sea, in an ocean without shores. If I add to it the strange behavior of the Passy Americans, the rude way they left unanswered what I wrote to them, the peculiar things they would like me to say, what I hear about Lee's conduct, what is attributed to you, etc. I doubt honestly whether I am awake, for unless I have offended at once common sense, fairness, honor, England, America, France, the king, his ministers, and the American commissioners, all I see seems to be one of those nightmares caused by fever in a sick man; and what I have to do to effectuate the most implicit submission appears to me just as difficult to guess. Whatever the wishes of the king may be, the pro and con at one cannot both tend to the execution of his orders. All of that is splitting my head. I therefore ask you for a cold and methodical conference with M. de Sartine. I daresay it is indispensable, and without this indispensable necessity, I swear to you I would need to rest rather than to do such a disgusting work as mine.

I have seen you sometimes as distressed as I am. It's your kindness I invoke. Grant, I beg you, that I hear what is expected of me, and that it be possible to do. Then neither you nor M. de Maurepas will find anything in me but the greatest energy in following orders, if they are not contradictory. A thousand times, pardon, and your orders.

15 December 1777, to Vergennes
(Ang. 526, fol. 255; S.F. 1778; Mor 3:227)

(I thought it necessary to send a postilion for the following news.)

Today it is not on my behalf that I am giving you the trouble of reading me, but to let you know that at the very same time that an express messenger left St.James for America, at full speed, at the same time an Englishman was sent to France, who arrived two days ago. Upon his arrival in Paris, he wrote Mr. Deane and asked for a secret meeting, and saw Mr. Deane yesterday morning, when he came home from Passy. They conferred a long time, had dinner secretly together, and around 7:00 p.m. Mr. Deane's valet went out to check if anyone was watching. He saw a carriage thirty paces from the house. He asked questions. It was in fact the carriage of our spy. But the driver had the order to say he was waiting for two ladies. Then the Englishman left on foot and the carriage followed him. He went into several cafs, wandered about as a man familiar with the town, took the Richelieu street to the boulevard, walked around as to make sure he was not followed, and finally came back, after a thousand detours, to the Hotel of the Royal Bath, on Richelieu street. The spy managed to make sure that's where the mysterious Englishman is staying. I think it is Mr. Smith, Lord Germain°s secretary, for I know from a good source that Mr. Heinson was expecting him last night, but as Heinson talks too much, it is obvious that the Englishman decided to do what he had to do, before advising Heinson that he had arrived.

I also warn you that I wrote Mr. LeNoir and asked him to have this mysterious Englishman tailed. Mr. Deane asked someone this morning if he had heard about the arrival of some important Englishman. They asked me about it. I answered I had no idea of it. What a lot of mystery!

If you haven't heard that there arrived in London a Hessian officer entrusted with complaining most bitterly about the way the Hessians are being sacrificed at every opportunity and threaten to leave the English service, I am telling you. In fact, they lost 782 men during the assault on Fort Island or rather Redband, which is nearby: 28 officers killed, as well as their two generals. The grumbling and the threat to quit are sure news.

The English have lost 195 men in Augusta; and the whole crew of a frigate of 26 cannons, which they called sloop. The black servant of M. de LaFayette passed to the service of an English officer in New York and said that the "Monseigneur" was dead.

The English Parliament is adjourned until January 20th, but this short interval will decide the fate of America or rather of England.

The stock of the Indies is at 163 1/4; the bank at 126 1/2; you see how the market fell. If France could seize this moment of fright and uncertainty, all the forces of the nation and all the English energy would not suffice to sustain the market. Everything would be amiss at once.

They bet 15 guineas against 100 they'll keep Philadelphia against the Americans until January 1st, and 30 until May 1st. But no one picks up the bet and all is in combustion.

This comes from last night's mail.

The most important in my letter concerns the Englishman and the mysterious dinner of yesterday in Paris. I keep an eye on everyone and although I am still ill, I try not to miss anything.

M. de Sartine, whom I had asked for a conference with you today, put me down for tomorrow at 9:00 at his house in Paris. It is not the same thing for me but I'll go anyway.

You may believe, M. le Comte, that I do not intend to persist, as you think, in changing the dispositions taken regarding my operations, but only to show the contradictions between the orders and the decisions made, which must be straightened out in order to do or prevent what has been decided. Once more, you cannot have the pro and the con at once.

Forgive my scribbling, and receive my respects.

17 December 1777, to Vergennes
(Ang. 526, no. 96; S.F. 1781; Mor 3:230)

The name of the mysterious Englishman is Wentworth. He is kin to the Marquis of Rockingham, a private friend of Lord Suffolk, used by all the ministers in difficult missions, holding on to the opposition as well as to the royalists: that is to say, ready to live at the expense of both. His mission is to discover where the relations of France and America are exactly and to feel the commissioners to find out what they think about it. Whether he was not satisfied enough with Deane, or whether he is trying to sound more than one plot, he is looking for a place to stay at the Hotel Vauban, where Captain Nicholson and Mr. Carmichael are staying.

This Wentworth speaks French as you do and better than I. He is one of the skillful men in England. He was on a similar mission in Paris last year.

I also know that two Americans, one of which is Carmichael, are about to leave for America with important letters. That's what we should know! But would we get to them? Would you want to? Would you throw some money through the window for this important job? You can see, M. le Comte, that the zeal of the house of the Lord consumes me. But do not write anything on this. Only fix a meeting with M. de Sartine for tomorrow or the next day at night, and let me know in your morning mail.

They say there was a riot in London, where many people died; but I have no direct news of it. They had that people cry "down with the ministry and war to France," which in good French means "peace with America." The moment seems supreme to me, and I beg you to hear me about it. Hey! Ireland, on which you never said a word. I say like Mr. d°Aranda: God, he is a Bourbon. Only the Bourbons don't want to be Bourbon.

I salute, respect and cherish you and assure you of my utmost dedication.

19 December 1777, to Vergennes
(Ang. 526, no. 101; Mor 3:231)

I felt last night the sweet influence of your kindness. If I did not obtain what I wanted, at least I perceived they were less directed against me than forced by the circumstances. To lose a lot of money is bad when one does not have much, but to bear in one's heart the sorrow of displeasing people when one does one's best, and the best that can be done, that's enough to sicken me to death. Receive etc.

P.S. M. de Maurepas told me two words yesterday about Prince Ferdinand of Prussia.[47] If he had the least fear not to succeed with him, I offer to help out, whenever he needs me to. I know a sure way to do it.

20 December 1777, to Francy[48]
(Lom 2:146-152; Mor 3:231-5)

I take advantage of every opportunity to send you news, and beg you to do the same.

Although this is the 20th of December 1777, my big ship has not left yet; but it is the lot of all the ships going to America. The ministry feared commerce would take away too many sailors at a time where they may be suddenly needed. The most rigorous orders have been given in all the ports, but especially in the one where I operate. It appears that the force and speed of my ship have caused Lord Stormont to raise a few shields. Thereupon, the ministry feared to be suspected

---

[47]Duke of Brunswick (1721-1792), a remarkable general and one of Frederick's most intimate friends. After 1766 he bacame a patron of the arts.

[48]Francy arrived in Portsmouth on December 1st, having left on the ship l'Heureux (the Happy) from Marseilles on September 26.

of encouraging an operation which in truth is done without and even in spite of them. As we were ready to set sail, my artillery was confiscated and I have been trying to get it back or replaced, which is what hold me back in the port. I am struggling against all kinds of obstacles, but I am struggling with all my heart, and I hope to succeed through much patience, courage and money. The huge losses all this is causing me do not seem to touch anyone; the ministry is inflexible; even the Passy Commissioners have vied to cross me, me, their country's best friend! At the arrival of the Amphitrite, which finally landed at Lorient a modest load of rice and indigo, they had the gall of claiming the cargo, claiming that it was addressed to them, not to me. But, as Voltaire put it: "Injustice in the end produces independence." They probably took my patience for weakness, my generosity for stupidity. I was as offended by the Passy commissioners objectionable behavior toward me, as I am attached to the interests of America. I wrote them a letter, of which I am sending you a copy, and they have not yet replied to it. Meanwhile, I had the cargo stopped by the Berard Brothers, of Lorient, and in so doing, I did not feel I was departing from the frank and generous way I have dealt with Congress, but only asserting the most legitimate right on the first meager remittance on an enormous advance. This cargo is worth only 150,000 livres. It is a long way from this drop of water to the ocean of my claims.

As to you, my dear, I believe you are there by now. I believe you obtained from Congress a reasonable payment on account, according to the circumstances. I believe that, following my instructions, you have been and are still purchasing tobacco,[49] I believe that my ship or ships will find their returns ready to embark, as soon as they arrive where you are. I hope too that if events delayed them here more than I expect, you will have followed our friend Monthieu's advice, and that you will send my at least by the Flamand and such other adjunct as you may give it, by using the additional quantity of munitions loaded on that ship by Landais, a cargo which can help me a little out of the straits where I am.

---

[49]This hope was deceived. Inflation was running wild in America and tobacco merchants were reluctant to sell. Most of the tobacco was being hoarded in the warehouses of Robert Morris (Augur, 201).

I don't know if I am flattering myself, but I count on the honesty, the fairness of Congress, as much as on mine or yours. Their commissioners here are not well-off, and need often makes people a bit unscrupulous. That's how I understand their recent unfairness towards me. I have not lost the hope to bring them back, by reasoning with them calmly and firmly, to kinder feelings towards me. It is unfortunate that the interests of this cause was entrusted to several persons at once. One alone would have succeeded much better, and in what concerns me, I owe Mr. Deane the justice to recognize that he is sorry and ashamed of his colleagues' behavior towards me, which is entirely Mr. Lee's fault.

I am also experiencing some unpleasantness on the part of the South Carolina congress, and I am writing by L°Estarguette to President Rutledge to ask justice of himself to himself. L'Estarguette will write you about the outcome of my presentation.

Throughout all these setbacks, the news from America overjoys me. Brave, brave people, who by their military conduct justify my esteem and the beautiful enthusiasm we have for them in France! Finally, my friend, I only want returns in order to be in a position to serve them anew, to cope with my own debts, so that I may continue to borrow in their favor.

It seems, if I can believe the news, that our Frenchmen have done marvels in all the battles of Pennsylvania. It would have been a shame for me, for my country, for the French reputation, if their conduct had not matched the nobility of the cause they have espoused, the efforts I made to procure employment for most of them, the reputation of their former corps.

The city of London is in a terrible turmoil. The ministry is at bay. The opposition triumphs, somewhat harshly. And the king of France, like a powerful eagle gliding over all these events, still reserves for himself the pleasure to see the two parties floating between fear and hope as to what he will decide, which must carry such great weight in the quarrel between the two hemispheres.

To prescribe pedantically what you should do, my dear friend, two thousand leagues from me, would be to imitate the silly English ministry who wanted to make war and direct the campaign from their offices. I have learned from that lesson: Serve me to the best of your ability. It's the only way you can do it and the only way you can interest the Americans themselves.

Do as I do: despise small considerations, small measures and small resentments. I allied you to a magnificent cause. You are the agent of a just and generous man. Remember that success depends on luck, that recovering the money due to me depends upon the concurrence of many events, but that my reputation belongs to me, just as yours is presently being made by you. Let it be good always, my friend, and all will not be lost, even if everything else should be lost.

I salute you as I esteem you and love you.

P.S. Here is what I think regarding my big ship. I cannot break my word to M. de Maurepas that my ship would only serve to carry to San Domingo 700 or 800 militia men and that I would come back without having reached the continent. However, the cargo of this vessel is very interesting for Congress and for me. It consists of soldiers' ready-made clothing, of cloth and blankets, etc. It carries an artillery of 66 brass cannons, of which 4 pieces are of 33 pounds, 24 of 24 pounds, 20 of 16 pounds; 12 and 8-pounds balls, plus 33 artillery pieces of 4-pound balls. Which makes a total of 100 brass cannons and much other merchandise.

I dreamt about it so much that I conceived a plan. You could secretly arrange with the Secret Committee of Congress to send one or two American privateers to the level of San Domingo. One of them will send his shallop to the Cape, or else he will signal as agreed for a long time by the American ships-- *they put a white pennant, arbor the Dutch pavilion to the great mast, and shoot three blasts of cannon*--then Mr. Carabasse will go on board with Montaud, Captain of my ship Proud Rodrigue. They'll manage for the American ship to capture my ship, under whatever pretext, and take it away. My captain will protest and write a complaint to Congress. The ship will be taken where you are. Congress will publicly disown the brutal corsair, free the ship, with excuses to the French pavilion. In the meantime, you will land the cargo, fill the ship with tobacco, and you will send it back to me promptly, with all the other ships you may be able to find. As Mr. Carmichael is very fast, you will have time to arrange this maneuver either with Congress or directly with a friendly privateer. This way, M. de Maurepas is no longer held by his word, I by my word to him, since no one can resist violence, and my operation will be successful in spite of all the obstacles that hinder my work.

That's the plan on which I beg you to go to work, my dear Francy, for my ship will sail before January 15,[50] and will be waiting to hear from you at the Cape.

After all I do, Congress will no longer doubt, I hope, that the most zealous partisan of the Republic in France is your friend, etc.

27 December 1777, Private Memorial
for the king's ministers[50]
(France 410, no. 20; S.F. 1814; Mor 3:208 or 4:43-50n.)

[1] As the crisis has reached a climax; as we are certain that the English people are crying out for war against us[51] and are making all kinds of offers to their king in this respect, such as to call immediately the militia and to pay for it, or for each Shire [in English in the text] to volunteer a certain quantity of troops and sailors, provided they be used against Spain and France--what remains for us to do?

[2] We still have three alternatives. The first is no good. The second would be the safest. The third is the noblest. But the right combination of the third and second alternatives is apt to make the King of France the first power in the world.

---

[50]Alas, hopes deferred! According to the post-scriptum added to this letter on 20 January 1778 (Mor 4:41), the Proud Rodrigue was still in port.

[50]Doniol dated this paper January 22, 1778, based on the letter to Vergennes of the same date. Lom nie had dated it 26 October 1777. Morton gave it under both dates. SF suggests "beginning of 1778." However, references to English politics indicate that it post-dates the news of Saratoga (in England, 4 December). Lord North's conciliation plan was announced in Parliament on 10 December 1777. Moreover, a letter to Vergennes dated 1 January 1778, mentions "a paper dispassionate and carefully thought out," submitted the previous saturday, i. e. 27 December 1777.

[51]After the news of Saratoga, and before Parliament adjourned for Christmas 1777, on November 27th, Lord Chatham, ill and barely able to stand, had made a pathetic speech, crying for "Peace with America, war against the house of Bourbon!" (Burnett 1941, 336).

[3]   The first alternative, which is no good, would be for us to continue doing what we do, or rather don't do; to keep on remaining passive while our neighbors are bustling about; to bide our time and wait for things to happen: because, between now and the 2nd of February, either the ministry will have changed, and Lords Chatham and Shelburne, who were offered Lord Germain's position for the first and that of Lord Suffolk to the second, if they would abandon the Whig party--which they refused to do--may change their minds and pretend for a while they have become Tories, in order to take power--and if we are unlucky enough for it to happen, can any one doubt that they will seize the first opportunity to sign the peace with America, at any cost, with one hand, and with the other the order to pounce on our ships and our possessions--which would give us both the Americans and the English to fight--or else, in spite of the outcry of the people and the difficulties; although people are going to protest against the administration when Generals Burgoyne and Howe confess "that they were only the instruments of an incompetent and despotic ministry," the present ministry will hold on. But since all of them equally agree that a war so detrimental to England must stop , and since the present ministry can no longer hope to sidetrack people on their past blunders, but only to cover them while leading the nation to hope they will soon make up for their losses at our expense--it is beyond doubt from the effervescence of public opinion, the small and large meetings held in London, that there will be at least a truce in America, in order to consider the grievances of the continent, and let England catch her breath. But once this first step is taken toward peace, we can be quite sure that it will be too late for France to declare herself in favor of America. Perhaps the head of the American delegation will already have passed over to England, and war against us will have started without any advice as the last one did.

[4]   Perhaps before we can save our merchant ships from the first blows of the English fury, one sixth of them will have been destroyed! It is certain, at least, that for the past two months, several English warships have been cruising in the Channel, but with destinations unknown so that no one in Europe knows in what area they are supposed to cruise.

[5]   Who knows if the last packets sent by the government to America are not carrying some armistice

and conciliation plan[52] which will not be declared in London, it is believed, until the packets will have had a chance to arrive at destination? Hey! if unfortunately the possibility of independence was suggested as a first condition, is there any doubt that the second one would be for the Americans to unite with England against us? Then, we would become the laughingstock of all of Europe, as the deadliest war and bankruptcy for all of our merchants would repay us for our sluggishness in taking a position.

[6] The worst alternative of all, therefore, is to go on today undecided, without starting anything with America, waiting for England to make sure we won't ever be able to, which cannot fail to arrive very shortly.

[7] The second alternative which I consider the safest would be to accept publicly the *treaty of alliance*[53] America has been proposing to us for more than one year; *with fishing rights in Newfoundland, mutual warranty by the contracting powers of their possessions, promise of reciprocal assistance or diversion in case of attack on one side and continuation of hostilities on the other; the whole accompanied by a secret plan to take over the English islands, with the sacred engagement between the three powers, American, French, and Spain, to assign categorically thereafter a meridian on the ocean between Europe and America beyond which all English vessels would be declared good prizes in peace as in war, those restless neighbors of ours having no longer any claim to the new continent.*[54]

[8] It must be admitted that as soon as the English know that they can no longer hope to negotiate with a country which has negotiated with us, they will immediately make war on us and declare us the aggressors

---

[52]This was factual: the Carlisle Commission was preparing conciliation bills (S.F. vols. 4, 5, 11 and 12).

[53]This is referred to as "the Plan of 1776" written by Franklin, Adams, Dickinson, Harrison and Robert Morris (JCC:5, 17 September 1776).

[54]This policy differs from the "generous and magnanimous" way the king of France treated with the commissioners in February 1778 (I am quoting Franklin's *Autobiographical Writings*, p. 434). Cf. *Observations*, paragraph 102.

as a result of our treaty itself.[55] But war for war, as it is today unavoidable, Americans, Spaniards and Frenchmen together are more than sufficient to tame that arrogant nation, should they be reckless enough to attack us.

[9] Another objection arises. It carries weight and I must not fail to answer it, especially since it comes from M. de Maurepas. It is to be feared, this minister says, that the American commissioners themselves do not have powers extensive enough, or sound enough, for us to be able to deal with them in such an important affair; or that their various hidden interests cause it to be divulged before its conclusion; or that Congress, whose members may vary at any time, shaken up by English corruption or intrigue, may refuse to ratify the treaty; or if it does, that the people themselves leaning toward England with whom they share the same language, the same religion, the same constitution and customs, and pleased to see themselves finally on an equal footing with their proud step-mother who tried to humiliate them so long, the people themselves, I say, soon will find a way to elude the clauses of this treaty. Then the king would have nothing left but equivocal allies, a dubious treaty, against a bloody and unequivocal war.

[10] To such consummate wisdom, I answer that, while weighing risks and advantages, you certainly have not failed to realize that in a decision forced on us by events, it stands to reason to leave something up to fortune, while investing it as best one can by all the precautions human wisdom can foster in such a major affair. Those precautions I shall indicate later, after I have exposed the third alternative, the one which appears to me to be suitable for the king of France in this delicate conjuncture.

[11] This last alternative--the noblest of all, whose consequences may meet the purpose of the second one, but without in any way compromising the dignity of the king and the faith he believes he owes to subsisting treaties--would be to declare to England in a good manifesto, which would also be notified to all the European nations:

[12] That the King of France, after remaining for a long time, as a consideration for England and through moral scruples, a passive and tranquil spectator of the

---

[55]This is what happened. See Gibbon, p. 124.

war existing between the English and the Americans, to the great detriment of French trade; informed by the debates of the English Parliament as much as by the success of the American troops[56], that in spite of the mighty efforts of England, during three successive campaigns, the force of events is finally freeing America of the British yoke; informed also that the best minds in the English nation agree in thinking and saying loudly in both houses that it is imperative to recognize immediately the Americans as independent, and deal with them as with friends, on an equal footing; that some of them go so far as to question, whether in this quarrel between two parts of the same empire, the old England is not, rather than the new one, the rebel to the common constitution; that in the midst of all these debates and from the information received from day to day, one is forced to wonder whether in getting ready for a new campaign England's purpose really is to fight America, or rather some other country they might see fit to bother.

[13] That the king knowing only too well that the English, while claiming to visit French merchant vessels and examine their relations with the American continent, have been insulting, vexing and tormenting his subjects, the French merchants, without any regard for the French pavilion nor for the sacred asylum of the French coasts landing; that the English take advantage of their private quarrel, to exercise an unfair and inflammatory visit on all the nations for whom the ocean used to be free; that his Majesty sees with sorrow his subjects the French merchants suffering an anxiety, more painful for them than an open war, being victimized as a result of his own courtesy for England; and the maritime commerce of his States languishing under political restrictions and prohibitions, on one hand and on the other, the very harsh inquisition of the English against all his enterprises. That this courtesy for England has led his Majesty, in spite of his status of neutral power, to worry American privateers about the nature of the asylum they would find in his ports, as well as the prizes they brought there; this austere policy causing misunderstanding between friendly peoples, has already suggested to several American privateers the unfortunate idea of capturing several French ships; that France has already suffered the consequences of such new undertakings, which may lead to cumulative reprisals and resentment to the point where people will be so confused

---

[56]This seems to refer to Saratoga, and justifies dating this memorial later than Lomenie did.

that very soon we won't be able to tell friends from foes, or who we are at war or at peace with. That moreover, his Majesty is in a position to fear that the two belligerents may turn together against him, because the Americans, who have been constantly and openly seeking the assistance and the alliance of France, and have been unable to obtain them, may unite their own resentment to that of England, so that both nations will wage a common war against France--a war the more unfortunate for the latter because it would be the results of the King's courtesy and considerations toward England, and his religious respect for subsisting treaties. That in this current state of uncertainty and agitation, his Majesty, forced by circumstances to make up his mind, will always, in accordance with his heart and his dignity, choose the most noble and disinterested one of all alternatives.

[14]   Thus, that without meaning to declare war against england, even less to make it without declaring it, according to the hateful usage which has become prevalent in this century; without even engaging in any negotiation prejudicial to the interests of the court of London; but as a consideration for the suffering and the just representations of his faithful subjects engaged in maritime trade, his Majesty, as a consequence of the neutrality he has always kept, will do no more than *declare he considers the Americans to be independent, and will regard them as such inasmuch as the trade between the two countries is concerned.* That he allows all his subjects to go trade in the American ports just as they are doing in the English ports; to exchange French manufactured products there against produce from these climes, in competition with all the European merchants who carry there their own countries products---for if his Majesty believes he should have consideration for his warring neighbors, he also think it fair not to let his subjects suffer any longer, in peace time, the privations and prohibitions no other sovereign of Europe seems to be imposing on his own. That while continuing to open his ports to the Americans as in the past, his Majesty does not mean to deprive the English of the right to compete there and procure for themselves French products, whose trade is free to all nations which are not at war against us. That by this moderate conduct toward every one, his Majesty believes he is giving to each one what can be expected from his justice and generosity.

[15]   That, with the intention to make very clear the most disinterested sentiments which motivate him, his Majesty is proposing to the two belligerent nations

his good offices in mediating their differences. Declaring besides, that his Majesty does not mean to importune England or America about accepting his mediation, nor to be offended if either refuses; but if any of the two nations, elated by their successes, or embittered by their losses, brings the least obstacle to the freedom of trade with its rival, at the first hostility against his war or merchant ships, his Majesty will consider himself no longer bound to any consideration for that unjust nation, and will contract with the other, without any scruples, so that this one only will benefit from all the advantages of his alliance and trade. His Majesty declares moreover that he will immediately take measures to fight back the insult made to his pavilion.

[16] Such is, more or less, the manifesto which I propose to the King's Council.[57] True, of course, it is that such writing, doing no more than extend the rights of French neutrality and establish a strict equality between the contestants, may very well irritate the English without satisfying the Americans. Stopping at that point may still leave England free to anticipate us and offer independence to America in exchange for an offensive alliance against us.

[17] In this chaos of events and universal conflict of so many interests, will the Americans not prefer those who offer them an alliance together with independence, to those who will only recognize that they were brace and successful enough to get their freedom? I would therefore, coming round to Count de Vergennes' opinion, dare to propose to join to the third alternative the secret clauses of the second one.

[18] That is, at the same time as I declared America independent, I would start negotiating secretly with her a treaty of alliance.[58] And as this is the time to answer Count de Maurepas' objection, and to keep him from worrying that the commissioners may have divided interests or insufficient powers, in order to procure all the securities possible with such an event,

---

[57]"It is rather curious," says Lom nie (2:160), "that, all things considered, the gist of this project suggested by Beaumarchais . . . is found in the official declaration to the Court of London of March 13, 1778."

[58]The double plan of alliance was adopted by Vergennes, i. e. one open treaty of amity and commerce, and one secret treaty of defensive alliance.

I would not conclude this treaty in France with the commissioners, but I would send secretly a faithful agent, who under the pretext that he was going to settle questions of trade between the two nations, would be specifically entrusted with the mission of finalizing the conditions of a treaty which would have only been started in Europe and only to contain the commissioners. I admit that, in order to carry public opinion in America and counter the influence of English intrigues and corruption, properly preserve the interests of France and consolidate all the main points our administration may wish for, I must reckon that, leaving aside all courtly considerations, our ministers will have to be very discriminate on the choice of this secret agent, for only the trust in his zeal and ability must limit his powers, in a country so remote from the cabinet and under such difficult circumstances.

[19] But this agent once well chosen; the trip promptly executed, those powers well placed; if the commissioners are requested to pledge in writing that they will not deal with England until the first news have been received from the French agent in America, you may be sure you have found the only remedy for the troubles that Count de Maurepas apprehends.

[20] At the very time when I would declare the independence, receive the commissioners' pledge and send my agent to America, I would start garnishing the ocean coasts with 60 to 80 thousand men, and I would give my fleet the most formidable air and tone, so that the English may not doubt that I am in earnest.

[21] During that time I would do my best to wrench Portugal away from England, even if I had to take them into the Bourbon compact.

[22] I would foster war in Turkey against Russia, in order to keep busy in the East those that England would want to utilize in the West. Or, if I felt I could not do much with the Turks, I would secretly have the Russian emperor flattered about my intentions not to oppose the dismembering of Turkey, with some compensation coming from Austrian Flanders--all means being good, provided they result in isolating the English and safekeeping Russian indifference toward them.

[23] Finally, if in order to save face as to the faith of treaties I did not ask for the restitution of Dunkirk, whose present state is the eternal shame of France, I would at least start a port on the ocean so

close to the English that they would have to consider my intentions of containing them as definitive and irrevocable.

[24]   I would cement, in every way possible, my bonds with America whose guaranty today alone may save our colonies. And since the interests of this new nation can never cross ours, I would bank on their engagements as much as I would distrust those of England. And I would never again neglect to keep down this perfidious and spirited neighbors who, after they have so much outraged us, display today more hatred toward us than resentment against the Americans who have deprived them of three-fourths of their empire.

[25]   But let us beware to spend in deliberations the one moment which remains for us to act, and that after wasting time and always say "it's too early," we may have to cry out very soon, with sorrow, "it's too late!"[59]

---

[59]Cf. 15 April 1777 to Vergennes: Those were Maurepas' words.

1778:   THE ALLIANCE, SUCCESS AND DISAPPOINTMENT

The news of Saratoga have reached Paris on December 5, 1777, and Beaumarchais the Statesman has done his job. He has not heard anything from the ministers. He continues his work of counter-espionage.

1 January 1778, to Vergennes
(Ang. 527, no. 3; S.F. 1815; Mor 4:9-11)

I hasten to let you know that a new envoy sent by Lord North arrived in Paris yesterday.[1] We have not lost track of him since he left London. His mission is to unsettle the commissioners, cost what may. He may even carry the safe-conduct from the king I mentioned to you. Some do believe it.

It's now or never time to cry: "Brutus, you are asleep!" But I am sure you are not asleep, and you can see that I am pretty much awake myself.

You may be sure that the English ministers are holding down the universal resentment only by assuring all their friends that they are working in earnest to make peace in America and that it is better for them to handle it than Lord Chatham, etc.

The king of England promised Lord Germain he will sacrifice Burgoyne and support him, but the people and the opposition will support the latter, and his arrival and the new session will decide everything that has not been decided before.

Thus peace with America appears to have been absolutely resolved. That's what I am told very explicitly, and it is connected with the arrival of the new agent. arrived.

As to me, I am told by the same source that the French ministry has granted assistance in cash to the commissioners through Mr. Grand; that the English ministers know it from good source and that I am out, which displeases no one in England. I believe it.

So I have lost the fruit of the noblest and most

---

[1] The envoy in question here was probably William Pulteney, (who changed his name from Johnstone) a Member of Parliament, who visited Franklin at this time and offered him a peace proposal (McSpadden ed., 437).

unbelievable labors by the very efforts which lead others to glory.

I have suspected it more than once by the strange things which struck my eyes about the Americans' behavior toward me. Wretched human prudence, you cannot save anyone when intrigue dogs his footsteps!

M. le Comte, you are one of the men on whose fairness I have always counted the most. You have even looked sometimes with kindness and respect on my active zeal. Before I perish as a businessman I request to be fully justified as agent and negotiator. I ask to turn in my accounting so that it may be proved that no one could have done as much with so little means, in spite of so many vexations.

It is certain that last summer M. le Comte de Maurepas permitted me to buy and send guns to America and promised me that when they had left, he would have me reimburse them in money or replace them in kind, because he feared some indiscreetness on the part of M. de St. Germain's entourage. I bought them, sent them on and have given in payment my notes which are going to mature and M. de Maurepas meanwhile seems to have forgotten his promise. This item and the purchase and loading of my Rochefort ship put me behind by more than 800 thousand pounds Sterling.

As my ship is being incredibly held back in port, everyone regards me as ruined and asks me for his money. Meanwhile, about to go under because I can't leave and pay, I still have not lost my mind. You could tell by the cool and reasoned paper that I handed you last Saturday.[2] But I confess I run out of courage and energy, when I am assured from England that MM. Grand have overtaken the trust I felt I had so well deserved.[3]

This wilts my heart. I carried on the thorniest duties. I now must prove that I have done a good job; and I will do so by submitting my accounts.

Thereafter if I have to declare bankruptcy and leave the country, may God lead my way! It will be

---

[2] I have taken this as a reference to the Private Memorial for the Ministers of 27 December 1777.

[3] Vergennes had granted 2 million livres to the commissioners in 1777 and another million was loaned to them in 1778 (Bemis 1965, 53, 93).

proved then that the king has lost a good servant, but neither events nor men will have the power of dishonoring me.

Enough of that for today. An agent arrived from England is much more important than the disgrace or the support of a private individual like me. I have just warned Mr. LeNoir about it.

May you be happy, Monsieur le Comte, this year and all the others. No one deserves it more than you do and no one wishes it for you as sincerely as Beaumarchais.

4 January 1778, to Vergennes
(Ang. 528, fol. 26; S.F. 1819; Mor 4:13

I will need a moment of your attention tomorrow Monday, after you have dinner. I would also want a moment from Mr. de Maurepas. Although my personal situation is very rough, the matter does not involve me but some novelties I must impart to you. I was on my way to see you yesterday afternoon when the silliest accident forced me to return from Chaillot to Paris. Today you are snowed under but tomorrow you will be free, and although it is rather urgent, I hope it will keep till then.

This cannot be put in writing, although it concerns something you are supposed to have written.

[8] January 1778, to Vergennes
(Ang. 528, fol. 211; S.F. 1830; Mor 4:52)

I was going to take to you and M. de Maurepas the reflections begotten by last night's insomnia. I was going to remind you of the orders to give to the Farmers-General not to oppress an era of one hundred years in favor of one of six, by obstructing returns from America.

I was going to beg you to remember how many times I have been publicly insulted by D'Eon whom I treat like a sister.

Finally I was going to tell you that while awaiting uncertain assistance, I am ready to go under as a businessman: and, by gosh, to start the whole hateful process, I am being assigned before the commercial tribunal tonight. No way out. So, instead of taking my reflections to you, I am sending them. Remember, I beseech you, that I am going to perish for the lack of

400 thousand livres and that I have requested them while proving that it is by stopping me everywhere that politics has strangled me.

But I will die with honor by working and proving I am right.

9 January 1778, to Maurepas
(Ang. 528 fol. 44; S.F. 1829; Mor 4:17)

If I am wrong to be worried about the decision France will take,[4] I do not mean to be. But among the reflections which torment and besiege me most, I try at least to sort out the most important ones and communicate them to you.

All that I read and hear about what's going on in America and in England convinces me more and more that these two nations, which appear so divided have never been so close to reconciliation.

Let's first recall that this war is not between two different nations; that consequently there is no prejudice nor hatred to embitter people's hearts when the time comes to lay down their arms. The debate is solely between the American colonies and the English administration. For some time English speakers have sounded brotherly, like people irritated to see their brothers persecuted; and that is the case more than ever in London. They are Englishmen, they are our brothers, our blood is flowing in their veins. We must make peace with our brothers, etc. Let us not forget besides that the Americans at the height of the war always show the greatest personal courtesy to Englishmen, as soon as they can stop regarding them as mercenary hirelings of the administration.

Burgoyne wrote his friends in london that his officers were moved to tears by the noble way the Americans treated them. All of that catches public opinion and softens the hearts. The king of England knows very well he can solve everything just by appearing to be disarmed by his people's tears, and he is ready to surrender.

Hey! How can the Americans refuse peace when they see the English people themselves driving their prince to propose it? When they see, from London to Philadel-

---

[4]Refers to the "Private Memorial to the Ministers," dated December 27, 1777.

phia, every Englishman open up his arms and cry: Brothers, we felt sorry for you and loved you. We did not stop presenting and defending your grievances, and at long last our cries and your courage together have touched the heart of a king who had been misled by the iniquitous hints, the barbaric and absurd policy of a few ministers. Let us no longer suffer from their mistakes. Brothers! There is no peace to make because we were never at war, and your liberty which the administration had failed to respect, is today, thanks to your courage, the safeguard and the warrant of ours. Let a simple and free confederation founded on the principles of the magna carta unite in one nation the two warring sections of this empire! We are not humiliated by your victory over us. Only Englishmen can beat Englishmen. This must not even be looked upon as a civil war among us; it is no more than a glorious insurrection against unfair parliamentarians and it makes us better acquainted with our brothers and teaches us how we can count on them to uphold the glory of the English empire!

I stop, M. le Comte, although this aspect of things strikes me very deeply. It's enough for me to call it to the attention of wise ministers. I am sure that they are aware of it, they will think it through.

What I want to establish is that perhaps you have counted too much on the two countries hating each other, so that you could always think you had plenty of time as that they were irreconcilable. And I see that they never were so close to make up, so that I reiterate: Quickly bind the Americans by a treaty, seize the last moment when they can still say proudly: France was the first to honor our success and to treat us on an equal footing. She is not on our side because she cannot defeat us, but because of her esteem for us and her generosity.

This great tool for carrying public opinion, M. le Comte, is still in your hands. If you make use of it quickly and adroitly, the English offers will arrive after the fact, and look more like jealousy than benevolence. Americans, you will tell them, it is less to be united with you than to wrench you away from France that the English are proposing peace to you. They would not think of offering it, if they did not know that now that you are independent and allied in interests and friendship with their rivals, you no longer need fear their blows in any manner, etc. etc.

That's what I cannot help but put before your eyes, once more, M. le Comte. But perhaps, ready to deal with them, you are afraid that the American delegation will fail to keep the secrecy needed by this important affair and by divulging it precipitate England's offers to America.[5]

But if you distrust one of the commissioners, I can work things out so that he will have to leave Paris. Then while he is away you can conclude an alliance, which should not be thwarted by your worries about the dispositions of the people of the north or the east of Europe; because nothing in Europe can balance the advantages or the losses connected with America.

Only if England and the north were by our fault united,--only then would the war be deadly for us. The loss of our colonies of the gulf and the most drastic diversion in Europe would be the least of the troubles to be feared. But let America be allied to the house of Bourbons, the wildest war England can make on us could only be equal or to our advantage.

But if General Clinton[6] is prisoner with his army, and if New York is back with the Americans, as the news already suggest, and when this is known in London, we no longer have years, months or weeks, but days and hours to make up our mind.

22 January 1778, to Vergennes
(Ang. 528 fol. 227; S.F. 1845; Mor 4:43)

This painful memorandum which at any other time and on any other subject I would have written in two hours, took eight days for me to write, as my head was engrossed with the awful mess of the matters it contains, about which matters I am requesting in it your justice while invoking your memory.[7]

---

[5]Cf. "Private Memorial" Par. 9. Arthur Lee was kept away during the negotiations.

[6]Sir Henry Clinton, new commander of the British forces had ordered the evacuation of Philadelphia and retreated to New York. False news.

[7]Doniol erroneously dated the "Private Memorial for the Ministers" January 28, based on this letter which refers to matters of accounting. Beaumarchais is threatened with bankruptcy.

For four days I even thought it had become useless because it was too late and I had given it up to work on my petition in bankruptcy. I have managed to get back on my feet for 12 or 15 days. But, for God's sake, is this a life? The more I try to show a good countenance, the more my inner difficulties increase. I have examined myself. I have not done anything wrong. While going through my papers to check my statement, I was struck by what I had to overcome for the past two years to get where I am. If I am to be helped, you cannot do it too soon or too secretly, for letters of exchange, like death, wait for no one. M. Necker especially must not be informed of it--I know too much on the subject not to insist on keeping it secret from him. If I am not to be helped, amen. I have done what I could and more.

I hear from sure source that my two Marseilles ships are certainly in Charleston. So, in spite of France and England, there are 66 cannons, 22 mortars, bombs and balls in proportion, 80 thousands of powder, cloth, tin, 25 thousands sulfur, and *my poor guns which have not been reimbursed* --all that is in America now, where I worked tirelessly to get it, and I had to deceive everyone and take frightful losses to do it in secret.

Ah! Monsieur le Comte, it's my bankruptcy statement which will show what an active man you have let be undone and dishonored, if you fail to prevent this horrible misfortune.

I don't have the heart to talk England with you, for in truth I am sad to death.

25 January 1778, to Vergennes
(Ang. 528, fol. 166; S.F. 1849; Mor 4:51)

I don't want to be so guilty as to leave you in the dark regarding the latest American news. I am sending you express the letter I just received on this subject, with instructions to hand it to you even in the king's council. The news is too interesting to be delayed even for one minute.

I have been working on since last night to tabulate for you my situation at approximately 60 thousand livres, more or less. On more than 9 millions that I compare in assets and liabilities, that's exact enough. My situation is superb over the long run, it's only my present situation which is worrisome.

If you help me out at present, I will vouch for the future. You will get my statement in tomorrow's mail.

Receive the homage of my gratitude and respect, and kindly send me back my Dunkirk letter so that I may answer it.

The Franco-American treaties will be signed on the 6th of February. He is not called in the negotiations nor even informed of them. Many of the Hortalez ships have left for America, but the big warship, Hippopotamus, now called Proud Rodrigue, is still held back. The merchant is in financial trouble and finally faces bankruptcy proceedings.

2 February 1778, to Vergennes
(Ang. 528, fol. 227; S.F. 1855; Mor 4: 55)

The affair I treat so painfully in the enclosed memorial[8] being foreign to you neither as a minister, nor as a man of wisdom, nor as a responsive protector, I have taken the liberty of addressing it to you, persuaded as I am that your mediation will most effective in this supreme moment.

While I am thus soliciting in Versailles, I cause interventions, suspense, I write, I fling myself about incredibly to try to parry that awful blow: but my impounded ship is the death of everything. Whatever I do, however I struggle, I feel myself going under. Seeing my work thus horribly repaid drives me insane.

When I say a hundred times: Give me back my ship which belongs to my creditors! Reimburse my guns! Am I asking for a favor? Isn't it a matter of strict justice to give me back objects which do not depend on any accounting to turn in or computations to check? And will anyone conceive that the ministry let their agent go under, risking everything, for want of fulfilling in all fairness their obligations to me on these two points?

If thereafter you refuse to help me, that will be a denial of favors about which in all rigor I will not be able to complain, since you are the master of it. It's on the basis of superior views that you ought to do it. But I have no right to force your hand. Too bad for me if I perish for want of this help. But to deprive me of

---

[8]This is a paper concerning the financial difficulties of Hortalez.

what I need to keep my credit and everyone's trust! Is that believable? Will that be conceivable?

Excuse me, Monsieur le Comte, I am losing my mind.

15 February 1778, to Vergennes
(Ang. 528, no. 158; S.F. 1863; Mor 4:65)

You seemed to take too obliging an interest in my situation for me to fail to let you know how overjoyed I have been since yesterday.

Yesterday morning, my teeth clenched with fury as I had no news, I waited for the time to close my register and refuse to make my large payment of the 15th which, falling on today Sunday, was due yesterday.

Read, Monsieur le Comte, what I received at 2 o'clock, what I replied this morning, see how exceedingly happy I am. I am no longer exposed to the disgrace of a bankruptcy, which whatever I did, I could not have justified without an involuntary and deadly indiscretion.[9] M. de Maurepas received me as an English corsair who would have insulted our pavilion. I did not open my mouth: I would have had too much to say. I withdrew, sad unto death. Not that I believed America's interest abandoned. I know it is not. The deep secret I resolved to keep after Mr. Deane's brother left, secretly from Bordeaux, carrying[10] ... but this will be the subject of another letter. It is right for M. de Maurepas to learn from me that, if the fear of an imminent misfortune made of me an eager solicitor, I am not lacking in virtue, this will be the best proof I can give of my resignation in bearing with the aloofness and scorn of those who protected me against it. . . Once more I am saved. A million thanks for what you have done for me.

I did not think I needed to wait for either M. de Sartine or M. de Maurepas' answer about my ship, or about the reimbursement of my guns, to reply what I have just replied to my agent in Holland.

If you do not too much disapprove my letter's style, Monsieur le Comte, send it back to me together

---

[9]The reason why the government bailed him out.

[10]Carrying the news of the Franco-American treaty of commerce. Although he had not been advised by Vergennes, the secret negotiations were known to him.

with my agent's letter, so that I may include them in my mail.

During my difficulties, I kept from confessing to you that I was aware of everything, had seen and read everything, and I pretended not to know only to warrant a discretion and faithfulness which should have pleased you, since they relate to the basic principles of honor. I will never forget the generous efforts you made to save me from going under.

18 February 1778, to Vergennes
(Ang. 528 fol. 377; S.F. 1864; Mor 4:68)

If you heard me, I perfectly understood you. But the word "jactance" [garrulity] you applied to a detailed confession does not quite render the purity of my intention. The purity of yours and your kindheartedness show in what you say. Accept my thanks.

I would like to find more ways to prove my discretion to M. de Maurepas. Nothing proves it better than the ability of swallowing everything, including one's own losses, without failing to be discreet even on objects for which one owes nothing to anyone. That's all I meant to say. Moreover, Monsieur le Comte, I will abide by your advice and keep silent.

In this time of press, like a gold sponge, I draw some from every direction. That's my excuse for having loaded in your mail in Marseilles approximately 30,000 pounds of gold bullion.

Mr. Durival wrote me to simplify the accounting of 2000 pounds of back interests, the capital of which is reimbursed in London. Only the form necessitates care because it is better to get out. I am going to write him what I think on the subject. It's a small chore I'll be glad to get rid off.

I have my ship, that's already a lot, and by giving it back to me M. de Maurepas shows a meritorious fairness. Should he be kind enough to add a reimbursement, on which my existence depends, I will remember that I have suffered greatly only to thank him that I no longer do.

23 February 1778, to Vergennes
(Ang. 528, fol. 407; S.F. 1868; Mor 4:70)

I am sending you open what I am writing to Count de Maurepas, less for the letter than for the accompanying abstract. After you have read it, kindly put a little wax under the envelope so that the packet will arrive sealed, and send it on to his address as arrived to yours.

---- Have you seen a bad diatribe in forty or fifty bad lines of verse entitled "Conversation between M. de Vergennes and M. de Maurepas?" Really, it is so bad that it cannot be called wicked.

Abstract of a letter from London (S.F. 1860, Mor 4:71)

A Jamaica express has arrived in London bringing to the king the news that two English frigates pursuing an American ship in the area of San Domingo, the latter rammed into shore near a fort (the name is so poorly penned I cannot read it). The fort raised its pavilion and reassured it with a cannon powder blast. That did not stop the frigates which came after the ship right under the fort. The fort fired twice to warn them. Thereupon the frigates destroyed the fort and finally set the American ship on fire.

This news which leads the people to fear that France will move is hastening the crisis for the ministry. In eight days, very likely, Lord Chatham will be in and Lord North out. They are waiting for him to present his bill, before they strike. Lord Chatham who was believed to be so weak, is working with a surprising energy to supplant the ministers. His friends doubt not that he will succeed. All in the opposition are waiting impatiently for that moment and it appears that Lord North walked into the trap set for him and will have neither the courage nor the means to get out of it. He will either resign willingly or be forced to. You may take this for certain.

That's the abstract faithfully copied. I thought I should pass this short information on to you, to use as you please.

What a time! No matter how one tries, it seems to me there is no longer any way to back out.[11]

---

[11] The treaty of alliance with America, secretly signed in Paris the sixth of that month, had not been ratified by Congress, nor notified to England.

28 February 1778, to Vergennes
(Mor 4:71-73)

The night before last, after I left Count de Maurepas, I stayed with M. de Sartine so late that I could not bother you during the only time of rest you have during the day.

Your wise and philosophical reply on the bad diatribe which I had mentioned to you, is a superb lesson for me who often get upset like a child against injustice or insult. You are farther than I in the career of patience, M. le Comte, and I must take you for a model. As to the diatribe, it is, as I said, too bad to be mean. I did not know then that there was one on everybody: between Maurepas and Necker; between the queen and Count d'Artois, between Monsieur et Madame;[12] between Voltaire and M. de Villette; finally, Miss d'Eon and myself. There is no end to it. It's not worth putting one's bonnet on crooked. No point paying attention to things as silly as they are reprehensible.

I was, day before last, taking to M. de Maurepas' a briefcase full of papers on my painful business. I could tell, by the ambiguous answers I received, what I already knew: The time of suspicion has arrived. Good, it will also be a time for vindication. The mole called meanness has started working underground. But there are in those reports of iniquities such absurd things that it is very surprising that a man as enlightened as M. de Maurepas should react to them. I am so eager to reassure him about myself that I begged him to let me give a detailed account as soon as possible.

Would it be too tiresome for you, M. le Comte, if I begged you to read it yourself? In two hours of work, you will see the whole thing. Because it is not only as a merchant that I want to be vindicated, but as a good Frenchman; and I must be able to speak freely to the one who will do this work with me. Render me this signal service, M. le Comte. At least, I will be sure not to be judged by enmity and the little good I have done will not be misunderstood or hidden.

I am including an abstract of a letter from London which deserves some attention. Also a report I believe I owe you on some silliness being done in this country,

---

[12]The king's brothers, Count de Provence (Louis XVIII 1814-24) and Count d'Artois (Charles X 1824-30).

which you will not approve of any more than I do, under the present circumstances.

Someone decided to recruit soldiers to send on to Georgia or Virginia. I was asked to give them passage on one of my ships. This project is of no use to America and good for nothing except creating a scandal with England. If you agree, M. le Comte, send me back the list of all those volunteer bandits. I will tell you what can be done to stop the useless outburst and stop it quietly.

Count de Maurepas had promised for sole reward for all my work, never to judge me without first having listened to me. He is not keeping his word to me. I promised him to always be a good and faithful worker, and I will keep my word to him, in spite of all that is being done to disgust me of it. I need not leave my office to know who is talking, what is being said, believed, and done to make sure of it. All that wilts my heart but will destroy neither my courage nor my zeal, nor my loyalty.

9 March 1778, to Vergennes
(Ang. 529, fol. 53; S.F. 1885)

I hasten to forward to you the one reply I received from England on the liberty taken by the Courrier de l'Europe, not that I believe you uninformed about it, but not to miss any opportunity to assure you of my respectful desire to serve.

On the 12th of January, in Boston, they said that General Howe had evacuated Philadelphia and that Mr. Adams was on his way to bring an answer to France.[13] That last item was whispered.

Deane has been recalled. The news have arrived in Paris on March 4. It will not take his friend long to address to the French ministers and to Congress a masterful analysis of the "Deane-Lee controversy." His suggestions for the diplomatic steps to be taken and for providing Deane with testimonies for a job well done will be followed.

10 March 1778, to Vergennes
(Ang. 529, fol. 56; S.F. 1887; Mor 4:75)

---

[13]On the treaty ratification.

After thinking it over thoroughly, whether or not in such austere a time I ought to keep silent or speak out on matters important to the public cause, everything considered, I believe it to be a matter of strict duty for me to completely sacrifice my personal interests in order to promote what concerns the great affair of the state.

I went to Versailles yesterday. I intended to warn M. de Maurepas regarding Mr. Deane's present requests, that it is most important for you to be sure you are aware of quite a few facts before giving your answer to him. He is supposed to go to Versailles tonight. If you have any regard for my good sense, please hold your reply or that of M. Gerard, until you and Count de Maurepas have heard what I have to say. I am sending this letter by a messenger who will bring me back your order as to the time I am to go to Versailles. You may well believe, M. le Comte, that if this information was not of major importance, I had rather stay home and work on my own vindication.

13 March 1778, to Vergennes
(Ang. 529, fol. 99; S.F. 1891; Mor 4:77)

I am sending you my work and my views on Mr. Deane's disgrace. My best reward will be your approval, because you see things as they are and without the emotion that sometimes fascinates people's eyes.

I am also enclosing the statement on English finances, which I have revised. There were a few errors. But the difference between the partial results for 1777 and 1776, with a stronger total for 1776, stems from the fact that we do not have the extraordinary expenses for the war and the fleet in 1777 and we had to approximate them by comparison as well as the quantity of troops and sailors added this year to the 1776 service. This observation is mine and comes after the fact. The accounts are accurate.[14]

13 March 1778, Secret Memorial for the King's Ministers
(Dea 2:399-406; Mor 4:79-86)

By character and by ambition, Mr. Arthur Lee was at first jealous of Mr. Deane. He finally became his

---

[14]More than three legal-size sheets of accounting (S.F. 1892), entitled "Incontestable proofs of the enormous expense of the war between America and England and of the total ruin which threatens the financial resources of that kingdom."

enemy, as usually happens in small minds more concerned with supplanting their rivals than surpassing them in merit.

Mr. Lee's relations in England and the two brothers he has in Congress have made him a prominent and dangerous man. His design has ever been to choose between France and England the power that would more surely promote his fortunes. He often made that clear in the libertine suppers.[15]

But in order to succeed, it was first necessary to dispose of a colleague so formidable, because of his intelligence and his patriotism, as Mr. Deane. He has succeeded by making him suspicious to Congress in many ways. Having learned that foreign officers, competing for military ranks, were unfavorably regarded by the American army, he has put the worst construction upon the zeal of his colleague who had sent them. As some of the officers escaped from our islands behaved in such a way as to justify the opinion the Americans had of them, Mr. Lee seized that occasion to assure Congress that Deane himself had sent, arbitrarily and in spite of advice to the contrary, these officers who were as costly as useless to the republic. And as Mr. Deane's powers were commercial only, this was seized upon to disavow everything he had done in this regard, which is one of the reasons for his recall.

A second reason lies in the officious letters continually written by Lee to Congress, to the effect that all the merchandise and munitions shipped by Roderigue Hortalez were a gift from France to America; that he had been so informed by Hortalez himself; so that some people in Congress looked with a jaundiced eye on the invoices and various requests for payment or purchase bearing Deane's signature, coming from a commercial house and under the strict condition of remittances to be made as soon as possible. Nothing therefore was easier for the politician Lee than to blacken the conduct of Mr. Deane, by representing it as the result of underhand maneuvers contrived to support demands for money in which he expected to share. This explains the astonishing silence that Congress has observed after receiving more than ten detailed letters from me--which silence has caused me to send out to them an intelligent and discreet man capable of getting to the bottom of all that intrigue.

---

[15]Social occasions attended by George Wilkes, probably connected with Freemasonry.

Today Deane, overwhelmed with troubles, finds himself rudely and imperatively recalled. He is called upon to explain his conduct and to vindicate himself regarding several unspecified charges.

Resentful, he had decided not to go, until Congress sent him a description of the charges and grievances brought against him, unwilling to deliver himself to his personal enemies without having taken with him proofs capable of refuting them. But I have persuaded him to change his mind.

In order to fully understand the importance of this recall at such a critical time, it is necessary, if I may be allowed to speak frankly, that others should be as persuaded as I am that England has much to do with Lee's doings. It is necessary to know that he has brought his brother the alderman from London, through whom he carries a secret correspondence; and after investigating many theories regarding the means by which England manages to keep perfectly informed of everything done in France, I was the more impressed with the idea that Mr. Lee is a double-edged sword, and that within four days of the arrival of letters recalling Mr. Deane and appointing Mr. Adams, Mr. Lee furtively sent his butler to London.[16] He left day before yesterday, at night. To what end this mysterious trip? How do they always know so precisely in London what goes on in Versailles? How were they immediately informed that there was a plan of treaty between America and France? Why have such strenuous efforts been made to bribe me to speak, unless by giving ground for insinuations, to involve me in Deane's disgrace and to ruin me in Versailles at the same time as he was ruined in America? The sending of that butler to London upon the news of Mr. Deane's recall is the key to everything.

Thus it is clear in my opinion that while England is sending commissioners to America, and Mr. Lee's relatives and friends exert themselves to facilitate in Congress the reconciliation of the two countries, there is at the same time an attempt to destroy by slander the two men known to be the most attached to the policy of an alliance between France and America, Deane and myself.

---

[16]Lee's butler, John Thornton, recommended by Franklin, was a spy in the employ of Under-Secretary of State William Eden (Potts, p. 202).

This honorable American, who until his arrival in France had never experienced the foul deeds which are a part of the politicians' game, has become confused and loses his head, and instead of going to America and face the storm armed with his innocence, he prefers to remain in France and await the complaints against him in order to refute them.

While this intrigue has gained some success in America, Mr. Lee, having use for someone in France to serve his double object of ruining me together with Mr. Deane, hit upon the Count de Lauraguais, a man whose resentment against me he might excite to the point of doing me an injury. To completely alienate my friend, it sufficed to show him the coded letter [18 July 1776] in which I had advised Lee to beware of talking on political subjects to Mr. de L., because it was expressly forbidden to me. Not that Mr. Lauraguais' French heart ought to be distrusted, but because every sensible man should avoid every indiscretion and tattle, remembering that in serious affairs whatever is not of utility is superfluous.

Armed with all of Mr. Lee's secrets, Mr. de Lauraguais felt he had more than enough grounds to sound me, and especially to borrow from me one hundred thousand francs which he needed. As I refused to talk and could not lend him the money, Lauraguais abruptly left me; and since that time the two politicians have behaved in such a way that Lauraguais--who like a child always triumphs too early-has spread in Paris the rumor that I was discredited in Versailles, that I was not told anything any more, that I was even suspected of treason, and that I was being tailed on this account. On his side, Mr. Lee did not fail to inform his friends in England that "America's lover" (that's what they call me) had been discredited and they had nothing to fear from me any more. This is the precise history, to date, of the intrigue that has produced Mr. Deane's disgrace and prepared what is asserted to be my own. The end of the thread once found, it is very simple to unravel the whole fabric.

All this may, indeed, seem very trifling, but since it is usually through trifles that important affairs are thwarted, it is imperative to note them, if only to guard against them.

So, far from looking at Mr. Deane's unexpected disgrace as unfortunate and far from encouraging his design of remaining in France to await the charges, I believe that his departure might turn out to be a lucky incident, and that too much trouble cannot be taken in order to accomplish this.

"Your complete defense," I said to him, "is in my portfolio. Lee accuses you of having arbitrarily sent officers to America and I have in hand a coded letter from that would-be politician begging me to send engineering and other officers to help America. That letter was written before your arrival in France. Mr. Lee claims he received from me assurances that all my shipments were gifts of France and that everything else was the result of your greed, but in that same portfolio I find the coded correspondence between Lee and myself, the proofs that my shipments were established by Lee himself in the form of an active and reciprocal trade and not otherwise. You have not, therefore, arbitrarily imagined that America needed the officers; and, moreover, in following since your arrival in France the precedents established by Mr. Lee, you cannot be guilty in the sight of Congress for having accepted as actual business what was begun with that understanding, and never has been called anything else by your false accuser, except with the intention of injuring you. This is what I propose to establish beyond cavil."

With such arguments and such defenses, I succeeded in restoring the courage of my disheartened friend. I persuaded him to face this brief tempest and I have promised him a memorial for Congress in which I would so clearly vindicate his activity, probity, and patriotism, that his enemies, confronted by the written evidence, would repent their imprudence.

But the departure of this American agent seems to me to be a matter of pressing necessity. The bearer of our agreements having been forced to disembark at Brest fifteen days after sailing from Bordeaux, two months have been lost.[17] The English commissioners arrived before him will divide, seduce or persuade Congress, if an able man is not there to oppose English intrigues by the inducements we offer. Hey! Who can be more qualified for this task than Mr. Deane? Convinced that he owes his disgrace to the enemies of France, he will support her interests in good faith and the more

---

[17]Deane's brother, Simeon, mentioned in the letter to Vergennes of 15 February 1778. According to Morton (4:67, n. 2), Simeon had left for America on 6 January 1778 with mission to announce the news of an eventual treaty between America and France so as to forestall any reconciliation between America and England.

willingly because his vindication and his standing in America cannot come except from France.

I would therefore dare to propose that, while I establish the first attestation, a second one be granted by the ministry regarding his wise and efficient behavior.

I would even wish for some particular token, like a portrait of the king or such other remarkable present, be given him to assure his countrymen that he not only was an honorable and faithful agent but that his person, his prudence and his exertions have always been agreeable to the French ministry.[18]

Mr. Deane firmly believes that France must not lose any time to come out publicly and strongly in favor of America.[19] Consequently, if he determines to leave, it is not an extraordinary request on his part to ask to be taken to Boston by a French fleet, so that this may help him counter effectively England's peace proposals and annihilate the intrigues of the English commissioners as well as those of Mr. Lee's friends.[20]

Without such an effort on our part, he believes our alliance will fail. I am also of the opinion that this demonstration would remove all obstacles to the alliance. But since many things may still delay the action of France, however favorable the disposition of the government, I think there should be no hesitation in profiting by the recall of Mr. Deane, to hasten the departure to America of a man loaded with personal honors and useful to our interests. Once justified before Congress, his opinion will carry weight. He will be persuasive and the more so because his enemies recently disconcerted will still be upset and disturbed by their defeat.

---

[18] Deane received a snuff-box decorated with a portrait of Louis XVI, studded with diamonds. He and Franklin were introduced to the Court. See letter to Baron von Steuben (Mor 4:95).

[19] Deane and Beaumarchais did not have to worry about this. The same day, 13 March 1778, the Marquis de Noailles communicated the treaty of commerce to the king of England, before it had been ratified by Congress.

[20] This was granted. Admiral d'Estaing's fleet arrived in Delaware Bay on July 9 (Dea 2:468).

If the ministry does not grant him the fleet he wishes for, he must at least have a frigate of the king. M. de Sartine will see to it. He must have a good vindicatory memorial from his good friend Beaumarchais, who will give it with pleasure.[21] He must have an honorable discharge for his performance, and that will be M. de Vergennes' job. Finally, I believe he must have a distinctive token of personal appreciation, and that must emanate from M. de Maurepas's hand on behalf of the king.[22]

There is not a moment to lose. The English did not propose reconciliation until, from their secret information, they were convinced that France was sending a treaty to America. Since the news of Mr. Deane's recall, why is Lee's butler running to London? If not to hasten the commissioners' departure so that they will finish their business before we even start ours?

It is important therefore that Mr. Deane, properly armed with documents, but with the appearance of grief, like a man suffering a disgrace, should sail for America; that what revives his courage should be concealed from others, and that his enemies and ours, anticipating an easy victory, should relax their precautions. I even propose to leave Paris, if desired, at the same time, like a persecuted man driven to despair. My lawsuit at Aix will furnish me an excellent pretext. But I also propose that a reliable man leave with Mr. Deane,[23] in order to bring back on the same frigate ordered to wait for him the results of Mr. Deane's action in Congress. Then our adversaries' schemes will react upon themselves, and their very efforts to injure us will hasten our success.

If those views appear sensible and are approved, as soon as I am assured of it, I will leave everything else and will not rest until I have soundly established Mr. Deane's vindication.

---

[21] See letter to Congress, 23 March 1778.

[22] This was done by Vergennes (Dea 2:434 and 436).

[23] That would be the former Foreign office clerk, Conrad Alexandre Gerard.

21 March 1778, to Vergennes
(Ang. 529, fol. 130; S.F. 1905; Mor 4:90)

I have already received the best reward for my work: The first step has been taken regarding England,[24] and America openly is the ally of France. Although I do not yet believe the ministry God-forsaken enough to declare war on us, I expect to hear the news any time. Everyone has made his campaign plans, and I think I calculated one which would be as safe as it is certain. It involves as much political work as martial. The sketch is already on paper, and I plan to offer it to you as soon as I can make a fair copy of it. Meanwhile, I am giving you as a sure thing that there are 14 English corsairs, armed with between 16 and 30 cannons, around Jersey and Guernsey islands, ready to bear down on our ships as soon as the whistle blows.

It is appropriate for you to know about this pirate den, before they undertake anything against our merchant vessels. In the past three months I heard that 44 of them, all French, have left from North America, that 5 of them have been captured as they were sailing out of Chesapeake Bay, that only two have arrived and the fate of the other 37 is still unknown.

They have just seized two American ships, one in destination of Nantes, the other one putting in on its way to Bordeaux, with French pilots already on board. That's what is shown in my notices from Nantes and St. Malo.

I am sending you a letter I received yesterday from my agent in America.[25] You will see there that this young man's ideas on Mr. Deane's recall are absolutely the same as those I stated in my last paper. You will kindly return it to me.

---

[24]The treaty of amity and commerce was notified on March 13th.

[25]Between his arrival in Portsmouth on December 1, 1777, and January 11, 1778, Francy wrote three letters. Only one is given in Morton (4:28), dated Boston, 11 January 1778. It was received on March 3rd. Most of the French officers, Francy said, were vexed and anxious to return home.

23 March 1778, to Congress
(Dea 2:428-31; Mor 4:91-4)

After congratulating your country and mine on the useful and noble alliance that France has just contracted with America, I owe it to truth, to Mr. Deane's honor and mine, to make the following declaration to you, which Mr. Deane will take to you.

Although I am known to you only under the name of Roderigue Hortalez, the signature I have adopted previously to veil my commercial operations with you, my name is Caron de Beaumarchais. Long before Mr. Deane arrived in France, I had planned to establish a commercial house powerful and zealous enough to face the risks of the sea and the war and take over to you the munitions and merchandise for the clothing of your troops, which I was told you needed very badly.

I spoke to Mr. Arthur Lee about this plan in London and not only did I ask him if he had some means of establishing this commerce between you and me, but I wrote him from France that, if he could assure me of the prompt arrival of returns in products from your continent, to pay for my shipments and enable me to serve you further, I might be able to motivate some wealthy friends of mine to join me in establishing this trade with you [6 and 12 June 1776].

Mr. Lee answered that the tobacco returns would slow down the operations [23 May, 14 and 21 June 1776], if I wanted them done promptly, but that he beseeched me to send meanwhile my munitions and merchandise. I replied that having solicited even the powers that be to enter secretly in my plans through considerable advances, and having not been able to obtain it, I had just formed a commercial company who would join me for those shipments on the condition of returns from America as prompt as possible [18 July 1776]. Mr. Lee having failed to answer that letter, I was working alone, Gentlemen, to form that company, when Mr. Deane came to France. From that moment on I no longer had any correspondence with anyone else. I conferred with him alone and it is on the basis of our mutual efforts, the powers from you he communicated to me, the details he furnished me, the explicit orders he made with me for merchandise and war munitions, and the reiterated promises he made me that you would pay for our supplies with prompt returns, that I was able to determine my friends to entrust me with sufficient funds for the first disbursements.

Hence it is with him alone, Gentlemen, that I have consulted in regard to your interests. He alone, acting in your behalf, did all the work necessary to overcome difficulties which arose on every hand, and without the reliance we placed in his promises, perhaps I would never have succeeded in putting together this enterprise which when he arrived was only a plan, still doubtful and wavering.

Although the returns he had pledged in your behalf have not arrived within the time fixed, causing considerable difficulties to us, we never reproached it to him because we saw that he was even more distressed than we were. But I dare assure you, Gentlemen, that had he not endeavored continually to sustain our confidence against the slowness of your remittances, I might have been forced by my friends to abandon an enterprise which presented only risks and almost no hope of profit.

When he informed me of the situation of the American forces, I recalled that Arthur Lee in his letters had insisted I should do my utmost to send officers, engineers and vessels.[26] I advised therefore Mr. Deane, who dared not take it upon himself, to get together a choice of engineers and to embark them on the first of my merchant ships. A few days later, having found a way to procure for you some artillery among the surplus of our arsenals, I advised him to add to the engineers artillery officers to accompany what I was sending. .I felt confident doing it inasmuch as I had under my eyes Mr. Lee's letter, asking "How do you think America will be able to fight against England if you do not send engineers and war vessels?" This last article lying beyond the powers of a commercial firm, I simply exerted myself to procure the others. Such are the reasons why we decided to send you some officers.

As I have never known anyone else but him, as my house never dealt with anyone else in France, and as the other commissioners have even denied me the most basic courtesies, I certify that if my zeal, my money advances and shipments of munitions and merchandise have been agreeable to the noble Congress, their gratitude is due to the indefatigable exertions of Mr. Deane throughout this commercial affair.

I hope the honorable Congress, rejecting any insinuation by which others would like to take credit for the success of our business, will take the word of

---

[26]See from Arthur Lee, 21 June 1776.

the man most capable of informing them, and who respectfully signs,

>   Your most humble and obedient servant,
>   Caron de Beaumarchais
>   Secretary of the king, Lieutenant general of his hunt,
>   known in America under the business name of
>   Roderigue Hortalez & Cie

29 March 1778, from Silas Deane
(Dea 2:438; Mor 4:96)

I find since you left Paris that it is impossible for me to wait for your return from Rochefort, before I set out on my journey.

The letter you gave me for the Congress, with the correspondence between you and Mr. Lee when in London, will help to throw light on some transactions, which by the envy of some and the wickedness of others, have been most strangely misrepresented.

It is unhappy that the short time allowed me to prepare for my voyage will not admit of our making at least a general settlement of your accounts; but the absolute necessity of my setting out immediately, obliges me to leave my other transactions in the same unsettled state.

As the letters and treaty sent out some weeks since will fully inform Congress of the state of their affairs in Europe, to know which appears to have been the principal motive of my being sent for, I hope to return to France early in the fall, immediately after which it shall be my business to adjust and settle with you the accounts of your several expeditions and disbursements for Congress whilst in America. I shall be able to do you that justice with Congress and my countrymen in general which you so eminently merit; and I flatter myself, be able to remove any ills impressions that may have been made by designing persons. I doubt not indeed but that Mr. Francy will have already succeeded in a great measure in this, and hope that he will procure you a large remittance, and that Congress will no longer delay to do justice to your early and important services in the cause of American liberty.

After the perplexing and embarrassing scenes you have had to pass through, it must give you the most sensible joy to find the object of your labors obtained, and to see an armament going out[27] which will convince America and the world of the sincere friendship of France, and their resolution to protect their liberties and independence. I again congratulate you on this great and glorious event, to which you have contributed more than any other person.[28] I have requested Dr. Bancroft[29] to wait on you, and to inform you particularly of the necessity I am of setting out before you return.

I shall improve every opportunity of writing you, and rely on being honored with a continuance of your correspondence and friendship. Wishing you may ever be fortunate and happy, I am etc.

30 March 1778, to Deane
(Dea 2:440; Mor 4:97)

As I am afraid you may already have left for America when I arrive in Paris, I am writing you on board the Proud Rodrigue in the roadstead of Rochefort to recommend my interests to you with Congress. No one knows better than you how devotedly I sacrificed my fortune and that of my friends to the interests of America.

The necessity to recover the funds I need made me decide to consign the Proud Rodrigue cargo to M. Chevalier, a Rochefort merchant and my supercargo in this area, to be sold upon his arrival on the continent, instead of sending it directly to Congress, like my other cargoes. I have nevertheless recommended M. Chevalier to give priority to the Committee of Commerce for the items which they may wish to get in the interest of the republic but, whether or not the committee takes anything, I ask you to take care of Chevalier, Francy and my captain and all that pertains to my business as I have taken care of yours and those of Congress in Europe.

---

[27] A French fleet under Admiral d'Estaing left in March and arrived in July in Philadelphia, with Silas Deane on board as well as the first French ambassador to the United States, C. A. Gerard.

[28] Vergennes saw this statement with a jaundiced eye, according to Beaumarchais (RC, Mol 476).

[29] Would Deane have kept Bancroft spying on Beaumarchais, even after he had been recalled? There is no greater dramatic irony in the life of the French playwright. But the poor "militia diplomat" probably was not an accomplice. Had he been that crafty, he would have taken better care of his own interests.

If some unforeseen obstacle had delayed the 50 thousand pounds Sterling account I charged Francy to obtain from Congress in order to purchase tobacco for me, I count on your friendship and gratitude to do whatever you can to expedite this matter right away. M. Chevalier, the bearer of this letter, received from me the express order to solicit your good offices for all the matters where you may be useful to him and I have no doubt that you will gladly oblige the one who remains etc.

10 April 1778, from Swinton
(Mor 4:102-3)

I have just heard that the Lords of the Exchequer have forbidden the exportation of any goods not accompanied by an official specific permission, and in consequence, the Courrier de l'Europe has been stopped at the Customs in Dover and sent back to London.

As I suspect this prohibition will not be lifted for quite a while, I hasten to consult you, Sir, and ask you whether it would not be appropriate for me to have the Courrier reprinted in Paris and promptly secure the minister's order to this effect. This alternative presents some drawbacks: 1) The people who refused to believe the Courrier was printed in London would be confirmed in their belief. 2) Two, six or perhaps ten sheets being reprinted, why not, people would say, the whole paper? In that case, what stock can be taken in a sheet revised, corrected and castrated by the Paris Censors? Such are the reactions to be expected in that event, and the Courrier would be regarded as an ordinary paper, deprived of the originality, the energy, and the liveliness which have henceforth made its reputation.

On the other hand the public are getting tired of the long delay suffered by this correspondence, the subscribers complain, and the would-be subscribers do not appear. The editors of other periodicals are beginning to spread unfavorable rumors which ought to be checked.

Please let me know what decision should be taken in this critical circumstance. Your extensive knowledge and understanding will suggest to you, I hope, some means which will reflect the intent of the government, whose orders it will always be my duty to comply with.

20 April 1778, from Vergennes to Sartine
(Ang. 529, fol. 336)

The American Commissioners, Sir, have just made representations to me relative to the discouragement shown by the maritime merchants in Nantes and in Bordeaux, who have been involved in trade with America. They are asking for convoys for the security of that trade. I can do no better, Sir, than to send you the translation of their letter.

Franklin and his new associates, Arthur Lee and John Adams, continue mistreating America's best friend by trying to take from him the value of the cargoes brought back on his ships. Theveneau de Francy, on the other hand, has succeeded in getting a contract between Hortalez and Congress, which is up for ratification by the Commissioners. The basis for the "Deane-Lee controversy" is alive and well in Paris. Did the king of France not furnish the secret aid to his ally? Do they have to pay Hortalez? Who is Hortalez anyway? The minister's "diplomatic" answer amounts to a betrayal of State secret, an admission of breach of faith, and an abandonment of his agent.

5 September 1778, to Benjamin Franklin
(Mor 4:226)

M. de Beaumarchais is honored to present his very humble homage to Mr. Franklin. He begs him kindly to let him know by the postilion delivering this letter, what day he will be able to confer with him and Mr. Lee regarding the *Thereze*. Letters from Nantes require M. de Beaumarchais to promptly give orders for the sale, time being of the essence.

10 September 1778, from the American Commissioners
(Franklin, Lee and Adams)
(Wha 2:708-9; Mor 4:226)

In a letter we have received from the Committee of Commerce of the 16th May, we are informed that they had ordered several vessels lately to South Carolina for rice, and directed the continental agents in that State to consign them to our address.

In the letter from Mr. Livingston to us, dated Charleston, S. C., 10th June, 1778, he has subjected the cargo of the Thereze to our orders.

In your letter to us, dated Passy, 8 September 1778, you demand that the cargo received in your own vessel should be sold, and the money remitted to you, in part for a discharge of what is due to you by Congress.

We are at a loss to know how you claim the Thereze as your proper vessel, because M. Monthieu claims her as his, produces a written contract for the hire of her, part of which we have paid, and the remainder he now demands of us. However, Sir, we beg leave to state to you the powers and instructions we have received from Congress, and to request your attention to them as soon as possible, and to inform you that we are ready to enter upon the discussion of these matters at any time and place you please.

But until the accounts of the company of Roderigue Hortalez and Co. are settled for what is passed, and the contracts proposed either ratified by you and us, or rejected by one party, we cannot think we should be justified in remitting you the proceeds of the cargo of the Thereze. We will, however, give orders to our agents for the sale of the cargo, and that the proceeds of the sale be reserved to be paid to the house of Roderigue Hortalez and Co., or their representative, as soon as the accounts shall be settled, or the contract ratified.

By a copy of a contract between a committee of Congress and Mr. Francy, dated the 16th of April last, we perceive that the seventeenth article, respecting the annual supply of twenty-four millions of livres, shall not be binding upon either of the parties, unless the same shall be ratified by Roderigue Hortalez and Co., and the Commissioners of the United States at Paris. We take this opportunity to inform you, Sir, that we are ready to confer with Roderigue Hortalez and Co. or any person by them authorized for this purpose, at any time and place that they or you shall appoint.

10 September 1778, to Vergennes from the Commissioners, Franklin, Lee and Adams (Wha 2:706-7)

By some of the last ships from America we received from Congress certain powers and instructions which we think it necessary to lay before Your Excellency, and which we have the honor to do in this letter.

On the 13th of April last Congress resolved, "that the commissioners of the United States in France be authorized to determine and settle with the house of Roderigue Hortalez and Co. the compensation, if any, which should be allowed them on all merchandise and warlike stores shipped by them for the use of the United States previous to the 14th of April, 1778, over and above the commission allowed them in the sixth article of the proposed contract between the committee of commerce and John Baptist Lazarus Theveneau de Francy."

In the letter of the committee of commerce to us, in which the foregoing resolution was enclosed, the committee express themselves thus: "This will be accompanied by a contract entered into between J.B.L. Theveneau de Francy, agent of P. A. Caron de Beaumarchais, representative of the house of Roderigue Hortalez and Co., and the committee of commerce. You will observe that their accounts are to be fairly settled, and what is justly due paid for, as, on the one hand, Congress would be unwilling to evidence a disregard for, and contemptuous refusal of, the spontaneous friendship of his most Christian Majesty, so on the other they are unwilling to put into the private pockets of individuals what was graciously designed for the public benefit. You will be pleased to have their accounts liquidated, and direct in the liquidation thereof that particular care be taken to distinguish the property of the crown of France from the private property of Hortalez & Co., and transmit to us the accounts so stated and distinguished. This will also be accompanied by an invoice of articles imported from France, and resolves of Congress relative thereto. You will appoint, if you should judge proper, an agent or agents to inspect the quality of such goods as you may apply for to the house of Roderigue Hortalez & Co. before they are shipped, to prevent any impositions."

On the 16th of May last Congress resolved, "that the invoice of articles to be imported from France, together with the list of medicines approved by Congress, be signed by the committee of commerce and transmitted to the commissioners of the United States at Paris who are authorized and directed to apply to the house of Roderigue Hortalez & Co. for such said articles as they shall have previously purchased or contracted for; that copies of the invoices to be delivered to M. de Francy, agent of RH&Co., together with a copy of the foregoing resolution; and that the articles to be shipped by the house of RH&Co. be not insured, but that notice be given to the commissioners in France that they may endeavor to obtain convoy for the protection thereof."

We have the honor to enclose to Your Excellency a copy of the contract made between the committee and M. Francy, a copy of M. Francy's powers, and a copy of the list of articles to be furnished according to the contract, that Your Excellency may have before you all the papers relative to this subject.

We are under the necessity of applying to Your Excellency upon this occasion and of requesting your advice. With regard to what is passed, we know not who the persons are who constitute the house of RH&Co. but we have understood, and Congress has ever understood, and so have the people in America in general, that they were under obligations to his Majesty's good will for the greatest part of the merchandise and warlike stores heretofore furnished under the firm of RH&Co. We cannot discover that any written contract was ever made between Congress, or any agent of theirs, and the house of RH&Co., nor do we know of any living witness, or any other evidence, whose testimony can ascertain to us, who the persons are that constitute the house of RH&Co., or what were the terms upon which the merchandise and munitions of war were supplied, neither as to the price, nor the time, or conditions of payment. As we said before, we apprehend that the United States hold themselves under obligations to His Majesty for all those supplies, and we are sure it is their wish and determination to discharge the obligation to His Majesty as soon as Providence shall put it in their power. In the mean time, we are ready to settle and liquidate the accounts according to our instructions at any time and in any manner which His Majesty and Your Excellency shall point out to us.

As the contract for future supplies is to be ratified, or not ratified, by us, as we shall judge expedient, we must request Your Excellency's advice as a favor upon this head, and whether it would be safe or prudent in us to ratify it, and in Congress to depend upon supplies from this quarter, because if we should depend upon this resource for supplies and be disappointed, the consequences would be fatal to our country.

16 September 1778, from Vergennes to Conrad Alexandre Gerard, French Ambassador in the U.S.
(Mor 4:229n.)

The commissioners have just sent me a new twofold request. The first point concerns the verification of Beaumarchais' account under the name of RH&Co. and the second the ratification of the contract which the Committee of Commerce has entered into with Francy, Beaumarchais' agent. Mr. Franklin and his colleagues want to know which articles were furnished by the king and which by Beaumarchais on his own private account, and they insinuate that Congress is persuaded that all or most of what has been sent was on His Majesty's account. I am going to reply to them that the king furnished nothing, that he simply allowed M. de Beaumarchais to help himself in the king's arsenals and replace the stores later [de se pourvoir dans ses arsenaux charge de remplacement]: that moreover, I will be pleased to see to it that they should not be pressed for the reimbursement of the military stores.

As to the contract entered into with Francy, the commissioners are empowered to ratify or reject it, and they are asking for my advice. As I do not know the house of RH&Co. and cannot answer for them, it is impossible for me to have an opinion either on its soundness or its faithfulness in fulfilling its obligations.

Kindly communicate these two answers to Congress.[30]

3 October 1778, to Vergennes
(Ang. 530, fol. 321; Mor 4:248)

I was far away from Paris when M. de Rayneval's letter arrived at my house. I was therefore unable to be at the specified time according to your orders. Since my return I have made a trip to Versailles, but I was kept so late with M. de Sartine that you had already retired when I came out.

I am now asking for your orders when your head freed of more important affairs will find it possible to give me some attention, of which I will not abuse. Telling you that after I returned from Provence I went to London for twelve days may give you the idea of the highest imprudence. However, in listening to me, you will perhaps become convinced that it involved the love of good more than any carelessness on my part. I only had to show a little pride in repulsing the silliest insult from the Under-Secretary of State *Portina*[31] by a rather vigorous reply *la francaise*.

6 December 1778, to Francy[32]

---

[30]Gerard to Congress, 9 February 1779 (Wha 3:203).

[31]This code name may refer to Under-Secretary of State William Eden who was in charge of espionage in France.

[32]There is in 1778 a heavy correspondence between Francy, handling the affairs of Hortalez in the States, and his boss. Fourteen letters were sent in triplicates or quadruplicates by

(Lom 2:152-6; Mor 4:284)

   I am dispatching you the corsair Zephir to warn you that I am ready to put to sea a fleet of more than twelve sails under the leadership of the Proud Rodrigue, which you sent back to me and which arrived in Rochefort October 1st in good condition. That fleet may contain from 5 to 6 thousand tons, outfitted absolutely in war. Act accordingly.

   If my ship Ferragus [alias Amelie and Romain], out of Rochefort last September, has arrived, hold it for the return until my fleet arrives. Its load was arranged between Monthieu and me. We loaded it based according to the list you sent me by the Proud, although to tell the truth, I am trying to get back into my funds rather than accumulate claims. Most of the cargo will therefore be tafia, sugar and a little coffee. Having a lot of room going we took the freight we found there; but on the way back we won't bring anything for anyone.

   So, English hardware, cloth, gauze, ribbons, silk materials, nails, canvas, gear, samples of several types of painted material, paper, books, brushes and generally the articles that you preferred are being sent to you. See to it that this fleet stay at the plank as little as possible; because, although it is powerful and well armed, notices of its arrival must not have time to get to the enemies in time for them to bar our return. Commerce, first; war, second.

   The fleet will get to you in February at the earliest, as it is scheduled to make a detour to our islands to provide them with supplies of flour and salt which they need badly, the product of which coming to us in bills of exchange drawn on our treasurers before the fleet returns, will put us in a position to cope meanwhile with the terrible disbursements that this outfitting has cost us. It will not sail until the first days of January.

   You will get, by the Proud all my accounts with Congress in order, including the insurance, and without

---

different channels, with the hope that one would reach its destination (Mor 4:28-31, 131-224, 272-277, and 297-303). There were more than one letter from Beaumarchais to Francy in 1778, but this 6 December letter is the only one extant. Francy, suffering from cultural shock, disparaged Americans in and out of Congress. Deane was too cowardly to be counted upon, he stated, based on the letters of the Commissioners to Congress, which he had seen.

policies furnished,[33] since I was my own insurer, and that it is a thing accepted unquestionably in European commerce, that either insuring or running the insurance risks entitles one to the payment therefor. The only consequence is that Congress will not pay for the cargoes they did not receive and which have been plucked in route on their way from Europe to America. I will include the exact statement of what I have received from Congress notwithstanding the faithless Passy commissioners, who disputed me each return cargo, and would have robbed me of the Thereze's if Mr. Pelletier, briefed by me, had not sold it out. This perpetual insult stirs my blood and has caused me to resolve not to have any more to do with the commissioners as long as this rascal Lee is one of them. The Americans must have a poor grasp of their own interests to leave in our court a man so suspicious and especially so discourteous.

I was promised, my dear, your captain commission[34] and I hope to have the pleasure to send it by the Proud; but don't count on it until you have it in hand. You know our country: It's so large that there is a long way from where something is given to where it is received. Briefly, I haven't got it yet, although it is promised.

The rest of the detail will arrive to you by the Proud. Hey! What would you say if I gave you a chance when it arrives to greet on board our friend Monthieu? He wants to very much; but it has not yet been decided.

I received no other money for Mr. Pulaski's[35] account except what he handed me himself, on which I just paid 100 Louis on his behalf. I will send you his account. He was supposed to write me but I have not heard from him.

---

[33]This question caused difficulties to Francy. Hortalez had stated in an early letter to Congress that the risks must be on them. As that would have been too onerous, he later asked for insurance costs instead.

[34]Francy wanted a captain commission, he wrote his boss, because it would allow him to be freed faster, should he be taken prisoner at sea.

[35] Casimir Pulaski, one of the officers sent by Deane and Beaumarchais. A Polish aristocrat, he was complaining about everything since his arrival in America. See Francy's letter of 14 August 1778 to Beaumarchais (Mor 4:206).

I approve what you have done for M. de LaFayette,[36] brave young man! You serve me according to my heart when you oblige men of character. I have not been paid yet for the advances you made him, but I am not worried. The same goes for M. de LaRouerie.

As to you, my dear, I will write you about what I want to do for you. I you know me, you must expect that I will treat you as a friend. Your lot henceforth is tied to mine. I esteem and love you, and you will see proof of it before long. Give my regards to Baron von Steuben. I congratulate myself, from what I hear of him, for having given such a great officer to my friends *the free men* and to have in a sense forced him to follow this noble career. I am not worried about the money I lent him when he left. I have never invested money with such pleasure since I put a man of honor in his proper place. I hear he is general inspector of the American troops. Bravo! Tell him that his glory is the interest on my money and I have no doubt that in that kind I will be more than repaid.

I received a letter from Deane and one from Carmichael.[37] Give them my love. Those are brave Republicans, and who would be as useful here for their country's cause as this base intriguer Lee is deadly. Both promised me the pleasure of soon greeting them in Paris, which will not keep me from writing them by the Proud Rodrigue, proud to see himself leading a small squadron, who I hope won't let anyone cut off their mustaches, and who even promised they will bring me back a few.

Adieu, my dear Francy.

---

[36] See letter from Francy (Morton 4:204) for the financial arrangements made by him to rescue the twenty year old Marquis, who had fallen prey to loan sharks. Francy advanced him the money he needed; the interest would not start running until the "Major-General" had stopped "fighting for the Republic." Contrary to common belief, the French government had not sent LaFayette to America but, on the contrary, had tried to stop him, not only in France but in Spain, from where he departed (RC, Mol 477d).

[37] This letter dated 3 September 1778 is extant only in French translation (Lom 2:567 and Mor 4:224). Carmichael, claiming he had forgotten his French, wrote in English. "We have as many intrigues and cabals here as you do," he noted, "and why not, since we are now the friends of Louis XVI."

12 December 1778, to Sartine
(France 530, fol. 399[38])

When the matter is very important and time is very precious, one can never recommend an affair too much to the man who handles a lot of them, and mishandles a few of them.[39] I therefore have the honor of asking you for:

A new letter to M. de Marchais, without which he swears to God he will not give one man to the Proud Rodrigue, who would become the humble Rodrigue, as it cannot be proud except through your kindness, without which it is nailed down in the harbor.[40]

Plus the order to deliver to me the fourteen[41] cannons, bombs, etc. as a compensation, instead of that so harsh word "cash," which is being thrown into our faces while our hands are full of legitimates complaints and we are asking to be paid for advances made and supplies furnished to the navy.

I cannot believe, Sir, I should be more mistreated by you than the puniest corsair because I am the most daring of them all. I am going to cruise across the ocean, convoy, attack, burn some mustaches, and capture a few pirates, and because I have 60 cannons and 160 feet of keel, I should see myself less welcome than those who do not get to our gasket! I trust in your fairness too much to have any fear. My Proud Rodrigue is fitted for war and carries no cargo. While the others will empty themselves out and fill up again, it will proudly cruise all over the American seas. There you have, Sir, the true destination. See for yourself if your wise ordinance is less applicable to it than to all the projects of frigates which are still only in the air, while the Proud Rodrigue is ready to plow the Atlantic as soon as you let him have some sailors.

---

[38]Lomenie(2:162-3) and Morton (4:292-3) give only an expurgated version of this letter.

[39] This opening sentence was left out by Lomenie, for obvious reasons: What a way to talk to the secretary of the navy!

[40]This last clause has also been omitted by Lomenie.

[41]This figure was also omitted by Lomenie.

If I came to you and asked you to build and outfit a vessel of such caliber, always able to serve as a ship of the king anywhere I should send it, would you refuse it cannons and the rank of squadron leader [capitaine de brulot] for its captain? Such meager encouragements for such great objects would be nothing to you. Then how can it be less valuable to you ready-made than if it remained to be built?

I beg your pardon but the multiplicity of the matters you handle might have concealed in part the importance of my outfitting dedicated to the triple purpose of encouraging French commerce through my example and my success, providing supplies to our islands windward or leeward, which greatly need it, and to lead to the American continent, in the most stormy weather,[42] a French merchant fleet so far-reaching that the new States will be able to judge thereby France's desire to sustain her new trade relations with them.

I submit these great concerns to your wisdom. Nothing, I daresay, is worthier of the attention and protection of such an enlightened minister.

13 December 1778, to Vergennes
(Ang. 530, fol. 403-404)

For lack of the seamen I cannot obtain, I was faced with the necessity of cutting down by half the superb fitting out operation which I had the honor of describing to you in detail at M. de Maurepas'.

Today I am threatened with the possibility of having to cancel it completely, lacking enough men to equip the Proud Rodrigue by itself. I do understand M. de Sartine's quandary, but I can only lament thoroughly that commerce is encouraged in words only, while it is stalled in fact and in sorry facts.

If the towns of Nantes and Bordeaux were to see me unload after all that I have said to the tradesmen, there would ensue a let down akin to despair.

I have the honor of sending you, but you alone, a copy of my letter to M. de Sartine [13 December]. I am doing more than I can do, I swear to you, and no subject

---

[42]The war between England and France had in fact started six months earlier. An English fleet under Admiral Keppel purported to search the Belle Poule off the coast of Brittany, 18 June 1778. The first firing shots ensued (Lom 2:161).

of the king deserves to be seconded more than I do. You can well say about me that the zeal for the country [la patrie] devours me and that I would gladly pay with a pint of my blood the slightest advantage for it.

The favor I ask of you is to recommend my shipping to M. de Sartine as an affair of threefold usefulness, without mentioning the news we received from Nantes yesterday and which was forwarded to M. de Sartine. In discussing it with M. de Maurepas, please decide whether it would do any harm to put it in the Courrier de l'Europe. It seems to me it can only be helpful, without any danger. Helpful, because in the height of the Parliamentary debates, such a cause of worry can only increase the parties bitterness and will especially hurt their chances of obtaining further subsidies. Without risk, because as soon as the news is out, the move on Halifax is over or has failed. A word will suffice, and you alone can give that word.

I would not know M. d'Estaing very well if I did not believe that he is furious he cannot do anything. Rest assured, M. le Comte, he is a true lover of glory. I am certain about it by the grief I feel: for he too has his arms full.[43]

But what can I do if I am denied the convoy for my fleet and if they also refuse to me the means of convoying my own ships as well as those of others. My private outlay amounts to more than six millions between my friends and me. The various ships that will join in will bring it to over nine. The English would give to such an enterprise at least four convoy vessels, and we, not a single frigate! How shall we manage?

You know, M. le Comte, the respect and gratitude I have for you.

20 December 1778, to Committee of Foreign Corr. (Mor 4:305-311)

---

[43]Charles-Hector, Count d'Estaing (1729-1794), had fought bravely in India with the army and was named admiral only in 1777. He was discredited after his first campaign in America and remained unemployed until 1783. A liberal, partisan of constitutional monarchy, he tried to save the royal family in 1792 and was condemned to the guillotine. He enumerated his services before the revolutionary tribunal and concluded: "When you have cut my head, send it to the English. They will pay you dearly for it" (NBG 15:455).

When Mr. Deane, your first commissioner, arrived in France, he found in me a zealous partisan of your cause, a fervent friend of your interests, and especially a solicitor, an ardent advocate with the king of France and his ministers in favor of your rising republic.

I have done more, Gentlemen. Not being enough of a capitalist myself to exhort by my example the courage of the French merchants who still hesitated to direct their operations toward your ports, I have managed to persuade several generous persons richer than I to entrust to my intelligence and probity considerable funds which I would employ in your favor by way of an honorable trade and under condition that I would establish between you and me a quick turnover of shipments and returns, so as to improve those funds, but loyally, generously and without extortion.[44]

If I made that promise to my associates, Gentlemen, it was based on the trust I placed in the word of your agent Mr. Deane, who kept assuring me that he was expecting incessantly vessels loaded with produce from your country, which would always be remitted to me as they arrived here. Then I started purchasing all kinds of stores for the clothing, the support and the armament of your troops.

I went further, Gentlemen. Your commissioner Mr. Deane being unable to find anyone who would rent out or sell to him vessels for the transportation of these goods, without the warranty of a local wealthy person, I offered myself to him. Not only did your commissioner find this warranty in my zeal and friendship, but I advanced to him upon that occasion approximately one hundred thousand ecus, which has not been repaid.

His correspondents in Bordeaux, he said, took advantage of his need to charge him too much for the money he had to borrow to subsist. He begged me to lend him some money promising he would repay me before long. I generously gave him what he needed. This has not been repaid.

He wanted to engage officers to cross over to America but considerable advances were needed: this new loan did not deter my zeal; he found it in my coffer, and this money has not been repaid.

---

[44]This refers to the high interest required of Americans in Europe at the time.

He inspired me in such a way that in spite of the obstacles of European politics, I unearthed and obtained on reasonable terms brass cannons and all sorts of war munitions which I loaded on our ships together with the clothing and guns which I bought elsewhere. But the same European politics still standing in the way of operations so useful to you, after I had hoped often-times for a covert protection on the part of the government, the English came to check me and soon I met only with obstacles. All my vessels, one after the other, were stopped in the ports, delayed or forced to take the islands for destination. That was the time, Gentlemen, when stimulated by the difficulties, I no longer spared money, or exertions, or any steps to soften these prohibitions or to elude them. But although everyone here is sympathetic to your cause, politics often being the stronger, it is only after enormous losses in time and money, incredible proceedings and exertions, that I was able to accomplish a portion of what I wanted to do for you.[45]

Mr. Deane saw my troubles and was often touched by it. Mr. Carmichael, a friend of Mr. Deane's and a confident in his affairs, who is taking this letter to America,[46] was constantly surprised by my courage and indefatigable zeal. I call on him to witness these facts before you. He will tell you whether a single American ever failed to find shelter in my house, he will tell you whether or not I treated them as brothers.

Through all these undertakings and exertions in your favor alone, Gentlemen, Mr. Franklin constantly showed me a disobliging aloofness, about which I would not complain if this aloofness did not go so far today as to unjustly attempt to take over the first cargo that came back to me on my vessel Amphitrite. Would you believe, Gentlemen, that this commissioner, a man of the highest merit besides, courtly with everyone in this country, and having dinner all the time at the houses of people most indifferent to the Republic, would you believe, I say, that this commissioner has not been polite enough to set foot in my house once during the whole year he has been in France? My friends have been outraged by this behavior, concluding that I had led

---

[45]The idea that he accomplished less than what he had planned, is also stated by Beaumarchais in the *Observations*, paragraph.

[46] This fact might support the hypothesis that Vergennes did not see this letter.

them into bad business since those I was obliging treated me so impolitely. I assured my friends that if Mr. Franklin did not want to meet me, it was, as he himself said it, only not to look as if he was criticizing or disturbing the work done before he arrived by his colleague Deane. However poor this reason to dispense with a courtesy which this commissioner refused only to me, my friends relied on my conciliatory interpretation of such a strange behavior. I distinguished between the deputy and the nation he represented. Unhappy with the former, I did not stop serving the latter. I continued to be for his colleague Mr. Deane the most responsive friend in every occasion, and whenever he needed it, my purse and my cares were at his service.

Today, Gentlemen, I have exhausted my money and my credit. As I counted too much on the returns promised so many times to me, I have gone in the red in my accounts with my friends, I have even exhausted other powerful help which I had at first procured, under explicit engagement to return or remit shortly.

After a whole year of waiting in vain on a total of five millions advanced for you, and after the commissioners eluded in every possible manner to remit one penny to me on the funds they have received, one of my vessels finally brought me something like 150 thousand pounds of rice and indigo, and that same Mr. Franklin who never wanted to meddle with my business, as long as I was advancing money, chose the first instance that a meager return was coming to my company to intervene in our affairs and hold back against us funds to which we were so rightly entitled, and moreover which have become so necessary to the maintenance and support of a credit without which I cannot proceed.

I therefore did not feel I was departing from the generous, frank and loyal way I have always behaved with you, when I firmly opposed Mr. Franklin's insulting behavior towards me. I had my own cargo stopped and seized in the hands of my Lorient correspondent, to whom those gentlemen your commissioners had the cheek to write that this cargo did not belong to me but to them and that monies therefrom were to be remitted to them alone.

I therefore beg you, Gentlemen, to find it agreeable if from now on I deal only with you directly. I have sent to you for this purpose my general agent M. de Francy with a magnificent cargo and my invoices. I am having this same agent hand you this present letter with the copy of the one I wrote your delegation in Passy three weeks ago[47], which delegation has not yet deigned to honor me with an answer.

So many insults, so many accumulated exertions have not however diminished my zeal for your interests. The letter I write to my agent, and have ordered him to communicate to you, will prove it to you beyond question, together with the testimony of Mr. Carmichael, a man as honest as well-informed and zealous on your affairs and who has unceasingly served the cause of the Republic. The testimony of this worthy friend will convince you that I am not saying one word here which does not even understate the exact truth.

---

[47]This letter dated 8 September 1778 (which I have not located) is acknowledged on 10 September by the commissioners, Franklin, Lee and Adams, who stated they had been instructed to examine the Hortalez accounts. They asked Vergennes his opinion on the matter. He gave an ambiguous diplomatic answer. Vergennes to the French ambassador in the U.S.(Mor 4:229,n.7).

1779:   FRUSTRATIONS, REFORM AND OPEN PROTEST

15 January 1779, from John Jay, "President of Congress"
(JCC 13:70-71)

The Congress of the United States of America, sensible of your great exertions in their favor, present you with their thanks and assure you of their regard.

They lament the inconveniencies you have suffered by the great advances made in support of these states. Circumstances have prevented a compliance with their wishes, but they will take the most effectual measures in their power to discharge the debt due to you.

The liberal sentiments and extensive views which alone could dictate a conduct like yours, are conspicuous in your actions and adorn your character. While with great talent you served your prince, you have gained the esteem of this infant republic and will receive the merited applause of a new world.
By order of Congress.

Beaumarchais pleads with the commissioners in a long letter where he attempts to explain to them why they are doing him "a grave insult" in denying his right to the cargoes returning on his ships. It is "a sacred claim" because it involves the honor of both countries, as he sees it, and a French policy for which he feels responsible.

10 February 1779, to Vergennes
(Ang. 531, fol. 50)

I have the honor of sending you my letter to the American Commissioners.[1] Read it, please, with your usual thoughtfulness.

I appear to be putting politics aside completely in this letter But you will easily see that I get back to it, imperceptibly, and that my letter, of which I am going to send a copy to Congress, is very apt to finalize the painful job undertaken by Mr. Deane to remove that wretched Lee, the most dangerous enemy of France.

I have just received news from Philadelphia which confirm me in my plan of bringing my complaints to the next session of Congress. An attack so combined from

---

[1]Dated February 13, below.

Europe and America should finally succeed. They consider war as almost over. But it's even more time for intrigues and cabals. Francy looks worried about the consequences of the quarrel between the Lees and Deane. We must not neglect any way of reinforcing the latter's cause, which is ours, and that is what I have in mind at this time when Congress counts on the continuation of my shipments and services.

By Francy's letter, I see that Congress is convinced today that they have no better friend in Europe than me. This opinion must make them consider very carefully the strong feeling I have about Lee's character and scheming.

That's my theme. Yours, Sir, is to correct me if I am wrong and especially never to doubt the reverence I have for your wisdom.

I have made it my principle never to doubt about whatever you seriously enter into.

I will send this letter only when you have approved it.

12 February 1779, to Sartine
(Mol 663)

I beg Mr. de Sartine to give orders to locate among the English prisoners a certain Nehemiah Holland, who was taken on the Saint-Peter, and to grant his freedom to M. de Beaumarchais, who wishes with all his heart to fulfill the engagement taken by Mr. Mulliers, an officer of the Irish Brigade, with an English privateer captain who not only set him free on a neutral ship, after he had captured him on the crossing from the continent to Europe, but generously offered his purse to him, asking him in return to try and obtain the freedom of his friend Nehemiah Holland, a prisoner in France.

In the horrible business of war, it seems one cannot encourage too much what pertains to generosity and deviates a little from English ferocity.

The feature of the English captain and the reward given it by the French minister will both be consigned in the Courrier de l'Europe.

However, the real reasons for the trade difficulties between France and her new ally rest elsewhere: in the administrative structure of France. The essential tobacco trade is not free in France. It is shackled by the monopoly of the Farmers-General. Beaumarchais, the economist, will attempt to obtain a reform the French tax system.

13 February 1779, to the American Commissioners
(RG 76)

Mr. Pelletier-Dudoyer, my correspondent in Nantes, informs me that he was served on your behalf with summons to deliver to your attorney the feeble load of rice and indigo arrived from Charleston for me on the ship Thereze, which Mr. Pelletier has sold at my request and the proceeds of which he has forwarded to me.

Surprised by this attack, I have instructed my Nantes attorney to reply that the person to address in this matter is not Mr. Pelletier but I, who gave the express order to hold back this cargo, for my own pressing needs; that I will take the noble delegates' action under my own responsibility. I likewise intend to call the national Congress of America to account for making to me such a puny remittance in return for the huge sums owing to me by the republic, whose word and written promise I have that they will discharge their obligations toward me as soon as possible.

As this discharge must finally take place, with all due compensation entailed by its tardiness, in spite of the exertions constantly made by worrisome minds to avoid or delay it. I would like if possible to avoid legal action in a court of admiralty, 200 miles from Paris, on a question which would in Europe appear unseemly between the noble delegates from America and the man known as the most zealous servant of the nation they represent. I have the honor of addressing you, Gentlemen, the exact account of the Therese cargo, with my acknowledgment that the proceeds have been remitted to me and should be credited against my claims (without prejudice to my recourse on the charterer for shipping expenses, etc.). This will suffice for unloading the ship between M. Pelletier-Dudoyer and you, as well as you, Gentlemen, toward your principals.

I have the honor to include herewith detailed information regarding the Amphitrite and Mercure return cargoes. The former not having been sold, and the other ships not having brought anything back from the continent, this will allow you to update your accounts with Congress on this matter.

Allow me, Gentlemen, to thank you for your mediation on the settlement of my accounts and compensation. I do not accept it for reasons I will spell out hereunder. Zealous friends who deal with my interests in America are taking measures to defend the honor of my character, of the services I rendered to Congress, and especially to defend my rights underhandedly [basely] attacked by certain correspondents [horrible intriguers] in Europe.[2]

If, following what I have the honor of writing you, Gentlemen, you do not withdraw your summons to prosecute my correspondent in Nantes for the recovery of a cargo which belongs to me and of which I hereby acknowledge receipt, I will conclude that your intention is to force me to go to court myself to fight back such an unseemly attack. Hey! How grievous it would then be for a zealous friend of America to be forced to defend my behavior, which will ever remain the same, and bring out in the open for self-defense in court, the following facts of which you are well aware:

That in 1776 I was eagerly solicited by Mr. Silas Deane, as one of the truest partisans the thirteen States had in Europe. That I was urged by this agent of the Republic in France to form a company which would agree to undertake huge shipments of artillery, merchandise and warlike stores, in favor of the Americans, who were deprived of arms and clothing; and on the explicit promise and word of honor of that delegate, that ships loaded with merchandise would come from America to match my shipments; that these shipments always consigned to me, would through an uninterrupted turnover and prompt discharge, enable me to make new advances to Congress, who would be deeply appreciative of it.

I would prove then that upon these promises and under the tradename of RH&Co., I formed my company and raised considerable capital in Europe, gathered stores, artillery, arms and munitions of all kinds.

I would prove, by a very extant agreement, that when the time came to send those shipments, Mr. Deane confessed to me that no one was willing to charter ships

---

[2]The manuscript intentionally shows the stricken words, given here in brackets. The handwriting also reflects, by the size and energy of pen strokes, the writer's feelings.

to him without considerable advances and caution in
France for all sums due; that in order to fulfil the
generous plan I had devised, I immediately advanced all
the sums requested by the charterer, and became caution
towards him for all sums owing by the United States of
America, and that I did not rest until all those ships,
tied down in our harbors through superior considerations, were on their way to America.

I would prove that another agent in London, as
well as Mr. Deane, having urged me, the one to send
officers to the continent and the other to lend the
money necessary for their pay and travel expenses, I did
not hesitate to advance the funds needed for that
purpose. That from that time on, carried away by my
zeal, beyond my capacities, I committed all of my
fortune and that of my friends, my credit and theirs, in
order to continue serving America. That many ships,
richly loaded with artillery, merchandise, clothing and
war stores, were expedited to the continent by me alone,
after incredible exertions and labors, physical and
mental, necessary to overcome the perpetual obstacles
placed in my way by European politics.

I would even have no qualms in proving that I
carried my devotion several times to the point of
supplying Mr. Deane with the monies necessary for him to
live on and discharge his debts, because he knows that I
honor and love him with all my heart; nor that I treated
all Americans as my friends and my brothers, having
offered to most of them my credit and my resources.

That, far from seeing any American ship arrive in
our ports with the returns from the continent so many
time promised and agreed upon, after a new delegation
for the past three years has exhausted all manners of
avoiding a sacred payment--by alleging either the
distress of the State or the difficulties of the ocean
crossing, etc. etc., all of the men I had just served,
obliged or employed (MM. Deane and Carmichael excepted),
have done their best to rob me of the honor of my labors
in Europe and have attempted to appropriate to themselves all the benefits of my shipments to America.

Then, Gentlemen, resentful of such a grave insult,
I would perhaps show that all the obscure speculators
[intriguers] that such an enterprise would be bound to
attract, huddled together to deceive the Congress on the
nature and the conditions of my shipments. They made me
appear in their eyes as the dispenser of public funds in
France, which the Republic would never have to pay back;
as the agent of the State for the distribution to the

Americans, as a simple gift, of all that I had so painfully gathered myself and shipped to them, as a sacred advance, as an exchange and a trade.

I might even go further, for owing no longer any consideration to such underhanded enemies [intriguers], I could very well name them and prove that they have not ceased by their insidious letters, extracts of which are in my hands, to prevent Congress from discharging their debt toward the generous servant and friend who had devoted himself to their country, and who came close to go under ten times, because he failed to receive the wherewithal to cope with his obligations.

And if the rankling pain from so much injustice caused me to break the discretion I imposed on myself, I would surprise the honest people of my country by adding that the noble delegates of the Republic (Mr. Deane excepted), carried away by these illusions [intrigues], have presumed to dispense with the most common civilities towards me, to the point of not setting a foot in my house, to the point of never letting me receive any answer from Congress to the more than twenty important letters, which I wrote them and forwarded to America on the very ships which brought such precious assistance to the Republic.

Hey! How startling it would be for all of Europe, if I divulged the fact that those noble delegates carried their insult and injustice towards me to the point of attempting to withhold from me the puniest returns belatedly arrived from America in exchange for my shipments, on the very same ships loaded for them under my own tradename and at my expense, and for which I had paid more than 11,000 louis, for two-thirds of the freight agreed upon and as a caution for all subsequent payments and all possible accidents.

What would people say, Gentlemen, if I added that, if I had not resolved to send an agent of mine to America to carry my bitter complaint to Congress, if that man had not arrived there, as well as MM. Deane and Carmichael, M. Gerard, who have opened the eyes of the honorable Congress, and who have informed me that, surprised to realize the injustice done to me upon false advice and insidious reports received from Europe, Congress had resolved to make amend for this wrong at the earliest--what would people say, Gentlemen, upon learning that without all those precautions by an honest man carried away by indignation, I would still be unaware that the enemies of the common good [horrible intriguers] made it a game to spread confusion, disinformation and ruin on an affair which has become as deadly for me as it has been beneficial to the new Republic.

Such are the justifications I would be forced to give publicly, Gentlemen, if you persist in wronging me and if you do not withdraw the scandalous summons made on M. Pelletier-Dudoyer on your behalf. Then, still distinguishing the honorable Congress which has been deceived, from their agents who are doing me wrong--I am sorry to say it but your actions are forcing me to do it--I would have seized and stopped in all our ports, with all our bankers or depositories, all merchandise, funds, that you may have in Europe. It would be my turn to drag you before the courts of my country and to force you to be fair with me, since so much devotion for your country has not succeeded in eliciting in you the least gratitude.

If I address this letter to the delegation collectively, Gentlemen, it is because I cannot do otherwise, the summons having been signed by the three of you. I do hereby attest that my complaints and personal resentment are directed only against Mr. Arthur Lee, the only author of the wrong I have suffered. I declare also that inasmuch as it depends on me, I will never have any dealings with that ambitious agent who, in order to harm his colleague Mr. Deane, has spread doubt and suspicion on all the work that this honorable man had done with me in Europe for the Republic. Such is the reason which obliges me, Gentlemen, to refuse any mediation on your part, any accounting in which Mr. Lee should be involved. I took the liberty of stating as much to the Congress and sent them the ciphered correspondence exchanged in London between that agent and myself. It will clearly prove both the hatefulness of his behavior towards me and the falsity of all his subsequent insinuations regarding the nature and the conditions of my shipments to America.

That if Congress, deceived, seduced, or led by reasons unknown to me, should continue to entrust their interests to that politician, I know him too well ever to consent, if I can help it, to have him enter in any way in my affairs.

Having disposed of the bone of contention, let us beware to give to England the pleasant spectacle of a public confrontation. It is not good for it to happen between you and the French trader who was the first by his work, his example and his advice to exhort our merchant ships to dare sail towards your perilous shores.

Consider, I beg you, that the opinion of such a failure would contribute more to deter our maritime merchants from American ventures than politics and all the treaties in the world can do to persuade them.

You, the delegates of a new trading nation, keep away from every mind the idea of such a wrong. You would not make anyone believe that the man who did so much to excite the hearts in favor of your cause could have wronged you in any way. And the French government, the constant and (before the treaty) often repressive witness of my exertions, would be bound to frown upon a suit destined to loosen a union based on the hope for an extensive trade between the two nations, a union sealed by an honorable alliance with America and sustained today by the greatest effusion of the gold and the blood of Frenchmen.

Such are, Gentlemen, the noble [great] considerations which led me to suffer so long without complaining. And it is in this spirit that asking the American delegation for justice on a summons imprudently assigned to my correspondent in Nantes, I still have the honor of being, of Mr. Franklin and Mr. Adams, the most humble and obedient servant.

P.S. Leaving aside, Gentlemen, the justice which I am entitled to expect from Congress and for which I hope, upon all the supplies furnished by me to the Republic, I have the honor of including herewith the invoice for the chartering of the first ships which I sent to the continent, and for which you have the agreement signed by Mr. Deane and myself, as caution for Congress. This deal, recently settled by you with the charterer for the sum of 351,400 ecus of which I paid 269,400 ecus in 1776, should be reimbursed to me at the earliest. As no verification is needed for merchandise sent to America in order to discharge such an advance made in France, in French ecus, and based on a paid invoice, I am asking today for the twentieth time to pay me those 269,400 ecus with interest, expenses, etc. due to me since October of 1776 and which I need very badly. Such is the reason why I called those ships I had chartered <u>my own ships</u> in my letter to you. They may belong to whomever you please, Gentlemen, after that sum of 269,400 # has been paid me by you. For more than three years, I have not sent the sheriff [huissier] to you either for this collection or many others. Am I asking too much when I beg you to put a stop to the scandal of summons assigned by you on my correspondent in gratitude for the mildness and honesty of my behavior toward you and the long patience with which I waited for you to discharge your debts.

13 February 1779, to Vergennes
(Ang. 531, fo. 31)

By sending you for perusal the copy of my letter of today to M. de Maurepas, I mean to inform you on the matter of the conference he was kind enough to grant me last night.

I go over my assertions several times because everything points to their importance. Please support this essential endeavor.

Before I send my packages to Rochefort for the continent, do you have anything for Mr. Gerard?

Francy writes me that this minister has started a plan of compensation of our artillery with sums due for objects supplied to Count d'Estaing.[3] That's charming. So much got on a bad debt. It is necessary for you to be willing to confer with me on this matter before I close up my packages, because while cleaning up the substance we must not change the form adopted,[4] and the more excited public opinion becomes in America, the less we should lend ourselves to malign interpretations.

I will have the honor of showing you my letters to Gerard and to my agent when you permit me to come and assure you again of my very respectful devotion.

13 February 1779, to Maurepas
(Ang. 531, fols. 32/55)

After last night's lengthy discussion, it seems that only a good summary can rest your mind, establish

---

[3] From Francy, 19 december 1778 (Mor 4:300). The French government owed Congress considerable sums for victuals furnished to the fleet. Gerard had suggested they be written off against the amount due Hortalez and that the "king would see to it that Hortalez would be satisfied."

[4] This kind of accounting would complicate and delay the response of Congress to Francy's demands for payment. See, in *Letters of Delegates to Congress*, edited by Paul H. Smith (11:467-8), John Jay to Jean Theveneau de Francy, 15 January 1779.

and organize all the matters which you were kind enough to hear me submit to you for your decision.

It is clear that, in the wavering state of public opinion in America, the affair of France is totally lost there if we suddenly cease to trade with that country, however difficult trade may become today.

Questions to ask yourself

Is it useful that France should continue to carry over to America all the stores they cannot do without?

A well-informed man must answer: It's indispensable. But the French merchants being able to trade there only by exchanging goods, must not the Versailles administration do everything possible to facilitate the flow of the one merchandise brought from America?

Sensible people will agree that this must one of the most important matters for our ministers to consider.

But since there is only one buyer of tobacco in France, which is the king's Farm, and since the flow of tobacco has become as necessary to the merchants as daily bread to the people, must the government allow a monopoly on tobacco to subsist in the kingdom and stop the flow of it?

Everything is lost if the government does not completely free the tobacco trade, or if it fails to treat the tax-farmer in the same manner as the baker. You sell at such price. You will buy at such other.

But the tax-farmer says: I must take advantage of the conditions of a lease I entered into when I bought tobacco 4 S[ols] if I am to pay 20 S for it today. I cannot give it for 3 S as when I used to get it for almost nothing, especially if I must give back 24 millions of it to the King.

Thereupon the Equitable Ministry cannot refuse to the tax-farmer an accounting between clerk and master, for the farmer must be compensated if, by a fact outside his management, he incurs a loss on the contract; but that's what remains for him to prove. I do not believe any of it, and for good reasons.

But in the case of a proven loss, must the king, whose revenues are all allocated in advance, inconvenience himself by lowering the price of his Tobacco Farm?

You do not think so? But who would keep the Ministry, whenever they believe the price is about to cause losses to the seller, from allowing the sales price to the consumer to rise? When beef becomes rare, meat in Paris goes up to 10 or 11 S. When wheat fails to arrive there, the price of bread increases in proportion. In those instances, the new tax is a matter of policy, as here it is a matter of high administration. And if you tolerate those variations on goods of first necessity, why not allow it on those of mere fancy?

Will an increase in tobacco price annoy the consumer more than to see the carriage-ride now costing 30 S in Paris as a result of a new contract? and if the interest of a particular company could persuade you to do it, *a fortiori*, when a great reason of State obliges you to support a magnificent plan, and when for it to succeed, you only have to allay the farmer's greed, which greed puts him today at the throat of the merchant, which merchant, disgusted by so many losses and hindrances, no longer wants to fetch tobacco in America, while taking there merchandise from France. Whence it follows that your manufactures which were beginning to double and triple production are going to fall instantly. Whence it follows most of all that your new ally, solicited by your enemies and wavering in its friendship towards you, not seeing the French flag wave in its ports any longer, will not fail to take the abatement of your trade as a pretext for coming to terms with the common enemy. Then all is lost.

One does not order a merchant as one does a soldier. One can only encourage him. Welcome therefore the prayers of your privateers today, when their co-operation is needed for our political plan to succeed and be assured that the tax-collectors will soon recover, through a rise in customs, the slight sacrifice has made on the purchase of an indispensable commodity-- or grant the freedom to trade in it, in exchange for a fee equivalent to your Farm price, or else allow a momentary increase in the price of this ammoniacal and corrosive product, a light tax upon the nose of all Frenchmen, permitting the tax-farmer to give for it a suitable price to the privateer. That's a very small evil for a very great good.

But in all these matters, Sir, the first desirable point is to engage Mr. Necker to start working seriously with me or anyone as competent. Time is of the essence, the shipping season is passing by, no one trades with America, and the English are doing their utmost to detach them from us. Let us not give them a pretext to do so.

Such is the summary of all I had the honor to represent to you last night, and such will be at all time the indefatigable zeal of the one who vowed to you eternal gratitude.

28 February 1779, to Vergennes
(Ang. 531, fol. 56)

I am pleased to walk before you, impervious to silly vainglory, still jealous and proud of your approval. I have the honor of sending you my last letter to Mr. Necker. you will see there that I am surrounded with schemers. But throughout adversity, ambush and hindrance, one must go forward if one wants to reach a reasonable goal.

My goal is to co-operate in safeguarding an alliance very useful for the future, but which now requires a moment of effort and sacrifice. Those who can encourage commerce are negligible next to those needed in the war, so that one cannot keep from bemoaning the fact that their voices are stifled in so many ways.[5]

27 February 1779, to Necker
(Ang. 531, fol. 79)

I have the honor to inform you that my conversation with Mr. Paulze[6] resulted in his making the two following offers:

1. That the Tax-Farm consent in granting me the transit throughout the kingdom, *to me alone and as a preference*. You know, Sir, as well as all of the king's ministers, whether my request is personal. I would blush to use so much force and solicit such considerable persons in my own interest only. Let me suffer in misery and let French commerce, so useful to the present situation as we know it is, thrive! What would people

---

[5]Note the constrained and ironic tone.

[6]A Farmer-General whom Beaumarchais had approached in the name of all the French merchants who traded with America. See to Mr. Paulze, 17 January 1779 (Mol 660-663).

say about me if, pleading for the common cause, I was satisfied to reap fruits for my private advantage?

Mr. Paulze finds no more disadvantage than you or I do in the transit agreement for all merchants, but he says that his colleagues are a long way from thinking as he does. All opt for a literal interpretation of the text which denies this transit to commerce, in their favor. Your firmness is much needed, Sir, if we are to prevail on this capital point. While waiting for that honorable effect of your kindness toward French commerce, I have refused the favor of transit which was offered to me personally. You would have done as much.

2. Mr. Paulze undertakes to have his company agree to bring the tobacco price from 80 # to 90#, which is the lowest which the merchants can offer to the Farm. He undertakes to do so if on my part I can get the administration to come to the aid of commerce and consent to sustain the sacrifice of 5# or less on that increase in their accounts with the Farm. Here all my patriotic fervor is less influential than the importance of the matter itself, of which you and Mr. de Maurepas are aware. I limit myself to the silent desire of seeing this encouragement given to those who trade with America, at a time when it is to fear that maritime traders will receive very soon the most distressing news about the vessels which left for our islands last december and january. But I think that the Farm is more than able to make this small sacrifice without losing anything.

The transit, first object of my prayers, depends on you alone, Sir. The division of the slight sacrifice between the Farm and the king, or the entire sacrifice to be borne by the Farm, is a point to be decided between M. de Maurepas and you. I plan to have the honor to see him on Monday, and you, if you agree, on Tuesday morning.

4 March 1779, to Vergennes
(Ang. 531, fol. 50/86)

I was unable to find a moment yesterday to pay my respects to you. I was on my way, with my head and my briefcase full, to get Mr. de Maurepas to get the Farm to agree through the mediation of Mr. Necker. I was taking to him the written proof of a new scheme which threatens to charge 40 thousand livres of duties for the tobacco stored with them by a Nantes house, if the owner does not let it go at 80#. He listened to me kindly, and that matter having brought another one up, we resumed conversation where we had left it on the day you and I talked about it. That conversation was important enough for me not to need to remind you of the subject involved.

After a lengthy plea, the tenor of which I will give you, I finally obtained the most important point of *the secret examination of proofs,* some of which have already passed under your eyes. Briefly, under the reciprocal condition of silence, with any one else than you; agreed that the conduct of an impartial and prompt examination is granted; agreed that you are the commissary, I the reporter, and that to start with, I will put again under your eyes the part already proven, with the evidence; that your conviction will trigger his, in a short work with you; that this first point established, he will give the secret orders I indicated to him, in order to obtain the proof of a few others promptly. For my great argument is that, in such a grave affair, the discovery even of one error in the *givens* is an important step towards the truth. Even supposing that a careful man should have been deceived in a few instructions, so difficult to obtain in those matters, his work may be so beautiful, so thorough, so methodical, that he should be deemed, even if mistaken, to be trustworthy and able to straighten everything. The deep knowledge of the laws and of the revenues of a kingdom are two points very rarely found together in the same subject.

Be gracious enough therefore to let me know (without further explanation for security's sake) when at your earliest convenience I may have an appointment of less than an hour with you. That's all that is required on matters already discussed. But time is of the essence, as I promised that all the rest would be known within three months, and until then I was promised everything would remain *in statu quo.* It appeared to me that the various errors which bother him *on the others,* increased his trust in you who do not make any. You, the enlightened friend of the public good, do not fail to support it in such a serious instance. I will spare you the unpleasant labor involved by doing it myself in Paris and you will only have results to verify and documents to examine.

Forced to go to Rochefort to recruit the sailors I need, I am going by dint of gold louis to attempt to gather enough of them to send on their way ten ships, which have been loaded for three months and ruin me by their delay, and which would have prevented the commanders of our islands to send away the merchant ships without escorts, as useless mouths, if the flour I loaded on last October had left on time and had arrived in January, as it could easily have. Big sighs are escaping from my chest as I write this.

I don't know whether I am committing an indiscretion in asking for your frank recommendation to the Grand Master of Malta[7] for the son of one of my good friends, who needs a small dispensation of <u>maternal proofs</u>, for everything else with the family is good. I am enclosing herewith his application in duplicate so that it may arrive in Malta with your letter, if you have granted it to us. What I can add in favor of the son is that never was anyone more worthy of a favor than his good and honest parents, in whose behalf I am soliciting you.

14 March 1779, to Vergennes
(Ang. 531, fol. 51)

I have the honor of sending you the faithful account of our last conference. The obligation of copying my original myself, because of the secret imposed, has delayed the letter until now.

I have given an elementary tone to this report so that if M. de Maurepas shows it to the king, his inexperience in so complicated an affair will not prevent him from grasping the truth of it. This manner caused my first report to be longer, but the next ones will only be shorter for it.

Our first work will be on the tax-farms of Lorraine. It is ready, as clean-cut on proofs and of a disproportion even more ticklish than salt, the tax-farmers' receipt is what they pay to the king. The farm of Paris will come next. And I assure you that our inquisitor explained to me very well how, before three months, he would have handed to the king 40 million without any taxation or borrowing, and how he desired that the reform plan start by bringing about a bed of

---

[7]The order of Malta, order of St.John Hospitaller. Younger sons of titled families sometimes were sent to it, so that they would not compete for the family title and fortune. Cf. "When he had an older brother, the pride of a very great name condemning him to celibacy, the order of Malta was his lot. Prejudice then appeared to cover the injustice done regarding two sons equal in rights" (MC, 4:13, Mol 184). Today the order is recognized in France. According to an allusion found in the work of Andr Malraux, General de Gaulle was grand master.

justice[8] to remove half of a twentieth ___ [9] to promise even greater remittances, a great way to obtain confidence for a new administration.

I plan to give my regards to Mr. de Maurepas tomorrow and to ask him to please postpone a certain decision of the Council concerning the *Caisse d'Escompte* [discount bank] which would place us in the complete dependence of Bank administrators. I understand nothing of what Mr. Necker ___ it may be my own fault.

You know, Sir, my respect and very inviolable attachment.

-- The Proud Rodrigue of 60 canons and the Zephir of 20 were setting sail a the moment the two ships of 44 were coming in, having been unable to hold on. This annoying deficiency making even more useful the cruising of my two ships. I console myself for the sake of the public good for the awful damage caused me by the forced departure of my fleet.

I cannot imagine anything else on the return of the two vessels of the king, except that they were sent out too hurriedly and they were poorly trimmed, which is only a delay, but the unfortunate commerce will pay for it.

Excuse my handwriting. I am writing in my bath, where I am shaking all over. I am including the paper I received from London listing their prizes on us as of march 5th.

17 March 1779, from Vergennes
(Lom 2:247-8)

If you will, Sir, get here tomorrow Thursday at 6 p.m. with your assistant, I will be able to give you a good session to continue the work started last week. I tell you in advance that I will have an assistant who has the complete confidence of the Mentor [Maurepas]. I wished for it because, in a matter of such importance, you cannot multiply observations too much.

---

[8]During that confrontation with the court, the king was in fact reclining comfortably on cushions.

[9]Illegible spot on the manuscript.

20 March 1779 to Countess Fanny de Beauharnais[10]
(Mol 663-4)

Your letter, Madame, has touched me deeply. Sweet friendship never painted its care so tenderly. I know you, honor you and love you for this letter. But how you grieve me by asking me to give your friend a help that I cannot procure. I esteem him and value his work very much.[11] Moreover, I believe one must do as much good as one can in order to be as happy as our condition allows; such is my natural feeling and the fruit of the reflections of my whole life. I hold on to it without ostentation or care for what others say or think about me.[12] Let's return to you, Madame.

Your confidence provokes mine and I must speak plainly. People are mistaken on the nature of my affluence as they are about the rest of me. I am not a strong capitalist, but a great administrator. My friends' fortune entrusted to my care forces me to be wary and scrupulous on the use of their funds, whence it follows that i can be of help to a suffering friend in the amount of 25, 50 or 100 louis, taking them on my own money, but that I cannot go further without putting in my register in paper the equivalent of the money I take out and I know too well the poor people cannot give solid equivalents to the funds they borrow. They are in difficulty because they lack those. It is therefore with much sorrow that I find it physically impossible to lend your friend the large sum of money he needs.

As to the personal loans which are gotten from my soft-heart all the time, my wretched reputation of wealth caused me to have accumulated so many that all the unfortunate of the kingdom seem to have gotten together to bear on my heart and choke it with pain at the same time. I can't open my mail without being depressed, sure as I am to find another unfortunate person I often cannot help out.

---

[10]The Countess was a writer, whose literary salon was attended by philosophers. "The energy which characterizes you and honors your epoch engages me in writing you," she stated (Lom 2:579). He wrote her again on April 5 and Dorat obtained assistance (Lom 2:259-266).

[11]Claude Dorat (1733-1780), a poet, was in need of a loan of 20,000 francs.

[12]A statement of the author's philosophy of service to others.

Such is my life: vast endeavors, little success; expensive living, meager fortune, and the eternal circle of the most painful correspondence with a host of unfortunate people whose troubles have become my own. If that friend of yours knows me well, he will tell you this is the truest picture I can give of my feelings and situation.

Be that as it may, Madame, invite our common friend to see me; since you trust him, I will too. We will talk about the Dorat affair; he will explain to me the nature of his circumstances, what he fears, what he hopes for, and when I am better informed, if I can help him out, you can be sure, Madame, that burying with religious discretion all that he wants to keep secret, I will do the impossible so that your trust in me will not be totally fruitless.[13]

21 March 1779, to Vergennes
(Ang. 531, fol. 105)

Kindly receive the second account of our conferences and keep me, I beg you, a small share of your kindness.

Tomorrow new materials will enable me to offer you a new abstract on Wednesday. My respectful attachment is inalterable.

11 April 1779, to Mr. Swinton
(Mol 664-5)

Since you do me the honor, my dear Mr. Swinton, to consult me on the great matter which brings you to France, I owe it to the esteem I have for you to think aloud with you on this affair: listen to me.

Give up, my friend, all sorts of intrigue and expense which would not lead you anywhere and could harm you, and remember what I am telling you.

England, burdened under the weight of the mistake she made by alienating America, must dread to increase its troubles by continuing a war with France, which will not give America back to her, and which by the forthcoming addition of the forces of the house of Bourbon,

---

[13]On April 5, having heard of the suicide of another person in distress, he wrote the Countess urging Dorat to see him (Mol 664).

and the turn things are taking in Holland, can throw her in the worst difficulties.

France, having no ambition at all to increase her power, has no interest in fighting that war. The only one she had at first in the quarrel between England and America was that her enemy should be so occupied by the uprising of her colonies that France would not have anything to fear from her rival, always unfair towards us, as is well known, when she can do it with impunity.

England does not even have the right to reproach us our treaty with America, although it is the sole pretext for her hostilities:

1. Because that treaty was concluded only at the moment when England was going to propose a similar one to America, and expose us to the resentment of that republic, which had not ceased for three years to solicit our alliance. Forced to deal with the English, about whom the Americans had so much to complain, if we had continued to refuse them, they would have reunited themselves with England in order to fall upon us and punish us, if they could, for having refused their alliance.

2. Because this treaty, the most moderate one of all, is not exclusive and does not even prevent England from entering into a similar one with the Americans as to trade, the day she will consider the thirteen colonies as an independent power.

Unless I am mistaken, that's the actual situation. Now you want to know at what price you can hope for peace. Here is what I think. Without being in the secret of the administration, I believe I know their minds well enough not to be mistaken in my conjectures:

If England requests as a basis for peace that France abandon the interests of America, I don't know any advantage that could balance especially in the opinion of our young King, such a cowardly behavior. But if England, sincerely desirous of peace, puts aside this unacceptable condition, I don't think it would meet with many obstacles on other conditions. It is neither through ambition, nor the love of conquest and of war, that we are fighting, but through a just resentment of the awful devices the English have used against us.

Briefly, the treaty with America which at first dealt only with a practical interest, has become for us an affair of honor in the first instance. Respect that treaty, you will find us much easier to deal with than you dared hope.

If you believe your offers may be modified, don't forget that Spain has become like a mediator between us. In that capacity, she has the right to expect good will on your part and she is perhaps the only vehicle today for a peace overture.

Your mission, my dear friend, appears to me therefore to be either impossible or extremely easy: impossible, if the rights of the Americans are not safeguarded; very easy if the ministry can find a way to save the honor of the English Crown while letting America keep the independence they have so well earned. And especially if England sends us honorable propositions through the Court of Madrid, whose guidelines invite us to listen to or receive nothing except through its channel.

I sincerely believe, my friend, that all the success of your affair is contained in this short instruction that I am giving you gladly, 1) because I think it is correct, 2) Because the opinion of a private individual like me is inconsequential.

Go back with this, so you will not be accused of doing here things I know to be as far from your principles as they are contrary to the good you want to procure to the two powers.

12 April 1779, Vergennes to M. de Montmorin
French ambassador in Madrid (Don 3:802-3)

We have here an English emissary said to be loaded with letters of recommendation for intriguers of both sexes, and letters of credit to try and bribe people. He has not spoken as yet either to Mr. de Maurepas or to me, but he has seen a person who works for us [Beaumarchais] and gave him to understand that they would give us anything if we would detach ourselves from the Americans; but this same person did not hesitate to answer himself that such a proposition would not be heard. This emissary appeared determined to write Lord North to obtain more specific instructions. I don't know what will result from this little game, but whatever they propose to us, I beg you to tell Count de Floridablanca that we will not hear anything except by the channel of the King of Spain or to transmit it to him.

This emissary is an Englishman who passes for a gentleman; he is the owner of the Courrier de l'Europe.

To tell the truth, Sir, I look at these attempts as ways to deceive us; the channel is improper; Milord North is not a man to start peace negotiations; he is undeniably trying to lead us to do something that would compromise us with Spain or with America. I subscribe to Count Floridablanca's principle that we will avoid the traps of England only by imparting everything to each other frankly and in good faith.

8 June 1779, to Vergennes
(Ang 531, fol. 224; Mol 665-6)

No one knows better than you how crafty wicked people can be. I am not writing to ask you to right a wrong that I am being done, because that is impossible, but to protect myself from the wrong that this horrible incident would do me if it became known to the king, without his having been forewarned, or to M. de Maurepas, or yourself.

When I arrived back from Bordeaux, I found two letters on my desk. They are unsigned; but the reason why they were written seemed to me worthwhile and without further ado I replied to them, as I always do according to how my heart and mind were affected. An article on French prisoners sent by me to the Courrier de l'Europe[14] before I left Paris was the first text on which the anonymous writer exercised his pen. He appeared indignant against the English; then he listed our shortcomings and seemed to wait for my advice to fix his.

Full as I was with the hateful cries I have heard everywhere against our navy and our ministers, I turn out a quick answer and send it to the address shown. Forgive me, Sir, and may the King forgive me if you disapprove of my warmth, and my true letter, of which I am sending you a literal copy, while sending you the original of the one which gave rise to it. A letter from me is running around now, disfigured, perverted and full of cynical liberties.

I can see I was trapped. I see that some people are trying to harm me by sending this to the king, as

---

[14] Dated March 7, 1179 this article (Proschwitz 1956, 357-9), appeared in the March 16 paper.

was already done regarding things supposedly said at my table.

The deep scorn I have for wicked people must not prevent me from protecting myself against them. I beg you to let the king and M. de Maurepas see my true letter, of which I have fortunately kept a copy. I vouch for its authenticity and I challenge anyone to produce another one signed by me.

I will not add one word: I know your equity and your kindness. Indiscrete scandal makes my blood boil and I become twice as French when I find people who act as if they were not. That's what makes me speak out loudly sometimes and why I replied to an anonymous writer who seemed honest to me.

If it is possible for you, Sir, to grant me a minute of your time this week, I wish to put under your eyes important matters relative to the Americans. I will receive your orders in this respect with the respectful gratitude and all the feelings that bind me to you.

4 June 1779, to an anonymous writer[15]
(Ang. 531 fol. 230; Mol 666-7)

I have found, Sir, upon my return from Bordeaux and Rochefort, the two letters you honored me with, one from Metz and the other from Paris.[16] Your patriotism deserves much praise, but it causes you to paint with too much fear our situation on the battlefield.

(I have received, Sir, the letter you honored me with. Your patriotism and your fears are right.)

The English have no military advantage over us. They have pillaged our commerce, as highway robbers attack carriages while waiting for the sheriff: perhaps he should have arrived sooner. But most of our ships were insured in London and we had over them four thousand more prisoners than they have over us.

(The British have pillaged our ships like highway- men but if our navy, instead of remaining idle in the

---

[15]The text of the allegedly apocryphal letter (6 June 1779, Ang. 531, fol. 280) is given in parentheses after each paragraph.

[16]Ang. 531, fol. 225-230.

ports, waiting for the decision of ministers who won't make up their minds, had only acted like the highway patrol, we would not have uselessly lost our commerce, part of which however is insured in London; which does not detract from the gross mistake our ministers have made in starting the war without preliminary precautions. It is true that we have taken more of their men prisoners than they did us, but our mistake remains the same.)

Our d'Estaing squadron is in the best shape and has all it needs, while Byron, having made the mistake of setting his land troops on the cemetery of America, perishes there obviously every day, not daring to try anything and with troops superior to ours.

(Count d'Estaing is in the best shape while Admiral Byron perishes on the cemetery of Saint Lucy, without daring to do anything. In spite of that have they not failed to recall him? And if he remains in place, is it not as a result of the ministers indecision rather than their expressed will?)[17]

The taking of Pondichery is not an advantage for the English to boast about either. A French frigate had left a year before with orders for Mr. de Bellecombe to evacuate the place at the first move of the English and to withdraw at Ile de France where the government had resolved a long time ago to gather all its forces, a little too scattered in India. The frigate arrived after the beautiful defense of M. de Bellecombe, who would not have attempted to do so uselessly, not being strong enough to hold on, if he had earlier received orders to retreat. Which does not detract from his merit.

(You say that they took Pondichery from us. It is another effect of our want of vigor to have sent a year before the order for M. de Bellecombe to withdraw to Ile de France. During that time the English grab everything in India, and to our shame do there whatever they want. They can't even dent their own colonies but they can

---

[17]Admiral d'Estaing, after arriving at the mouth of the Delaware in July 1778, had failed to provide General Sullivan assistance for a combined assault on Newport. His fleet had suffered in a hurricane, and after refitting in Boston he set sail for the West Indies. Although recalled, he returned to American waters and tried an unsuccessful assault on Savannah.

take ours away from us! Which removes nothing from M. de Bellecombe's merit.)[18]

As to the constant mistreatment of our prisoners by the English, as there can be no excuse for such cruelty, I thought it my duty to publish it as a punishment for their crime; that's all a private individual could do, while waiting for the government to react, which we must hope for from their wisdom.

(I have published the cruelties of the English against our prisoners. What more can a private individual do? Would it not be up to the government to react to all that, if they could feel anything? But all their wisdom consist in wallowing in an indolence that passes for prudence. Generally, in our affairs, there may not be three men in their true positions.)

Be that as it may, you can believe, Sir, that France has never been in such an advantageous position. Has she not given peace to Prussia, Russia, Turkey? Has she not isolated England from any kind of ally in Europe? Is she not keeping that power in check through the movements we take on our coasts? Has not our alliance with America consolidated that independence which takes away from the English Crown the whole Northern continent? And has not our political cabinet, the most able and the first of Europe, acquired universal influence on the actions of all the militant powers? Spain is armed and ready to thunder. Holland is resolved to defend and maintain her trade and the freedom of the seas. Sweden, Denmark and Russia join in that honorable plan: What remains for England? A deadly isolation, total exhaustion in men and money, intestine dissensions, the loss of America, and the fear to lose Ireland. It is true that as a revenge for San Domingo it has taken from us the foul rock of Saint Lucy, but while pretending to threaten our possessions of the Gulf can't you see they are trying to hide how afraid they are for theirs?

(Be that as it may, we gave peace to Germany and Turkey. Our alliance with America, if we don't let it slip away, removes a precious jewel from the English Crown, and our diplomacy is the only one which has some influence in Europe. Still how many matters left behind!)

---

[18] In India, France was losing ground. Pondichery had capitulated on October 17, 1778.

That is the respective statement of their advantages and ours. Whoever does not feel the extreme superiority of our position poorly reads the great book of the events of the century.

(Such is the state of current affairs.)

Let's dismiss the alleged faults of Count d'Estaing and the outcry of the envious. Let us not judge lightly a man big enough to be above the outrage, by printing every anonymous insult addressed to him. Let us look solely at the good condition of his fleet after such a laborious campaign, at his indefatigable vigilance, and the concert of praise from all soldiers and sailors. Let's look at the efforts made by his enemies to denigrate him. One does not get hoarse bad-mouthing a man who has not done anything to think about. A contemptuous pity is what should be given to mediocre people, and the anger of the rivals of a good man is perhaps a more flattering and sure homage than his friends' praise.

(Count d'Estaing is denigrated because the ministers have chosen him; and the ministers have allowed the foreign gazettes heap insults on this brave man as if it was not a duty to defend the man you have appointed. But every one cares only for his own appointment, nothing more.)

I am stopping short on this subject, because my opinions do not add anything to the matter, and I have much business to attend to.

(I stop on this inexhaustible subject, because having nothing to do with all that, I need neither feel sorry about it nor speak about it. It's enough to see how things are and to shrug and keep quiet. Let us mind our own business.)

If it has been my pleasure to ease the mind of a gentleman who appears to be very good Frenchman, it is because carried away by the torrent of bitter critics who spend their lives belittling our advantages while our enemies waste not one minute in blowing theirs up, he fears for us and has asked me how I felt about it. I hastened to tell it to him in a couple of words, assuring him of all the feelings his letter inspire in his very humble servitor.

(I believe I am writing to a gallant man and I am answering him as he addressed me with the frankness and esteem, etc.)

18 June 1779, from John Jay to the French Ambassador
(Barnett, 4:274)

I enclose you Acts of Congress of the 5th and 18th instant respecting Bills of Exchange for two millions four hundred thousand livres tournois principal, and four hundred and thirty two thousand livres interest drawn on you in favor of M. de Beaumarchais, and payable in the several sums, and at the respective times specified in the enclosed schedule. Sensible of M. de Beaumarchais' efforts to serve these United States, and of the seasonable supplies he has from time to time furnished, Congress are earnestly disposed to make him this payment. They would gladly have done it in produce; but the state of our finances, and the hazardous navigation render it impracticable.

We flatter ourselves that you will be able to discharge the respective drafts with punctuality. If difficulties occur you will have time to represent them to Congress, who will exert the means in their power to prevent any loss or disappointment to M. de Beaumarchais.

24 June 1779, to Vergennes
(Ang. 531, fol. 277)

I have the honor of sending you the letter requested by M. de Maurepas, and which runs around under my name. I would not have permitted myself such an insolent thing, had I not been ordered to do so. I spoke to Mr. LeNoir [Chief of Police] who is going to do some research about it.

I am not sending you the manifesto I have received from London last Monday, because I think you had it before Mr. Almadovar received it from Spain. It seems to me that following the serious complaints involved, the Spanish declaration is rather contorted.

By the 15th no news had been received in Bayonne regarding the departure of the Cadix fleet, although mail has come from that city. That's what I hear today from Bayonne.

If the book is as strong as the preface is long, we can expect beautiful things from that nation. But I don't know why, I always have a bit of ice in the corner of my brain, labelled *Spain*. No matter how I try, I can't get excited about that. God grant that I be wrong.

12 July 1779, from Count d'Estaing
On board the Languedoc, Grenada Island
(Lom 2:164-5)

I only have time to write you, Sir, that the Proud Rodrigue has kept its post on the line and has contributed to the success of the king's forces.[19] You will forgive me for having used it so well, as your interests will not suffer, rest assured of it. The brave Montaud, unfortunately, was killed. I will forward very soon the *statement of "graces"* [acknowledgment of services rendered] to the minister, and I hope you will help me solicit what *your* navy has so richly deserved.

7 September 1779, to Sartine
(Lom 2:165)

I thank you for forwarding Count d'Estaing's letter. It is noble of him to have thought at the moment of his victory, that a word from him would be appreciated by me. I take the liberty of sending you copy of his note, for which I pride myself as a good Frenchman and rejoice as the passionate lover of my country, against arrogant England.

My brave Montaud believed he could do no better to prove he was worthy of his trust than to get himself killed. Whatever the result may be for my business, my poor friend Montaud died in the field of glory. I feel a childish joy to know that those Englishmen who have been tearing me up in their papers for the past four years, will be able to read there that one of my ships contributed to the taking of the most fertile of their possessions.

And Count d'Estaing's enemies, and yours especially, Sir, I can see them gnawing their fingernails, and my heart jumps with joy.

11 September 1779, to the King
(Lom 2:166-7)

Sire,

I do not ask you for compensation for my work.

---

[19]In the recent naval battle between Admiral Biron and Admiral d'Estaing. The ship was convoying ten merchant ships when it was called upon to join the French forces off of Grenada.

Your wise ministers know I would be supremely happy if it was always useful to Your Majesty.

I do not ask you for compensation for the Proud Rodrigue campaign, too much honored that a ship of mine has deserved the Admiral's praise while fighting with a victorious squadron.

But Sire, war is a game for kings, which crushes private individuals and wipes them out like dust. The Proud Rodrigue was escorting ten other merchant vessels engaged in commercial operations, equally useful to the State in another way.

The death of my first captain, thirty five men out of service, the wrecking of my ship, the most mistreated in the squadron (three cannon balls in the side, four at the floating line, two of which have gone clear through, five in the masts, which ruined them, one in the great pump, which tore it to pieces, forty in the sails which pierced them full of holes, and the rest in the rigging, which chopped them up); the complete exhaustion of sailors suffered by my other ships when they arrived at Fort Royal, in order to complete the crews of the squadron; the order given to the Proud Rodrigue to repair and follow the squadron; the obligation for me to send new orders to the head of my fleet, and the impossibility for this fleet, which has already lost eleven ships, to leave under escort of the Proud Rodrigue for its true destination for more than three months: all of that, Sire, ruining my company whose funds advanced were enormous and postponing the returns which should have been now coming, forces me to implore your Majesty.

Let me not perish, Sire, and I am happy. The service I am asking for is of little importance.

I am advised from Grenada that I have been charged with 90.000 livres for the urgent repair of the Proud Rodrigue. On more than two millions I borrowed this year for my fleet, I have left to pay only 100,000 ecus, half on the 25th of this month, half on the 10th of October. I beg Your Majesty to please order the modest sum of 400,000 livres be lent to me, for a few months, from the Royal Treasury. Count Maurepas knows by experience that I am faithful in my engagements. When the considerable funds I expect arrive from Martinique, where my merchandise has been sold, I will reimburse the Treasury capital and interest.

It is only after an accounting, impossible today, which will submit the statement of my losses to the ministers that I will call upon Your Majesty's justice for their reimbursement. It is as a favor that I am asking for the short-term loan of 400.000 livres which is required as a result of this campaign to keep from perishing one of Your Majesty's most faithful subjects, whose undoing would bring about a general discouragement.[20]

11 November 1779, to Maurepas
(Mol 668)

I may not have yet the strength to jump out of bed to go visit you but no illness will ever prevent me from expressing my gratitude to you.

They want to steal 33,000 livres from me and, adding interest for twenty years of silence, they double the sum. That's 66,000 livres. Plus some 12,000 livres for expenses, and there I am, obliged to pay 80,000 livres to the people who for twenty years have owed me 46,000 l. and on the only ground that, loathing suits as I do, I have not bothered them.

You kindly heard my friend. I ask only to consign and to count: I never said anything else. This is denied, judgments having been taken against me by default while I was away. Form, form, that awful bailiwick of the legal profession, serves as a blanket for the iniquity of an atrocious request.

Consign and count, that's the object of my request. To pay cash, if I owe anything, that's the favor I am begging for.[21]

You promised to help me. I am counting on your kindness. Your words are always straightforward. You help people without ceremonies, whenever you can. That's what I adore in you.

If my poor Prince de Conti was still alive, I certainly would make him ashamed he was unfair towards you. He used to recommend to me never to depend on you.

---

[20]The loan was granted and the amount deducted from a two million livres indemnity payable in several installments, the last of which was paid him in 1785 (Lom 2:167n).

[21] The suit in question was that of the Aubertin family, relatives of Beaumarchais's first wife.

Passion blinds people. He had no inkling of your kind and merry soul as if he had never seen you. For two years he kept me from frequenting you. And you, Sir, although you knew that I was one of his closest associates, you have never shown me anything but kindness, loyalty, kind protection and frank guidance. So, I am more touched than I can say and really regret that this unfair, obstinate enemy of yours should not be with us any longer. He trusted me and I would have made him change his mind. Your most grateful servant would have brought back to you a heart which was blind on your account.

Excuse me, Sir. I love to talk about him because he was like a father to me, and I like to talk about him before you because, although I have not deserved it, I find in your attitude with me all the characteristics that endeared him to me.

I am taking the liberty of enclosing herewith a short Instructive Memorial on the petition which will be reported Saturday by Mr. Amelot to the Council of Dispatches.

I have just sent to M. de Vergennes a paper, poorly written because I am ill but at least, because it contains true facts, capable of countering victoriously the insidious accusations of the Saint-James cabinet about our alleged perfidies.[22]

My gratitude and my respect for you are as sweet to my heart as they are inalterable.

16 November 1779, from Vergennes
(Ang. 532, fol. 170)

I have received the letter you did me the honor of writing me, as well as the memorial enclosed therewith, for which I thank you. I think you can without inconvenient publish a refutation of the allegations of the *Justificative Memorial of the Court of London* regarding your shipments to America, but I would like very much to see your work before you send it to the Courrier de l'Europe.

---

[22]See Introduction, page 44ff.

OBSERVATIONS

SUR

LE MÉMOIRE JUSTIFICATIF

DE LA COUR DE LONDRES;

PAR

PIERRE-AUGUSTIN
CARON DE BEAUMARCHAIS,

Armateur & Citoyen Français;

DÉDIÉES A LA PATRIE.

Facit indignatio versum.
Juv. Sat. I.

A LONDRES, A PHILADELPHIE;
Et se trouve par-tout.

1779.

OBSERVATIONS ON THE JUSTIFICATIVE MEMORIAL OF THE COURT OF LONDON[1]

FIRST MOTIVE FOR WRITING

1]   If a private citizen may be allowed for a moment to dare intermeddle in the quarrel of the sovereigns, it is when called by them to judgment in Justificative Memorials[2] addressed to the public of which he is a member, he sees himself personally cited upon facts turned into accusations of perfidy against the enemies of those[3] sovereigns; which facts, presently more truthfully, may be used to vindicate the indicted power, to give everyone what belongs to him.

SECOND MOTIVE FOR WRITING

[2]   If it is an accepted practice among kings to maintain at great expense, at each other's court, some lavish inquisitors whose real merit is as much to elucidate what is being done in the country where they reside, as to spread there without any scruples the falsest notions about current events, when such falsehood can be useful to their august constituents;[4] at least, no people before had ever seen a magnificent ambassador pushing the dissimulation of his profession so far as to mislead the people of his own country in his ministerial dispatches, in order to augment the

---

[1] See Introduction, "A Political Opuscule."

[2] The ambiguous plural (which Gudin had removed) indicates that the previously published French papers are included besides that of Gibbon. In the same manner the plural "sovereigns" includes the <u>people</u> of England, France and the United States. "Everyone" at the end of the paragraph includes the private citizen himself. For the contemporary readers who had read Gibbon's writing, there was no ambiguity. It meant all those who sympathized with the American cause in England and France as well as in America: "The secret enemies of peace, of Great Britain and perhaps of France herself, had, however, the criminal adroitness to persuade His Most Christian Majesty that he could, without violating the faith of treaties, declare publicly that he received among the number of his allies the rebellious subjects of a king, his neighbour and ally." Gibbon, p. 140.

[3] Gudin: "his sovereigns" rather than "those sovereigns."

[4] Reminiscence of Voltaire, VL14 1:40.

misunderstanding between nations, or to increase his own substance and prepare his own advancement.[5]

This is however what transpires today from the examination of the alleged facts concerning the trade between France and America cited in the Justificative Memorial of the king of England, based on the faulty reports of Viscount Stormont[6], whom I name here without scruples, because he seemed to invite me to do so himself, by making use of my name and my shipping operations to accuse France of "perfidy."

========================

[4]   If it entered my plan to discuss the basic question which divides the two courts today, I would not need to establish, by the particular facts which concern me, that our ministers not only have shown England more consideration than they owed to her, to the nature of subsisting ties, but, through complacency for the court of London, have remained well within the limits of the undisputed rights of any indifferent and neutral power. It is through international facts, known to all of Europe, that I would dismiss the charge of perfidy, so many times leveled against France in that Justificative Memorial; and I would throw it back upon its authors so thoroughly as to leave no doubt about the truth of my assertion.[7]

[5]   Indeed, what nation is it which presumes today to smear us with the suspicion of perfidy, so self-righteously clamoring for honor and the faith of treaties? Is it not that same English nation, systematically unjust towards us and whose morality with us has always been contained in that maxim, a thousand times applauded in London, in the mouth of the great statesman

---

[5]The first motive is clandestine because it addresses political theories and criticizes the French government. Hence the deliberately muddled style. The second is ostensible. It introduced the argument ad hominem, and is burlesque in style. The English ambassador's reports were "faulty," because incomplete.

[6]David Murray, Viscount Stormont (1727-1796), peer of Scotland, and English ambassador in Paris 1772-78.

[7]*This paragraph warns the reader that the question of international law, dealt with in the following pages, is not the writer's main concern. The tone of Paragraphs 5-15 indicates that Beaumarchais is enjoying the narrative of the privateers' exploits against the no less spirited British navy.*

Chatham: "If we wanted to be just toward France and Spain, we would have too many restitutions to make. To weaken or to fight them is our only law, the basis of our success?"[8]

[6] Is it not that same nation whose outrages and usurpations have never had any other bonds than those of its power; who has always made war on us without declaring it; who, in 1754, after having assassinated Mr. de Jumonville, a French officer, in the midst of a meeting called in Canada in order to agree on peace terms and fix boundaries,[9] started the war of 1755, without any reason or semblance of reason, by unexpectedly seizing, in time of peace, 500 of our ships,[10] and who ended that same war, in 1763, by the most tyrannical abuse of the advantages that the hazard of battles had given them over us in that unjust war?

[7] Is it not that predatory nation for whom the most solemnly sworn peace is never anything but a truce granted to her own exhaustion, and quickly terminated by the most shocking hostilities?[11] Who, already in 1774, had allowed her commanding officer in Senegal, a certain MacNamara, to capture a French merchant ship from Nantes, which was never returned?[12] Who, in the year 1776, after all kinds of outrages perpetrated against us in India, insulted on the Ganges three French ships, Sainte Anne, Catherine and Ile de France, and bombarded

---

[8]*Cf. the 7 December 1775 memorial to the king.*

[9]*In the Ohio valley the French had built Fort Duquesne where Pittburg is now located, and the English raised nearby Fort Necessity. It was commanded by George Washington when Coulon de Jumonville (1725-1754) tried to stop the construction.*

[10]*This is referred to in French history as the "attentat de Boscawen," i.e. the outrageous attack of Admiral Boscawen who captured the French fleet in time of peace. According to DNB the admiral seized only three merchant ships on june 10, 1755, and the rest of the fleet escaped in the fog.*

[11]*The hyperbolic tone here shows that this is not the real priority in the writer's intentions.*

[12]*Additional details on these and similar incidents can be found in a paper written by Beaumarchais for the French government, entitled "Abstract of various matters which are grounds for complaints against the court of London" (Ang. 530, fo. 444-7). The officer in question "stayed drunk from morning to night and inflicted on everyone the most vexatious treatment."*

them at the pass of Calcutta, smashing our rigs, killing and injuring our sailors, and, adding insult to injury, immediately sent over surgeons to take care of the wounded? An outrage for which all the merchants of India, irritated and dismayed, have not ceased to seek redress and revenge from the king of France.[13]

[8]   Was is not that same nation again who, always faithful to her system, had given orders to attack us in India without warning, one year before the outbreak of hostilities, and to drive us out of all our possessions, as irrefutably proven by the date of the investment of Pondichery in 1778: and who, imperturbable in her arrogance, does not blush to have her demure writer seriously contend: "that it is below the dignity of his king to examine the dates when these facts occurred," as if, in any quarrel, it was not recognized that the aggressor is the only one to blame?[14]

[9]   Was it not that always provoking nation, who during that same time of peace, arrogating the right of search and visit on the whole ocean, made sport of trying our patience by stopping, insulting, and vexing all our merchant ships, even in sight of our shores?

[10]   Was it not a sailor of that same nation who was cited by Captain Marcheguais of Bordeaux, when the latter stated that he had been stopped in March of 1777, 130 leagues from the coast of France, that they fired at him eight times, broke off his rigs; and that even after he sent over four men and his assistant to have his passports checked and to prove that they were in order, he nevertheless saw ten scoundrels come aboard his ship,

---

[13]The English forced the French ships to undergo the search.

[14]Beaumarchais parodies Gibbon's bombastic style: "It is not consonant with the king's dignity to seek to discover the epoch or the nature of the correspondence which these agents had the address to engage in with the ministers of the court of Versailles" (p. 132). And as to who started the hostilities: "The court of Versailles cannot fail to acknowledge that the king of England, after having recalled his ambassador, announced to his Parliament the conduct of His [French] Majesty as an act of hostility of formal and premeditated aggression .... hence it is somewhat futile to search out orders sent to the East Indies or to mark the precise day when the fleet of England or France ...." Historians give different dates to the beginning of the war: May 4, 1778, date of the ratification by Congress of the treaties (Lecky 1916, 347), May 24, date of Louis XVI's alleged declaration of war (Madaule, 2:149).

bust his bales, upset the whole ship, loot it, take him prisoner and keep him, he, the sixth, aboard their ship as long as it pleased them to see him swallow the poison of insult and the grossest outrages?

[11]   Was it not also some English captains who, in that same period of peace, seized several ships from Bordeaux, the Meulan and the Nancy among others, on their way out of the Cape, and grossly mistreated their crews, although their destination was France and they did not carry munitions of war? That a certain Captain Morin[15] was stopped at Preachers' Point, the landing of Martinique, and led to Dominica, in spite of papers in good order for the French Cape and S. Pierre de Miquelon? Our Admiralty files are full of such complaints and declarations made in 1776 and 1777 against the English, that people so loyal in their behavior, which today accuse us of perfidy!

[12]   They would seize our merchant ships even as they were landing in our islands. They would chase their enemies all the way up to our shores and would blast them so closely that their bullets hit the ground and they had no qualms answering with broadsides our Captains complaints about their improper behavior. Witness the Chevalier de Boissier who, carried away by his indignation, felt obliged to chastise such insolence by gunning down an English frigate near the Cow Island [Abaco island] and forcing him to limp back to Jamaica in the worst of shapes.

[13]   They would gun down ships already inside French harbors. Witness that merchantman, fired at and stopped short in the jetties of Dunkirk, and forced to come out again at all risks and be searched by an English revenue cutter shamelessly waiting to do so in the roads.

[14]   Did they not go so far as to attempt outrageously to burn American ships within our docks? An insult witnessed in Cherbourg and which cannot be attributed to anybody's carelessness, since it was a corvette of the king, its captain in uniform, sailing out of Jersey by express order of the court with the promise of three hundred guineas, if he carried out their insulting project.

---

[15]The ship involved here is the Seine, chartered by Beaumarchais, and of course the papers in question were false, or "ostensible" papers, according to a well-known practice described by Beaumarchais in the 16 April 1776 letter to Vergennes.

[15] These complaints and a thousand similar ones came from all directions to the ministers of France, who able, and perhaps obliged to cry out against England at such excesses, nevertheless would be so moderate as to be content to file their complaints with the English ministers, whose replies, often as ludicrous as the sailors' behavior was odious, stated in substance that "either the information was mistaken, or the captains were drunk, or it was a misunderstanding, or even that they were perfidious Americans sailing under English colours." Never any other reason, much less justice. And that's the scrupulous neighbor, the candid friend, the equitable and moderate people who accuse us today of perfidy!

[16] Who is it the author of the Justificative Memorial is trying to mislead in Europe? Is he trying to divert the English people's attention away from their government's insane behavior, while trying to inculpate ours? By accusing our ministers of having deceived the French people and their king, do they hope to smother the cries of the English people who clamor in their ears these dreaded words: Give us back America and the blood of our brothers. Give us back our trade and our millions swallowed up in that abominable war. Our rivals' perfidy did not cause all these losses. Yours did. Hey! What do the French ministers have to do with America's independence?

[17] When France at the last peace, gave possession of Canada to England; when long before that time, the clairvoyant Mr. Pitt predicted that "if the Americans were allowed to forge even the irons of their horses, they would soon break loose the chains of their allegiance;" when the same Lord Chatham predicted again in London in 1762 "that the cession by France of Canada would cause England to lose America;" when the jealousy of all the colonies for the privileges granted to the new possession, and their uneasiness about the establishment of a monarchism which seemed to threaten their freedom[16], caused them to protest and rebel; when after concussions and bad treatments the Americans sounded the alarm and threw the yoke of harsh England, while restricting the extension of the great word "home" [patrie] to the bounds of the continent; had France anything to do with the motives for that rupture? Did

---

[16]Inspired by the Declaration of Independence regarding British laws establishing "arbitrary government" in Canada. Other allusions to the Declaration need not be footnoted.

her intrigue or perfidy blind the English ministers to the consequences of that frightening rumor which they affected to scorn?[17]

[18]   The fire of discontent was smoldering all over America. But when at the time of the Stamp Act in 1766, the conflagration lit up in Boston spread out to all the northern cities; when the bloody uprising of that town led its inhabitants to demand proudly the recall of the governor and the lieutenant of Massachusetts-Bay; when the affair of the revenue cutter of Rhode-Island forced the British to recall these two officers, and to repeal the imprudent Stamp Act; did the intrigue or perfidy of France have anything to do with those events preparatory to the liberty of the colonies upon which the English administration then barely deigned to open their eyes?

[19]   Soon the fatal tea tax, the transfer of important cases to the mother country, the installation of tribunals appointed by the court, and a thousand other outrages against the freedom of the colonies, made all citizens take up arms and finally form that great body which has become so fateful for the English of Europe, the Congress of Philadelphia. Was this kind of imprudence and blindness on the part of the cabinet of Saint-James the fruit of the gold, intrigue or perfidy of our administration?

[20]   Did we instigate the cadets' uprising, General Gage's hostilities in Boston, the proscription of tea in all the colonies, and all those great moves which warned the universe that America's time had arrived at last;[18] while the English ministers, like that Duke Olivares,[19] so famous for the insidious account he gave his king, Philip, about Duke Braganza's rebellion, were likewise deceiving their king, George, and perfidiously deluding him with the most absurd hope of subjugating America?

---

[17]Paragraphs 17 to 23 are partially drawn from Beaumarchais' letter to Congress of 10 September 1777.

[18]Beaumarchais had read Common Sense, a translation of which was found in his papers.

[19]Gaspar de Guzman, Duke Olivares, was minister of Philip IV of Spain, during the 1640 rebellion of Catalonia and Portugal. Bragance fought for Portuguese independence and became king of Portugal in 1643. He had been secretly helped by Cardinal Richelieu.

[21] Did France's intrigue or perfidy inspire the vigorous efforts of a people driven toward independence by tyranny, when the English ships were so proudly sent back to Europe? Did France incite the English obstinately to send them back to America, and the Americans obstinately to refuse them and burn their cargoes?

[22] And the outbreak of hostilities between the two peoples, and the armaments on both sides, and the shameful Lexington affair, and Bunker's Hill; and the treachery of the English in arming the slaves against their masters in Virginia; and even worse in counterfeiting the paper money in order to discredit it, a kind of poisoning theretofore unknown; and all the horrors which have led America to publish her independence at last, to sustain it by force of arms, have they been the fruit of French intrigue and perfidy, or that of the greed, pride, folly and infatuation of England?

[23] Did we see France then availing herself of the rights of the most ancient, most profound, most legitimate resentment, to kindle strife and rebellion among her unfortunate neighbors?

[24] A tranquil spectator, she forgot all the breaches of faith of England, and the interests of her own commerce, and the great reason of State which allows, which perhaps directs a country to take advantage of the divisions of a natural enemy to prolong their troubles or to weaken them, when the experience of more than a century has proved that there is no other way to render them just and loyal with us.

[25] Thus, although, obviously, Saint-James palace did not deserve the courtesies the Versailles palace lavished upon them in such a major occurrence, France nevertheless remained strictly indifferent and passive about the intestine quarrels of her unjust rival.

[26] To reassure this worried rival, she declared that she would keep the most exact neutrality with each of the two nations; and has religiously kept it until the time when reason, prudence and the force of circumstances, and above all concern for her own security, have obliged her publicly to change her conduct, for fear of becoming a victim thereof herself, openly to show herself under another aspect.

[27] But why, at the instant of neutrality, did England not dare to look at it as a breach of faith on the part of France and bring it up as an infraction to subsisting treaties? The fact is that she knew very

well that the issue which aroused her colonies could not be likened to those seditious movements that even success cannot justify and that the prince has the right to punish in kingdoms more absolute.[20]

[28]	The fact is that the generic word king the latitude of which is so wide that none of those who wear it have like conditions, functions, powers or rights; the fact is that this title, so difficult to bear, has quite different connotations in countries subject to a one-man government such as the peaceful French monarchy, and in mixed and turbulent governments such as England's royal-aristo-democracy[21]. An act which on the part of Languedoc or Alsace in France would rightly have been considered as a crime of lese-majesty [high treason] in the first degree, was in England but a simple question of law, subject to examination by every free individual.

[29]	The fact is that the refusal, by order of the king, to do justice to America, and the redress by dint of cannon balls of her long grievances were to be considered there as the greatest abuse of authority, as a total subversion of constitutive laws, and as a most dangerous usurpation for a prince of the House of Brunswick; for he ought not to forget that a similar uprising had caused the crown to pass to his house, but on condition that he should wear it as an English king [in English in the text] and not in the manner of the king of France.

[30]	The fact is that the vehement protest of the colonies about the right not to be taxed without representation, and the right to be judged by their peers in the form of juries [in English in the text], had found so many supporters in England that it kept and still keeps the nation divided on a subject so relevant to the civil rights of every English citizen.

[31]	The fact is that even in Parliamentary debates and in some writings by the most respected men in both

---

[20]"The approbation which the court of Versailles has just given to the revolt of the American colonies would not suffer it to condemn the uprising of its own subjects in the new world or those of Spain, which would have more powerful motives for following the same example, if they were not dissuaded therefrom by the calamities into which these unhappy colonies have plunged themselves" (Gibbon, 142). Note the litote "kingdoms more absolute."

[21]Cf. *Common Sense*, on the English Constitution.

houses, doubt on this subject was carried to the point of questioning openly whether the English themselves were not more rebellious to the common constitutive charter than the Americans.[22]

[32]   The fact is that Milord Abingdon,[23] one of the most upright and enlightened men in England, went so far as to propose in front of the whole house, that the opposition withdrew from Parliament and that they set on record as the cause of their secession (a new word he made up to describe this national insurrection) that Parliament and the prince had exceeded the limits of their powers in that war. Above all, that Parliament, being composed of the representatives of the English people, should not have played the odious farce of the servants-masters[24], and sacrificed their constituents' interests to the ambition of the prince and the ministers.

[33]   The fact is that in case of such abuse, the people had the right, he said, to recall powers so ill-administered, because such a decision as that of the American war belongs to the people only in their capacity as supreme legislator and first founder of the English constitution.

[34]   So, if it was an issue, even in England, who was more rebellious to the constitution of the English or the Americans, a foreign prince was even more likely not to bother examining the issue which divided the two nations, and to remain cool in their quarrel, and such was the position taken by the king.

[35]   That refusal to judge between the old and the new England; that equitable and uncontested principle of neutrality for the king of France once set down, destroyed in advance the whole lot of subtle objections escaped since then from the mouths of the logicians of Oxford, Cambridge and London. That is, whether the king of France ought not to open or close his ports to the

---

[22]This paragraph and the next five are partially drawn from the memorial to the minister of navy, 19 september 1777.

[23]Willoughby Bertie, fourth Earl of Abingdon (1740-1799) was a friend of John Wilkes, with whom he travelled to Europe and visited Voltaire in Ferney in 1766. He published several works in support of the American cause, as well as the cause of Ireland and later on the French revolution.

[24]The representatives are the servants of the people.

ships of both or only one of the belligerents. Whether he ought to restrict the rights of his commerce by complacency for a nation which does not respect the rights of anyone, and especially, whether he ought not to prohibit his merchants the ports of the American continent while receiving the Americans in his own. Questions, obviously, as vain to ask as useless to answer. For, by the absolute right of his neutrality, the king owed both nations an absolutely equal treatment, whether he admitted or rejected their ships.

[36] So, just as it would be contradictory for France to open her ports to English, Danish, Dutch and Swedish vessels and to forbid her French merchants to go trade in London, the Baltic sea, the Zuyderzee and so on, while receiving American ships in her ports on the same footing as those of all other nations, France could not, without contradiction, deny her own merchants the freedom to do business in Boston, Williamsburg, Charleston, Philadelphia, since everything had to be equal.

[37] Such were, according to my opinion, the strict conclusions which France ought to draw from her neutrality, regarding her commerce. And if the king of France, forgetting the long resentment of his forefathers, was willing to show consideration to his unjust neighbors at war with their brothers, His Majesty ought to have believed a fortiori his justice involved in not imposing on his faithful subjects the maritime merchants, in time of peace, prohibitions and limitations that no other European sovereign seemed to impose upon his subjects.

[38] To leave all our ports open and free to all nations which were not at war with us, and not to deprive the English of the right to exhaust through trade all our French products, while leaving to the Americans the liberty of buying them from us, in free competition--was that not at once, on the part of the king, to keep the courtesies granted foreigners and to maintain the protection essentially owed by any equitable monarch to the commerce of his states?

[39] Well, while frankly declaring, and according to my own opinion, that such was the conduct the king of France ought to follow, I am forced to confess that,--be it moral delicacy, austerity, on the part of a youthful and virtuous king whose heart has not aged, has not been consumed in that anger, that desire for revenge against the English that his ancestor kept on into his grave--be it love for peace--be it our ministers' regards for the predicament of unjust England,--or I know not what blind

complacency for the representations of Viscount Stormont, who kept on harassing them,-- while recognizing the French merchants well grounded in asking protection for the commerce they wanted to open with America, the king's ministers have always kept with the merchants the most excessive rigor. If anything can lead them today to repent for their condescension, is it not the honest writer of the Justificative memorial, trying to establish as an indication of their perfidy, that anxiety which was but a perpetual and painful struggle between their repressive authority and the very active efforts of a commerce enlightened on our true interests?

[40]   When to all the reasons which militated in my petitions in favor of French commerce, I added, with a liberty that only a great patriotism can excuse, when I added, I say, that it would seem very strange to all of Europe that the king of France should be patient enough to let his tobacco Farm pay up to one hundred francs a quintal for that useful commodity,[25] even to let it run out of it, while America overflowed with it; that if the war between England and her colonies should last another two years, the king, because he had refused to avail himself of his most incontestable rights as a neutral, risked to see the twenty-six or thirty millions of his tobacco farm totally compromised; and that, because it pleased the English who could no longer supply us with this produce, insolently to forbid our purchasing it from the only country in the world where it was raised---a kind of audaciousness so intolerable that in London itself people joked about the meek way we put up with it.

[41]   When, through all those arguments and others of the same nature, I urged our ministers to untie the hands of the French commerce--as it cannot be supposed that it was for want of understanding that they did not relent toward us--one must conclude that an excess of condescension for our enemies made them deaf to our entreaties! An excess all the more surprising that it was easy to guess what experience proves today, that they would never receive any thanks from the other side of the Channel.

[42]   Now, if I have demonstrated that after several centuries of a legitimate resentment, and according to the principles of Natural Law which alone regulate the relations of nations and kingdoms with one another,

---

[25]It was useful because it was a State monopoly and produced revenue.

France could without any qualms seize all opportunities to get even with England and to weaken her by encouraging the movements of her colonies--and that she did not do it.

[43] If I have demonstrated that by following England's own example, by imitating her behavior, France could have taken advantage of the predicament into which the American war plunged her natural enemies, and could have pounced on her merchant fleet, or on her Gulf possessions--which far from getting us into the war, would have condemned England to an eternal peace--and that through tenderness of conscience and honor, she did not want to do it.

[44] There only remains for me to prove, according to the quotations of the Justificative Memorial concerning our commerce, my person, my views and the alleged cooperation of the ministry; there remains for me to prove that Viscount Stormont--against the truth, against his information, and against his conscience--has not ceased to send to his court very insidious, very false reports about the behavior of ours. And that is what I shall do presently.

[45] I will start by agreeing frankly and straightforwardly that the French merchants, among whom I belong, have, in spite of the court,[26] shipped clothing, arms and munitions of all kinds to America; and that if they did not multiply these shipments further, it is because the severity of our administration has not ceased to hinder their operations. And I will admit this, not only because it is the truth, but because I believe that under the circumstances French merchants were bound by no other duty than not to hurt by their speculations, the political interest of the king of France.

[46] They could even afford to ignore if the king, through austerity, frowned upon their efforts; for under a prince so kind, so just, there is a long way between the misfortune of displeasing him and the horrible crime of disobeying him. Besides, the English writer who makes in his Justificative Memorial such a false application of the word smuggling to the ventured expeditions of our commerce--doesn't he know, or does he pretend not to know, that a merchandise whose exchange or sale is free in a certain kingdom, does not become

---

[26]This is not agreeing with, but contesting Gibbon's allegations. A sure way to baffle the censors.

contraband there just because its exportation or its destination may be detrimental to a foreign power; and that the merchant, who is never a party to treaties between kings, does not have to study them except inasmuch as they may cross or favor his speculations?[27]

[47]   On what basis, therefore, should a merchant owe any consideration to foreign rivals, enemies of his commerce? By the very nature of things, in maritime warfare, the unfortunate merchant is condemned to bear by himself the whole weight of the losses incurred by the state without ever obtaining compensation. During land warfare at least, while all the stipendiaries of royalty fight it out with cannon or guns, over a piece of territory, a city, a country, some piece of real estate whose income will compensate the attacking prince for the expenses incurred during the conquest, the townsman, the merchant, the burgher, who have not taken up arms, await the outcome fearlessly and remain free owner of their property--provided they pay the new master the tribute exacted by the previous one, with a few exceptions here and there.[28]

[48]   But as it is written that no one ever fights except for some loot; that if man is a born looter, war and especially naval war will awake that passion in him which the checks imposed by law have only lulled into sleep. And as in the maritime war in question, there is no real estate to conquer in order to cover expenses and give subsidies, and as the battlefield in the end still belongs to the fish--when the noble mad dogs separate, go away, or sink, all the heroes of the ocean are agreed among themselves, as the first return for their costs, and according to the morality of wolves, to run forthwith onto unarmed peaceful merchant ships and without reason, pity or shame, to grab the property of the merchant who cannot fight back; and later on, if they meet again face to face, to attack and tear one another up. So that when peace comes, when the tired states finally do justice or have mercy on each other; or when forcing each other's hand in proportion of their successes, they compensate each other for their losses; the poor maritime merchant, who hasn't even been men-

---

[27]"That brilliant apparition, the Armed Neutrality of 1780, that lighted for the moment the immediate field of diplomacy and left so luminous an after-glow lingering over the whole domain of international jurisprudence" (Bemis 1965, 113) was conceived by Beaumarchais five years earlier.

[28]Reminiscence of Voltaire, VEM 2:811-812.

tioned, who has lost everything and who recovers nothing, remains alone, dispossessed by such unpunished robbery done to him, who wasn't at war with anyone!

[49]   This abominable state of things which makes the merchant the first victim of the quarrels between kings, cannot but leave in his heart an inveterate hatred for the foreign enemies of his commerce and his property. Moreover, no one, who does not have an infernal heart, could deny him the only resource left to him against so many accumulated perils, that is, seizing every opportunity, every way of making his speculations prompt and lucrative.

[50]   So, in spite of Viscount Stormont, who makes of the French merchants the vile instruments of our ministers' perfidy, the hope of balancing the risks with the advantages involved was sufficient to make us trade with America; and our calculations being stronger than any ministerial hints, we believed the only thing we had to do was not to hurt the known interest of the prince who governs us. However, in spite again of Viscount Stormont, and the British cabinet, and the manifesto writer, none of us ever supposed he owed unjust England the delicate courtesy of refraining from trading with a country which had become their enemy. All of us on the contrary surmised that the Americans having more pressing needs as a result of their war with England, would set a higher price on the commodity they required. Such has been the general vehicle of French commerce.

[51]   As to me, moved by a natural liking for freedom, excited by a reasoned attachment for the brave people who have just avenged the universe of English tyranny, I confess with pleasure that, seeing the incurable foolishness of the English ministry who presumed to enslave America through oppression and England through America,[29] I dared foresee the success of the Americans' efforts to free themselves. I even dared think that without the intervention of any government, of any of the maritime giants they approached, the humiliation of proud England could very well

---

[29]Cf. Lord Chatham in Parliament: "I rejoice that America has resisted. Three million people, so dead to all the feelings of liberty as voluntarily to submit to be slaves, would have been fit instruments to make slaves of the rest."

presently be achieved by those "vile cowards"[30] so despised by the other continent, assisted by a few merchant vessels sailing unbeknown from this one.

[52]   I further confess that, full of these ideas, I dared by my words, my writings and my example, give the first impulse to the courage of our manufacturers and merchants; and that I have never believed, in spite of what has been said, that I was remiss in my duties as a good subject toward his sovereign, when I formed a maritime corporation, established strong commercial ties between America and my house and undertook to buy and ship from Europe all of the objects which could be useful to my brave correspondents, the "vile cowards of America."

[53]   But, if I did not expect the protection of the court,[31] I confess that I was far from believing that Viscount Stormont, whose main business was to harass our administration, would be so influential as to drive them by his crying to carry a severe and theretofore unheard of inquisition on the merchants' business, and to stop their speculations.

[54]   But since this purpose of his mission, which he has only too well fulfilled to the best advantage of England, has unfortunately ruined the French merchants' enterprises, why is it that ungrateful Viscount, who in his ministerial reports so emphatically cites nine or ten vessels freighted by me for the Americans at the end of 1776, and who distinguishes them so subtly from my frigate Amphitrite,[32] has failed to inform his court that our ministry, stunned by his complaints, had lost tract of the protection which they owed us perhaps;[33]

---

[30]A frequent British insult at the beginning of the war. On February 10, 1775, Lord Sandwich, minister of the navy, said in Parliament: "They are raw, undisciplined, cowardly men."

[31]The hypothetical construction is a clandestine stylistic device. It is ambiguous: did he or didn't he expect the protection of the court? (Cf. MF 2:19.)

[32]"The nine large vessels freighted and equipped by a certain M. de Beaumarchais and his partners in the month of February 1777, are not to be confounded with the Amphitrite, which carried at about the same time a great quantity of munitions of war and thirty French officers who enlisted with impunity in the service of the rebels." Gibbon, 134. "Subtle" is ironic.

[33]Clandestine reticence invites the reader to think.

and far from granting it to us, they had crushed our trade by their prohibitions and in particular had almost stifled to death my new-born company by laying a general embargo on all my ships?

[55]   In vain did I argue then that having to put up with British customs at sea and standing to lose everything thereby, without any hope of appeal if caught near American shores with merchandise prohibited by England, was risky enough without having France helping out to thwart even further her merchants' endeavors. The inflexible ministry strictly required all those ships to make their expeditions to our islands and certify in writing they would not go to the continent.

[56]   What could have motivated the ambassador to hush with his court the exceeding courtesies he received from ours? Why did he hide that on December 10, 1776, the minister of the navy stopped all my ships and had them searched thoroughly at LeHavre? That there were in that port at the time the Amphitrite, the Romain, the Amdrom de, the Anonymous, and several others; and if the first, already engaged in the roadstead, managed to escape the search, all of the others had to submit to it and so strictly that they were publicly unloaded to the great damage of my enterprise?

[57]   Why, in the joy he must have felt, didn't he add that, unable to expect any term, any softening of these prohibitive orders, I was forced to dismantle all of my shipments? For it is notorious that if some of the ships were able to leave later on, it was not until May or June of the following year, and their names and cargoes first had to be changed and the strongest assurances given that they would go only to our islands in the Gulf! Will his lordship deny that they did go there, knowing that one of them, the Seine, was, as a reward for my obeying orders, captured at Preachers' Point, the landing of Martinique, to the great outrage of all the inhabitants who witnessed it, and taken to Dominica where, without any other form of process, the English flag was hoisted and ours thrown overboard amidst cheering and the meanest bonfires?

[58]   How could that profound politician, that ambassador now a minister, fail to write his court that the same embargo was laid upon all my ships in Nantes. That the Therese, immobilized in that port, was not allowed to leave until June 1777, after the most thorough visit ascertained that she did not carry any munitions, and after the Captain pledged he would go to San Domingo, where he did stay for more than a year, as

did the Amelie, again to my greatest damage, since four Bermudian vessels I had bought there to carry to the continent the cargo of these European ships have all been captured, either while going there or coming back?

[59]   Why has he not advised his court that in January 1777 my Amphitrite having put at Lorient, the ministry, in answer to his request, held it there, claiming that several officers were on board to go offer their services to the Americans?

[60]   How could he omit to state in his dispatches that the court had ordered the most considerable of these officers immediately to rejoin his regiment in Metz and explain his behavior, and when they heard that the officer was refusing to obey, they sent a messenger to Lorient with orders to put him under arrest, break him and lock him up in the Nantes castle for the rest of his life[34]--a hardship he escaped by running away alone and almost nude, never daring thereafter to return to the ship. That the minister did not allow my frigate to sail until the Captain certified in writing that he would only go to San Domingo, under all sorts of penalties inflicted on him when he returned, should he fail to obey.

[61]   But another point comes to mind, and I am not supposed to bring it up since the king of England's writer has left it out.[35] The French court, a foreign power, indifferent and neutral, objected to the noble use some officers, most of them not French, wanted to make of their leisure time in favor of the Americans. But what was it to them for which side they would exert their courage? By what kind of excessive complacency for the English ambassador did our ministers establish such an inquisition against the partisans of America, when it is proved by the fact, that the nephew of Marshall Thomond, Milord Clare, Count Bulkley to be exact, the most ardent Englishman ever suffered in the service of France, obtained from them without any difficulty permission to go to London and seek service against America?[36] If the answer to this problem is beyond me, it will be obvious to everyone as it is to me, by comparing these two policies, that our obliging ministers should have found favor with this terrible

---

[34]A familiar phrase coming from Sartine.

[35]Ironic clue to the real purpose of the writer.

[36]See Bulkley's letter to Vergennes, 22 December 1779.

ambassador, and that his zeal and accomplishments would not have seemed less important to his country and would equally have led him to the ministry where he was burning to be promoted, if instead of slandering our court, he had kept his well-informed on the results he was obtaining every day.

[62]   Although politics is nothing but a sublime imposture anywhere, no ambassador has ever taken such liberties with the sublimity of his. It was reserved to Viscount Stormont to offer the universe a dignified example of it. "France, he says, was sending these troops to America!" Hey! Great politician or politico, are there many reasoners like you in England? And do you think that the Congress who hasn't seen fit to keep a single one of the engagements taken before me by their agents in Europe with the officers I sent them, who even refused service to most of them after they arrived, would have been so inconsiderate with our court--had they thought these generous warriors were sent to them by a king whose friendship and assistance they were so eagerly soliciting? And how do you think the king of France would have viewed these officers being sent back home, if that prince had been involved in arranging their departure? One has a good time being illogical in London!

[63]   This last reflection in itself is a ray of light revealing what all of us really are, Englishmen, Frenchmen, workers and reasoners.

[64]   Truly, my eager zeal for my new friends could have been wounded by the meager welcome shown to some honest fellows I had myself induced to leave their homes to go into their service. My efforts, my pains, my advances in this respect were enormous. But I was sorry only on account of our unfortunate officers; because in refusing those services, the Americans showed a sort of ambition, of republican pride, which attracted my heart and showed me a people so ardent in conquering their freedom they feared to diminish the glory thereof by letting foreigners share in their perilous fight.

[65]   My soul is made this way: In the worst troubles, it seeks whatever good may be found therein, as a consolation. Thus, while my efforts bore so little fruit in America, and the English tried to corrupt everything around me to reduce it even further, some cowardly enemies in my own country accused me of being in the pay of the British court and warning it about the departures of our merchant ships so they could capture them. Sustained by my pride, I would not defend myself

and left them to their shameful deeds, making sure I would never soil my paper with their names. The idle people in Paris envied my good fortune, regarding me as a favorite of the authorities, while, poor plaything of circumstances, alone, deprived of rest, lost to society, dried up with insomnia and worry, exposed in turn to suspicion, ingratitude, anxiety, reproaches from France, from America and from England, working night and day, struggling to reach my goal through thorny thickets, I was getting exhausted and making little progress. But I would take heart again at the thought that a great people soon would offer a haven of liberty to all the persecuted people of Europe;[37] that my country would be avenged for the humiliation imposed upon her by the treaty of 1763, which limited the number of ships she was allowed to maintain;[38] that the obscure veil, the funeral crepe hanging over our port of Dunkirk for the past sixty years,[39] would at last be torn off; that at last the sea would become open to all the trading nations and Marseilles, Nantes and Bordeaux could compete with London and become the cabarets of the universe. I was sustained by the hope that a new system of politics was going to dawn in Europe, and that England once put back into her proper place, the French name would be loved, cherished, respected everywhere. I would also add that I hoped the present reign would be exalted as one of the most beautiful of the monarchy, if in this austere and abrupt writing,[40] I had not ruled out any praise, even that of the young king who gives us such great hope by the wisdom of his views and his simple and true love for good, at an age when most men distinguish themselves only by follies, ridicules or quirks.

[66]   This bright future would bring back my courage and even my gaiety, to the point that when an English minister quipped to me about the Amphitrite that I was a good politician but a poor businessman, I answered in

---

[37]Cf. "This new world has been the asylum for the persecuted lovers of civil and religious liberty from every part of Europe," and "O receive the fugitive and prepare in time an asylum for mankind." Thomas Paine, *Common Sense*.

[38]This assertion was the pretext for the condemnation of the writing. Editor Gudin (1809) cut it out.

[39]The treaty of Utrecht in 1713 had forced France to destroy the fortifications of Dunkirk.

[40]Ssarcastic. It is the opposite of austere and abrupt.

the same vein. Let him wait awhile, time would tell who would succeed better, I in my little business or he in his big administration.

[67]	Under such circumstances, it stands to reason that the Saint-James Cabinet would have been overjoyed to learn from their ambassador that when the Amphitrite returned, my Captain, accused of disobedience, was scandalously arrested and thrown into jail although his log book proved he had only yielded to superior force, and that having been 90 days in route and 35 unable to figure out where he was, he had been ready to die of misery when he was washed onto the continent. But his crime was to have cast anchor there. I am quite sure on the contrary that Lord North would have been very grateful to his ambassador, had he learned from him that the awful face he showed our ministers cost my unfortunate captain three months in jail, and me two thousand francs, for a compensation I felt I owed him, to pay for Viscount Stormont's tantrums.

[68]	That's how every fact entered in the Justificative Memorial from the ambassador's reports is false, insidious or contrived. See him reporting as a crime the sailing from Marseille in September 1777 of a ship of mine, the Happy, and dissimulating at the same time that this most unhappy of ships had been in the harbor for ten months, all equipped, loaded, ready to go, and at the Viscount's request, stopped and publicly unloaded twice by order of the minister; and that it was only after those scandalous and damaging happenings that this ship, which has ruined me by such a long demurrage and such enormous expenses, obtained permission to leave port loaded with food supplies only and without munitions of war. For if it stopped in another port to complete its cargo, which wasn't even a third of its capacity, that was a fact our ministers had nothing to do with, since it happened out of the kingdom and beyond their reach.[41]

[69]	Thus, when that memorial mentions my Dunkirk operations, it is careful not to confess that the administration, always as strict toward me as they were courteous with the English ambassador, gave the express order to search all the ships listed in that port by the Stormonian inquisition, and ruthlessly to unload them if they had on board any munitions of war. That one of them, Marie-Catherine, already engaged in the roads when the order arrived, succeeded in slipping away and sailed

---

[41]A good example of a revelation of secret activities.

to Martinique with a load of artillery insured in London itself. But all the others were searched, unloaded and forced to go in ballast get some freight in America. In the meantime I was unable to reload my military cargo, so severe and continual was the government's attention to prevent it.

[70]   That's what Viscount Stormont could have told his court. He would have honored his vigilance and not betrayed the truth, which is what politicians worry the least about. He ought to have added even that irritated by what happened to me in Dunkirk, and having learned that the English commissioner named Frazer, odious because of his job and personally detested in that port, had dared corrupt one of our good coasting pilots and many French sailors and caused them to defect, I procured every legal proof of this shameful deed. But I failed to have the insolent commissioner prosecuted by our government for this crime of l se-nation[42] and the reason was, I remember it well, that the English ambassador might have taxed as recriminations my exertions in the matter. I will tell everything. This is not the place or time to flatter anyone. A writing meant to call out the bluff of England in her Justificative Memorial must not in turn be accused of an imbecile partiality for France.

[71]   But the last straw of bad faith in the English ambassador's reports is the insidious account he gives his court on the Hippopotamus, that ship I named Proud Rodrigue and which had the honor since then of being considered, by General-Admiral d'Estaing, worthy to contribute to the success of the king's arms near Granada--which was not what the mealy-mouthed memorialist calls "gazette triumphs" won at the printing press, but honest-to-goodness victories, won with cannon blasts.

[72]   It's the insidious account he gives his court regarding the alleged "fourteen thousand muskets I was to load therein and of the other munitions of war for the use of the rebels" mentioned in the Justificative Memorial--no other operation having been more openly, more cruelly molested in order to please Lord Stormont. Here are the facts. They will be found conclusive.

---

[42]This is a neologism coined by Beaumarchais he first time, on the model of "lèse-majesté" (high trea treason against the nation, not the king.

[73]   So many ships stopped in our ports, so many unloadings carried out by superior orders, so many operations fallen through or delayed, so much gold and so much time wasted, and above all the enforced obligation to execute rigorously the prohibitive orders of the court about war stores--all that had finally changed my shipping plans.

[74]   Soon, learning that the English had captured many of my ships and that I could not operate freely except by forcing the respect of the corsairs, I had a third party buy at a public auction, in April 1777, the Hippopotamus, a ship of the line which was being sold for the king at Rochefort. It was put in dry dock right away to be fitted out in war and merchandise, and all its cargo, about a million's worth, consisting of wine, brandy, dry goods, and without a single weapon, a single case of ammunition, was immediately transported to Rochefort, to sail as soon as possible.

[75]   But that fatal ambassador, whose main business was to lay waste our commerce on the land while the pirates of his nation insulted and pillaged it on the sea; this profound politician who amused himself half of the time annoying the ministers in France, and the other slandering them in England, proceeded to Versailles there to lament . . . so lamentably about that ship, saying I claimed to fit out for commerce and was in fact arming a warship for the service of the Congress, that the court was shaken up.

[76]   Upon that new crying, the ministry, absolutely unaware that I had any part in this venture, carried out under an assumed name, gave to the Commandant and Intendant of Rochefort the most precise orders to discover discreetly the name and object of the real owner of that ship. I heard about the court's inquiry, and from the port addressed, under an assumed name, the following memorial to the minister of the navy. If I include it here, it is because its character and style can better than all my arguments, give a just idea of the relations which existed between the administration and the commerce of France.[43] [. . . .]

[85]   This memorial, intended to set down the Proud Rodrigue's true destination and disarm the court, produced the opposite effect by giving me out. They thought they recognized me, and as the ambassador kept

---

[43]See Roderigue Hortalez, Hugaly et al to minister of the navy, 28 August 1777, which is quoted here [par. 77-84].

on clamoring against my ship and against my person, the ministry while they lifted the temporary embargo laid on all the other merchant ships adamantly ordered mine to stay put and gave it no hope of sailing at any time.

[86] As I intended to equip it with bronze pieces, so it could sail easier as a war or merchant ship, I had at great cost purchased and transported, of that kind of cannon, the quantity needed. A new order wrested from my Eumenides,[44] arrived and forced me to sell my artillery back at a loss while still maintaining the embargo on my ship.

[87] In vain did I personally offer to the ministry to embark on that ship some of the king's troops for San Domingo, so as to make sure of its destination. In vain did I propose to undergo the most rigorous visit so that they could certain no munitions of war entered in the cargo of the Proud Rodrigue. In vain did I certify in writing that the ship would be back within six months with produce from San Domingo, under the penalty of losing both the ship and its load if I failed to do so. The Ministry was inexorable; and in spite of the enormous expense of a double purchase, double transportation and costly exchange of artillery; in spite of the loss resulting from a million's worth of cargo kept in abeyance a whole year; in spite of protestations induced by despair that I would sue the administration for my losses before the king himself, which I am now in the process of doing; the ministers remained faithful to their word extorted from them by the English ambassador and never consented to lift the embargo, and I am sorry to declare that I did not obtain justice until after the treaty of commerce between France and America was notified in London by the Marquis of Noailles, when the English ambassador abruptly withdrew--that is, more than one year after the outfitting and loading of the Proud Rodrigue.

[88] That's what Viscount Stormont was very careful not to write his court and what he would not dare deny today. I am leaving out a thousand other facts distressing for our commerce and especially for me, because this extract will more than suffice to show the credi-

---

[44]The 1780 edition reads Eumenides (the well-meaning deity, used as a euphemism), i.e. the ministry, while the 1779 edition read "wrested by my Erinys" which would then apply to Lord Stormont. Gudin settled the question: "wrested by the English ambassador."

bility of the long Justificative Memorial narrative and allegations.

[89]   When Viscount Stormont resided in Paris and there would circulate some political lie, some false news more or less detrimental to the Americans; the deputies of Congress questioned would reply: "Don't you believe it, Sir. That's pure Stormont."

[90]   Well, Reader, the same thing can be said of the Justificative Memorial: It's pure Stormont, except for the style, which while a little dragging in translation, would not lack in charm or in sound logic[45], if the writer was not always forgetting that Lord Stormont furnished the data and that he is writing for unjust England, who by her usurpations, bad faith, arrogance and despotism stands in a class by herself, apart from all human societies.

[91]   For, if kingdoms are large isolated bodies, more separated from their neighbors by the diversity of their interests than by the barriers, fortifications or seas around them, if their only relations are those of Natural law, i.e. those imposed on them by the need for self-preservation, well-being and prosperity; and if these relations, diversely noted down under the title of Law of nations, have for general principle, according to Montesquieu himself, "to do what is in their own self-interest with the least possible harm to others,"[46] it seems that England, having put all her conceit in departing from this common law, has chosen for fundamental principle to make herself odious and formidable to the whole world with no resulting advantage to herself.

[92]   Add to this damnable principle the convenience of violating treaties and flouting all conventions, under the pretext that her king sharing his authority with the Commons and the Lords, cannot prevent his spirited nation from carrying on abuses which subsist even though disowned by the prince. Put all these notions together, I say, and you will have a feeble idea of the audacious people who today accuse us of perfidy.

---

[45]On the side, the author agrees with Gibbon.

[46]"The law of nations is founded on the principle that the nations must in peace do one another as much good and in war as little harm as it is possible without hurting their own true self-interests." Montesquieu, *L'Esprit des Lois,* Book I, Ch. 3. See also the 7 December 1775 memorial to the king.

[93]   But indeed, if the king of England cannot always be made answerable for his people's infractions to subsisting treaties--with whom are we keeping faith? What! You Englishmen would tie us down while believing yourselves free? Strange and superb nation, which must be admired for your patriotism and the Roman staunchness you are showing in your present misfortune;[47] but which it is time to humiliate in order to punish and repress the horrible abuse you have always enjoyed making of your prosperity.

[94]   Insane stepmother who expect love from your children when you purport to put them in chains only to exhaust the blood of their veins and use it in your prostitutions! If the time has come for your example to teach the nations that no politics succeeds and endures but that which is founded on universal morality and on the reciprocity of duties and courtesies . . . .

[95]   If your ministers, blinded by an ambition inept in its views and mistaken in its implementation, have imprudently carried their oppressive system on your colonies and have forced them to take up arms and adopt as a motto this terrible, instructive and sublime line of our great Voltaire: "Injustice in the end fosters independence."[48]

[96]   And if, as a result of the uneasy arrogance which never allows you to enjoy any liberty but that founded on your brothers' oppression, you Englishmen will have to cry also over the loss of Ireland, so long and so unjustly abased by you. Repent, beat your breasts, blame yourself, and stop accusing your neighbors for the storm and the infinite troubles that you alone have brought upon your unfortunate country.

[97]   I have proved by your horrible ways towards us that we owed nothing to you except anathema and vengeance--and yet you Englishmen are the aggressors!

[98]   I have proved that if France had obeyed the impulse of the most legitimate resentment, she ought to have helped America, anticipating her needs and hastening the hour of her independence; and yet you Englishmen are the aggressors!

---

[47]This sincere praise of England makes sure the reader does not go astray.

[48]From the play "Mahomet." This line is also cited in the 20 December 1777 letter to Francy.

[99]   I have proved that turning against the honor of our ministers the effect of their condescension for your predicament, you try to heap upon them the indelible ridicule of having continually stopped with one hand what you accuse them of having encouraged with the other; that instead of thanking them for the meager benefit America got from the weak efforts of our commerce, you ascribe these efforts to their perfidy--in that respect, Englishmen, you are most discourteous and ungrateful aggressors. Yet, never mind insults. That's how you defend yourselves, that's well known; and when a bad reputation is acquired, one might as well make the best of it. We know that in your English style the "perfidy" of France is like the "cowardliness" of the Americans who have forced your troops to lay down their arms and who have driven you out of their country. Go ahead and insult everyone!

[100]   But to talk nonsense for the sole pleasure of insulting people! Nonsense in a serious writing submitted to all the reasoners of Europe! Isn't it availing oneself of all manners of being audacious? For after all, if the king of France had planned secretly to aid America, he would at least have wanted to do so effectually; and in that case, it was not difficult to see that by the loan of one million Sterling to the United States, a kind of balance would have immediately been restored between the currency and the paper of their country, which would have sustained the public trust and ambition, would have increased the soldiers' eagerness by the reality of their pay, and perhaps would have enabled the American without any other aid to terminate their war promptly[49]--an act of economy or liberality which would have saved us close to 400 millions which our military protection has already cost us.

[101]   Therefore, if the morality or the noble politics of the king of France prevented him from choosing this course of action, it is because that king, young and virtuous, did not want to permit what he could not avow. All his subsequent conduct is the proof of that assertion.--But why did such a just king suddenly renounce his neutrality to ally himself with America? --Listen to me, Reader, and weigh my words. That's the end of everything.

---

[49]Beaumarchais' original proposal in the Hortalez memo. The writer still thinks that it would have been possible to help the insurgents and keep the peace.

[102]   After he had long remained a passive and tranquil spectator of the ongoing war, the king of France, informed by the debates of the English Parliament and by the success of the American troops, that in spite of the efforts of England during three consecutive campaigns, the force of events was finally separating America from England; informed also that the best minds of the English nation agreed in thinking, in saying loudly in both houses that it was imperative immediately to recognize the independence of the Americans and deal with them on an equal footing--the king no longer able to mistake the real object of the English armaments when he saw the English people cry out for war against him, offer to call the militia at their expense and to supply a certain number of soldiers per county, provided they be used against France; having besides assured himself that the English admirals who had flatly refused to serve against America were nevertheless being appointed as commanders of squadrons which could no longer threaten her; too certain finally that millions were being scattered and efforts being made to divide the opinion of Congress as well as of their commissioners in France; and above all well aware of the secret hope entertained in London to involve the Americans in a joint war with France, by suddenly granting them independence, in order to punish her for having rejected America's alliance for three years; urged by so many accumulated motives, the king resolved, but publicly and without mystery, without declaring war on England, much less making it without declaring it according to the odious practice they have established--without even wanting to initiate negotiations prejudicial to the court of London, and as a modest consequence of the neutrality he had adopted, the king, I say, finally resolved to recognize the independence of America, to sign a treaty of commerce with the new United States--but without excluding anyone, not even the English, from competing for that commerce.

[103]   Indeed, if the rules of justice, of prudence, and the care of his own security have not permitted the king to defer any longer that recognition of an honorable liberation and of an independence which England soon intended shamefully to acknowledge and turn against us--at least it must be granted that no action as interesting, as great, as national, was ever taken with more moderation, candor, nobility and simplicity-all characteristics absolutely opposed to the "perfidy" with which English insolence has tried to smear France and

her king in the Justificative Memorial--which was to be proved.[50]

[104]   As to me, whose interests dwindle to nothing besides such great interests; a mere private citizen, but a courageous one, a patriot and a sincere friend[51] of the brave people who have just conquered their freedom;[52] if it seems surprising for my weak voice to join in with the thundering mouths arguing this great issue--I will reply that one needs power only to uphold a wrong and that a man is always strong enough when he has reason on his side.[53] I have suffered great losses. They have made my work less useful than I had hoped to my independent friends. But as it is less by my success than by my efforts that I should be judged, I still dare claim the noble salary I promised myself, the esteem of three great nations, France, America and even England.

---

[50]*Quod erat demonstrandum.*

[51]Cf. "Let the names of Whig and Tory be extinct; and let none other be heard among us than those of a good citizen, and open and resolute Friend, and a virtuous supporter of the RIGHTS OF MANKIND, and of the FREE AND INDEPENDENT STATES OF AMERICA." (*Common Sense*)

[52]A polemical assertion in 1779. Gibbon said: "The event is still in the hand of the Almighty."

[53]Cf. Rousseau, *Du Contrat Social*, Ch. 3. and MF, final vaudeville.

17 December 1779, to Vergennes from Duke of Praslin
(Ang 532 fol. 199-200; Observations, 1780 ed. p. 44-47)

I received a few days ago a brochure entitled *Observations on the Justificative Memorial of the Court of London by Pierre Augustin Caron de Beaumarchais*. I didn't pay attention to it at first because I rarely read such brochures, especially the political ones, but the noise this one created among the public incited my curiosity, and I can hardly express how surprised I was to find on page 37 the following passage: "But my courage was reborn each time I thought ... that my country would be avenged of the humiliation it had been subjected to by the Treaty of 1763 limiting the number of vessels they deigned to allow her to keep."

If this writing, Sir, was the work of a private individual, without any mission, who did not take the trouble to read the Treaty he is talking about, I would have scorned the erroneous assertion it contains; but it passes among the public as having been published under the authority of the government. Consequently, one must believe it contains only true statements, and the part I had in the making of that Treaty does not permit me to regard with indifference the above-mentioned item which involves my honor as well as that of the nation, and the memory of the late king. You certainly know, Sir, that there is no article in the Treaty of Paris which fixes the small number of vessels which Great Britain deigns suffer France to keep; that even in that treaty (in which there is no secret clause) there isn't a single word that could allow such inference. And if you wish to take a look at the negotiations which preceded it, you will see that such a clause was never proposed. The British ministers, with whom we dealt, knew very well the advantage of their position and they were quite ready to insist on peace conditions proportioned to their success. But, Sir, I owe them this justice: They thought nobly. They knew the regard which is due great powers. They never made insulting propositions and I dare say they knew me well enough to foresee how I would have responded. I will also add that the late king, who knew how to carry the dignity of his person and the independence of his Crown, would never have allowed his ministers to put such a clause under his eyes. Peace was then desired by the whole kingdom; it was even thought to be a necessity, but I assure you peace would not have been made if our enemies had offered it at the price of dishonor.

Moreover, Sir, this alleged limitation of our naval forces, belied by all the clauses of the treaty is even more denied by the fact of the restoration of our navy. It is notorious that it was almost down to nothing in 1763 and since that time, work has been going on publicly in all our ports to put it again on the most respectable shape it has been since the beginning of the Monarchy. When I left this ministry, France had already 64 ships, without counting those in the shipyards, ten or twelve more, and approximately 55 large frigates or corvettes. The English saw this restoration with a worried and jealous eye but they never complained about it. They knew they had no right to, and you can believe that if the Treaty of Paris had authorized them to do so, they would not have overlooked such a useful and glorious title.[1]

I have perhaps expounded too long on an error which is evident. But, Sir, being today in the position I formerly was, you can better than anyone else share my feelings, and I believe you will agree that it behooves the justice and the dignity of the King to have the article I am denouncing publicly refuted. I am not afraid to say that he owes it to the memory of his grandfather, to the honor of his Crown and to that of the nation he governs. I do hope, Sir, that you will kindly show His Majesty my just and respectful complaint, with the arguments on which it is founded, and let me know the orders he deems necessary to take.

17 December 1779, from Choiseul to Vergennes
(Ang. 532, fol. 171-2; *Observations*, pp. 47-50)

I have received, Sir, from the author, a writing entitled *Observations* ... I am told, Sir, that this work was read to you. It is impossible to doubt from the manner in which it is presented that it has the authorization of the Government. Based on this opinion, I am sure that you will find it natural that I should call your attention to the fact that the writing contains a misstatement of fact and of common sense, on which it is just, proper and even political, to inform the King and the public authentically.

M. de Beaumarchais, on page 27 of his memorial, after a truly touching picture, theretofore unknown to Europe, of how he was beset with anxiety, dried up with insomnia, how he suffered from suspicion and reproaches coming from France, America and England, says that his

---

[1] Historians credit Choiseul with rebuilding the French navy after 1763, but contemporary opinion was that it was insufficient, poorly budgeted, and short of trained seamen (Gudin 1888, 198).

"courage was renewed every time he thought that his Country would be avenged from the humiliation imposed upon it by the Treaty of Paris, which limited the number of ships it was permitted to maintain." That is the false and absurd allegation which I am taking the liberty of denouncing to you.

You know the Treaty of 1763, you know that nothing is so untrue and implausible as what M. de Beaumarchais dares assert. If you have been apprised of the negotiation of this Treaty, which must be in your office, you have seen that peace was offered by England first and that in spite of her successes, England had too much respect for the King of France to make any such humiliating proposition to him.

The minister of the navy cannot be unaware that most of the vessels used in the present war were given gratuitously to the king in 1762 by the various bodies and communities of his Kingdom, and that they were built immediately after the peace of 1763. Thus there can be no difficulty in publishing the falsehood of the assertion made by M. de Beaumarchais. But I have the honor of calling your attention to the fact that this false information, in a writing supposed to have been approved by the Government, may have dangerous consequences.

First His Majesty could be misinformed on such an important fact. His Majesty knows that his ministers are aware of M. de Beaumarchais' memorial. Naturally, he must believe that whatever is said in this memorial about the last war is accurate. His noble and sensitive heart must surely be aggrieved the existence of such a condition in the treaty, so humiliating for the memory of the late king and such a disgrace for the nation he governs. I believe, Sir, that it is just and urgent for you to inform His Majesty and submit to him the letter I have the honor of writing to you. I will even ask you to tell the king that, however obedient I may have been to the wishes of the late king out of duty and respect, I would not have set my signature to an article so contrary to the honor of his reign.

M. de Beaumarchais's positive assertion would give something else to fear, if it was not pulverized in its principle by the king's authority with the greatest authenticity. You know, Sir, that foresight is essential in politics. As formidable as the king's forces may be, as great his power and influence in Europe, and whatever talents one may have in managing this respectable power, the outcome of wars depends on so many hazards that sometimes misfortunes happen even in the best planned campaigns. Far from me to fear any reverse in the present war, but who can answer for the events of another war? And if these events led to the desire or need to seek peace, would the English, who at Geertruidenberg did not think of limiting the forces of France, who in 1763 did not even consider making such a proposition, would they not be authorized by such a memorial where this proposition is set as a fact, a memorial approved by the French government, to advance as a condition of peace, without fear of revolt from a government or nation who imagined they had already suffered that yoke?

I beg your pardon for going over this point at such length. I had to yield to the concern I must take in it. And I thought that when M. de Beaumarchais imparted to all of Europe his feelings about the controversy between England and America, and his intention to sustain the honor and the rights of the French Crown, I could well let you know my feelings on a matter which involves the late king's reputation when I had the honor of being his minister.

18 December 1779, to Vergennes
(Ang. 532 fol. 204)

I have given a lot of thought to what you told me. The solution you prefer may have a terrible effect. At least do not rush it. Nothing goes so fast as the *Courrier de l'Europe*. I can, under the sole name of the author of the *Observations*, in the next issue, have an erratum inserted which will satisfy everybody. I plan to send it to you, and if you and M. de Maurepas do not find it sufficient, you can return to your decision. After a suppression, it will be impossible for me to have it inserted in the *Courrier*.

But if I remove from the text the sentence in question, saying something very noble and appropriate to refute the sentence myself in a footnote, it will seem much simpler for an honorable man to retrace his own steps frankly than for the administration to blame a writing designed to honor France and the king as they should be. People would feel that the ministers have been offended because they were cleared of perfidy only by showing their condescension toward England. Whereas the erratum I suggested has all the strength and nobility of a free retraction and does not commit any one. Can you imagine the argument England could draw from such a suppression? You suppress the whole work for a couple of words which can be removed beautifully?

An error of fact is easy to retract. But to disavow a writing which uplifts the heart and soul of all good Frenchmen (excepted the Court, where there is little patriotism); to suppress the entire writing of a true patriot, for which I have already received twelve hundred enthusiastic thanks! People in London will openly say that all I have asserted is false since, without explanations, you mention "questionable assertions." They will draw therefrom a public disadvantage against France, and nothing will save me. Above all, the reproach of perfidy will come back with all its strength.

I entreat you to weigh my arguments. See my correction before you suppress. My personal interest concerns me much less than my country's interest and the honor of the ministers whom I respect and to whom I address these reflections.

As to the reading committee, as I have not set foot out of my house, it is not difficult to imagine that everyone thought, without my saying so, that in a country where the press is not free an honorable writing cannot even appear under "tacit permission," which is another reason not to choose the suppression over a free denial by the author. Forgive me, Sir, it is from my inn that I am scribbling.

19 December 1779, Suppression Sentence
(Ang. 532 fol. 209; *Observations*, 1780, 50-51)

The King, informed that there circulates among the public a certain printed work entitled ...., His Majesty noticed with surprise, besides various rash statements and hazardous qualifications, that the said author has stated as a fact the existence in the Treaty of paris of 1763 a clause, either public or secret, limiting the number of vessels France would be able to maintain. This allegation being entirely contrary to the truth and belied as much by the treaty which contains no secret clause as by the actions which have preceded and followed it, His Majesty deemed it inadvisable that such false and absurd assertion should remain standing. Considering moreover that the said writing was published and circulated in violation of the Regulations of the Library; His Majesty, in his Council, upon the advice of the Keeper of the Seals, has ordered and does hereby order that the said writing entitled .... be and remain suppressed. It is further forbidden and prohibited by His Majesty for any publisher, printer, bookseller and others, to print, sell, trade in or distribute said writing. Ordered to all those who have copies thereof to turn them in to the Registrar of the Council, within a fortnight, so they may be suppressed. Ordered further by His Majesty that this judgment shall be printed, published and posted everywhere needed. Enjoined the Lieutenant General of Police in Paris to execute the present judgment.

Rendered by the State Council in the presence of His Majesty, in Versailles, the 19th day of December, 1779. Signed: Amelot

19 December 1779, to Vergennes
(Ang. 532 fol. 268)

I am enclosing with this short memorial and my letter to the editor of the *Courrier de l'Europe*, the copy that M. le Duc de Choiseul returned to me with his handwritten notes on p. 35 about the two words I have already mentioned. The letter or short message attached thereto comes from the Abbess of Saint-Louis, sister to the Duke, and far from having snubbed me, they sent someone three times to get my answer. They wanted to know if someone had prompted me to hurt the Duke's feelings in this manner. My oral answer was that I knew no one cowardly enough to do so. That the pride of my character would make me flee forever from anyone who would think me capable of so doing, but that in acquaintances, friends and protectors, I had always been happy enough to associate only with noble and generous souls. As to my answer about the article on page 35, I had them read my letter to the *Courrier*. They appeared to be delighted. They insisted on taking copy of it. I answered: If a great misfortune does not happen me between now and Tuesday, I will give as many copies as desired. If it happens, I will owe nothing anyone anymore and that's the end of my French, if not my human career.

I beg of you, M. le Comte, after you have conferred with Count Maurepas, kindly to return to me the *Courrier* article, the Choiseul copy, and the note from Madame his sister. I will tell more to M. de Maurepas if I have the good fortune of paying my respects to him.

I am going back to bed for I have a fever.

19 December 1779, to the Courrier de l'Europe
(Gudin 1809, 7:256)

While asking you to publish these observations in a supplement, Sir, I also request that you change a word misprinted on page 35, during a hurried writing and proof-reading. In the first copies which have come out one can read: "When I thought my country would be avenged of the humiliation imposed on her by the Treaty of 1763 which fixed the small number of vessels they deigned to consent to her." This printing error states a fact justly considered as false and absurd, since no number of vessels was fixed by any clause of the treaty, either public or secret. Substitute the word "agencies" which is in the manuscript, to the word "vessels" which is not there, then the sentence will have mathematical accuracy and will state an unquestionable fact.

19 December 1779, to the ministers
(Lom 2:172-5; Mol 669-70)

If a warrior fighting for his country ought not to receive a dishonoring slap as he trips over the rough terrain, would it be fair for the king to throw among scandalous libelers whose works may be suppressed, a writer who has repulsed with force and dignity the dark imputations of his country's enemies, because with a hundred thousand others, he has fallen into an involuntary error, but an easy, even advantageous one to correct adequately?

When a man who only vied for the honor of being on the side of reason does not blush to admit publicly that he has made a mistake, and can draw therefrom a great benefit for the cause he is fighting for, is there any harm in letting him straighten things up by himself?

What can be more forceful in correcting a ventured assertion than an open and free denial by the author, when he can broadcast it as rapidly as his writing? Is it fitting to reward zeal, hard work and patriotism with the dishonor of suppressions intended for the punishment of deliberate pranksters, gangrened culprits and impenitent sinners?[2]

Before dealing so cruelly with me, I beg the king's ministers to read what I am sending to the Courrier de l'Europe, to that of the North.[3] The same thing substantially will appear in all public papers, with the promise to all those who will send back their faulty copy that they will receive two correct ones.

---

[2] Hyperbole indicates a tongue in cheek tone, the letter being "written for the galery," to be read in "salons."

[3] An English publication edited by John Wilkes.

I beg them also to consider that to discredit such a writing by a shameful judgment will rob it of all that is good and praiseworthy in it, and will give back to the accusation of perfidy contained in the English manifesto all its force, by canceling the great principles of the reply.

By the pain I am already suffering therefrom, I feel that I will not be able to survive its hateful effect. I am losing my mind and I have spent a most cruel night.

A relative of Duke of Choiseul has just sent me a copy earmarked by him with these words in page 35: "This fact is false and absurd." The very words of the judgment. He has dictated it himself! False? That's the right word since the fact is untrue, but *absurd?* After Dunkirk and its English commissioner, who can, without bending his head, dare call absurd anything concerning the sea and us, however hard it may be?

To destroy a French port ten leagues from the enemy upon their request, and to keep this port in ruins under the disgraceful inspection of their commissioner, that is what is absurd and what has been going on, under our indignant eyes, for the past hundred years.

I speak to French hearts. I must be heard. Allow me, Milords, I beseech you, to make amend. I can do it honorably and fruitfully; but I feel by the pain which chokes me that I will die of sorrow if you have the cruelty to deliver my person and my work to the degradation of a stigma.

My friends would only have to publish the twelve or fifteen hundred exalted letters which I have received in the past six days and in which good citizens poured their hearts in their thankful approval.

Where one says: "I will place this writing on the shelf with Tacitus, Cardinal de Retz, Price and Sidney,[4]

---

[4]Tacitus was a Republican. Retz led the opposition against Richelieu and Mazarin. Algernon Sidney, English Republican, beheaded on June 26, 1683, wrote "from my youth I endeavoured to uphold the common rights of mankind, the laws of the land and the true Protestant religion against corrupt principles, arbitrary power and popery" (DNB 18:209). Richard Price, British philosopher and friend of America, published *Observations on Civil Liberty and the Justice and Policy of the War with America*, 1776.

for no monument as noble and worthy of the nation will ever honor the present events."

Where another writes: "The author is afire with patriotism, his pen sparkles. T'is true man does not do anything great unless a great passion inspires him!"

Where a third one confesses that he was ill informed on the matter and that everyone in France used to think France was wrong, but the question is finally settled.

Where all thank me for my zeal and my courage in a country where so few people have so little of them for the glory of France. Such letters from my fellow-citizens could show this peculiar fate of mine that I cannot do any good without suffering from it. He wanted to work and supply arms for his country, they would say, his shipments were stopped, he wanted to write and defend the honor of France, his writings were suppressed. His nation esteemed him, the authorities crushed him. He had no other choice but to die or leave the country.

For pity's sake, through mercy if I cannot get it through justice, don't break my heart with a suppression while you are bearing with a Linguet! He has insulted all of you, I have respected you. He did the *Aiguillonnade* and I the *Observations*. What a difference in both the work and the reward!

If such an atrocious judgment is given, I will be like a severed limb, dead, cut-off completely, and I don't want to owe France anything anymore but the last sacrament or a passport.

I beg your pardon, but I am in despair.

19 December 1779, from Vergennes
(Ang. 532 fol. 206)

I will forward your observations wherever you want, but I warn you that it is too late for them to have any effect. Orders have been given and have gone out as I had told you. I am sorry you are taking it so hard. Truly there is no reason for you to feel bad. You committed an error, the more serious because you could have easily informed yourself. May I call your attention to the fact that the manner you propose to make amend is not very obliging either for those who were concerned or for the nation itself. Where would her energy be if she had known about and stood for such a humiliation as the one you propose? The similarity you suggest with the demolition of Dunkirk is anything but just. That place was requested by Louis XIV and sold out by a weak and wasteful prince.[5] At he peace of Utrecht, the two prevailing powers did not want it to remain in the hands of France. The latter could not agree to its passing into the hands of a neighboring power, then a rival, who would have had too easy an access to the interior. Demolition was decided upon as a middle term, a conciliatory expedient. There was nothing there to outrage the nation. We could have ceded Dunkirk as we did any other place in the past.[6] After that, it should not seem strange to you that we regard as false and absurd your assertion concerning the limitation of ships and you are wrong to suppose we would take our judgment from the Duke of Choiseul. Truth is one, just like falsehood. All sane minds see it the same way. Check your comparison and see for yourself whether it is not improper.

Learn to accept, Sir, what you cannot prevent.[7] I don't know if your priest will give you the last sacrament, but I am not promising any passport.

Be ever assured of my sincere esteem.

P.S. Enclosed is the earmarked copy. I cannot return your other writings until I have communicated them.

21 December 1779, Vergennes to Duke of Praslin
(*Observations*, p. 50-51; Ang. 532 fol. 215)

You are quite right, Milord, to complain against the passage found in the writing entitled . . . which supposes a limitation on the number of ships which France was allowed to maintain. The king and his council were as shocked as you were by that absurd and mendacious statement. Although this is the writing of a private individual without any mission, who was careless enough to write according to some common prejudice[8] without taking the trouble to inform himself by reading the articles of the 1763 treaty, or by consulting people

---

[5]Charles II, "in a bargain glorious for the buyer and shameful to the seller" (VL14 1:326).

[6]Vergennes' cold and unpatriotic heart shows here.

[7]These words are repeated by Count Almaviva, MF 4:8.

[8]A reminder, offensive to Choiseul, Vergennes' enemy.

who could, and consequently, that his error cannot become dogma or bear serious consequences, His Majesty nevertheless deemed it advisable to destroy every trace of it.

I am enclosing, Milord, a copy of the Judgment rendered by the king in his council: I hope you will find it satisfactory in every way.

22 December 1779, to Vergennes from Count Bulkley
(Ang. 532 fol. 218)

Upon my return from the country, I happened to see a brochure entitled .... I cannot tell you how surprised I was to find that the author took the liberty of writing about me as follows: "that the Count Bulkley, the most ardent Englishman ever tolerated in the service of France, was easily obtaining from them permission to go and solicit service against America ...." and as, in these few words I find at once atrocious slander and punishable insolence, I hope, Sir, that you will deign to consider the just remarks I am taking the liberty of making on this subject.

You well know that when I asked for the permission to go serve with the English army in America, I stated and repeated tirelessly that I had no other purpose than acquiring new knowledge in a profession I like and to which I have devoted most of my life. There was at that time no other was going on but that of England against the Americans. The name I bear being an insurmountable obstacle for service with the latter, I did not have any choice. But the minute circumstances changed, I came back to France, and if the epithet "ardent" can be applied to me, it is because of the way I have continually solicited for the past two years the minister of war to be sent against the English for whom I am suspected of so much partiality. I don't have to comment on the expression "tolerated in the service of France," it deserves only scorn, but I hope, Milord, that you will kindly see to it that you do not let go without punishment such false and insolent remarks against a general officer who has always served without reproach, and who right now has no other desire than to find a way to prove his zeal for the glory of the State and the arms of the king. I dare ask you to let me know what His Majesty has decided in this respect so that I may inform of it the persons to whom I have the honor of belonging and who have been as stunned as I by this impudent libel.

P.S. I came back ill from the country. That's why I did not go and pay my respects to you.

December 1779, from Grimm et al
(*Corr. litteraire, philosophique et critique*, 12:353)

In the *Expose of the motives* . . . by M. le Comte de Vergennes, one could admire the candor and simplicity of a style as little ambitious as the views presented therein to the impartial judgment of all the powers of Europe. England's answer to such moderate declaration, while it may lack all the precision, dignity, required by that kind of writing, did offer at least the conclusions of a rather resourceful logic, and if one cannot always find in it the tone most appropriate for the spokesman of his nation and sovereign, yet one can recognize the ingenious pen and the excellent mind of that estimable writer who had the courage to undertake the execution of a work for which the illustrious President de Montesquieu has left us only a sketch,[9] although a sketch which bears the mark of his genius. M. de Beaumarchais has had the honor of being mentioned in the English Memorial as having been charged with directing the first shipping expeditions made by France in favor of the Americans. Consequently, he has felt authorized to vindicate his country and his king of the accusation of perfidy these shipments have served as a pretext for, in the eyes of our enemies.

How could M. de B. resist the temptation to meddle in that august quarrel? How could he fail to grab such a beautiful opportunity to publish a manifest of his own hand and authority? Worthy as it was of so bold a genius, the idea did not have all the success he had expected. These *Observations* were found to be indifferent for the vindication of the French ministry, and not any more effective in reassuring the honest individuals who had become interested in the author's shipping operations. It was found that the tone permissible with a Goezman of the Maupeou Parliament was not suitable in speaking to the ambassador of a respectable nation. That there was neither wit, nor good taste in applying to Lord Stormont the ridiculous epithets of "big politician" or "politico;" in saying of a false news that it was "pure Stormont;" in predicting with patriotic frenzy that at last Marseilles, Nantes and Bordeaux would be able to become "the cabarets of the universe," etc. It was found even a little more absurd, in a writing meant to vindicate the reputation of France, to

---

[9]The paraphrase refers to Edward Gibbon.

proffer certain facts which dishonor her and which are not proved by any valid evidence; to dare publish that there had been in the treaty of 1763 a clause limiting the number of vessels England deigned to allow France to keep. It is mostly this last bit of indiscretion, not to use another word, that the government deemed advisable not to tolerate. They had not paid attention to it at first; apparently it was only upon the request of M. de Choiseul, personally compromised in that strange assertion, that the brochure was prohibited. It is noteworthy that since the prohibition, it has not sold any better than before.

22 December 1779, from L. P. de Bachaumont,
(*Memoires secrets*, 14:320-32)

The Dukes of Choiseul and Praslin have been offended by the Observations of the "sieur de Beaumarchais" as he speaks of the last peace in words most outraging for those who were the authors of it, and dares allege that by a secret stipulation England had limited the number of vessels France could maintain. Consequently they have filed a complaint with Count Vergennes. That minister has reported to the council Sunday and a judgment resulted which suppressed the book, but strangely enough does not inflict any penalty on the writer, who is known -- which confirms the rumor that in spite of his impudence, he would not have dared publish such a libel without first communicating it to the ministers.

[26 December 1779] One can see a letter from the Duke of Choiseul to the Count of Vergennes, containing his complaint against the "sieur de Beaumarchais's libel. It appears that there is another letter from the Duke of Praslin, and that the Duke of Nivernais, plenipotentiary at the last peace, has joined in. It was upon those diverse requests that on December 19 the council's judgment of suppression came about. The suppression is motivated . . . They say that the Duke of Choiseul's letter is diffuse and careless. His cousin's seems to be better composed, more precise, noble and firm.

What is peculiar about this anecdote and proves the fickleness and inconsistency of the ministers, is that the *Observations'* author, known, whose name appears on the title page and is recalled in the Council's decision, implicitly accused of libel towards the authors of the peace treaty, at least declared to have broken the laws of the Library--which has caused so many others to go to jail--is remaining free and unpunished, a strange situation which leads one to believe that the "sieur de B" was authorized to publish this writing; it is a slap given by the ministers on that villain's cheek, according to the wits of the Court.[10]

27 December 1779, to Count d'Estaing
(Lom 2:169-70)

Most worthy and most respectable Admiral, who may well be attacked, but never discredited, since you made use of the navy of this sovereign only for the service of another as mighty as he is fair, let's hope he will do justice to both of us, in showering you with honors and making up for my losses.[11]

You will receive whenever you can the homage of this sovereign, your servant, who did not wait for your brave feats to appreciate you, and who fought a hundred times with the tongue against the army of rascals who were doing you wrong while you were parrying so valiantly against the enemies of the State. The most urgent for you is to take care of your health, which we all need so much, and if perchance you planned to write an apology for your military career, as it is being implied, I beg you to chase away that idea while crossing yourself for it's a temptation from the devil. Don't, I beseech you, on behalf of all those who honor you and namely on behalf of an aged and famous gentleman who loves you and yearns to see you sitting by his side, baton in hand, at the great tribunal of honor, whose duties you fulfill so well.[12]

I take the liberty of sending you, to give you a good laugh, my last political opuscule, which did not have the good fortune to please everyone. If you can

---

[10] Cf. "How did you like that slap you recently received?" the Count asks Cherubin. "He received it on my cheek: That's the way the lords do justice," Figaro answers (MF, last act, last scene)

[11] On 6 July 1779 the Proud Rodrigue joined Count d'Estaing in a battle off of Grenada, won by the French. The warship suffered a loss of two million livres. See 12 July 1779 letter from d'Estaing, who alludes to "your navy"--hence the word "sovereign" which alludes to Beaumarchais himself.

[12] Lomenie's note here reads: "No doubt, M. de Maurepas, who wanted Admiral d'Estaing to keep silent regarding the attacks made against him during his campaign" (2:170). The famous person in question is one of the twenty Marshalls of France, among which the writer hopes that the admiral will be soon take his place.

grant me fifteen minutes of your time, you will certainly overjoy the one who is, with the most respectful devotion, at the end as at the beginning, and in the course of all the years, worthy and respectable Admiral, your very humble servant.

1780-1798: THE AFTERMATH

Beaumarchais, maritime trader, narrates what happened to his flotilla of merchant ships and to the war ship which was to convoy it. Beaumarchais, the only loyal friend left to Deane, solicits Vergennes on his behalf. He will go through the storm of the French Revolution without hearing anything from his Friends, the Free Men of America, and in the end he asserts that, although he may have been a dupe, he regrets nothing.

26 February 1780, to Francy [in America]
(Marsan, 9-14)

I am taking advantage of the first opportunity to acknowledge receipt of your two letters of October 6th and 9th, from Williamsburg, and of the parcels enclosed (the letters of exchange from Congress, its Resolved [in English], its letter to Mr. Franklin, the one addressed to me, etc. I also acknowledge receipt of the duplicates of the first parcel of October 6th, and the quadruplicates of the fifty-six letters of exchange, as well as your letters of December 24 and 26, from York.

The first parcel announced that neither the Proud nor the fleet it convoyed had arrived at the [Chesapeake] Bay, and how grieved you were that the whole fleet had been attached to a royal convoy. "Two millions, you said, will not make up for the loss caused by this fatal delay." But I was even more grieved in Europe, I who knew what you didn't. Engaged by patriotic views and the wishes of the ministry, I had agreed, in October 1778, that my ships, ready to sail for Virginia, should take the long way by our islands to carry supplies needed by our troops there. I, who knew that in spite of all the pledges that my crews would not be touched, my loaded ships had been delayed from October 1778 to May 1779, had stopped over four or five times, needlessly and at great cost to me, from one French harbor to the other, and that finally, at the last minute, M. de LaMothePiquet[1] had ordered Montaut to follow him to Martinique, although his ship-papers were for San Domingo. I, who knew that after this unfortunate flotilla arrived at Martinique, Count d'Estaing had picked the cream of my crews, and taken the Proud along to Grenada, where Montaut had been killed; that M.

---

[1]With Counts de Grasse and de Vaudreuil, one of the three admirals who were sent to help d'Estaing in 1779.

d'Estaing having returned too soon for my ships to load merchandise from the islands for the continent, most of them had sailed away empty; that the same impossibility of loading up at St. Domingo, where M. d'Estaing put in briefly, had not helped at all. But what I did not know any more than you did, is that my unfortunate merchant flotilla had been led by the king's squadron from St. Domingo to Savannah, where the Proud, being still engaged in service under Count d'Estaing's orders, the other ships, waiting for their convoy to go to the Bay, had remained in Charleston; and that on October 26th, Count d'Estaing returning to Europe had ordered M. de Grasse to go with seven vessels to refit at Chesapeake and to convoy my ships there; that the Proud, running out of every supply and full of sick people, having gone to join the fleet at Charleston while that fleet was just going out to meet with M. de Grasse, they had crossed each other without meeting, and that M. de Grasse, having preferred going to St. Domingo rather than obey orders to the Bay, not only were my ships coming from Charleston left unprotected, but he took with him three English flutes that Count d'Estaing had ceded to me, in order to do his best to start as he could compensating me for the ruinous military campaign he had led my flotilla into.

The result of all that, as I learn from your letters of December 24 and 26, was that most of the unfortunate merchant ships have fallen into the hands of the English and that the Proud had a hard time dragging itself to the general destination. What a mess of trouble and losses! It's enough to lose one's head. Were honor or head affected, all hope would be lost. Let's bear with it therefore and go on working and spending money. As soon as exact figures will allow me to accurately compute my losses, I will ask the king and his minister to deign recall their engagement and compensate me equitably. But such recoveries are based only on fixed losses, and leave behind all the advantages which would have resulted from a good trip. One year lost. More debts, returns failing to arrive, the impossibility of resuming the preparation for a new trip or the exceeding difficulties of such new preparations, and all the immeasurable losses of such a deadly campaign, all that makes me shudder. As long as honor and head remain whole, let's go on working. *Courage and truth*, you know that's my motto.

You are entertaining false hopes for me when you think that the letters of exchange will be negotiable in Europe. Were they as secure as they are believed to be unsound, a delay of three years makes them useless in

Europe. Thus, after three years' waiting, all I get for payment is a partial remittance payable three years hence! What company can sustain such delays without going under?

I have to look for new resources in Europe since so little is coming from America. You are the only one who knows what I am going through.

You inform me that the new ambassador with Congress [Chevalier LaLuzerne] is against me. I was not in Paris when he left for Philadelphia. I don't even know him. Certainly he did not get such orders from M. le Comte de Vergennes, who would be as surprised as I am if he knew it. Be as courteous with him, when you are in Philadelphia, as required by his position. But continue to carry on your business steadfastly with everyone without letting petty personal ill-will bother you. You are entrusted with just and honorable matters and, if the Chevalier carried things to the point of harming our interests, your duty is to take accurate note of it and to send me some proofs. It will be up to me to obtain justice in Versailles.

All your worrying about the consequences of my association with our common friend is very obliging, but nothing contained in your letter "for me alone" from Williamsburg, on October 8th, has happened. The detour to be taken by our islands, to which I agreed for the sake of our ministers, demanding greater forces than those I then possessed, we got together for this operation which the military campaign makes so unfortunate. But I am in such straitened circumstances due to my enormous advances before that venture, that our friend cannot and must not protest if the first returns are on my past account since the present has only produced losses for me. Therefore carry on as before. My interests, for so long in jeopardy must be your first concern. My love for my country's success will leave me only with my last breath. Such as you witnessed it, such it is today. All of our shippers are discouraged and refuse to fit out and load for America. But if the French pavilion is never seen on any coast, the Americans will look at the treaty of commerce with France as illusory, and the necessity to get from Europe what they need will slowly drive them back to England, and we will be left holding the bag. That's why I want to encourage by my advice, my associations and my example, all those who I believe have enough spirit and courage to take advantage of it or at least to serve the country.

I am enclosing herewith a printed reply [the *Observations*] that indignation has wrenched from me against the manifesto or *Justificative Memorial* that the Court of London has given of its conduct.

2 December 1780, to Vergennes
(Dea 4:265-6)

It is with extreme circumspection that I venture to speak today of a matter that has no direct relation to my personal affairs, but I cannot keep the silence I had pledged to myself when I see an honest man suffer as a result of the injustice or rather the ingratitude of his native country which he served with so much zeal. Poor Mr. Deane has been sent back to Europe to conclude all the business he had undertaken for Congress.[2] He expected to find here monies of his own to enable him to live here until his return to the continent, where the settlement of his own accounts would reimburse him for all the advances he has made to his country during the period of his political mission in France. Through either the dishonesty or the negligence of his friends or agents, he now finds himself in Paris deprived of the strictest necessary. He has applied to Mr. Franklin, who informs him that he has no instructions to furnish him with money. I am the only person with whom he has opened his heart and shown a bitterness which borders on something more fatal. I find myself in such straits that I could offer him help only in the future. But after he left, I pondered that it may be politically quite imprudent to push to despair people who have rendered great services to the State, which is what that wretched newborn republic is doing constantly to men of merit who have espoused its interests. I can already see defections so deadly to its cause that I cannot but shudder at such examples. M. Deane belongs to the French party and his devotion in this regard accounts for nearly all his enemies in America. Do you think, M. le Comte, that French policy could ever do anything more generous and appropriate than what I dare propose to your wisdom? One thousand louis[3] granted to this unfortunate former negotiator would uplift his heart to a

---

[2]After the congressional hearings on his mission, Deane declined the $10,500, in depreciated paper money, offered him for his expenses and services. He arrived in France for the second time on July 27, 1780, and stayed with Franklin in Passy. After going over Beaumarchais' accounts, he moved to Ghent, Holland.

[3]Here the Deane Papers translation erroneously reads "one million louis."

gratitude from which some day France may draw the greatest service. He has a beautiful soul and a sensitive heart. He cannot do without a prompt assistance, however you may wish to offer it, as a gift or a loan. This money will perhaps bear the highest interest. The deep emotion with which he talked to me about his country, himself, his son who is in school in Paris, his present situation, and the ingratitude which is the cause of it, makes me shudder.

I would never, M. le Comte, offer you a pointless or irresponsible suggestion. I leave this one up to your wisdom. My duty is done. For some time it has been quite hard to do; and the people who hinder the important operations in regard to America of the government and of the enlightened merchants who are eager to add some usefulness to your great works--those people, I say, seem very guilty to me! I refrain from further comment and only assure you of the devotion, etc.

Passy, 9 December 1780, from Deane to Rayneval
(Dea 4:268-9)

Your obliging letter of the 5th[4] did not come to my hand until yesterday morning, and I have since been confined to my chamber by a severe cold, which prevents acknowledging in person the sense I have of the seasonable assistance offered me by Count de Vergennes.

I must, therefore, pray you to make him my grateful acknowledgements and to assure him that I will improve the first moment my health will permit me to convince him that no imprudence or neglect of mine has been the cause of the difficulty in which I find myself involved, and from which he has generously offered to relieve me.

I hope in a few weeks to have my accounts finally and fully stated, and my affairs so arranged as to be able to repay the sum lent me. But no time will efface from my mind the sense I have of his kindness.

21 April 1781, to the President of Congress
(RG 76)

Gentlemen,

When in 1776 your commercial agent, Mr. Silas Deane, arrived in France, seeking to procure for you

---

[4]Vergennes' secretary's letter to Deane, 5 December 1780, is missing. Beaumarchais' advice was followed.

prompt assistance in war stores and in merchandise and unable to offer any other security than his word and his orders from Congress, he met with the refusal of business people, who do not operate without securities. As he was most embarrassed in this regard, he made my acquaintance and found with me what he had looked for in vain elsewhere: friendship, trust, money. We agreed that I would furnish him all the necessaries to clothe and arm 30 000 men; that I would add artillery, if I could, and would send artillery and engineering officers; that the first shipments would be ready before October 1776; that by then Mr. Deane would have procured some ships in order to transport them to Boston; that those ships would be sent back by you, loaded with tobacco which would be remitted to me upon arrival as payment; finally, that all my advances would be reimbursed within one year; which would enable me to continue my shipments and you your returns, without interruption or delays. I had the honor then to write you to this effect.

I purchased the goods, I procured arms and artillery and I had all of those stores warehoused in different ports, agreed upon by Mr. Deane and myself. But no ship having ever arrived in France on your behalf, Mr. Deane tried to charter European vessels to carry the stores to you, but he did not succeed. He soon had to confess his new difficulties and although I had already carried my advances to the maximum of my ability, I felt I had done nothing at all if the cargoes were to stay in our ports. So I exerted myself again and procured him an advantageous charter for all my merchandise. I became his caution (and yours) for the payment therefor, and I had to pay three-fourths of it in advance to hasten the ships departures.

I had the honor then to send you a statement of account and to ask you to hasten your returns because I could not proceed further without receiving remittances from you. I overcame all the obstacles which the politics of England (and even France) opposed to my undertaking, but it was only after enormous cares and disbursements that the ships were finally able to go, some straight to Boston, the others to the French Cape, according to the amount of risk involved. You were again thoroughly informed by me and apprised of the need for you to send to the Cape the boats necessary to pick up the cargoes waiting there for you, while I would purchase in St. Domingo a few small, fast Bermudian ships to help carry the stores to the continent. Thereafter each ship carried letters from me to you, in which I constantly reminded you to keep the promise made by your agent, Mr. Deane. I have never received any reply from you.

Whenever my ships brought back some meager cargoes, your commissioners took hold of them or fiercely disputed them to me.[5] As a result, my friends became so discouraged they no longer wanted to participate in my efforts and I was forced to discontinue my shipments. I sent an agent to America to learn from you directly the reasons for your silence and strange behavior. Whereupon I was most surprised to learn through Mr. de Francy, my agent, all the tricks used to explain my operations in such a way as to lead you to believe you would never have to pay me, people boasting they had procured for you, as a pure gift from the king, what I was sending you according to the specific conventions made between me and Mr. Deane, the only person I ever dealt with.

Not knowing how to write you any more, I gave to my agent Mr. de Francy general powers to represent me with you. When I sent my ship Proud Rodrigue with a considerable load, I did not address it to you as I had the others, because of what I had learned about your attitude, but in order to make sure that you would be able to take advantage of what I was sending, I requested my supercargo to contact Mr. de Francy and have him offer it to you first. The supercargo's difficulties with the English language, however, and two or three misunderstandings, caused him to sell out that superb cargo to the Virginia government at a ridiculous price.

Since then, Gentlemen, I have received some 2 400 000 livres worth of letters of exchange, excluding interest. But these, maturing three years hence, were of no use to me. The ruinous deals I had to make to keep afloat then were my only reward for serving you--that is, financially, for I do appreciate the letter of January 15, 1779, you honored me with. It was the first gratifying word I had received from America and it confirmed to me that it was only by error that I had been deprived of answers to all of my letters.

Mr. Deane came back to France and my account which in the rush of his departure he had failed to regulate, finally was verified and closed. I hope therefore, Sir, that having had enough time to convince yourself it is fitting for you to help out the person who so willingly

---

[5]See letter to the commissioners, 6 December 1777, and to Vergennes, 10 February 1779.

supplied your country's needs, you will kindly check the statement submitted and remit me funds in Europe.

11 September 1781, to Deane
(Dea 4:458-9)

As we were settling our accounts together, I had a new opportunity to delve with you into the facts relating to the first and difficult mission you received from Congress in 1776, to seek aid for your countrymen in Europe, and to purchase all the supplies and munitions you could procure for them, without any other title, funds or credit than your orders from Congress.

I was also reminded of the zeal, the care, the perseverance, and the labor with which you started and followed through the delicate endeavors involved in the shipments I made to America. If your enemies have subsequently succeeded in belittling the merit of your political and commercial conduct in the opinion of those you represented, it is a great misfortune for your country and for you; and, as the first and constant witness of the services you performed for your country, I cannot but deplore it. Those efforts of yours, Sir, inspired me with the greatest regard, esteem and friendship for you, and our ministers and all enlightened men in our nation have also invariably recognized your sagacity, ability, and irreproachable conduct.

It occurred to me that in going over our accounts, you mentioned that Congress had stipulated a commission of five per cent upon all the purchases you might succeed in making. Although you did not pursue the subject, I suspected that you are at present somewhat anxious in regard to the fulfillment of that promise. For myself, as my incentive in sending aid to my friends was much less to make a profit than to help a brave people to win liberty, the supreme good of mankind,-- I could not see without distress their first representative, and one whose ability and exertions have rendered me such efficient aid, remaining uncompensated.[6]

I have, therefore, decided, Sir, to offer you, and I beg you to accept, a commission of two per cent on all remittances that I may receive from Congress, either in money or in merchandise, for the mass of the purchases made for them in Europe which are included in our accounts; only in the event that your enemies prevail in

---

[6]Deane soon found himself without means of support, and lived his final years in total estrangement.

influencing Congress to withhold from you the promised commission rightly due to you on these purchases.

This letter, Sir, will serve as your title on me, my heirs and assigns, for the two per cent commission I offer you, supported only by the affidavit that Congress has done you the injustice of denying you any commission on these transactions. This is but a poor compensation for your labors, but I deduct it from a commission of ten per cent allowed to me, which as you know, is far from repairing for the immense losses suffered by me in consequence of those purchases, my shipments, and the delay in payment extending over so many years. Accept this commission, then, I beg of you, as a token of the esteem and affection, and every consideration with which I have the honor to be, Sir, etc.

3 June 1782, to Robert Morris
(Wha 6:469-70)

The health of poor Francy not yet permitting him to hazard another voyage to America, I find myself obliged (to my very great loss and regret) to postpone the hope of closing and settling all my accounts with Congress until he has sufficiently recovered to travel, he alone being able to resume the thread and exposition of an affair which he has already pursued with so much assiduity for three years.

From one merchant to another, the extract of the account adjusted in France by the authorized person who has ordered and vouched all my advances, and which I have the honor herewith to address to you, would be sufficient to completely settle my account. But my business deals with the United States, who have entrusted the administration of their most valuable interests to an assembly of citizens--a Congress, whose members are continually changed and are liable to view anterior transactions, which may have been thoroughly investigated previously, with the same uncertainty and ignorance of circumstances as if they were new business. Hence the necessity of having my accounts adjusted and settled by the same agent who has already presented and discussed them according to the vouchers in his possession, which M. de Francy will do as soon as his health permits him to cross the ocean.

In the meantime, Sir, I have the honor of addressing you a faithful abstract of my accounts [Wha 6:470-3] as they have been settled by Mr. Deane, with whom alone, on behalf of Congress, I treated. His misfortunes, the malice with which his character, naturally mild and even, has been aspersed, and the complaints which I have heard about in this country against certain of his writings (of which I have not seen any) since the English papers made them public,[7] have not changed the opinion I had formed of him; and I will always do him the justice to say that he is one of the men who have contributed the most to the alliance of France with the united States. I will even add that his laudable endeavors in the most difficult times merited, perhaps, a different recompense. I see *there are intrigues among Republicans as well as at the courts of kings*. This digression (which a compassionate feeling for a man worthy of a better lot forces me to write to you, to you, Sir, who have loved him as I do), this digression excused, I resume my affair.

I request of you, Sir, to engage Congress to assist me at the very first opportunity, by bills of exchange like those I received in 1779. Although they are not yet be payable, and although I have been obliged to undergo the heaviest losses to make them serviceable, I cannot bear the weight of my unpaid claim on America (which would suffice to enable me to pay my debts in Europe) without having at least a title thereof in hands. Neither Congress nor I should look too closely to losses which I may incur in negotiating that paper. It is one of the unavoidable consequences resulting from the nature of the things involved. Do me therefore the justice, Sir, of remitting to me as soon as possible at least a part of what is due me in bills of exchange, reserving any objections until Francy may be able to go to Philadelphia. My very embarrassed situation will cause me to receive this strict justice from Congress as a favor, and I shall be greatly obliged to you therefor.

---

[7]Thirteen letters written by Deane, in May, June and september 1781, to friends and family in the States were intercepted
   by the British and published in the *Royal Gazette*. Although contained only Deane's personal disillusioned thoughts, raised a furor in Congress and he was branded as a traitor. February of 1782 he wrote a long letter (Dea 5:39-58) to Frank who replied: "It appears that your resentments and passions overcome your reason and judgment" (Van Doren 513). In regard, one of Deane's biographers keenly remarked: "Men who revolutions have too much at stake to judge wisely those acc of deviating from the revolutionary line. . . . Many, no doubt self-protection, joined the hue against him." James 1975, p. In 1789, the much-maligned patriot died on board a ship which to take him back home. His heirs, in 1842, obtained his vind tion and a sum of $37,000.

14 July 1783, to Congress[8]
(NA Microfilm 247, Roll 67, Item 54)

Now, Gentlemen, allow me to delve seriously into the facts of this great affair in the presence of the venerable Congress, always subsisting but often composed of new members to whom the nature of my claim and the justice of my complaints are not sufficiently known (if I may judge by the terms of the 20 November 1782 resolutions communicated to me by Mr. Barclay, your consul general).

This complaint, Gentlemen, does not deviate from the profound respect which I profess for the venerable Congress before whom I have the honor of pleading. It is, on the contrary, the strongest proof of the high value I attach to the esteem and opinion of the brave people to whose cause I have dedicated my life; and the greater the disparity between a private individual in Europe and the noble nation you represent, the more that man's exertions and toil deserve your esteem and I daresay your gratitude.

Will you not deign, Gentlemen, to do justice to the first European who provided you with generous assistance? Every citizen of the thirteen States owed his energy, his fortune, his person and his life to the common cause, to his country. But I, Gentlemen, a stranger to your pretensions, your debates, born a French citizen, living quietly in my own country, and who worked diligently for yours, was I to expect I would be reduced to the shame of claiming much misunderstood rights and tiring you with my complaints?

Will you recall, Gentlemen, those unhappy times when crushed by war and English persecution, you were sending secret emissaries to all the powers of Europe, the time when you called in vain on the large commercial houses of these different States without obtaining from them any assistance? I alone, then, Gentlemen, a subject of a monarchic State, without any other incentive than my love for the good of mankind and my admiration for the virtuous efforts which promised it to you; I had been working for two years to make you friends in Europe, to excite hearts and minds in your favor.

The only newspaper apt to give freely to our French people just notions about your rights and the wrongs

---

[8] I have omitted the first six pages which deal with accounting.

committed against you by the Old England was the Courrier de l'Europe. I am the one, Gentlemen, who solicited and obtained its admission into France in spite of considerable difficulties.[9]

I am the one who composed the first articles which were published there in favor of your cause, and which established its justice upon principles now adopted by all sensible people in Europe.

I am the one who sought your friends and secret agents in England at the peril of my life, who promised them to do my best with our ministers, who came back to plead your cause in France, and to remind powerful men, who knew it better than I did, but were uncertain and cautious because of your situation, and the king's policy and youthfulness, that the separation of England and America was the most important issue which should occupy the French government.

I was the first to solicit the assistance required by your situation in a memorial where I strongly established the nature and extent of neutral rights, made application of my principles to the present circumstances and explained how we could assist you in applying them. But I could obtain only a certain, very limited tolerance for the energetic zeal of a company of merchants which I formed, whose activities not only the government did not want to enter into, but would punish at the first sign of publicity. See upon this subject, Gentlemen, my correspondence in ciphers with one of your secret agents, Mr. Arthur Lee, then residing in England. It will be laid before you.

At the same time, your official agent Mr. Silas Deane arrived in France; but alone, without money, without credit, without any relations and even unable to speak French. I made his acquaintance in Bordeaux. My love for your great struggle soon attached him to me. He implored my zeal and my assistance. Later on he came to Paris to inform me about his powers and his difficulties. He applied to the ministers in vain, returned to me, knew my courage and my candor, and finally began with me the work of soliciting, planning and carrying on the shipments I made you successively and which have never caused me anything but trouble.

But what kind of a deal, Gentlemen, do you think this agent made with me? Ardent prayers were his

---

[9]See letters to Vergennes, 8 September and 5 December 1776.

applications, which we shall call orders. My only guarantee of payment were his promises. The reward he offered me, in truth, was to be forever counted among the first friends of America, and I surrendered.

No one then, Gentlemen, came to me in your name without showering me with praise. All that can swell the pride and vanity of an ordinary man was offered to me. Above all, I was told, I would forever be cherished by v virtuous people as one of the first supports of its freedom. My admiration for the cause they pleaded and which you sustained so nobly with your arms exciting my heart and mind much more than their words, I gave myself entirely to your service and, giving up everything else, I became the agent, the apostle and the martyr of your cause in Europe. <u>Read my answer to the English manifesto of Gibbon, in which I was called the instrument and the perfidy of our ministers</u>.[10] But above all, read my correspondence with Mr. Deane, and read it carefully, Gentlemen. It will prove to you my labors, my efforts, my disappointments and tireless exertions. It will show you what a single man could do for you, a man who now blushes to have to justify before your assembly his conduct and his generous methods.

Surely, Gentlemen, had I been but an ordinary merchant, eager to take advantage of your plight, is there a single advantage I could not have exacted from you? I would have fixed any profit which greed prompted me to extort from you, and I would have gotten it. Far from me these vile motives and mercenary concerns. From the Frenchman that I was, I became an American, a political merchant, a maritime trader, a writer. I imparted my enthusiasm to able but timid souls, and formed a company under an unknown name. I gathered merchandise and warlike stores in all our ports, always under fictitious names. Your agent was supposed to procure vessels to transport these stores to America, but he could not find a single one and I again, redoubling my zeal and efforts, succeeded in procuring them for him in Marseilles, Nantes, and LeHavre, paying out of my own pocket two-thirds of the charter in advance and standing surety for the remainder.

Should the most severe orders threaten to thwart my operations everywhere, what I could not accomplish by daylight was executed after dark. Should the authorities order the unloading of my ships in one harbor, I would send them further on into the road to reload silently.

---

[10]This refers to the *Observations* (Emphasis mine).

Should my ships be stopped under their surnames, I would change those proscribed names right away or would simulate a sale of the ship, and would reload them anew under ostensible ship's papers. Should written certificates be required of the captains that they would only go to our islands in the Gulf, a powerful gratification made them yield again to my wishes. Should they be sent to prison for disobedience when they came back, I immediately doubled their gratification to keep up their zeal, and with gold I consoled them from the rigors of our policy. Trips, messengers, agents, gifts, rewards, I spared nothing to carry on. Once on a sudden counter order which would have cost us a departure, I dispatched to LeHavre by land, post-haste, twenty pieces of cannon which would have delayed us ten days, had they come by boat from Paris.

Thus I scattered gold everywhere to remove the obstacles I constantly found on my way. I felt it would have been an insult to the nation I served ever to doubt that they would put in their gratitude the same generous feeling that moved me, and so I spent gold for them as if it was straw, happy to be able at such a price to help them out quickly.

And when your agent, Gentlemen, admired and encouraged those sacrifices, telling me how eternally grateful his country would be, I was far from imagining that once free, far from honoring the engagements entered on their behalf, that nation would send new agents to sift minutely one at a time every thread of my shipments and presume to settle again all my accounts already closed and to impose on me after seven years of waiting and suffering the insulting discussion, the minute calculation of every item of my advances; and forgetting my character and my services, would treat me in the end as a petty retailer who should be only too happy to receive a commission and some money for the rags he purchased in Europe.

By what inconceivable subversion of all principles, Gentlemen, have I experienced nothing but ingratitude, injustice and hardships from the time of my shipments to this day in everything which relates to your service? Not only did the returns so solemnly promised to arrive in Europe within one year at the most, never appear in our ports, but when my own vessels, for millions in advance, have brought me some trifling cargo of merchandise from the continent, I was obliged in order to obtain them to argue with your commissioners who claimed them under the pretext that they needed them. To wrangle them from me they went so far as to sue, and was

I not forced in turn to threaten to complain to our ministers, to France, to America and to all of Europe?

If the startling character of this narrative leads you to believe that I am exaggerating, Gentlemen, see on the returns of the Amphitrite, Amelie, and Thereze, my letter to your commissioners, the letter I wrote to Count de Vergennes, the answer I received from this wise minister, and his reproaches for the vivaciousness of my words, although he kindly acknowledged the rightness of my resentment and complaints.

Only the most rightful indignation, Gentlemen, could have altered my character and my style with your agents and might possibly excuse its bitterness. But compare this severe letter, Gentlemen, with those I had the honor of writing you in 1776, full of the ardent zeal which made me espouse your cause. In reading them, Gentlemen, you will appreciate how vexed and bewildered I felt to have never received from you any answer and to have sought in vain for three years a solution to this incredible problem.

In truth, Gentlemen, I was not aware that everyone trying to obtain credit with you for what I was doing by myself, deceived you basely on my account. To believe those honorable intriguers, I was only an obscure ghost serving as a cloak to cover the generous gifts which each of them claimed he had obtained gratuitously from the king of France, and while I was overburdening myself with loans, payments, interests, and ruinous transactions in order to survive while awaiting returns which never would come, on the continent people were satisfied to make use of my shipments, without even taking the trouble of acknowledging receipt.

So many outrages, Gentlemen, your obstinate silence, the lack of returns which Mr. Deane excused as he could on the hardship of the time, have finally forced me to send you a representative of my business, to whom I have promised, on all sums recovered, a two and a half per cent commission, which I have charged to you. The same Mr. de Francy has again the honor of laying my claims before you.[11]

Through him I have heard about the base and vile attempts which have been made to ruin me in your esteem.

---

[11]Francy, however, was too ill to travel and was replaced by LeVaigneur.

To his efforts I owe the tardy recognition which you made of my claims, and the bills of exchange you sent me in 1779, payable three years from date, for merchandise advanced more than six years earlier, and which was supposed to be paid within six months.

Finally, with him in 1781 my accounts were settled by Mr. Silas Deane, with whom he had served as my interpreter at a time when we did not yet speak the same language, in 1776.

I am sending him today, Gentlemen, to hand you this letter and to ask justice of you, to submit to you the credit and debit of my business with you, to request liquidation and receive payment. I expect of you Gentlemen, an honorable treatment, such as my zeal and my conduct toward you have given me a right to expect, and as the repayment of a sacred debt does not compensate for services rendered, when you have done me justice, I ask you, Gentlemen, for public marks of your esteem. Let them be the noble reward for my exertions on your behalf in Europe, where I have not ceased for eight years to solicit our ministers through continuous memorials on the political and commercial interests of your new republic. These wise ministers do exist, they will testify in my favor. They have many a time wondered at my incessant active zeal, for they were aware of the serious grievances I had against those I served so wholeheartedly. Give me, therefore, Gentlemen, what I deserve by distinguishing the devoted friend who supplied your needs from the people that your misfortunes have enriched. Do not lengthen my ordeal by delegating to other judges the settlement and the recognition which I must receive from you alone.

If I should be unfortunate enough not to obtain that honorable justice for so many proofs of attachment, outraged and mortally wounded, what could I do? Should I, Gentlemen, shaking the dust off my feet on all my relations with America, demand justice at the bar of Europe by publishing what I have done, advanced, suffered and kept secret to this day for the support of your cause and the preservation of your honor?

You will not reduce me Gentlemen, to this horrible extremity. My heart, my conduct, and your fairness assure me of it. People noble and free today, rival of the proudest sovereigns, friend and ally of my king! you will feel that it is just, honorable and without risk to your reputation to remember today that a private individual in Europe had the courage to espouse your interests when they were despised by all, and that he dared send you at the peril of his health, of his fortune and of his life, the first generous aid that you received from our continent.

2 July 1787 to the President of Congress[12]
(RG 76)

The most zealous, the most ancient and I daresay the most patient of America's creditors has the honor of asking you today for justice and for the belated justice of Congress whose President you are. The constitutional form of those congressional assemblies which gives each member a perpetual movability, is as contrary to the interests of foreigners who have claims against your government as it is advantageous to the country. The result of the perpetual changing of members is that affairs which cannot be terminated in six months, forced to be reviewed by new members to whom they are unknown, will languish, suffer delays and too often be forgotten. That's what has been happening to mine for the past twelve years.

This painful situation, Sir, has lasted so long that all honest and enlightened men in the Republic must feel sorry for it and sympathize with me for the wrong I have been suffering with an extraordinary patience for nearly twelve years that I have been creditor of the state, i. e. its creditor before it was certain to become a state.

The person charged with presenting this letter to you,[13] Sir, will submit to you the important services I have rendered to your country, my generous agreements with your agent in Europe in 1776 to aid with arms and munitions, clothing and dry goods, a virtuous people who lacked everything.

I do not mention my zeal although no man in Europe had devoted to you the like of it, and that, at a time when fear and uncertainty froze everybody's heart and closed all purses to you.

I attest before you that none of the conditions for which Mr. Deane had pledged to me his country's faith in 1776 has been accomplished, not a single one. My goods,

---

[12]There was no "president of Congress" but John Jay was Secretary of Foreign Affairs. Congress resided in New York and the Constitutional Convention, in Philadelphia.

[13]It was the French merchant, Chevalier, for many years an associate of Beaumarchais'.

my vessels, my armaments and my munitions have arrived to the continent, or in the warehouses agreed upon in our islands at the beginning of 1777. Abundant and prompt remittances were solemnly promised to me. A perpetual and uninterrupted circulation was to feed this trade, established on the trust I had in those virtuous insurgents and sustained by the most active and generous zeal ever demonstrated by any individual. But penury and disorder were such in your country, Sir, that it took almost three years for me to receive a single answer to my urgent letters. Only one of your port employees acknowledged receipt of my huge cargoes. Never any remittances came back to me to enable me to continue my services.

By the end of 1777, tired of waiting for returns which would not come, I had the honor of sending you, Sir, a representative of my business, Mr. de Francy, with general powers to deal with you. He stayed in America for three years, during which he was barely able to obtain for me a partial payment in letters of exchange maturing in three years, which amounted to a credit of six years for debts which were supposed to have been discharged within the year.

Finally in 1778, Mr. Silas Deane, Sir, your only commercial agent had verified all my accounts, only the final signature remained to be affixed as agent of the United States; my employees were busy making triplicates, one for you, one for him, and the third in my hands, as my authentic title; when his mysterious departure[14] from Europe with the fleet of Count d'Estaing suspended the only formality remaining to be given to my statements of accounts.

This delay caused me great hardships, Sir. He apologized to me before leaving, in a letter he addressed to me in Rochefort where I was on business for you. He asked me to be patient and assured me he would soon return and finalize everything. In the meantime, my interests would not suffer, on the contrary he would see to it that his country would make remittances, either in money or in tobacco, to the best, the most devoted friend America had in Europe.

All those promises accomplished was to make me lose a year and a half and await his return more impatiently.

---

[14]Deane had left incognito from Toulon with four other Americans who were to help pilot the fleet off the coasts of America. See Admiral d'Estaing to Deane, 1 April 1778 (Dea 2:447).

He returned in 1780 without any other mission, he said, but that of settling all the supplies for which he had been responsible in Europe so that they would be paid to me with the first monies available to the state.

He did review our accounts, finalized them. They only needed his signature, but he verified everything as commercial agent of the United States and no one, Sir, came to contest his title with me. No letter from the continent, emanating from any authority, ever came to raise any doubt in my mind that the only man with whom I had dealt about the interests of America, who alone had been appointed and empowered by his country to obtain aid on credit from European merchants, who alone had followed and shared all the work I did over a long period of time to achieve those important supplies, was still empowered to close the accounts involved. I could not have any doubt about it since no one else was able to discuss the articles involved; since all my letters on this subject had remained in his hands, as his letters in mine; no one else could appreciate the care, the zeal with which I had handled those thorny operations and the great sacrifices I had been forced to make to carry them out, which is genuinely proved by the correspondence.

This account closed by him, I solicited from Congress the aid I needed to face my obligations in Europe, an aid, Sir, to which I was entitled since the aid furnished by me to that nation which I asked to remit for it, had been received and consumed by them six years before, in a time of great need, and had greatly contributed to secure their precious freedom.

Who could have doubted, Sir, that a partial payment so needed and so long solicited, on such a sacred debt should have been made to me at the earliest if difficulties prevented Congress to discharge the whole debt.

I waited in vain for that aid from 1781 to 1783. Then, Sir, the only answer and payment I received was to see a new agent of Congress arriving, charged, I was told, with the mission to discuss, close and settle all the large European suppliers' accounts. It was Mr. Barclay, Sir, and I pointed out to him that my accounts had already been discussed and closed in 1781 by Mr. Silas Deane, your first agent, that they needed only to be settled; that based on the former statement, I had already closed and settled my own accounts with everyone else here.

Mr. Barclay told me that he could not acknowledge Mr. Deane's actions; and I could not agree to lose the only title I had of the advances I had made in 1776 to the American insurgents, closed in 1781 by the only agent I had dealt with. I agreed that Mr. Barclay could check it. Mr. Barclay wanted to destroy it. After debating for a long time, we agreed that I would send Congress a copy of the account closed by Mr. Deane and of the correspondence, with documents in proof properly authenticated, so that the sovereign might judge the facts of the case. I did. Two years passed and for only reply to that account, to a long letter somewhat lofty, copy of which is attached herewith,[15] I received in 1785, by the same Mr. Barclay, the curt declaration that Congress would agree to nothing, would send nothing, would pay nothing, until he had himself closed my account.

Then it appeared obvious to me, and I beg your pardon for it, that one was trying to gain time, using any pretext to avoid paying. Protesting against your agent Barclay's contention and not consenting in any way that Mr. Deane's statement of account could be destroyed by him, I handed out to him all the documents which had accompanied the first one to enable him to make a statement concurrent with but not necessarily destroying the other.

Eight months, Sir, were spent in accomplishing this huge task. The insurance I had taken was at issue. We agreed to take the advice of two maritime merchants, Messrs. Beaux and Texier, in Bordeaux. Their advice was that of all European business, that insurance costs are due on all cargo delivered which incurred its risks, whether the shipper had it insured or insured it himself.

The article of the commission due me was also submitted to them and their advice, after taking into account the time, the danger and the work involved, and especially the exceeding trust by the house making such courageous and risky advances in war time, was (they gave it in writing) that no European house would have taken less than a 60 percent commission. Mr. Deane had set it at 10 percent.

This long process once finished, I had thought, Sir, that whatever difference there would be between Mr. Barclay and Mr. Deane statements, whether or not I

---

[15] The 1783 letter to Congress given above.

accepted it, I would at least receive from him the amount thereof. I was far from expecting what happened to me. Mr. Barclay notified me that his mission involved only discussing; far from being able to settle my claim, he did not even have the right to close my account, but only that of sending his advice to Congress, that it was necessary for his work and my documents to be taken to America and submitted to his principals, who had refused to look at them when I had submitted those to them in 1783.

Having no recourse against this incredible treatment, deprived of my capital for more than ten years, hopeless to obtain justice from the nation I had helped out, I had to submit to this new postponement. Mr. Barclay assured me, at least, that I would not have to wait very long for an answer from the Honorable Congress.

The packets left in 1785. They were received the same year by Congress. We are in July 1787 and neither Mr. Barclay nor I have any reply from them. Is there in the annals of any nation on earth a single example of such a denial of justice?

And yet, on 19 August 1776, your agent Mr. Deane, wrote me the following: "I know there is no difficult task you will not undertake for the service of the united colonies of America and their gratitude must equal, if it cannot surpass, your generous exertions in their favor at a time so important and so critical."

And on 29 March 1778, he wrote me as he was leaving France: "After the perplexing and embarrassing scenes you have had to pass through, it must give you the most sensible joy to find the object of your labors obtained, and to see an armament going out which will convince America and the world of the sincere friendship of France, and their resolutions to protect their liberties and independence. I again congratulate you on this great and glorious event, to which you have contributed more than any other person."

And on 15 January 1779 the Honorable John Jay, President of Congress, wrote me . . . And on June 18 of the same year, in support of that letter, the same President of Congress wrote to Mr. Franklin. [see supra]

And on 17 December of the same year the very respectable Mr. Jefferson, then governor of Virginia, wrote to my agent Mr. de Francy: "I am very sorry that the unfortunate depreciation of the paper money, which no one was expecting at the time of the contract between the supercargo of the Proud Rodrigue and the State, did involve in the common loss Mr. de Beaumarchais, who has so well deserved this country's gratitude and has aroused our greatest veneration by his love for the true rights of man, as well as his literary reputation and genius."[16]

Kindly compare, Sir, the past with the present, and the United States' present behavior with mine at all times.

In 1776 you asked, obtained, received aid from me, which you used up in 1777. You were only an insurgent people. In 1787 I cannot obtain any accounting, any settlement, any reply from you, and you are a sovereign people. Such an incredible forgetfulness, too well known today in Europe, Sir, has been used by evil-minded people as a pretext to torment me in Paris. Despicable hacks in my country went so far as to have it printed in libels, among other insults, that I had sent the American insurgents spoiled merchandise, defective arms and bad munitions since after ten years' waiting I had not yet been paid by a independent people. Others, even more despicable, have dared assert it and the idle public believed them.[17]

I could fight the insult and prove beyond doubt that at the time the merchandise left, it was remarked by some busybody that if the goods happened to be of poor quality, it would be too late to remedy it when they had arrived on the continent; that this was reported to me by Mr. Silas Deane as a remark that he and his colleagues considered as insignificant; but that, indignant, I stopped the ships and insisted that two American appraisers, Mr. Williams, nephew to Mr. Franklin, and Mr. Carmichael, today your minister in Spain, be sent to Nantes, to LeHavre, bust all bales, open all crates; I proved on the report they made and the samples they took, that everything was of excellent

---

[16] I am translating back into English the French translation given by Beaumarchais. I have not found the original English letter in the *Papers of Thomas Jefferson*, as edited by Julian P. Boyd. Statements to the same effect are found, however, in letters from Meriwether Smith, 24 and 25 June 1779 (3:14-15).

[17] As the Revolution approaches, personal attacks on prominent people become virulent. He will defend himself on many counts, including those, in his Petition to the Paris Commune of September 1789 (RC, Mol 468-479).

quality. I received many apologies and much praise. MM Carmichael, Williams and Franklin being alive and the correspondence between Deane and me being in your hands, those facts can be ascertained. Verify them, Sir, I pray, on the original paper entitled: "In the name of God. Business Journal of Affairs between Silas Deane, acting on behalf of the thirteen united colonies, and Caron de Beaumarchais, on behalf of Roderigue Hortalez and Company" (the tradename under which, as you know, Sir, I was operating). You will find there the following letters: [8 January 1777, from Deane; 10 January 1777, to Deane; 24 January 77, from Deane and 19 February 1777, to Deane] I had, therefore, in my hands the wherewithal to refute that insult which was the deed of the most despicable rabble existing in my country, the pen-pushing rabble [la canaille plumitive]. But I was afraid that in so doing I would bring onto your country a universal blame. I scorned the scoundrels as any honest man must, and I reserved my reply for more important occasions, in more pressing needs.

But how long, Sir, do I have to wait for a people who has become free and sovereign in America to discharge its debt toward a private individual in Europe who not only dedicated his life and his fortune to them but by his zeal and labors contributed more than any one else to warm French opinion in their favor and persuaded France to take their side. Your agents recognized it and the many proofs thereof are such that your country's honor would suffer direly if what I am complaining of with you was made public in Europe.

Read the letter I wrote on this subject in 1783 to the President your predecessor. Someone told me that several members of Congress misinformed about the services I rendered and the justice of my complaints had found my letter *illiberal*, and I, Sir, patient as I am, I found that opinion of my letter, the silence kept about it, and the way Congress generally behave with me, very remote from that virtuous people who, when my services were less forgotten, wrote me through the hand of their leaders what you have read, and did me the honor to toast and drink to my health in public in one of the dinners given by Congress to the French ambassador, as the best friend America had in Europe. I learned about it from my Mr. Carmichael, then a member of Congress, today your ambassador in Spain, and from Mr. de Francy, my general agent, who were both guests at that dinner. But all that is changed today.

If the United States is not financially able to discharge their debt to me now, is there any consideration that would prevent them to fix the balance due, send me a few partial remittances, or at least set the terms of my future reimbursements and in the meantime send me the interest accrued on the outstanding sums. Think about it, Sir, how wrong it is to have forced me to solicit for eleven years the payment of a sacred debt, without offering a solution to such a legitimate request. What can be surmised here from the vicious circle which appears to have been adopted with me: We will reimburse nothing to Mr. de Beaumarchais until his accounts have been regulated by us; and we will not regulate his accounts so that we will not have to reimburse him at all. Perhaps a people having become independent and powerful can look at gratitude as a private person's virtue, below them, but nothing can dispense a State from being just and especially from paying its debts.[18]

I dare hope, Sir, that touched by the importance of the affair and the force of my reasons, you will honor me with a prompt official answer regarding the decision Congress will take: either to regulate and settle my accounts promptly as an equitable sovereign should; or to choose arbitrators in Europe to judge the points at issue, insurance and commission, as Mr. Barclay had the honor to propose to you in 1785; or to write me plainly that the American sovereigns, forgetting my past services, refuse to do me justice. Then I will advise as to what I should do regarding my despised interests, my wounded honor.

London, 9 December 1792, an open letter
Courrier de l'Europe, 11 December 1792 (Mol 703-4)

My poor wife, and you my darling daughter, I don't know where you are, or where to write you, or any one who might give you any news, as I learn that the seals have been affixed for the third time on my house in Paris and that I am under accusation for the wretched affair of the guns from Holland, and for an abomination of a more serious kind, added thereto to do away with me faster. I ask all the honest people who read the foreign gazettes to have the humanity of letting you know, my dear ones, that it is from London, from his hospitable and generous land where all the people who are persecuted in their own countries may find a comforting shelter, that I beg you not to worry about me. I

---

[18]Commercial probity was one of the main topics in Beaumarchais' early dramas.

see you grieve, the four of you. My daughter's tears fall on my heart and break it: But that is the only thing I cannot bear.

The National Convention, deceived by the cruelest tissue of nonsense ever to have come out of an informer's mouth, has on the faith of the Lecointre[19] deposition issued a decree of accusation against me. But those who have misinformed Lecointre, aware that such accusation would not stand a three-minute examination, have plotted to smear me in such a way as would sink it all. They denounced me as having written Louis XVI, listing me among those who are conspiring against French liberty. But this charge, more serious than the first, is even more groundless. Don't worry, my wife and my two sisters! Dry your tears, my dear daughter: They disturb the serenity your father needs to clarify with the National Convention the serious matters they need to know, so as to throw those abject calumnies back into the hell out of which they came.

I have never written Louis XVI about the revolution, either for or against, and if I had, I would be proud to proclaim it. We no longer are at a time when men of courage needed to belittle themselves when they wrote to powerful people.[20] Equal to the task, I would have imparted to that prince such truths as might have prevented his misfortunes and those which tear apart our unfortunate France.

The only direct relations I ever had with that king, through the channel of his ministers, go back to the first year of his reign, eighteen years ago, when he was just stepping up to that throne from which a weak personality, many mistakes and fate itself have just removed him so pitifully.

I am very far from betraying my country, for whose liberty I have long wished and then sacrificed a great deal, and all those vile accusations brought up against me at the National Convention would be the most abject abominations, were they not also the most stupid nonsense.

---

[19]A deputy at the convention, who had been used by Beaumarchais' enemies.

[20]This statement should be taken into account while assessing the 1775-78 correspondence of Beaumarchais with the French king or ministers.

But the Senate, which was taken aback, is made up of just people and I have not yet been heard. My enemies hoped undoubtedly that I never would be. By arresting me abroad,[21] they flattered themselves that as I would be brought back home under the odious suspicion of treason, hired murderers would have repeated on me the scenes of the 2nd of September,[22] or that the infuriated populace would have executed me on the way before it had been possible to undeceive them. It is the fifth time in four months they have attempted to have me killed. Without the generous intervention of a magistrate of the Commune[23] (whom I will name in my memorial with gratitude), who fetched me out of the Abbaye[24] six hours before all exits were locked, I would have suffered the same fate as so many innocent victims.

If I do not prove unquestionably, to the satisfaction of my country and of all of Europe, that all this horrible plot is but a vile villainy concocted to achieve a gross trickiness, and if there is one line written by me to Louis XVI in the past eighteen years, I say woe on me, anathema on my property, and I run and place myself under the sword of justice.

I am writing a petition to the National Convention to beg them to distinguish the ridiculous affair of the guns from the very serious accusation of a culpable correspondence. Before clearing myself of the first accusation, I must be either washed clean or dead, on my defense regarding the second. But in the name of God,

---

[21] The National Convention had ordered him to go to Holland and get the 60,000 guns he had contracted for on their behalf.

[22] During the September massacres. He had gone to the country during the day, and upon returning to Paris that night, he barely escaped from the house of Pierre Manuel who had saved his life before. The killers, having missed him the night before, were looking for him. He walked for three hours and found shelter with "some good country folk."

[23] Pierre Manuel, a writer of merit, a revolutionary leader of high integrity, after disparaging Beaumarchais in an article (see to M. Manuel, 16 April 1792, Mol 697) became his friend . He resigned as prosecutor of the Paris Commune after the death sentence was voted for the king, and went home to Montargis, not to hide (Manuel 1:2), but to serve the "Friends of the Constitution" by writing. He was guillotined on November 14, 1793.

[24] Abbaye de St. Germain des Pr s, a prison where the September massacres took place.

my dear wife, if you want me to be able to use my head, keep your daughter from crying.

10 April 1795, near Hambourg, to the American people (RG 76)

PLEA OR PUBLIC PETITION

OR REQUEST FOR JUSTICE

after twenty years suffering
addressed to the whole American people,
their collective person and
their representatives whoever they may be,
whenever they may receive it,
by Pierre Augustin Caron de Beaumarchais,
the undersigned French citizen

Sovereign American People!

Will you be great, generous, and especially just enough to allow a European who is proud to have rendered you perhaps not the most considerable but certainly the most authenticated services, to ask you publicly to do him justice against yourselves.

Nearly twenty years ago, finding myself in the height of a situation where adversity instills in a strong man the desire to exert well all the faculties of his soul, since I was wandering, persecuted, unjustly proscribed from my native country (which has since then vindicated me),[25] I conceived the noble project of serving with all my strength an insurgent and troubled people who voted and fought to preserve their encroached freedom. That was the American people. I too was suffering from abuses of authority, which doubled the energy with which I devoted myself to that people, from whom I wanted to ask as my sole reward to be admitted to the high rank of citizen of their country. I served them therefore, those virtuous people, with an indefatigable zeal, and my success would have met my hopes better if I had been better seconded.

Be that as it may, American Nation! the facts I am going to submit to you have an unquestionable certainty. The proofs I am giving have all the evidence needed in a legal discussion. The last alternative I suggest is noble enough to merit a fair treatment on your part. It is to you alone that I appeal from your own actions. I can no longer postpone it. For twenty years now I have

---

[25]This refers to the 1774 "blame" suffered by the author.

been asking for justice in vain. I will not mention the troubles I went through. After the horrible mass of those I have witnessed around me for the past five or six years, I would feel very contemptible if I mentioned mine. But I am old and very ill, and perhaps so ill that I cannot hope to live long enough to see the end of my affair in the form in which I am bringing it up now.

There is even in my present situation a similarity with the one I was in when I first decided to devote my services to you and I hope it will help my present endeavor. I was wandering, persecuted, unjustly proscribed from France when I was fortunate enough to serve you usefully. After a cycle of twenty years, there I am again wandering, persecuted and proscribed from my native country, which I served ardently, without belonging to any faction, hating persecutions of all kinds. My fortune is under siege, without the least pretext therefor, and I have just taken in this respect the same vigorous steps I am taking with you. I am asking justice from France against herself, with the same forceful means, and a courage more dangerous. May those last efforts of a banished man, dying in squalor somewhere in Europe, be of some benefit to my most unfortunate daughter, the only child I leave behind, without fortune or protectors.

I am going to set before you the great issue which concerns us in a way incisive enough to make you want to find out on what grounds a man dares believe himself entitled to talk to you this way. I will tell you: American people, you have been in my debt for twenty years, in an unfair and intolerable manner. When I have proved my case, let whoever must, blush in shame. But it will not be any of the men to whom I appeal today. Those who should have blushed are no longer around. Their successors will be my judges.

Do you realize, American people, that the most despotic kings in Europe, even in France, always granted to their subjects the right to take them to court; always permitted their justice administration to decide against them whenever necessary. It was seen as a kind of tribute to the fairness of the sovereign that justice could be claimed against him, since he could have been unjust had he wanted to, supposing, of course, that he could have been taken at fault. It is the same kind of reasoning which brings me to request justice from yourselves, in this petition, or whatever you may call this request of mine, since I admit I do not know the precise procedure that I should follow in this matter. Let us therefore disregard formalities and look to the facts of the case.

Facts

In 1774, forced as a result of a grave injustice arising out of a troubled period, to move to England, I studied there in depth the important issue which set you against what was then called the *mother country*. It soon appeared to me that she was entirely wrong. What people would indeed call upon themselves the troubles entailed in a great revolution, were they not impelled by unbearable wrongs! Centuries of experience have taught us that the uncertain advantages that can be expected are reserved for posterity, while all the sacrifices are the lot of the courageous generation which take up arms. Yours is the only exception to this general rule: You were able to enjoy very soon the fruit of your struggle, and you owe this advantage to your geographical position. And I contributed a lot to it: Yet you prosper, and I suffer.

Wise men who heard me often speak to this important issue and support your cause, soon sensed that the one who saw it under so many aspects was certainly able to serve it well in some. I succeeded in forming in various places, which are hardly suspected,[26] a secret association which made me the referee and the dispenser of the means and funds we put into it together.

After the death of King Louis XV, in France where I dared return, I dared show to the ministers of a youthful king the great usefulness which resulted for the French from the possible weakening of their natural enemies,[27] if the American people was assisted in throwing off the yoke of their proud oppressors. But it stands to reason that no one would have listened to a

---

[26] Because they included England.

[27] Beaumarchais had mixed feelings about England. He loved it as a land of freedom, but as a French patriot he resented her arrogant rule over the seas. A 75 page monograph published without date or author's name, entitled *The Wish of all the nations and the interest of all the powers in the lowering and humiliation of Great Britain* has been attributed to him, as well as a 145 page work published in the same manner and entitled *Influence of the despotism of England in the two worlds*. The first was probably published in 1778 and the second in 1781. Both attributions have been contested by Proschwitz (1956, 176-7). The alleged dedication by Beaumarchais to Franklin of the first work mentioned above, found in Aldridge 1957, p. 123 is mistaken.

banished man, who had been considered as almost lost, had he not begun by proving that he came possessed with large means, and only asked for a certain tolerance for his commercial operations. I proved that France was to benefit from it, since as I had already advised my foreign associates that I intended sending to our common *friends (Excuse me, that was a name they gave me then)* only French goods, hoping in this manner to obtain strong support in France. That strong reason did in fact sway them. In Versailles, obtaining the required tolerance was uneasy, even though I took all risks upon myself. None of the ministers being willing to assume the responsibility of leading a king so youthful and inexperienced as Louis XVI to agree to a project which could be far-reaching. I am the one who succeeded in persuading this prince, to the amazement of the two ministers who heard me speak to the issue before him, Messrs. de Vergennes and Maurepas. But the mere tolerance I asked for was so restricted it greatly hindered my secret shipments. My course of conduct then, I will one day bring it out in the open, was dictated by this hindering and did not allow me to realize a fourth of the good I had planned to do for your sake. But it will be proved to you that I did almost the impossible.

I was not happy with a man who, like the stagecoach fly in the fable, used to set himself as your spokesman in England, and with whom I had begun a correspondence in ciphers. This ardent and ambitious man, this Englishman, was Arthur Lee. I was aware he was only representing himself and not you in this matter. The relationship was distasteful, and I had been ready for a while to drop it, when you sent to France in 1776 a courteous, friendly and knowledgeable man, who soon looked for me. That was Silas Deane. The hot-headed Arthur Lee never forgave him his arrival in France.

Be sure to see the letters exchanged between us in 1776, 1777 and 1778, which show the form in which our relationship was initiated in order to pursue your dearest interests. These letters are found at the head of the account closed by him since then, in 1781. You have had it now for 15 years. Upon learning from this correspondence how enthusiastically I undertook to serve you, you may wonder that my best title upon you was that I did not *require any*, I did not request any other contract than the promise of a virtuous gratitude. Any bargain between us? There was none. I would have thought it insulting for the American people to doubt that they would be grateful. It never occurred to me that they would ever be unfair after benefiting from such devotion. The basis of all the precautions I felt

I had to take with your agent Silas Deane, is contained in a letter dated July 22, 1776 (q.v.). This phrase at the end explains it all:

"As I believe I am dealing with a virtuous people..."

O American people, that was my only contract, my only title upon you. What I am complaining about today is that breach of trust I have had to take for twenty years, a trust such as there is no other example in the history of any country. The percentage dealers may laugh at the blind confidence which made me neglect to take the precautionary measures they all take. But those who share the feeling which motivated me, the probe and discriminating people, will lament the hateful consequences of this generosity of mine. I lament even more the need for me to prove it publicly after twenty years, when I think that, had I stooped to take those mercantile precautions, no stores would have reached you, since I met with one hundred obstacles for each possibility.

I worked day and night, so that in the space of five months I was in a position to send you my first four ship-loads. The others followed soon thereafter, those you received, as well as those which did not arrive and whose losses were great.

This correspondence between Silas Deane and me, which I am having printed so that each one of you can read it, will show you five or six things equally important to know, indispensable to the judgment you must bear upon me. It is that my only objective was to be useful to you. That I disregarded anything which excluded that purpose. That nothing stopped me from fulfilling that wish of my heart. That I did it with a zeal, a selflessness which could be called *filial*. This correspondence indicates briefly the obstacles I had to overcome, although only about a thousandth of them. That of all the promises and pledges taken with me on your behalf, none, not one of them, has ever had the least effect.

According to your agent Silas Deane, he was supposed to receive several American vessels to take away my ship-loads--not a single bark did arrive. He wanted to procure some in France, and everyone turned his back on him as soon as he offered in trade his personal guarantee or the pledges of America. I had to add this expenditure to all the others, or else nothing would have gone. See my letter of August 22nd, in answer to

Deane's anxiousness, letter of August 19th, and you will have an idea of the friend you had in me.

I was promised you would pay me by all kinds of returns within six, eight months, or at the most one year, which should have given our business the proper turnover. Not a single remittance ever came back to me from America, except the little that my own vessels were able to pick here and there and bring back to me from the continent, and after twenty years, my accounts are not yet settled.

You were supposed, I was told, to answer me in three months at the most on the important decision I had been kind enough to leave up to you (which no other merchant in the world would have done in my situation), i. e. the decision left up to your equity to accept my shipments either at the usual sales price or at the purchase price in Europe, with the insurance, the costs and an amicable commission. This excess of noble confidence did bear the seal of the greatest selflessness. And (who will be able to fathom it?) three years later, all my shipments received and used up, I did not have even a word from you acknowledging receipt! Never an answer to the most important letters came to me on your behalf! Never did you attend to that choice that I left to you so nobly! on the manner in which you would pay me. Content to have received the fruit of my work, you seemed to leave up to chance the task of compensating me for it--and I challenge anyone to give of this a reasonable explanation! The grief this caused your agent and his excuses of all kinds are very nobly expressed in the letters he wrote me. These ingenuous letters prove the justice of my complaints because they teem with testimonies to the manner in which I have served you. If it were not for those letters, at the head of the account, I would in addressing so many reproaches to you look like a madman making insane demands, or else that it was deemed necessary to quibble with me to punish me, during twenty years, for a demerit I know not.

These letters and the manner in which my shipments were made did deserve, I daresay, an honorable treatment on your part, and up to the day when the worthy Mr. <u>Hamilton</u> and the probe assistants who helped him do his job (after seventeen years) have examined my accounts in an equitable fashion, although it is full of errors to my disadvantage, the Americans have dealt with me so unfairly that you will be stunned and the good people dismayed, after you have seen the proofs; with the exception of one instance, when the Congress secretly informed by Silas Deane of the nature of the services I had not ceased to render you--the most essentials of which could not be put in writing without risking to ruin your great cause--the Congress, regretting its conduct towards me, finally realized that I had been wronged and were noble enough to admit it and attempt to make up for it. In one word, they showed they were just. Any national public assembly usually are just when they are no longer misled by intriguers. And I must, my American readers, to encourage you to bear with the boredom of this prolix request, include herewith the letter from Congress and the one they addressed to Benjamin Franklin, the head of your delegation to France in 1779.

When I read those letters I forgot the displeasure which had forced me, to send to the Congress, Mr. Theveneau de Francy, as my representative, at the end of 1777, with the explicit mission of clarifying the enigma of this long silence. Silas Deane himself had left in 1778 with the Count d'Estaing's fleet, and it was only in 1779 that I received the true explanation for it, followed by the above letters. But that sort of amend made by Congress did not furnish me any means of sustaining our great trade, since, three full years after the departure of my shipments, they were sending me as payment some bills of exchange drawn on their agent in Passy, maturing three years hence. What businessman, what corporation could have kept up its credit with that kind of payment, in paper which had absolutely no currency in Europe! I lamented it on account of my creditors without reproaching it to Congress and the little they had written me, <u>the only letter I have ever received from them in twenty years</u>, warmed up my zeal for them again, and I hope to prove to you, just men of America whom I ask for justice, when I deal with the political part of this great affair, that in spite of the delay and the token character of your partial payment, I multiplied my services.

I had sent you a shipment in 1778, purchased for more than one million, on a man of war of 52 canon, belonging to me, a huge load from which the Virginians, on whose shores the ship landed, have alone richly benefited. I have not been paid for it yet. Thereafter, I had sent to South Carolina another shipment of a smaller size, on the urgent request of Mr. Rutledge, the President of that State. I still have not been paid for it. Finally, in 1779, I had succeeded in warming my friends up again and sending you another ship-load twice as large. But when it was about to set sail, the ministers of France exacted from me the complete sacrifice of your interests and mine, so that I might carry urgent supplies for them to their islands of the Gulf--an obedience involving losses and abuse of authority which were the subject of a suit between the ministry and me, and that King Louis XVI was fair enough, after several years, to allow to be judged against himself and in my favor. But those losses, abuses and late compensations have nevertheless ruined any possibility for me to render any more services to you. It is in that political memorial, today a matter of mere curiosity, that you will learn about your three-year bills of exchange, the losses I took on those without your having benefitted from them, the mistakes you made in the arrangement, which you tell me today you made in 1783 with the ministers of that time, to acquit yourselves towards them, about which they made sure I would not be informed. Then you will know how much better it would have been for you to deal with me and what I could have obtained for you from the youthful king who governed France (or rather, the unfortunate, who let it be governed by others in his name) either as a matter of justice or of goodwill. And you will be convinced when I recall for you the great favor I had obtained from him for you, which saved you more than a million in debt, which the ministry wanted to have you pay and which was entered in my accounts in spite of myself, without the strict probity of this king, who did not understand politics, and without the vigorous plea I made in your favor, in presence of two ministers, MM. de Vergennes and Maurepas. The little I am telling today has no relationship with what happened since then in France and is anterior to it by more than ten years. It is for my security that I have stated that.[28] Less than a year ago, for all the fortune that you are keeping from me, I would not have dared stating it, because, in my absence, it could have cost their lives to my wife, my daughter, my sister. Fortunately this horrible period is over.

Let us resume my sad petition. In 1781 your former agent, Silas Deane, came back to France. Pardon me if, while I ask for justice, I am obliged to establish certain facts for which I will be most honored to furnish proofs. They require a historical background for they contain the whole issue we are debating and one cannot establish in a few lines what embraces twenty years. Silas Deane came back to France to finalize, as he told me, all the accounts of the suppliers with whom he had done business, and that he was starting with me.

---

[28]Having had anything to do with the royal government during that period deserved a ticket to the guillotine.

What, I said to him, are you also bringing back from that country the shameless idea that I can be counted among greedy suppliers? You who saw me serve it with such benevolence. Have I not left up to them the choice which they have not yet made, to fulfill their obligations towards my company as they preferred to do it, and in the manner which would seem easier for them and most honorable for me?

Silas Deane taking my hand, assured me that insulting me was the furthest thing from his mind. Your shipments to Congress having ceased in 1778, they considered you almost as a deserter of their cause. I told him again what had happened when my man of war arrived in Virginia in 1778, how my 1779 shipments destined for Congress, had been ordered by our ministers to go to our islands. Your agent, Mr. de Francy, Silas Deane told me, said as much to Congress who found it difficult to believe. But finally, convinced by me that it was not your fault if you suspended your shipments, as it was not theirs if they could not pay you on time, Congress asked me to obtain from you, in spite of your dissatisfaction with their prolonged silence on the alternative you were giving them, that the settlement take the amicable form of purchases made on their behalf in Europe, with all costs and expenses, as well as insurance and a commission proportioned to the efforts involved. Then, looking unhappy, he confessed that he had so many enemies in his country that he would not have been charged with this mission if they had been able to find someone else as able as he to persuade me to accept this kind of sacrifice. But after he had secretly revealed to them the nature of the last services that my courage had rendered to you with King Louis XVI himself, against the advice of his ministers, a secret only he and Mr. de Francy were cognizant of in America, they had no longer insisted on that point. Then, begging for forgiveness, he confessed that in spite of the injunction to keep silent, he had felt it necessary to take Mr. de Francy as a witness while he was telling them in detail about those services. Such services, he had told them, that should I refuse a settlement of my accounts in the form they desired, the result would be a real loss for them of more than a hundred thousand livres.

Before making up my mind, I sent my agent, Mr. de Francy, to my foreign associates who knew that I had complete trust in that young man. It was through him only that I corresponded mysteriously with them, unknown to any other clerk or employee of mine. They relied on me to decide. His trip lasted three weeks. During that time Arthur Lee who never lost an opportunity to torment his opponent, had an American hint before me that Silas Deane was not to be trusted as he no longer held a public mission, on anything. I passed this on to Deane, whose answer was clear-cut. He told me to go visit Mr. Franklin and ask the same question to that respectable man. So I did, and asked him: Have you or someone else, Sir, been charged by Congress with the express mission of settling my accounts in France? If you did, what are those orders, whose first point must be to order you to let me know what Congress has decided regarding the manner in which my account is to be assessed either on the basis of a simple sale or of an amicable commission, a choice that I left up to them in 1776, and about which I have been waiting for an answer more than four and a half years--we are in 1781--so that I in turn may decide whether or not to accept this belated decision?

Mr. Franklin, struck by the strength of the argument, replied that he had received no such order; that he thought I would do well to receive those documents from Mr. Silas Deane himself, who was a most honest gentleman, and to rely on what he would tell me. Which I did. And I have been convinced since then that this Congress, now so particular about taking precautionary measures against me, would not have neglected then to have the man they had charged with scrutinizing my shipments item by item, if they had done so, to have that man inform me of the choice they had made on the manner of settling our accounts and that the settlement would be done, subject to whether or not I would accept the suggestion. For it was before my ships had left that this should have been decided and not five years later, when all risks and losses had materialized.

And yet, I declare frankly here that if such a thing was done, if that choice had been made, even in 1781, by the Congress of that time, if someone was charged by them to notify me about it in France, if that was done, and if, whether or not I adopted it, I refused to admit anyone as a third party during the discussion of these accounts with your agent Silas Deane who was indispensable in the matter, *I am wrong in this respect,* and I stand ready, as a punishment, to submit to a review the question under another form than that which resulted from Silas Deane's accounting. Then will it be better understood, that spirit of devotion and extreme generosity which made me sacrifice my own interests to those of the American people when I accepted that settlement. Then, however, a few more millions will have to be paid over what is owed me according to Silas

Deane's accounting. And although my affairs in France are presently in disorder, I will find the papers of that time which will clarify everything.

This question thus cleaned up, it is clear for both you and me that it was your own interest which made you had continue Silas Deane's mission to finish with me what he had so ably started, the mission of settling in 1781 my accounts in Europe, *which he alone was in a position to do well.* That he settled them to your greatest advantage. That his accounting, any error excepted, has been the constant basis of your situation towards me. That I do not invoke any other. That neither you nor I have the right to alter its foundation, nor any of the conditions under which I consented to it. Finally, that your examiner Barclay, who forced me on your behalf, in 1785, to review these accounts with him, refusing to regard as irrefragable Silas Deane's settlement, was unable to answer the question I put to him as to the other: Have you been charged by Congress to tell me what alternative they chose regarding my offer of 1776, since they believe it behooves them to disregard my services? Have they charged you to tell me how they intended to fulfill their obligations to me, either as sales according to the customary price of the merchandise at the time they were received or on the basis of an amicable commission (which never was given) me to make purchases for them in Europe, as you cannot destroy the basis, the form of a settlement made four years ago by someone else, without having received an order to propose another one to me, which I should either accept or reject? Mr. Barclay, appearing before me as surprised as the most respectable Mr. Franklin had been, confessed that he had received no such order to the effect he should start by asking such a question, that he had only been told: " You will settle the account of Mr. X," without mentioning any decision either on the substance or on the procedure, or anything else on the subject.

Will you then be surprised, virtuous men I invoke, if I tell you that a scornful smile was my only answer to Mr. Barclay's reply. He felt the impact of it and I have had no reason to complain about his behavior thereafter. But then I notified him that while he could well examine all my accounts with Silas Deane, he could not destroy any part of them, and I asked him if he wanted for his own security that I have a notice sent to him by an officer, based on the inexplicable silence they had maintained in this regard for nine years after I had made the offer. He assured me this was unnecessary, and we set out to work on the audit, severely, but without assuming any basis destroying Silas Deane's settlement.

Men of learning! I have no intention of availing myself of the immense advantage that this uncontested narrative would give me over you in court. I appeal to your sense of equity now, for it is you alone I take for my judges. It's enough for me to have stated the facts, without exposing their motives, which I am reserving for my political memorial, if I am forced to give it. But it would be regretfully since, as you know, men of understanding, one does not stir the cesspool of politics without giving vent to some mephitism [stench]. And I, indeed, know only too well that when I address a great Nation with all the respect due them by any individual, I cannot charge their representatives of sundry eras with the wrongs I owe only to a few men's intrigues. It would be unfair.

CONCLUSION

Sovereign people of America! I am only asking you, as an honorable treatment which I believe I deserve, to agree to submit to arbitrators named by both you and me all the points in controversy between us. In 1785 I had requested an arbitration in Europe and the place I chose was perhaps the reason why my request remained unanswered. If it was feared then that I would have too much of an advantage in Europe, I will prove to you I do not want any today by submitting to it in America. I even in advance gratefully accept, in the requested arbitration, the severe Mr. Hamilton for the political part. If you consent to adjoin to him an attorney for the legal part, a businessman for the commercial part, I will be satisfied and will not appeal the judgment of such arbitrators, once I have well informed them.

I will beg the State of Virginia, and that of South Carolina, to adopt the same solution for all the monies they owe me, whether they agree to the arbitrators named by you, or they want to appoint some others. Requesting from them and from you but what is due me based on strict equity, <u>disregarding all matter of gratitude</u>. And for my only reward for the zeal I showed you, to be recognized by all of you as <u>a good citizen of America</u>, without renouncing my French citizenship, unless an atrocious injustice forces me to abjure it, which must not be presumed, since according to what letters tell me, the reign of justice has replaced in my country the system of terror; and that for a year now they have not cut people's heads without wanting to hear them first, when they can prove that they are a thousand times right.

But being in a terrible state of suffering and illness, I have almost lost the hope of being able to go submit my rights to the arbitrators I have requested. Do not deny me at least to give me public writ, which can serve as a basis for the claims of my daughter or my heirs when I am no longer here (that petition will be the first of their legal documents), that Mr. Hamilton and his assistants have recognized in your name that in January 1791, you were indeed my debtors for a sum assessed by them to two millions, two hundred eighty thousand, three hundred thirty one livres, seventeen sols, eight deniers tournois. Not that I recognize this faulty evaluation of your future settlement as the exact payment for what you owe me, but I adopt it, if I must, as a minimum of debt at last recognized by you, and below which I cannot be brought.

The affidavit I am asking for is but a needed precaution in the event of my imminent death. If I recover my health, and if you grant me the arbitration I have requested (such as King Louis XVI did not deny me in 1782 against himself in a question of indemnification which had a lot to do with you), I agree to prove to these honorable arbitrators that not one of the objections which have prevented me from being paid by twenty years could have been sustained in normal business practice. Most of all, I will prove, by exposing before them the motives of the steps taken in your behalf with the French Republic[29] in order to try to learn from it whether you could be exempted or not from paying me one million of your debt, under the pretext that <u>King Louis XVI might have charged me twenty years ago to make you a gift of it on his behalf</u>. I will prove to our arbitrators that this last undertaking, which costs me three years, is so strange in law, in politics, in commercial usage, that I hope to lead them to tell you just men, willingly that I have given you the highest mark of my respect and that I have once more deserved your benevolence by not agitating it here publicly as I could.

And now, it remains for me to state the facts of

---

[29]Gouverneur Morris, U.S. ambassador to France, to Buchot, Foreign Minister, 21 June 1794. Buchot handed out the 10 June 1776 receipt signed by Beaumarchais, which in 1786 Vergennes had refused to give to Mr. Grand, banker for the U.S. See Introduction, page 40.

which I request an affidavit, accompanying them by my declarations, for which I also request an affidavit.

Sovereign People of America!

I beg you to order, directly or through your representatives, that an affidavit be given me of the declaration that I make to you in several articles, in the form the most respectfully legal and as formally as I can, ill as I am, sixteen hundred miles away from you, in a garret, deep in the highest Germany, in 1795, to serve in the event of my death, to my daughter, or my heirs, when they come before your courts of law.

1. That in 1776, 1777, 1778, and up to 1782, inclusively, I have sent you, in the way of trade, various mighty ship-loads for your most pressing needs; that I have not contracted with your commissioner beforehand; and that I have furnished this aid only for the sake of seconding your virtuous efforts to recover the first good of man in society: his freedom.

2. That I have furnished the most authentic proof of what I have done and why, in the correspondence between your avowed commissioner and me, which correspondence is given in front of the accounts settled by him, on your behalf, on April 6, 1781. Not of the mass of my shipments but of those which have reached you; all that which did not arrive being assumed as a loss by me, and with my full consent. Which makes the decision of Silas Deane a sacred proof of debt for you, since it contains the ultimatum of the sacrifices I can make.

3. That I left up to you the choice, in 1776, of the manner in which you would see fit to receive all that I sent you and to pay me for them, either on the basis of the usual price, at the time of arrival, or on an amicable basis as purchases made for you in Europe, with the expenses, costs, assurance and commission proportioned to the difficulties and losses I might have incurred.

4. Of the sad declaration I am forced to make to you that in 1781, more than four years after you received all that I sent, when Silas Deane came back to France to settle my accounts in your name, you had never replied to my offers on this important alternative. And even that, for reasons into which my respect prevents me to delve, you never made that choice so important for you, neither before, nor during, nor since that settlement of my accounts: and that in order to finalize them, I had to be content with the verbal invitation Silas Deane made to me in your name to adopt the ami-

cable way of a commission (which never was given me) to make purchases for you in Europe, which I have accepted merely because it suited you best. This is what I will prove best if this question arises between your arbitrators and me.

5. That since this settlement of 1781, I have not ceased asking for payment, efforts of which I have just heaped proofs and have placed them under the eyes of the worthy Mr. Hamilton, in the lengthy letter I wrote him on _____,[30] which each one of you can consult at his house. A payment I have not been able to receive as yet, although it has been nearly twenty years that my advances and my services were agreeable and useful to you, and all my cargoes have been consumed.

6. But most of all let it be attested that I seize the late admission the Honorable Mr. Hamilton made in your behalf in his 1793 report, after seventeen years of waiting on my part, that you were my debtors in January 1791 for a sum of 2,280,331 livres, 17 sols, 8 deniers tournois. Not that I mean to accept it as the exact balance owed me, which I cannot do, but I take it as a minimum of sums owed finally recognized by you and below which you will never be able to lower my claim, as was attempted in 1788 in a faithless report--whether I live long enough to go and demonstrate (after acknowledging my gratitude to Mr. Hamilton) how faulty his calculations were to my disadvantage; or whether death which is tailing me takes me away before the discussion which must finalize everything before our arbitrators.

7. Of the most precise declaration which I make that <u>I have never received from King Louis XVI, from his ministers, or anyone in the world, either one million or one schilling to offer you as a gift</u>. That all the gold I have used to serve you as a zealous friend, as a loyal merchant and on the only basis of an equitable commerce, was collected by me, in France as well as in other European States, only as participation, loans or cash flow. That all my creditors less patient with me than I had to be towards you, have not given me twenty years to close and pay their accounts, and that, if some of them have not yet been paid (which question does not concern you as debtors), it would be only another reason for you to enable me to do it by fulfilling your own obligations towards me.

---

[30]The blank is in the manuscript.

8. Finally, of what I am declaring now: that upon learning from you today, which I have never been aware of, about the sort of accounting the ministers of France made with you in 1783, an accounting in which I was not invited to take part and with which I have absolutely nothing to do, by the very fact that I was not a party to it, which should have been indispensable if, after 12 years, you were to try to invoke it as a last resort to postpone or avoid paying me. And I declare here formally that it is only out of respect for you that I will postpone shedding full light on the matter until arbitration. And I hope to have the arbitrators admit it and declare to you willingly themselves that such discretion of mine today further entitles me to your benevolence.

Virtuous Americans! I had concluded this petition by a concise summary of my unrecognized rights, terse and conclusive. After I have condensed in concise sentences what I have perhaps weakened in the long narrative that precedes, I had, in order to draw the necessary consequences, established in figures the strict balance of what you owe me in total, by deducting from that debt the monies I have received and balancing the interests on sums owed and those on sums paid at their different dates, the resulting table appeared incontestable. Before offering it to you, I planned to leave certified copies of it with some public men in Hambourg, London, Basel and Paris, so that in the event of my death, my daughter or my heirs would be able to recover those documents, and find everywhere judges of my judges, should I not obtain the satisfaction I am entitled to. An accident[31] I had last night causes me to change my plans, which could have been considered as the beginning of adversary procedure, into something more fitting in my present condition.

As a result of either excessive grief, fatigue, or overwork, I fell last night into a state of exhaustion so long and so total that I seemed to have reached the end. It was the second warning nature has given me in the last month. But the last one was such that it would be stupid of me not to heed it. Whether because in the supreme moment when we feel we can no longer hold onto existence we see things in a new way, or because the inability to carry things on to a useful conclusion finally makes them seem unimportant to us--I am changing all the computations in my summary into an ardent pray-

---

[31]This accident remained unknown and some biographers have alleged suspicions of suicide.

er, and although   feel an excruciating pain in my heart because of the state in which I am leaving my only daughter, without support, without protector, I prefer it this way. Thus, no longer arguing to establish and prove my rights, I will only try to appeal to your sense of justice and turn it into pity for my orphan daughter.

And so that none of you will feel offended by any abrasiveness in my complaints, I will compare your Congress and its successive assemblies to one of your rapid rivers, always fecundating, sometimes dangerous. To the unfortunate who would try to hold it accountable for a shipwreck occurred on its course, could the river not reply: I did not cause your losses. You may complain but do not accuse me! I am the same river always, but never the same water?

O virtuous Americans! The stormy weather has passed away for you; the muddy waters have run out. You enjoy in peace the fecundating river. If in this long petition I have reached my goal of reminding you of services almost erased by such a long lapse of time, if I have proved to you (<u>which means the most to me</u>) that although I was a complete stranger to you, I have cared for you in your difficult days with an indefatigable zeal and helped you recover your freedom; if, in 1779, the Congress composed of your then representatives, did not feel humiliated to recognize my services and the purity of the motives which attached me to their cause in the two letters quoted above, and if it was then determined after reading my correspondence with your agent Silas Deane, which he put before them and which will again be put before you; ponder the meaning of the last sentences of Deane's last letter as he was leaving France, on March 29, 1778.

Sovereign People of America! If those memories produce in you their natural effect, you will not be less fair than the 1779 Congress. Reward me in the person most dear to me, let the compensation for what I suffered for you finally benefit my daughter after her father is gone. Allow me in dying to place her under your protective ward! Let me quote an anecdote to remind you of the sweet gratitude owed past services. I have not fetched it in the archives of the nations of antiquity, to whom our historians seem to have given such high characters only to humiliate us by comparison, or to inspire in us the desire to emulate them. No, Citizens, it is drawn from the most modern history, that of the French Revolution. While discord among us fed the fire of strife between all parties fighting over a weakened authority, when the great word <u>liberty</u>, at first so sweet to say when it was accompanied by the sublime decree of <u>a declaration of peace to the whole universe</u>, seemed to offer us only the firebrand of a conflagration that would consume all of Europe, while heads were falling by thousands under the executioners' ax; someone introduced to our restless assembly the widow of Jean-Jacques Rousseau. That name immediately appeased the discord and fury, and without even considering that this great man's writings had not had in mind the sole happiness of France, the entire nation applauded the decree instituting a pension to his widow.

Americans, my rights over you are much more direct. It's you I served, you I wanted to serve. I never received from it in my life anything but bitterness as a reward, and I die your creditor. Allow me to leave you my daughter to endow with what you owe me. Perhaps, because of other wrongs which I can no longer challenge, she has nothing left at all, and perhaps Providence saw to it that, through your delayed payments, a resource would be left to her after my death against complete misfortune! Adopt her as a worthy ward of the State! Her mother, unfortunate also, my widow; her mother will bring her to you. Let her be regarded by you as a daughter of a citizen!

If, after these last efforts, after what has just been said, against all possible appearance, I could still fear that you might reject my request on the objects for which I am requesting an affidavit, if I could fear that you would refuse me or my heirs any arbitration, desperate and ruined, as much in Europe as by you; and your country being the only one where I could without shame hold my hand out to the inhabitants---what will remain for me to do if not to beg Heaven to grant me another moment of the worst health to permit me to make the trip to America. Arrived among you, my head and body weakened, without the strength to sustain my rights, should I then, proofs in hand, have myself carried on a stool to the entrance of your national meetings, and holding out the bonnet of freedom, of which no man more than I contributed to decorate your head, I should cry out to you: Americans, give alms to your friend, whose accumulated services have had no other reward? Date obolum belisario!

Ne varietur.

12 June 1796, to Chevalier & Cie, U.S.A.[32]
(extracts Dals me, *Le Figaro*, 27 October 1928)

After three years' suffering, three years of banishment entailing incalculable losses, my dear friend, I have just received my re-entry diploma, as valid as can be. It is dated June 2 and signed by the Directory.[33] I have received it today in Hamburg and in three days I will be in Paris, as estranged from all that has happened there for the past three years as the unfortunate LaPerouze would be if fate brought him back to us.

I cannot stress too much how surprised I am that I have not heard from you since August 3, 1795. Is some devil after me? Is the entire world beleaguered to intercept my correspondence with my dearest friends? Or do you have nothing to tell me? Are you tired of dealing with a man constantly crushed? He is rising again. Put an end, I beg you, to this depressing silence. . . .

1 September 1798, to Chevalier & Co. in New York
(excerpts printed in Le Figaro, 27 October 1928)

The French Republic which owes me from 12 to 13 hundred thousand livres, having just referred me to the twelfth commission, which is going to review my accounts, at a time when I thought I was about to leave to settle all of mine in the fatal continent where you live, I am tied down until I am through with that new business which has just been imposed upon me. But I swear to you that once this new shackle is removed from me, I will not remain fifteen days in Paris, and whether or not the government has entrusted its business to me[34], I will not tarry any longer and will go take care of my own affairs. Then I will take with me the funds necessary to my trip. I do hope we will not be at war with them and that it will not be enough to be a Frenchman in America to be denied justice in that fatal continent . . . I have no other means of support while waiting for that new decision except from loans. As they are due in four to five months from now, you may judge how I feel about your being so slow in sending me my viaticum [trip money]!

---

[32]The French merchant formerly associated with him had married and settled down in Long Island, New York.

[33]The executive branch of the French republic.

[34]He was soliciting an appointment as ambassador or delegate to America.

1798, to Talleyrand,[35] then Foreign Affairs minister (Lom 2:520-1)

I was smiling last night at the magnificent compliment you paid me when you said that I was everyone's dupe. Being duped by those one has obliged, from the scepter to the shepherds's crook, is to be a victim and not a dupe. Even if I could have kept at that price all that base ingratitude has taken from me, I never wished I had done otherwise. That's my profession of faith. I don't mind what I lose myself, but what affects my country's reputation or happiness wears out all my sensibilities. When we make a mistake, I become angry like a child, and although I am neither "fit for" nor employed "for anything," every night I repair in my mind our errors of the day. That's what makes my friends say that I am a dupe, everyone else being supposedly concerned only with himself. What a doggone country if that was true of everybody! But I am sure, very sure, of the contrary.

When will you see my little dupe's deal?[36] You will not find it devoid of interest: You will find resources there for the past, the present and the future--the future, the only time that exists for us, the other two having gone away while we talk about them.

---

[35]Charles de Talleyrand-Perigord (1754-1838), a former bishop of the Catholic church, who in November 1789 fathered the scheme of the *assignats*, a paper currency based on the confiscated assets of the Church. The two men had met while in exile in Germany.

[36]According to Loménie, this refers to a paper concerning the current difficulties between France and the United States.

CHRONOLOGICAL TABLE

27 April 1775, to Louis XVI 59
21 June 1775, From Vergennes 63
23 June 1775, Vergennes to Count de Guines 64
London, 14 July 1775, to Vergennes 65
26 August 1775, from Vergennes 66
Before September 1775, to the king 67
21 September 1775, To the king 69
22 September 1775, to Vergennes 72
Paris, 22 September 1775, to Vergennes 73
23 September 1775, from Vergennes to the king . . . 74
Paris, 23 September 1775, to Vergennes 74
Versailles, 24 November 1775, to Vergennes 81
7 December 1775, to the king 82
8 December 1775, Vergennes to Viscount Stormont . 86
[before 13 December 1775] 87
15 December 1775, to Sartine 89
15 December 1775, to the king 89

Paris, January 1, 1776, to Vergennes 91
January 7, 1776, from d'Eon 92
London, January 14, 1776, to Sartine 93
22 January 1776, Vergennes to the king 94
[29 February 1776] To the king only 95
16 April 1776, to Vergennes 107
London, April 16, 1776, to Vergennes 100
London, April 19, 1776, to Vergennes 105
April 26, 1776, from Vergennes 108
26 April 1776, from Vergennes 110
London, April 26, 1776, to Vergennes 111
London, 26 April 1776 to Vergennes 116
2 May 1776, Vergennes to the king 118
Versailles, 2 May, 1776, from Vergennes 119
London, 3 May 1776, to Vergennes 121
London, 8 May 1776, to Vergennes 124
10 May 1776, from Vergennes 127
London, 11 May 1776, to Vergennes 128
London, May 1776, to Vergennes   131
London, 17 May 1776, to Vergennes 131
London, 23 May 1776, from Arthur Lee 133
Paris, Friday, 24 May 1776, to Vergennes 133
Paris, 5 June 1776, to Vergennes 133
Paris, 6 June 1776, to Arthur Lee 134
Paris, 10 June 1776 [Receipt]   134
12 June 1776, to Arthur Lee 134
Versailles, 13 June 1776 135
London, 14 June 1776, from A. Lee   136
16 June 1776, to Vergennes   . . .136
21 June 1776, from Arthur Lee   137
Bordeaux, 21 June 1776, to Vergennes 137
Paris, 3 July 1776, to Vergennes 138

439

Versailles, 13 July 1776, to Vergennes	139
13 July 1776, Barbeu-Dubourg to Vergennes	139
16 July 1776, to Dr. Dubourg	140
18 July 1776, to Arthur Lee	142
Paris, 18 July 1776, to Vergennes	142
Paris, 18 July 1776, to Silas Deane	143
20 July 1776, from Deane	144
Paris, 22 July 1776, to Deane	145
22 July 1776, Deane to Conrad A. Gerard	147
24 July 1776, Deane to Beaumarchais	147
Paris, 25 July 1776, to Vergennes	148
Paris, 26 July 1776, to Vergennes	149
Paris, 26 July 1776, to Deane	151
27 July 1776, from Deane	152
Paris, 2 August 1776, 7:00 p.m., to Vergennes	152
Versailles, 11 August 1776	153
Paris, 13 August 1776, to Vergennes	153
Friday, 16 August 1776, to Vergennes	154
18 August 1776, Hortalez to Com. of Sec. Corr.	157
19 August 1776, from Silas Deane	160
29 August 1776, to Vergennes	160
6 September 1776, to Vergennes	161
15 September 1776 to Com. Sec. Corr.	162
18 September 1776, to Deane	164
21 September 1776, to Vergennes	165
25 September 1776, to Vergennes	166
14 October 1776, to Vergennes	168
14 October 1776, to Deane	170
[End of October 1776] To Count d'Aranda	172
9 November 1776, to Vergennes	172
12 November 1776, to Vergennes	172
21 November 1776, to Vergennes	174
1 December 1776, to Congress	175
2 December 1776, to Vergennes	176
Versailles, 9 December 1776, to Vergennes	177
10 December 1776, Vergennes to Lenoir	179
16 December 1776, to Vergennes	179
17 December 1776, to Deane	181
29 December 1776, to Vergennes	182
7 January 1777, to Vergennes	185
7 January 1777, from Vergennes to Gerard	185
8 January 1777, from Deane	186
11 January 1777 to Hughes Eyries, LeHavre	186
13 January 1777, to Vergennes	188
27 January 1777, to Vergennes	189
28 January 1777, to Francy	190
30 January 1777, to Vergennes	191
1 February, 1777, to Vergennes	192
3 February 1777, to Vergennes	192
4 February 1777, to Vergennes	193
8 February 1777, from Deane	194
10 February 1777, to Vergennes	195

10 February 1777, to Théveneau de Francy	196
11 February 1777, to Vergennes	197
18 February 1777, to Vergennes	198
19 February 1777, to Deane	199
20 February 1777, to Vergennes	200
24 February 1777, from Deane	201
28 February 1777, to Congress	201
1 March 1777, to Sartine	202
2 March 1777, to Vergennes	203
7 March 1777, to Vergennes	204
8 March 1777, to Vergennes	205
22 March 1777, to Vergennes	206
24 March 1777, from Deane	207
30 March 1777, to Maurepas	210
30 March 1777, to Vergennes	212
3 April 1777, to Vergennes	213
6 April 1777, to Vergennes	214
11 April 1777, to Vergennes	217
15 April 1777, to Vergennes	220
4 May 1777, to Vergennes	221
4 May 1777, to Deane	221
2 June 1777, to Vergennes	221
9 June 1777, to Vergennes	223
12 June 1777, to Francy	224
1 July 1777, to Vergennes	226
1 July 1777 (afternoon), to Vergennes	227
19 July 1777, to Vergennes	228
9 August 1777, from Deane	229
28 August 1777, to Sartine	230
7 September 1777, to Deane	231
10 September 1777, to Congress	233
10 September 1777 to The Secret Committee	234
19 September 1777, to Sartine	241
30 September 1777, to Vergennes	246
1 October 1777, to Vergennes	247
11 October 1777, to Vergennes	249
Marseilles, 17 November 1777, to Robert Morris	250
3 December 1777, from Sartine to Vergennes	251
3 December 1777, to Silas Deane	251
3 December 1777, from Silas Deane	252
5 December 1777, to Vergennes	253
6 December 1777, to Vergennes	254
6 December 1777, to American Commissioners	255
7 December 1777, to Vergennes	256
11 December 1777, to Vergennes	257
12 December 1777, to Vergennes	257
13 December 1777, to Vergennes (For you alone)	259
15 December 1777, to Vergennes	260
17 December 1777, to Vergennes	262
19 December 1777, to Vergennes	263
20 December 1777, to Francy	263
27 December 1777, Memorial for the ministers	267

1 January 1778, to Vergennes 277
4 January 1778, to Vergennes 279
[8] January 1778, to Vergennes 279
9 January 1778, to Maurepas 280
22 January 1778, to Vergennes 282
25 January 1778, to Vergennes 283
2 February 1778, to Vergennes 284
15 February 1778, to Vergennes 285
18 February 1778, to Vergennes 286
23 February 1778, to Vergennes 286
28 February 1778, to Vergennes 288
9 March 1778, to Vergennes 289
10 March 1778, to Vergennes 289
13 March 1778, to Vergennes 290
13 March 1778, Secret Memorial for the Ministers 290
21 March 1778, to Vergennes 297
23 March 1778, to Congress 298
29 March 1778, from Silas Deane 300
30 March 1778, to Deane 301
10 April 1778, from Swinton 302
20 April 1778, from Vergennes to Sartine 302
5 September 1778, to Benjamin Franklin 303
10 September 1778, from the American Commissioners 303
10 September 1778, to Vergennes from same . . 304
16 September 1778, from Vergennes to Gerard . . . 306
6 December 1778, to Francy 308
12 December 1778, to Sartine 311
13 December 1778, to Vergennes 312
20 December 1778, to the Committee of For. Corr. 313

15 January 1779, from John Jay 319
10 February 1779, to Vergennes 319
12 February 1779, to Sartine 320
13 February 1779, to the American Commissioners . . 321
13 February 1779, to Vergennes 327
13 February 1779, to Maurepas 327
28 February 1779, to Vergennes 330
27 February 1779, to Necker 330
4 March 1779, to Vergennes 331
14 March 1779, to Vergennes 333
17 March 1779, from Vergennes 334
20 March 1779 to Countess Fanny de Beauharnais 335
21 March 1779, to Vergennes 336
11 April 1779, to Mr. Swinton 336
12 April 1779, Vergennes to M. de Montmorin 338
8 June 1779, to Vergennes 339
4 June 1779, to an anonymous writer 340
18 June 1779, from John Jay 344
24 June 1779, to Vergennes 344
12 July 1779, from Count d'Estaing 345

442

```
7 September 1779, to Sartine  . . . . . . . . . . .  345
11 September 1779, to the King  . . . . . . . . . .  345
11 November 1779, to Maurepas . . . . . . . . . . .  347
16 November 1779, from Vergennes  . . . . . . . . .  348
Observations on the Justificative Memorial . . .    349
17 December 1779, to Vergennes from Praslin  . . .   378
17 December 1779, from Choiseul to Vergennes  . . .  379
18 December 1779, to Vergennes  . . . . . . . . . .  381
19 December 1779, Suppression Sentence  . . . . . .  382
19 December 1779, to Vergennes  . . . . . . . . . .  383
19 December 1779, to the editor of the Courrier  .  384
19 December 1779, to the ministers  . . . . . . . .  384
19 December 1779, from Vergennes  . . . . . . . . .  384
21 December 1779, from Vergennes to Praslin  . . .   387
22 December 1779, to Vergennes from Count Bulkley .  388
December 1779, from Grimm et al . . . . . . . . . .  389
22 December 1779, from L. P. de Bachaumont  . . . .  390
27 December 1779, to Count d'Estaing  . . . . . . .  391

26 February 1780, to Francy . . . . . . . . . . . .  393
Passy, 9 December 1780, from Deane to Rayneval  . .  397

21 April 1781, to the President of Congress  . . .   397
11 September 1781, to Deane . . . . . . . . . . . .  400

3 June 1782, to Robert Morris . . . . . . . . . . .  401

14 July 1783, to Congress . . . . . . . . . . . . .  403

2 July 1787 to the President of Congress  . . . . .  409

9 December 1792, an open letter  . . . . . . . . .   416

10 April 1795,  to the American people  . . . . . .  419

12 June 1796, to Chevalier & Cie, U.S.A . . . . . .  437

1 September 1798, to Chevalier & Co. in New York .   437
1798, to Talleyrand . . . . . . . . . . . . . . . .  438
```

WORKS CITED

Aldridge, Alfred Owen. Franklin and his French Contemporaries. New York University Press, 1957.
Allen, Gardner W. A Naval History of the American Revolution. 2 vols. New York: Russell & Russell, 1962.
Augur, Helen. The Secret War of Independence. Boston: Little, Brown & Company, 1965.
Bachaumont, L. P. de. Mémoires secrets pour servir à la République des Lettres en France depuis 1762 jusqu'à nos jours. 18 vols. London: J. Adamson, 1777-1789.
Bailey, Thomas A. A Diplomatic History of the American People. New York: Appleton-Century-Crofts, 1955.
Barzun, Jacques. Clio and the Doctors. Chicago and London: The University of Michigan Press, 1974.
Burnett, Edmund Coty, ed. Letters of Members of the Continental Congress. 8 vols. Washington: Carnegie Institution, 1921-36.
Bemis, Samuel Flagg. The Diplomacy of the American Revolution. Bloomington: Indiana University Press, 1965.
_____ and Grace Gordon Griffin. Guide to the Diplomatic History of the United States, 1775-1921. Washington, D. C.: 1935.
Boyd, Julian P. "Silas Deane: Death by a Kindly Teacher of Treason?" The William and Mary Quarterly, 1959, 16:167ff, 319ff and 515-550.
_____, ed. The Papers of Thomas Jefferson. 17 vols. Princeton University Press, 1950-1960.
Broglie, Duke of, ed. The Memoirs of the Prince de Talleyrand. 5 vols. London: Griffith, Faran, Okeder and Welsh, 1891.
Conway, Moncure Daniel. The Life of Thomas Paine. 2 vols. New York: G. P. Putnam's Sons, 1892.
Corwin, Edward. French Policy and the American Alliance. [1916] Archon Books, 1962.
Echeverria, Durand. Mirage in the West: A History of the French Image of American Society to 1815. [Princeton University Press, 1957] New York: Octagon Books, Inc., 1966.
Fay, Bernard. Revolution and Freemasonry, 1680-1800. Boston: Little, Brown & Company, 1935.
Grimm et al. Correspondance littéraire, philosophique et critique. Maurice Tourneux, editor. 16 vols. Paris: Garnier, 1879-1882.
Guizot, François. The History of France from the Earlier Times to 1848. Tr. by Robert Black. 8 vols. Boston: Aldine, 1898.
James, Coy Hilton. Silas Deane: Patriot or Traitor? Michigan State University, 1975.

Lecky, W. E. F. The American Revolution. New York: Appleton & Co. 1916.
MacKenzie, Norman, ed. Secret Societies. New York: Holt, Rinehart and Winston, 1967.
Madaule, Jacques. Histoire de France. 3 vols. Paris: Gallimard, 1943.
Manuel, Pierre. La Police de Paris Dévoilée. Paris: Fievée, 1793.
Morris, Richard B. The American Revolution Reconsidered. New York: Harper & Row, 1967.
Murphy, Orville T. Charles Gravier, Comte de Vergennes: French Diplomacy in the Age of Revolution. State University of New York Press, 1982.
Pinsseau, Pierre. L'étrange Destinée du Chevalier d'Eon. Paris: Clavreuil, 1944.
Potts, Louis W. Arthur Lee: A Virtuous Revolutionary. Louisiana University Press, 1981.
Proschwitz, Gunnar von. "Beaumarchais et l'Angleterre," Revue d'Histoire Littéraire de la France, 68:501-11.
_____ Introduction l'étude du vocabulaire de Beaumarchais. Paris: Nizet, 1956.
Roberts, J. M. The Mythology of the Secret Societies. New York: Charles Scribner's Sons, 1972.
Robiquet, Paul. Théveneau de Morande: Etude sur le dix-huitième siècle. Paris: Quantin, 1882.
Van Doren, Carl. Ed. Franklin's Autobiographical Writings. New York: Viking Press, 1945.
Vier, Jacques. Le Mariage de Figaro: miroir d'un siècle, portrait d'un homme. Archives des Lettres Modernes: 1959.
Voltaire. Essai sur les moeurs et l'esprit des nations et sur les principaux faits de l'histoire depuis Charlemagne jusqu'à Louis XIII. René Pomeau, editor. 2 vols. Garnier, 1963.
_____, Le Siècle de Louis XIV. 2 vols. Garnier-Flammarion, 1966.
_____ Précis du Siècle de Louis XV followed by Histoire du Parlement de Paris. Firmin Didot, 1850.
Weisberger, R. William. "Benjamin Franklin: A Masonic Enlightener in Paris." Pennsylvania History, 1986:165-180.

Abingdon   244, 358
    Secession, term coined by,   358
Affiery   101
Aix   139
Amelie 200, 227, 233, 366, 407
Amphitrite   181, 185, 190, 199, 202, 233, 251, 255,
    264, 315, 321, 364, 366, 368, 407
Andromede 365
Anna-Suzanna 251
Anonymous   226, 365
Armed neutrality xiv, 362
Arnold   115, 117, 249
Artois, Comte d' 288
Barbeu-Dubourg 28, 34, 43
    complains about Beaumarchais   139
Barber of Seville 19, 161, 190
Barberin 193
Barclay   403, 412, 413, 429
Barre   97, 114, 127, 258
Bancroft   28, 40, 43, 140, 148, 152, 301
Beauharnais, Fanny de 335
Beaumarchais
    and music   17
    and "Republican pride"   50
    and the "lost million"   43, 434
    letters to Congress not yet located   13
    subsidies   38
    expresses his loathing for "a sort of chores"   87
    his ideas fearfully presented to the king by
        Vergennes   74
    private trade aid will remedy the lack of funds
        76
    secrecy in aid necessary to avoid war   75
    State policy and morality 83
    accused of imprudence by Vergennes 89
    admires England   123
    alarmist reports as to islands in the gulf   95
    disapproved of, by Barbeu-Dubourg   140
    enthusiasm is beneficial   1233
    gathers gold coins in London for mysterious use
        134
    gives alarmist reports to the king   95
    one million subsidy dated 5 June 1776   134
    the English government is about to fall   94, 100
    signs letters to Vergennes only when his hand-
        writing poor   132
    Vergennes' reply written by his son   118
    warns Vergennes about intrigues 89
    gratefulness pledged by Deane   160
    outlines treaty between Spain, France and America
        171
    receives one million from Spain 153

    recovers his civil rights: "deblamed" 161
    suggests Courrier de l'Europe be censored by himself 165
    and French officers under DuCoudray 189
    and loans to Commissioners 208
    and European politics 275
    and French officers in America 265
    and liberty 234, 363
    and private enterprise 193, 258
    principle of neutrality 245, 316
    Sartine's opinion of, in 1777 251
    in disgrace with the ministers 279
    saved from bankruptcy 285
    stops "volunteer bandits" to go soldiering in America 289
    threatened with bankruptcy 279
    believes that right makes might 377
    patriotism 360
    political motivation 364
    principle of compensation of good and evil 21, 367
    asks for his daughter to be regarded as a US citizen 436
    finds himself without money in 1798, living on loans 437
    his reputation means more to him than money 435
    hounded by hired murderers 418
    misattribution of writings to him 47, 422
    planning to go to America 437

Bellecombe 341
Bellegarde 193
Berard Brothers, 251, 255, 256, 264
Bing 129
Bordeaux 137, 142, 150, 155, 368, 404
Bouille, Marquis de, 195, 228
Brazil 162
Breteuil 130, 131
Brissot 30
Broglie 62
Bulkley 366, 388
Bunker's Hill 356
Burgoyne, General 166, 249, 254, 257, 277, 280
Burke 129, 258
Byron, Admiral 341
Cagliostro 27, 30
Caisse d'escompte 150, 334
Canada 351, 354
Carabasse 200, 262, 268
Carleton 117, 166, 177
Carlisle 118
Carmichael 155, 186, 195, 262, 266, 310, 315, 323, 414

Catherine (ship) 192, 225
Cavendish 129, 258
Chalotais, Marquis de (ship) 194, 227
Chartres, duc de 20, 26
Charles I 85
Chastellux 192
Chatham 64, 72, 98, 235, 259, 268, 277, 287, 351, 354, 364
Chaumont 140, 165, 189, 213
Chevalier 230, 231, 301, 409, 437
Chinon forest 18, 202
Choiseul 22, 25, 34, 47, 132, 379, 383, 385, 390
Clinton, General 282
Clugny 34, 132, 154, 204
Colbert 35
Commerce 74
    irony about attitude of the administration toward commerce 228
    struggle of, with French government 360, 363
Common Sens
    quoted in Westminster Gazette article 213
Congress 231
    deliberations immediately known in England 159
    letter to, missing 175
    plan of reciprocal trade with, 155
    compared to a river 435
Conti, Prince de 20, 62, 152, 347
Contraband 362
Conway 129
Corsica 70, 109
Courrier de l'Europe 46, 161, 254, 289, 313, 320, 339, 348, 381, 383, 384, 404, 416
Courrier of the North 384
Crawford 258
Currency 141
D'Aiguillon 25, 34, 93
D'Aranda 131, 139, 170, 176, 214, 215, 217, 263
D'Ennery 180, 187, 190
D'Eon 7, 23, 24, 61-65, 92, 102, 104, 123, 127, 199, 206, 279, 288
D'Estaing 44, 313, 327, 339, 341, 343, 345, 370, 391, 393
D'Ogny 165, 225
D'Orleans 26
D'Orvilliers 44
D'Ossun 215
D'Ostalis 223
DaPunte 31
Dartmouth 124
Deane 28, 38, 39, 42, 140-3, 155, 157, 160, 180, 181, 189, 212, 217, 250, 255, 265, 288, 292, 295, 299, 310, 314, 320, 322, 396, 397, 399, 401, 404, 407, 412, 413, 423,

      425-428, 430, 432, 435
         certifies all of Hortalez' invoices   175
      "The most honest man" in Beaumarchais' opinion
         255
      and Paul Wentworth   260
      works well with Beaumarchais   222
      and peace proposals 207, 303
      sagacity and irreproachable conduct 400
Deane, Simeon   285
Declaration of Independence   162, 168, 176
DeCrosne, police minister   35
DeGoy 187, 188
Dickenson 110, 120
Diderot   29
Dorat (French poet)   336
Dorsius (Dorsies)   255
DuBarry   22
Dubourg, Dr. (See Barbeu)   152, 165
DuCoudray   160, 172, 177, 180, 182, 185, 190, 192-4,
         197, 203, 229, 366
Dumas, Alexandre   29
DuMenil de St. Pierre   108
Dunkirk 223, 228, 368, 370, 385, 387
Dunsmore 133, 167
DuPonceau   47
Durival, Foreign office clerk, 183, 188, 286
Duverney   (see Paris-Duverney) 13, 16, 161
Dutch
      make use of ostensible ship papers   106
      trade with America   105
Elizabeth   128
Ellis   125
Emery   225
Eyries (merchant) 182, 186, 229
Farmers-General   38, 174, 279, 328
      must agree with Hortalez about a good price for
          tobacco   77
      give permission to unload American ships carrying salt
fish   158
Fautrell, Captain 252
Ferdinand, Prince, of Prussia   263
Ferragus (ship) 308
Ferrers   24, 66, 92
Figaro   x, 28, 105
Flamand (ship) 232, 264
FloridaBlanca 215, 338, 339
Forth, Parker   216, 246
Fox 114
Francy   52, 196, 222, 232, 233, 250, 251, 261, 295,
         301, 304, 305, 307, 320, 327, 399, 408, 410,
         414, 425, 427
      illness prevents him from working   401

Franklin 27-8, 38, 39, 42, 53, 180, 182, 201,
        251, 255, 257, 303, 316, 396, 414, 425,
        428, 429
    French diary partially destroyed 15
    lands in Nantes 180
    and peace proposals 205, 208
Frederick the Great 259, 263
Freedom
    America's and England's, both threatened 363
French Revolution
    short-lived declaration of peace to the universe
        435
Gage, General 236, 355
Garnier 101, 121
Gates, 254
Genet, George Clinton, re Hortalez 39
George III
    deceived by his ministers 355
Georgia 130
Gerard
    Conrad Alexandre, 43, 147, 153, 185, 306, 327
Germain, Lord, 96, 118, 129, 177, 208, 210, 277
    one of his private secretaries, spy in Paris 205
Gibbon, Edward 45, 46, 50, 349
Goezman 25
Grand 530, 253, 277, 278
Grand Orient 26, 27, 30
Gravina, Italian publicist (1664-1718), 86
Granada 370
Grim, Frederick Corr. lit. 40, 368, 389
Gribauval 193, 197
Grimaldi 119
Grotius 86
Gudin 1, 28; in London 92; 349, 363
Guerchy 63
Guilds 9, 55
Guines 88, recalled 99, 123, 132
Hamilton 53, 424, 430, 433, 434
Happy (ship) 222, 232, 369
Hardy 232
Hartley 129
Heinson 259, 261
Hessians 111, 261
Hippopotamus 230, 370
Holdernesse 122
Hopkins 196
Howe 124, 125, 128, 245, 249
    and reconciliation 117, 166-7, 289
Hortalez 38, 39, first mention in corr. 77, 156
    to have priority with Congress for cargoes shipped
        155; 298
Hugalis 40, 128

India   351
Independence (ship)   212, 248
Ireland   101, 105, 118, 122, 342, 374
Jay   42, 52, 319, 344, 409, 413
Jefferson   15, 40, 52, 413
John the Painter affair   208
Johnson   114
Joseph II   33
Jumonville   351
Keppel   124
LaBlache   18, 75, 110
Laclos, Choderlos de,   8
LaFayette   261, 310
Lalande, Jerome   28
Landais   233
Langdon   252, 255
LaLuzerne   395
LaMothe-Piquet   393
LaPerouze   437
LaRochefoucault   194
LaRouerie   310
Lauraguais   25; one of the best-informed men on English politics 67; 107, 108, 112, 115, 120-2, 124, 136, 293; close friend to Arthur Lee 133; devoted to Turgot 13;1;his letters to Vergennes transmitted by Beaumarchais 122; Lee must not confide in him 141; no longer confided in by Beaumarchais 135 Vergennes concerned about him 126
LaVoisin Affair (Poison)   6
Lecointre   417
Lee, Arthur   24, 43, 52, 79, first mentioned to king 96, Vergennes refuses to see him 110; says tobacco returns are difficult 135; 132-4, 137, 142, 251, 255, 265, 290, 299, 310, 319, 325, 404, 422, 428
Lee, General   122, 126, 130
Lee, William   292
LeHavre   365, 405
Lenclos, Ninon de   105
L'Enfant (Lenfant)   196
Lenoir   35, 179, 192, 279, 344
L'Estarguette   265
Lexington (ship)   248, 356
Letters patent
    delay in receiving civil rights restoration papers   156
Linguet   25, 205, 210, 386
Linsing   25, 107, 111
Littleton   118, 124, 129
Lorges   172

Louis XIV 34, 84
Louis XV 27, 33, 421
Louis XVI 33-4; 59;
    approves paper 110; easy to persuade 211; 209, 345;
    requires elementary explanations 333; 368, 375, 417,
    418, 422;
    let others govern in his name 426, 431, 433
Macnamara 351
Madison, James 53
Malborough 118, 258
Malesherbes 138, 177
Malta, order of 26, 333
Mansfield, Lord 116, 123
Manuel, Pierre, revolutionary politician and author 8, 25,
    34, 418
Marie-Antoinette 30, 33, 288
Marie-Catherine (ship) 233, 369
Marly 135
Marriage of Figaro 16, 31, 364, 377
    hypothetical construction, comic device 364
    allusions in 391
Marsan, Jules, editor 2
Marsan, Prince 206
Marseilles 368, 405
Marshals of France
    judges in questions of honor 92; 392
Maurepas 34, 91, 134-6, 139, 154, 156, 176,
        177, 192, 195, 206, 210, 212, 223,
        254, 259, 278, 285, 290, 313, 327,
        333, 344, 347, 383, 426
    financial paper written to, by Beaumarchais
        169
    suspicious of American alliance 274
Mercure (ship) 200, 202, 233, 324
Mistral 187
Montaud 266, 345, 393
Montaudouin 109, 112
    receives subsidies 119
Montbarey, war minister 193
Montesquieu 50, 58, 83, 86, 373
Montgomery 117
Monthieu 37, 169, 189, 262, 302
Montmorin, French ambassador in Madrid 338
Morande 22, 30
Morin (ship captain) 202, 353
Morning Post 92
Morris
    Gouverneur, ambassador to France 53
    Robert 42, 229, 237, 401
Mozart 31, 57
Nantes 102, 108, 175, 180
    location of American commercial agency 259; 303,

453

331, 365, 368, 405
National Convention 417
Natural Law 360, 373
Naval war
    follows the morality of wolves 362
Navy, French 385
    whether or not it was in shape at the time 379
Necker 34, 173, 283, 288, 329, 331
Neutrality 101, 404
    principle established and then forgotten 358
News from America (given by Beaumarchais to
        Vergennes) 108, 120, 247, 249, 254
Nicholson 262
Nivernais 47, 390
Noailles (Marquis de, ambassador) 372
North, Lord 71-2, 95, 120, 128-9, 258, 287, 338, 369
    and English finances 116
    ridiculed in Parliament 113
North Carolina 111
Observations   some public surprised no penalty
        inflicted on the writer 390;
    sent to Francy in America 396
Olivares 355
Pacte de famille (Family Compact) 60
Paine Thomas 28
      Common Sense 355, 368, 377
Paris-Duverney 18
Patriotism 169, 390
    of Englishmen 374; 384, 386
    minimal at court 382, 339
Paulze 330
Pelletier-Dunoyer 206, 309, 321
Penet 166
Perrier 250
Pitt, William, Lord Chatham 49, 71; first a Commoner 84
Pliarne and Penet, 86
Poland 83
Pondichery 341, 352
Portugal 71, 163
    Beaumarchais advises Congress to declare war
        against 164
Praslin 47, 378, 390
Press
    "tacit" permission to print 382
Price 112, 385
Protestants, and civil rights 16, 211
Proud Rodrigue 266, 301, 308, 311, 334, 345, 370-1, 399
Provence, Count of 33, 289
Prussia 259, 263
Puffendorf, publicist 86
Pulaski 309
Pulteney, William (envoy) 277

Quebec 121
Rabelais 123
Rayneval 47, 307, 397
Republican pride
    opposed to monarchical honor 367
Retz, Cardinal de 385
Rochefort 242
Rochford, Lord 18, 69, 101-105, 108-10, 122-3
    comes to Paris to investigate 153
Rockingham, Lord 72, 96, 98, 262
Rodrigue 47
Rohan 27, 30
Romain (ship) 180, 365
Rousseau, Jean-Jacques 26, 29, 51, 377, 436
Rullecourt 1654
Rutledge 232, 265, 425
Saint-Germain, Minister, 138, 148, 156, 160, 166, 174,
        175, 193, 197, 203, 278
Saint Lucy 341, 342
Sandwich, Lord 130
    called American soldiers "vile cowards" 364
Saratoga 38, 42, 254
Sartine 35, 60, 63, 72, 111, 115-6, 134, 154, 177,
        191, 192, 198, 202, 259, 262
    told to refuse permission to Beaumarchais 185; 285,
    288, 302, 311-313
Sartre, Jean Paul 57
Sayer (Sayre) 259
Sawbridge 129, 258
Scaliger, Giulio Scaligero, Italian Renaissance philosopher
    86
Seine 186, 200, 202, 233, 365
Serre de la Tour 30
Shelburne 96, 98, 116, 259, 268
Sidney 385
Smith (Schmitz) Lord Germain secretary 213, 259, 261,
        273
South Carolina 108, 425
Spain 343; as a mediator 338
    mistreats American privateers 168
Stamp Act 355
St. Paul (Colonel) 109, 113, 148
Steuben, Von 310
Stormont, Lord 50, 86, 107, 111, 123, 153, 213, 241,
        251, 390, 350, 360, 363, 367, 371-3
Suffolk 262, 268
Sully's Plan (mentioned by Beaumarchais) 211
Swedenborg 14
Swinton 30, 168, 336
Taboureau 204
Tacitus 385
Talleyrand 54, 438

Tarare (opera)   57
Temple   208, 258
Texier (Tercier)   25, 105, 109, 121
Thereze   208, 227, 233, 303, 309, 321, 365, 407
Thornton, A. Lee's butler and spy   292
Thurne, Baron de (Goezman)   25
Ticonderoga   229, 248
Tobacco   40, 53, 79; necessary for continued aid   134;
    promised by Hortalez to the Ferme-generale   156
    158, 170, 176, 241, 246, 298, 302, 328, 331
Tocqueville   58
Townsend   259
Turgot   34, 131
Utrecht, Peace of   387
Vergennes   28, 34, 36, 42, 426
    and the "lost million"   53
    suppresses pamphlet   47
    England's wealth is a swelling, French economy is
        healthier   120
    gives permission to use French ships to Commissioners
    185
    hides dealings to Beaumarchais   185
    Beaumarchais' irony about his patriotism
        198, 212
    concedes England right to stop French vessels   228
    help Beaumarchais with financial difficulties   221
    re Beaumarchais' account with Congress   256, 306
    his views object of satire in Corr. lit.   389
Vignoles   60
Voltaire   7, 21, 28, 55, 106, 264, 288, 349, 362, 374, 375
Washington   117, 129, 167, 229, 249, 250
Wentworth   260, 262
Westminster Gazette   213
Wilkes   21, 71, 106, 258, 259
Williams   186, 231, 414